THOMAS FISCHER

# DISTRIBUTED MEMETIC ALGORITHMS FOR GRAPH-THEORETICAL COMBINATORIAL OPTIMIZATION PROBLEMS

T0135748

# DISTRIBUTED MEMETIC ALGORITHMS FOR GRAPH-THEORETICAL COMBINATORIAL OPTIMIZATION PROBLEMS

Vom Fachbereich Informatik
der Universität Kaiserslautern
zur Verleihung des akademischen Grades
**Doktor der Ingenieurwissenschaften**
(Dr.-Ing.)
genehmigte Dissertation

von
Diplom-Informatiker **Thomas Fischer**

*Wissenschaftliche Aussprache*
12. Dezember 2008
*Dekan des Fachbereichs Informatik*
Prof. Dr. Karsten Berns, TU Kaiserslautern
*Vorsitzender Promotionskommission*
Prof. Dr.-Ing. Stefan Deßloch, TU Kaiserslautern
*Berichterstatter*
J.-Prof. Dr.-Ing. Peter Merz, TU Kaiserslautern
Prof. Dr. Martin Middendorf, Uni Leipzig
*Zeichen der TU Kaiserslautern im Bibliotheksverkehr*
D 386

Bibliografische Information der Deutschen Nationalbibliothek

Die Deutsche Nationalbibliothek verzeichnet diese Publikation in der
Deutschen Nationalbibliografie; detaillierte bibliografische Daten sind
im Internet über http://dnb.d-nb.de abrufbar.

ISBN 978-3-8325-2178-3

Logos Verlag Berlin GmbH
Comeniushof, Gubener Str. 47,
10243 Berlin
Tel.: +49 030 42 85 10 90
Fax: +49 030 42 85 10 92
INTERNET: http://www.logos-verlag.de

# CURRICULUM VITAE

| | |
|---|---|
| 1997–2003 | Technische Universität Darmstadt, Darmstadt, Germany<br>Major subject: Computer Science<br>Minor subjects: Mathematics and Human Computer Interaction |
| 2000–2001 | Högskolan i Skövde, Skövde, Sweden<br>Exchange student within the Erasmus program |
| July 2003 | Diploma with distinction in Computer Science, Technische Universität Darmstadt |
| 2003–2008 | Technische Universität Kaiserslautern, Kaiserlautern, Germany<br>PhD student financed by a grant of the PhD program of the Dept. of Computer Science |
| December 2008 | PhD defense |

# ABSTRACT

In this thesis, three different graph-theoretical combinatorial optimization problems have been addressed by memetic and distributed algorithms. These three problems include the well-known 'Travelling Salesman Problem' (TSP) and the two communication problems 'Optimum Communication Spanning Tree Problem' (OCST) and 'Routing and Wavelength Assignment Problem' (RWA). The focus of the research presented in this thesis was on developing techniques to handle large instances of the above problems, where 'large' refers to problem sizes larger than those addressed in related works or large enough to pose a challenge for state-of-the-art heuristic solvers. For the TSP, a large number of publications and algorithms are available, so here research centers on how to solve large problem instances either by reducing the size of problem instances by fixing edges of a problem instance or by distributing the computation in sets of cluster nodes. For the OCST, a given local search algorithm was modified to handle large problem instances. The new local search algorithm was embedded into a distributed memetic algorithm with problem-specific recombination operators. For the RWA, most components of a distributed memetic algorithm were developed for this thesis, including local search, recombination, and distribution. To handle large problem instances, the algorithm was enhanced by a multilevel component to reduce the problem size.

# ZUSAMMENFASSUNG

In der vorliegenden Dissertation wurden drei kombinatorische, graphen-theoretische Optimierungsproblem mit memetischen und verteilten Algorithmen behandelt. Zu diesen drei Problemen gehört das bekannte Handlungsreisendenproblem (TSP) und zwei Kommunikationsprob-leme: Optimaler Kommunikationsspannbaum (OCST) und Strecken-planungs- und Wellenlängenzuweisungsproblem (RWA). Der Schwer-punkt der Forschung wie in dieser Dissertation vorgestellt lag auf der Entwicklung von Techniken um große Instanzen der o. g. Probleme zu bearbeiten. Hier bezieht sich 'groß' auf die Problemgrößen, die größer als die in vergleichbaren Publikationen sind oder eine Herausforderung für moderne heuristische Lösungsalgorithmen darstellen. Für das TSP sind bereits eine große Anzahl Veröffentlichungen und Algorithmen bekannt, sodaß die Forschung auf diesem Gebiet sich auf das eigentlich Lösen von großen Probleminstanzen entweder durch das Verklein-ern der Probleminstanz selber (Fixiern von Kanten) oder durch die Verteilung der Berechnung in einem Rechnerverbund konzentriert. Für das OCST wurde ausgehend von einem existierenden lokalen Such-algorithmus ein Algorithmus für große Probleminstanzen entwickelt. Diese modifizierte lokale Suche wurde eingefügt in einen verteilten, memetischen Algorthmus mit problemspezifischen Rekombinations-operatoren. Für das RWA wurden die meisten Komponenten eines verteilten, memetischen Algorthmus einschließlich der lokalen Suche, Rekombination ud Verteilung für diese Dissertation entwickelt. Um große Probleminstanzen bearbeiten zu können, wurde der Algorith-mus um einen Multilevel-Komponente erweitert, die die Größe von Probleminstanzen reduzieren kann.

PUBLICATIONS

The content of this thesis has in parts previously appeared in the following publications:

[27] BAUER, K., FISCHER, T., KRUMKE, S. O., GERHARDT, K., WEST-PHAL, S., and MERZ, P. Improved Construction Heuristics and Iterated Local Search for the Routing and Wavelength Assignment Problem. In VAN HEMERT, J. and COTTA, C., editors, *EvoCOP 2008 – Eighth European Conference on Evolutionary Computation in Combinatorial Optimization*, volume 4972 of *Lecture Notes in Computer Science*, pages 158–169. Springer, March 2008.

[63] FISCHER, T. Improved Local Search for Large Optimum Communication Spanning Tree Problems. In *MIC'2007 – 7th Metaheuristics International Conference*, June 2007.

[3] FISCHER, T. and MERZ, P. Embedding a Chained Lin-Kernighan Algorithm into a Distributed Algorithm. In DOERNER, K. F., GENDREAU, M., GREISTORFER, P., GUTJAHR, W., HARTL, R. F., and REIMANN, M., editors, *Metaheuristics – Progress in Complex Systems Optimization*. Springer, 2004.

[65] FISCHER, T. and MERZ, P. Embedding a Chained Lin-Kernighan Algorithm into a Distributed Algorithm. In DOERNER, K. F., GENDREAU, M., GREISTORFER, P., GUTJAHR, W. J., HARTL, R. F., and REIMANN, M., editors, *MIC'2005 – 6th Metaheuristics International Conference*, Vienna, Austria, August 2005.

[5] FISCHER, T. and MERZ, P. Embedding a Chained Lin-Kernighan Algorithm into a Distributed Algorithm. In DOERNER, K. F., GENDREAU, M., GREISTORFER, P., GUTJAHR, W. J., HARTL, R. F., and REIMANN, M., editors, *Metaheuristics – Progress in Complex Systems Optimization*, volume 39 of *Operations Research/Computer Science Interfaces Series*, pages 277–295. Springer, October 2007.

[66] FISCHER, T. and MERZ, P. A Memetic Algorithm for the Optimal Communication Spanning Tree Problem. In BARTZ-BEIELSTEIN, T.,

AGUILERA, M. J. B., BLUM, C., NAUJOKS, B., ROLI, A., RUDOLPH, G., and SAMPELS, M., editors, *Hybrid Metaheuristics, 4th International Workshop, HM 2007, Dortmund, Germany, October 8–9, 2007, Proceedings*, volume 4771 of *Lecture Notes in Computer Science*, pages 170–184. Springer, October 2007.

[7] FISCHER, T. and MERZ, P. A Distributed Chained Lin-Kernighan Algorithm for TSP Problems. In *Proceedings of the 19th International Parallel and Distributed Processing Symposium (IPDPS 2005)*, Denver, CO, USA, April 2005. IEEE Computer Society Press.

[8] FISCHER, T. and MERZ, P. Reducing the Size of Traveling Salesman Problem Instances by Fixing Edges. In VAN HEMERT, J. and COTTA, C., editors, *Recent Advances in Evolutionary Computation for Combinatorial Optimization*, volume 153 of *Studies in Computational Intelligence*, pages 243–258. Springer, 2008.

[9] FISCHER, T. and MERZ, P. Reducing the Size of Travelling Salesman Problem Instances by Fixing Edges. In COTTA, C. and VAN HEMERT, J., editors, *EvoCOP 2007 – Seventh European Conference on Evolutionary Computation in Combinatorial Optimisation*, volume 4446 of *Lecture Notes in Computer Science*, pages 72–83. Springer-Verlag, April 2007. Candidate for Best Paper Award.

[67] FISCHER, T., BAUER, K., and MERZ, P. A Distributed Memetic Algorithm for the Routing and Wavelength Assignment Problem. In RUDOLPH, G., JANSEN, T., LUCAS, S., POLONI, C., and BEUME, N., editors, *Parallel Problem Solving from Nature – PPSN X – 10th International Conference*, volume 5199/2008 of *Lecture Notes in Computer Science*, pages 879–888. Springer, September 2008.

[68] FISCHER, T., BAUER, K., and MERZ, P. A Multilevel Approach for the Routing and Wavelength Assignment Problem. In KÖPPEN, M. and RAIDL, G., editors, *Workshop on Heuristic Methods for the Design, Deployment, and Reliability of Networks and Network Applications (HEUNET 2008) at the International Symposium on Applications and the Internet (SAINT 2008)*, pages 225–228, Turku, Finland, July 2008. IEEE Computer Society.

[12] FISCHER, T., BAUER, K., and MERZ, P. Solving the Routing and Wavelength Assignment Problem with a Multilevel Distributed Memetic Algorithm. *Memetic Computing*, 2009. to appear.

*First I would like to thank my supervisor Peter Merz. His advice in our scientific discussions provided me with valuable feedback during the process of developing and evaluating ideas and concepts within my research.*

*A thank you goes also to my second thesis examiner Martin Middendorf for taking his time to assess and give feedback on my work. Furthermore, I would like to thank all my co-authors who were involved in the research projects that contributed to my thesis. Special thanks go to Kerstin Bauer for stimulating discussions on the RWA project and to both Steffen Wolf and Matthias Priebe for many more discussions and support both as friends and fellow PhD students.*

*I would like to thank the PhD program of the Department of Computer Science at the University of Kaiserslautern for financial support which gave me the freedom to pursue my field of research.*

*Last, but not least, I have to thank Jana who told me I could do it and who made sure I did not lose sight of real life. And mere words cannot express how grateful and thankful I am to my wonderful family for their constant encouragement and support.*

# CONTENTS

## LIST OF FIGURES

LIST OF TABLES

# INTRODUCTION

*Combinatorial optimization* problems as discussed in this thesis are problem types where items have to be selected from a larger set, reordered, or combined. The objective is to find a solution to the problem which has lower cost or higher quality, depending on the problem instance. An *objective function* is used to evaluate the quality of a solution and to compare it with other solutions.

Combinatorial optimization problems have a high relevance for different applications, such as scheduling or transportation. One example within the area of computer science is in the design of network topologies. Here, network connections have to be established that minimize total costs, maximize throughput, or minimize delay, depending on the communication requests of participating network nodes.

In general, combinatorial optimization problems can be categorized into one of two complexity classes. Class P contains 'easy' problems where the time to find the best solutions grows only polynomially with the problem size. More interesting are problems in the class NP, which are NP-hard, as no efficient algorithms are known for these 'hard' problems.

Combinatorial optimization is a field of research that aims to solve these hard problems: the objective is to find good or even the best solutions for these problems. Different types of approach exist and these can be roughly categorized into two classes. In one class, exact algorithms try to find provable optimal solutions. One drawback here is that exact algorithms are usually very expensive in terms of computation time. The other class is about finding good, but not necessarily optimal solutions using *heuristic algorithms*. Heuristic algorithms can find near-optimal solutions faster than exact algorithms. They use concepts from different origins, such as sociology, biology, or physics, to find sufficiently good solutions for practical applications.

This thesis addresses three NP-complete combinatorial optimization problems from the area of network design and communication. The first problem is the classic *Travelling Salesman Problem* (TSP). In its original definition, a salesman has to travel to his customers, visiting each once on a round trip before returning home. For communication networks, this problem is relevant to designing ring networks or overlays, where the distance between two 'customers' represents the communication costs or latency between network nodes. The second problem is the *Routing and Wavelength Assignment* problem (RWA). Here, a number of nodes are connected in a network of optical links, where these nodes exchange optical signals. If no direct connection is available, intermediate nodes forward these signals. Each optical signal uses one of several colors (or wavelengths) so no two signals on the same link may use the same color (otherwise they can not be separated later). The optimization aspect is to select both the route through the network and the color of the signal for each communication request. The third problem is the *Optimum Communication Spanning Tree* problem (OCST), where, contrary to the RWA, network links can be freely established between nodes as long as all nodes are connected by a spanning tree. Each pair of nodes requires some amount of bandwidth for communication and contributes to the total cost, which is the product of the allocated bandwidth and the length of the network links used to route the communication. The optimization objective is to find a network that spans all nodes and where the total communication cost over all node pairs is minimal.

This thesis describes the development of algorithms to solve problem instances for the problems above. Using heuristic algorithms, the objective is to find solutions for *large problem instances*. In this context, 'large' refers to problem instance sizes that are not addressed in the related literature or sizes that reach the limit of available computer systems, terms of both computational requirements and memory storage. This target is pursued with a two-fold strategy.

Firstly, the computation is distributed between a set of computers using a communication framework. In this framework, each computer is an independent island using an heuristic algorithm to optimize its own solution for a given problem instance. From time to time, islands are allowed to exchange their solutions and to integrate the findings from other islands into their own solution. As this approach combines biology-inspired evolutionary algorithms and local search (which is also a type of heuristic algorithm), each island performs a *memetic algorithm*. Given that the computation is distributed, the whole system is called a *distributed memetic algorithm*. Using distributed memetic algorithms, better quality solutions can be found in the same time than with non-distributed algorithms or similar solutions can be found in less absolute time.

Secondly, techniques are used to simplify the problem at hand by reducing its size. Once a problem instance has been reduced, this simplified instance can be solved, for example, by established heuristic algorithms. For best results, the problem reduction algorithms have to be problem-specific. For the TSP, segments of the route are fixed, i. e. changes on this part of the tour are forbidden, but other parts can still be changed. For the RWA, the problem size is reduced by decreasing the number of optical signals (communication volume) between each node pair. For the OCST, it is expensive to determine the costs of solutions during the process of finding better solutions. The cost function computation is sped up by counting less accurately and accepting some error in the solution's cost.

Results show that the algorithms presented in thesis allow large problem instances to be solved more effectively than previous approaches.

This thesis is divided into four main chapters: the first chapter introduces the concepts of heuristic and memetic algorithms and the distribution of computation; the three remaining chapters each address one of the combinatorial optimization problems outlined.

# FOUNDATIONS

2

This chapter sets out the foundations and definitions used in later chapters.

## 2.1 MEMETIC ALGORITHMS

*Memetic algorithms* (MA) are a class of algorithms that combine ideas from both evolutionary computation and local search algorithms. *Evolutionary algorithms* are nature-inspired search techniques that use operators such as mutation, recombination, and selection on a set of candidate solutions. *Local search* algorithms perform a sequence of directed exchanges on a candidate solution, 'walking' towards better solutions until reaching a *local optimum*. Details of these algorithms will be discussed in the remainder of this section.

### 2.1.1 *Combinatorial Problems*

The term *combinatorics* describes the part of mathematics that deals with sorting, permutating, or selection of discrete elements. It is partially related to probability theory (for example, how many 'three of a kind' hands exist for poker or what are the chances of getting one when drawing five random cards?) and graph theory (for example, how many different spanning trees exist in a given graph and which one is the minimum spanning tree?).

In the following discussion and in the context of this thesis, a *problem* is an abstract description of objectives to be achieved. Examples are finding the shortest path between two locations or sorting numbers non-decreasingly. A *problem instance* is a concrete example of the problem formulation, such as the set of numbers $\{1, 5, 4, 2\}$ for a sorting problem. A *solution* for a problem instance is a selection, assignment, or arrangement of the problem instance's elements so that it fulfills the objectives of the problem formulation ( for the sorting problem, for example: $\langle 1, 2, 4, 5 \rangle$). An *algorithm* in this context is a sequence of rules describing how to find a solution for a problem given the problem instance. For the sorting problem, the rules describe how to rearrange elements to get a sorted list as solution. Algorithms may employ memory (taking previous actions into account when making internal decisions) or randomization (given alternatives for a decision, each one may be chosen with some probability).

Combinatorial problems can be either formulated as *decision problems* or *optimization problems*. A decision problem formulation questions the existence of a valid solution for a problem instance that fulfills the requirements and constraints of the problem; the answer is either 'yes' or 'no'. In optimization problems, a large number of feasible solutions is usually available and the 'best' solution has to be found. Solutions are evaluated by an *objective function* (also called a *cost function*). In simple cases, a solution with the maximum objective value (*maximization problem*, e. g. maximize gain) or the minimum objective value (*minimization problem*, e. g. minimize cost) has to be found. Several objective functions can be used simultaneously (*multi-objective optimization*, [41]). No 'best' solution can be determined here but solutions are sought from the set of dominating solutions along the Pareto frontier. Any optimization problem can be formulated as a decision problem by placing a bound $b$ on the objective function and finding solutions that are at least as good as $b$.

Generally, combinatorial optimization problems can be divided into groups by their complexity class. Complexity classes describe, simplified, the effort (time or computation steps) necessary to solve any problem instance of a problem in this class. For combinatorial optimization, two complexity classes are of interest: (a) complexity class P contains all problems that can be solved by a *deterministic Turing machine* in polynomial time; (b) complexity class NP contains all problems solvable by a *non-deterministic Turing machine* in polynomial time [42, 82]. Turing machines are simple yet powerful theoretical concepts to manipulate data (correctly, 'symbols'), given a set of rules, an alphabet, tape-like storage, and an initial state, executing the set of rules starting from this initial state. Starting from an initial configuration, a Turing machine has to find a sequence of state transitions to reach one of several possible final states. Once such a final state has been reached, the Turing machine has accepted the initial input (for example, the problem instance of a decision problem) on the tape. In deterministic Turing machines, each rule translates into only one new state, whereas in non-deterministic Turing machines a set of new states is available. As non-deterministic Turing machines can simulate deterministic Turing machines, it holds that $P \subseteq NP$. One of the most important open questions in theoretical computer science is whether it holds that $NP \subseteq P$ and thus $NP = P$. It is commonly believed that $P \neq NP$. Examples of problems in P are sorting, where even simple algorithms find solutions in $\mathcal{O}(n^2)$, and finding shortest paths in graphs (e. g. using DIJKSTRA's algorithm [58]).

A problem $A$ is said to be *NP-hard* if every other problem $B$ in NP can be polynomially reduced to it (operator $\leq_p$), i. e. there is a function $f$ that transforms every problem instance in $B$ to a problem instance in $A$ in polynomial time. Whereas an NP-hard problem does not have to be located in NP, a problem $A$ is said to be *NP-complete* if $A$ is NP-hard and is in NP. The NP-completeness refers only to the decision variants (e. g. Is there a tour of length $b$ for a given TSP instance?), but most literature applies the term 'NP-hard' to optimization variants, too.

For NP-hard problems, no 'efficient' optimal algorithms are known, as current algorithms require exponential time to find solutions. As optimization variants of NP-hard problems play an important role in many applications, a common approach is to relax the problem's original formulation by either simplifying the problem or settling for non-optimal solutions. The three optimization problems discussed in this thesis are examples of NP-hard problems.

### 2.1.2  *Heuristics and Local Search*

A large variety of algorithms have been developed for combinatorial optimization problems. Exact and heuristic algorithms are well-known types of algorithms. A simple exact algorithm performs a complete search on all possible solutions for a given problem instances (enumeration) and terminates either with an optimal solution or with no solution if no such thing exists. A more elaborate example for an exact algorithm is branch and bound [123]. Here, the search for a solution is performed by traversing a search tree, where each tree node represents a subproblem of the original problem and the root node represents the original problem instance. Each branch represents a decision on whether to include or exclude a solution component from all subproblems in the subtree attached to this branch. For graph problems, a binary search tree can be used. At each branching point here, one branch forces the inclusion of an edge in all its subproblems, whereas the other branch forces the removal of the same edge in all its subproblems. For each subtree, bounds (e. g. the lower bound for minimization problems) on the best possible solution in this subtree can be determined. If this bound is above the best-known solution, the whole subtree can be pruned (removed) from the search. Once all subtrees have been evaluated, the best-found solution has to be an optimal solution.

Generally, finding optimal solutions with exact algorithms comes at the price of excessive computation time requirements. An alternative approach uses *heuristics*, which are designed to find (near-)optimal solutions in much shorter time. In contrast to exact algorithms, these algorithms do not give any guarantees on the feasibility or quality of the resulting solution (optimality or even worst-case excess). Given that both exact and heuristic algorithms operate only on models of problems that exist in reality, optimal solutions for the model are not necessarily optimal for the corresponding real-world problem. Thus, due to their lower computation time, heuristic algorithms are the better choice for practical applications.

Heuristic algorithms can be grouped into problem-specific and more general, problem-independent *metaheuristics* (Sec. 2.1.3). Problem-specific heuristics can be grouped again into *constructive* or *improvement* algorithms. In practice, construction heuristics create initial solutions that are used by subsequently applied improvement heuristics. The most simple construction heuristics create initial solutions by choosing or arranging elements at random[1] from the problem instance so that this process results in a valid solution. More sophisticated construction heuristics consider structural approaches or problem-inherent information. For graph problems, the closeness of nodes can be used, for example, for nearest neighbor tours or minimum spanning trees. Construction heuristics differ in the quality of their solution, the time required for construction, and the usability for local search. The last point refers to the observation that improvement algorithms may be limited in their search by the initial solution provided by the construction heuristic.

Improvement heuristics, on the other hand, modify an existing solution with respect to a given optimization objective (e. g. cost or size). A prominent class of algorithms within improvement heuristics are *local search* algorithms. Within local search algorithms, the set of all candidate solutions for a given problem instance is called search space $S$. Depending on the local search algorithm, only a subset of $S$ contains feasible solutions. A *neighborhood* relation $\mathcal{N} \subseteq S \times S$ defines the relation between two solutions. Two solutions are said to be neighbors if the local search employs a move operation that modifies one solution to re-

---

1 Given a number of feasible choices, each choice may be selected with some probability.

sult in the other solution (e. g. by exchanging edges for graph problems).
A neighborhood graph is defined, where each solution $s \in S$ is a node
and a node is connected to another node if the other node's solution is
in its neighborhood. The neighborhood of a solution is generally much
smaller than the whole search space. The local search algorithm starts
with an initial solution $s_0$, which is the initial element in a sequence of
solutions $\langle s_0, s_1, \dots s_k \rangle$ through the search space, terminating at some
(feasible) solution $s_k$. It must hold for each $0 \leq i < k$ that $(s_i, s_{i+1})$ is
an edge in the neighborhood graph and $c(s_i) > c(s_{i+1})$, where $c$ is a
cost function on solutions that has to be minimized. (This relation is reversed for maximization problems.) The above sequence thus resembles
a directed 'walk' (*trajectory*) through the neighborhood graph. In each
step, a subset of solutions in the neighborhood of the current solution
is evaluated and one solution is selected to be the new current solution.
The selection of a new solution is determined by some (stochastic) rule
and may take into account an internal status (acting as memory) before
performing the move operation. This selection can either follow *first
improvement* (greedy, checking neighbors sequentially, the first solution
better than the current one is chosen), *best improvement* (steepest ascent,
checking all neighbors, the best one is chosen), or some more elaborate
rule. A local search terminates in a *local optimum*, where no solution in
the current solution's neighborhood has a better objective value. The
definition (including size) of neighborhood and the strategy used to
walk through the search space are crucial for the performance of a local
search algorithm.

The general structure of a local search procedure is given in Fig. 1.
An example for a more sophisticated local search is the Lin-Kernighan
algorithm for the TSP [129] (see also Sec. 3.1.3).

### 2.1.3   *Metaheuristics*

Local search algorithms find solutions that are optimal compared to the
solutions in their neighborhood (thus 'local optimum'), but not necessarily optimal compared to all possible solutions (no 'global optimum').
In practice, local search algorithms are embedded into a higher-level
algorithm that takes care of escaping local optima, as local search algorithms can not do this on their own by definition. The most simple
approach is to restart the local search multiple times, reaching different
local optima due to either stochastic elements in the search or different

```
1: function LOCALSEARCH
2:     i ← 0
3:     sᵢ ← INITIALIZATION
4:     while ¬TERMINATIONDETECTED(sᵢ, N(sᵢ), memory) do
5:         sᵢ₊₁ ← CHOOSE(sᵢ, N(sᵢ), memory)
6:         i ← i + 1
7:     end while
8:     return sᵢ
9: end function
```

Figure 1: Generic structure of a local search algorithm. The function TERMINATIONDETECTED checks if there are better neighbors in the neighborhood of solution $s_i$; CHOOSE selects a new current solution from the neighborhood.

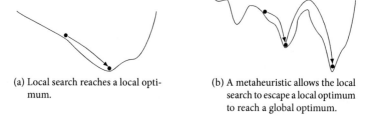

(a) Local search reaches a local optimum.

(b) A metaheuristic allows the local search to escape a local optimum to reach a global optimum.

Figure 2: Visualization of moves in the search space.

initial solutions. The best found solution over all local search runs is used as the final result of this 'meta' algorithm.

These 'meta' algorithms are called *metaheuristics* [84, 87, 31, 83], where the word stems from the Greek words 'μετά' ('beyond') and 'ευρισκειν' ('to discover') [139]. Metaheuristics are usually seen as higher-level algorithms that guide an underlying heuristic, such as a local search through the search space (see Fig. 2). This guidance can either help the subordinated heuristic to escape local optima or sample the search space to identify more promising search space regions. Metaheuristics are usually less problem specific (and thus easier to adapt to new problems) compared to the underlying heuristic.

According to BLUM and ROLI [31], metaheuristics can be classified by the following properties:

- nature-inspired or not inspired by nature

- single solutions or population-based

- static or dynamic objective function

- single or multiple neighborhood structures

- using memory or memory-less

The most prominent meta algorithms range from early variants such as *simulated annealing* (SA, [118]) and *tabu search* (TS, [85, 86]), through nature-inspired approaches such as *ant colony optimization* (ACO, [59]), *evolutionary algorithms* (EA, see Sec. 2.1.4), and *memetic algorithms* (MA, see Sec. 2.1.5) to 'synthetic' algorithms like *iterated local search* (ILS, [131]).

*Simulated annealing* (SA) is inspired by the annealing process of metals (metallurgy), which cool down over time while slowly adopting their final form [118]. Simulated annealing allows local search algorithms to escape from local optima by accepting worse neighboring solutions with some probability. This probability is defined by an exponential Boltzmann distribution that depends on the potential quality loss and the current temperature $T$. High temperatures at the beginning of the algorithms lead to acceptance of both better and worse solutions (thus, random walk), whereas low temperatures towards the end of the algorithm favor the acceptance of better solutions only (thus, resembling the original local search). Different strategies for cooling down or optionally reheating $T$ as the central parameter have been proposed, where the most common strategies follow an exponential temperature decay.

*Tabu search* (TS) uses a short-term memory to escape from local optima [85, 86]. This memory, called *tabu list*, stores components of the last visited solutions in a queue of limited length (usually in FIFO order) and forbids visiting neighboring solutions with components (*attributes*) contained in this tabu list. The tabu list's length (*tabu tenure*) is the central parameter, as small values support concentration on a small search space region, whereas large values support exploration of search space. The *aspiration criterion* is met once a better solution is available but blocked by the tabu list. In this case, the blocking gets overwritten to accept the better solution. Variants of TS use a frequency-based tabu list instead of the standard recency-based list.

*Variable neighborhood search* (VNS) addresses the problem of local optima by changing the neighborhood once such a local optimum is reached [146]. A local optimum in one neighborhood may be sub-optimal in another neighborhood, allowing the search to continue. Once

```
1: function ITERATEDLOCALSEARCH
2:     s* ← INITIALIZATION
3:     s* ← LOCALSEARCH(s*)
4:     while ¬TERMINATIONDETECTED(s*, 𝒩(s*)) do
5:         s' ← PERTURBATION(s*)
6:         s'' ← LOCALSEARCH(s')
7:         s* ← CHOOSE(s*, s'')
8:     end while
9:     return s*
10: end function
```

Figure 3: Generic structure of an iterated local search algorithm. The function TERMINATIONDETECTED checks if e. g. the solution as converged; CHOOSE decides based on an acceptance criterion whether to keep either $s^*$ or $s''$ as new $s^*$.s

a solution is a local optimum in all available neighborhoods, the search stops. A variant of VNS is *variable neighborhood descent*, where a set of neighborhoods $\mathcal{N}_1, \ldots, \mathcal{N}_k$ is defined in increasing size but not necessarily including each other. Once the local search in one neighborhood has converged to a local optimum, the search switches to the next larger neighborhood, which is more expensive to search but may contain better solutions. If an improvement has been found in a larger neighborhood, the search switches back to the smallest and thus cheapest neighborhood $\mathcal{N}_1$.

*Iterated Local Search* (ILS) is the base for many high-performance metaheuristics, utilizing the idea of perturbing local optima to escape them [131] (see Fig. 3). Iteratively, ILS perturbs the current solution and performs a local search until reaching a local optimum. The new local optimum is kept, based on an *acceptance criterion* (e. g. if it is better than the previous iteration's solution), otherwise the old solution will be restored. The perturbation step is usually a random, problem-specific mutation step with a variable strength. A too-weak perturbation is not sufficient to escape the local optimum, whereas a too-strong perturbation (although leaving the local optimum) may degrade the solution's quality. Aspects of ILS include the choice of initial solutions, perturbation, and more sophisticated acceptance criteria (e. g. considering SA-like strategies or restarts).

### 2.1.4 Population-based and Evolutionary Algorithms

Whereas single solution metaheuristics can concentrate their whole effort on one solution, it may be beneficial to maintain a set of solutions. Motivations for population-based algorithms include nature-inspired background, missing effective local search for a given problem, or avoiding premature convergence. Prominent examples of population-based metaheuristics are *evolutionary algorithms* (EA, see Sec. 2.1.4), *memetic algorithms* (MA, see Sec. 2.1.5), and *ant colony optimization* (ACO).

*Ant colony optimization* (ACO) [59] is a nature-inspired algorithm that uses the concept of artificial ants and pheromone trails. In nature, ants put traces of *pheromones* (chemical signals) on the path they traverse. Other ants can detect those traces and follow them, assuming they lead to a food source. This is a self-energizing process, as more often used paths receive more pheromones. In ACOs, artificial ants can be applied to any problem where a construction heuristic using partial solutions is possible. Each ant builds its own solution and whenever it has to choose between a number of alternative components to add, its choice is probabilistic, depending on the strength of the pheromone value assigned to each component. Pheromone values get updated (increased) by different strategies and strengths. For example, a component is rewarded if it was chosen by an ant and the reinforcement's strength depends on the solution quality. Pheromones evaporate over time, leveling the values assigned to each component. ACOs can be enriched e. g. by applying a local search on solutions constructed by artificial ants [105].

*Evolutionary algorithms* (EA) are nature-inspired, iterative algorithms to solve optimization problems. Based on a 'population' of individuals, operations similar to natural evolution are applied to members of the population striving to improve the quality of the population's members.

The foundations for evolutionary algorithms were laid in the 19th century, most prominently by DARWIN, LAMARCK, and MENDEL. DARWIN propagated the idea that more individuals are constantly born than actually survive (e. g. due to limited resources). Given that individuals differ to some degree, those that are fitter in adapting to their environment have a better chance of survival and thus reproduction. The term used for this fitness selection process is *natural selection*. Whereas DARWIN stated that individuals do not change during their lifetime, LAMARCK claimed that individuals can change themselves to increase their fitness. The former theory is assumed to be the correct one for biological systems;for optimization purposes, however, both theories can be combined. These high-level theories on evolution are complemented by the genetic mechanisms inside both biological and artificial individuals.

In 1865, Mendel performed experiments on plants to examine the rules and effects of inheritance (*Mendelian inheritance*). Mendel's laws, however, remained 'undiscovered' until 1900, when they were rediscovered. Mendel's and Darwin's theories were combined in 1920 into modern evolutionary theory [190] (found in [144]).

In the 1950s, initial work was done on evolutionary computation as summarized by [20, 70], but evolutionary approaches did not become popular before the 1970s. Three main branches of evolutionary computation emerged:

Genetic Algorithms (GA) were propagated among others by Holland [104] and Koza [120], where optimization problems have to be solved. A special feature of the canonical GAs is the representation of solutions as binary strings.

Evolutionary Programming (EP) propagated for example by Fogel [71], where programs in form of a finite state machine should evolve in the context of artificial intelligence to allow the prediction of results for unknown input data.

Evolution Strategies (ES) propagated by Rechenberg [167] and Schwefel [177] focus on optimizing parameters in real-world experimental environments.

A typical objective for both EP and ES is to find an input for a function $f : \mathbb{R}^n \to \mathbb{R}$ that optimizes (w. l. o. g. minimizes) the result. It has been argued in [145, p. 152] that since the 1990s there is no longer any significant difference between these three approaches due to the exchanges of components and ideas between them.

Several terms have to be defined for the following discussion. A set of *individuals* (e. g. candidate solutions) form a *population*. Each individual has a (numeric) fitness value associated with it, which is both an absolute measure and allow the comparison of any two individuals. A weaker formulation only requires the ability to compare two individuals to determine which one is fitter. An evolutionary or genetic framework iteratively applies a number of evolutionary operations (see below) on single population members or whole subpopulations. In the context of evolutionary algorithms, an iteration is called *generation*. The structure of an evolutionary algorithm is depicted in Fig. 4.

```
1: function EVOLUTIONARYALGORITHM
2:     i ← 0
3:     P_i = {s_i^0, … s_i^{p-1}} ← INITIALIZATION
4:     while ¬TERMINATIONDETECTED(P_i) do
5:         P_i' ← RECOMBINATION(P_i)
6:         P_i'' ← MUTATION(P_i')
7:         P_{i+1} ← SELECTION(P_i'', P_i)
8:         i ← i + 1
9:     end while
10:    return BESTIN(P_i)
11: end function
```

Figure 4: Generic structure of an evolutionary algorithm. Fitness evaluation is not shown as an independent function; rather, it is an intrinsic function of an individual in the context of the optimization objective.

There are three main operators applied during a single generation of an EA:

RECOMBINATION (OR CROSSOVER)  is an operation which takes the features (or components) of two or more *parent individuals* and creates one or more *offspring*. Common approaches are to split two parents in two parts and combine each two complementary parts to two offspring (one-point crossover) or to create one offspring that contains features common to two parents, with the missing features taken at random from one parent or created from scratch. Most approaches use only two individuals as parents, but multi-parent recombinators are possible, too. The idea is to merge good features of the parent individuals and to amplify these features in the offsprings. Therefore, recombination performs a weak *intensification* in the search process. Recombination may be applied with high probability values (> 0.5) in evolutionary algorithms.

MUTATION  is applied to single individuals (unary) and changes features of the individual at random. The mutation operator acts as a *diversification* step, as mutated individuals' features may differ from any other individual's features. Newly introduced features may allow an evolutionary algorithm to enter so far unexplored regions of the search space. Single mutation steps are usually performed with low probabilities (< 0.1), but may be applied multiple times on a single individual. In genetic algorithms, a typical mutation step is toggling a bit; for ES, a normally distributed random value is added to a floating point value, and in graph representations, a single edge may get exchanged.

SELECTION is applied once a set of offspring individuals has been created[2] after mutation and recombination. This step determines which individuals will form the next generation's population. There are basically two selection schemes. In the $(\mu + \lambda)$ selection scheme, the next generation is selected by choosing from both parents and offsprings. For $(\mu, \lambda)$, $\mu$ many individuals are chosen from the set of offsprings and it must hold $\lambda \geq \mu$. Different strategies on how to chose the next generation's individuals exist. In *proportional selection*, the probability of an individual to be chosen depends on its fitness compared to the fitness values of other individuals. Similarly, the *rank-based selection* orders individuals by their fitness and the selection probability depends on the individual's position in this ordering. In *tournament selection*, a subset of at least two individuals is selected from the population and the best individual from this subset is selected. It is common practice to ensure that the best individual always survives (*elitism*) even if it was not chosen by the above selection strategy for the next generation.

Recombination operators can be classified by the following properties, according to RADCLIFFE and SURRY: [164, 165].

RESPECT states that components (*formae*) common to all parents must be part of any offspring, too.

TRANSMISSION requires each component that occurs in an offspring to come from a parent (and not be created somehow else).

PROPER ASSORTMENT means that if there are non-conflicting components in the set of parents, it must be possible to create offspring that contain both components.

Both mutation and recombination are not only specific to the problem, but also depend on the *representation* of individuals. Based on the idea of biological genomes, fixed-length numeric vectors (real or

---

2 Selection strategies may also be used when selecting which individuals will be mutated or recombined with each other.

natural numbers, binary digits) are versatile representations that allow, for example, the description of permutations or weight vectors. Other representations include symbolic expressions (formulas or whole programs) or graph structures. Different representations are due to different historical backgrounds (GAs favored binary strings originally, for example) or application-specific reasons (like maintaining feasibility after mutation or recombination).

For some problems, it is necessary to distinguish between the *genotype* and the *phenotype* representation of an individual. The former describes how an individual is represented within the evolutionary algorithm, whereas the latter is the individual's actual 'shape'. In biological terms, the genotype is a life-form's genome, whereas the phenotype is the fully developed body. An evolutionary algorithm applied to a graph-theoretical problem may use a weight vector as the genotype, where the phenotype is the resulting spanning tree when adding the weight vector to edges and computing a minimum spanning tree. Both mutation and recombination are applied to the genotype, but selection uses the phenotype to evaluate an individual's fitness.

For initialization, the representation of individuals may be filled with random data to create individuals evenly distributed in the search space. Although this approach allows any solution in the search space to be reached in theory, practical approaches show that these random initial solutions are far too expensive to optimize to a competitive solution. It is therefore more common to start with reasonable initial solutions such as those created by a construction heuristic. It may be possible to run an evolutionary algorithm for an unlimited time but termination criteria, such as those discussed in Sec. 2.1.7, are used in practice.

### 2.1.5  *Memetic Algorithms*

The main advantage of evolutionary algorithms is their robustness: without specific knowledge of the problem to solve (assuming a fitness function is still given), evolutionary algorithms are able to find increasingly better solutions over time. Furthermore, using a population instead of the single solution in other problem solving algorithm avoids stagnation. The main drawback is the missing determination towards good solutions because no solution-generating component of an EA is a strong intensification operator.

Local search, on the other side, is a search technique with strong intensification that lacks diversification. Both local search and evolutionary

```
1:  function MEMETICALGORITHM
2:      i ← 0
3:      P_i ← {s_i^0, … s_i^{p-1}} ← INITIALIZATION
4:      P_i ← LOCALSEARCH(P_i)
5:      while ¬TERMINATIONDETECTED(P_i) do
6:          P_i' ← RECOMBINATION(P_i)
7:          P_i'' ← MUTATION(P_i')
8:          P_i''' ← LOCALSEARCH(P_i'')
9:          P_{i+1} ← SELECTION(P_i''', P_i)
10:         i ← i + 1
11:     end while
12:     return BESTIN(P_i)
13: end function
```

Figure 5: Generic structure of a memetic algorithm. Function LOCALSEARCH applies a local search operation on each given individual.

algorithms can be combined into a new algorithm class called *memetic algorithms* (MA, sometimes *genetic local search*, see Fig. 5). Here, the population-based framework including mutation, recombination, and selection is kept from EAs and local search is introduced as a 'directed' mutation. In practice, this local search's directed mutation is expected to lead to better results than random mutation because it becomes more unlikely that a pure random change results in an actual improvement with increasing fitness. Thus, a memetic algorithm contains components for both diversification or intensification in the search process. Memetic algorithms have been successfully applied to a number of combinatorial optimization problems. Disadvantages of memetic algorithms include their higher complexity (see below) and higher runtime due to more expensive operators.

The term *meme* was coined by DAWKINS [53, ch. 11] as a simplification of 'mimeme' (to imitate something). A meme is an unit of 'cultural transmission' such as a tune, scientific theories, or how to make fire. The primary concern of memes is replication, which is achieved by longevity, fecundity, and copying-fidelity. Like genes, memes strive for survival against other memes in the competition for resources (such as attention). In addition to this selection process, memes get modified during transmission or recombined with other memes. The difference between genes and memes is that the latter evolves much faster, thus improving the fitness of the carrier during its lifetime. Furthermore, an individual may incorporate previously unknown memes over time, which has only a limited analogy in biology.

Memetic algorithms have been most prominently proposed by Mos-CATO [148, 149]. They have been successfully applied to various combinatorial optimization problems, such as the TSP [143] (see also 3.1.3), timetabling [5], or VLSI floor-planning [193].

In terms of parameter and operator choice, the design of a memetic algorithm is challenging compared to both evolutionary algorithms and local search. For MAs, it is not sufficient to design both components independently as the interaction between the EA and LS component has to be considered. It is favorable if the EA operators (recombination and mutation) use a different neighborhood compared to the local search. For example, the changes resulting from an application of the 'inversion' mutation operator applied to a TSP solution are easily reverted by a 2-opt local search [96]. Furthermore, unlike early genetic or evolutionary algorithms, memetic algorithms make use of more sophisticated, problem-specific operators used for recombination or mutation. For the TSP example, a well-known mutation operator is the double-bridge move (DBM, [134, 135]); for recombination, operators such as EAX (edge assembly crossover, [152, 151]) or DPX (distance-preserving crossover, [77]) can be used.

### 2.1.6 *Lower Bounds*

Heuristic algorithms including the algorithms presented in this thesis do not guarantee to find global optimal solutions. Indeed, a heuristic algorithm cannot determine whether a solution is optimal or large its excess is above an optimal solution's quality. Determining the relative quality of a solution is related to the problem of defining a good termination criterion, which tells an iterative algorithm to stop once a sufficiently good solution has been found.

To evaluate the objective value of a solution found by a heuristic algorithm, a known optimal solution is usually required to compute the solution's excess. Due to the NP-hard of the underlying problems, the computation of optimal solutions requires prohibitively large computation times and thus optimal values are often not available. In cases where no optimal solutions are known for a problem instance, *lower bounds* can be used instead. Lower bound algorithms do not provide any solution, but instead give a minimum for an optimal solution's objective value (given that the problem under consideration is a minimization problem). Finding good lower bounds is not trivial. Although it requires less computation time than finding optimal solutions, is still considerably time consuming.

Two different principles exist to determine lower bounds. Either an estimation can be made based on the problem instance's properties, or some constraints of the problem formulation can be relaxed to make the problem easier to solve. Simple estimations of lower bounds are usually easily available, but these are often far below the optimal solution. Lower bounds computed by relaxations of the original problem are usually more expensive in terms of computation time, but yield much better results.

### 2.1.7    Termination Detection

For (simple) local search algorithms, termination is given once a local optimum is reached, i. e. no more improvements can be achieved by the local search algorithm. For more advanced algorithms such as iterated local search algorithms or evolutionary algorithms, there is no inherent termination criterion in general. For these algorithms, a termination criterion has to be defined, based on the search history and the current state. A termination detection algorithm is useful because continuing the search beyond a certain point will cost computational time without yielding better solutions. To avoid wasting time, the search has to be stopped once this point is reached. In probabilistic algorithms, however, the possibility of finding better solutions can never be excluded. Here, the algorithm is stopped once it has converged, i. e. the probability of finding improvements in the foreseeable future is negligibly small.

In practice, two types of termination criteria are used, depending both on the given problem instance and the algorithm. Firstly, the criterion may be defined by the setup. Here, the algorithm stops once a given solution quality level (e. g. known optimum or given excess) or a given limit in computation time or number of iterations or search steps is reached. Secondly, convergence has to be detected by the performance so far. Here the algorithm stops, for example, if no better solution for a given computation time or number of iterations or search steps has been found (suggesting that no improvement is expected in the near future).

## 2.2 DISTRIBUTION

### 2.2.1 *Distributed Systems*

A *distributed system* [50, 19, 192] is a network of individual computers placed at different locations and connected by a communication system to exchange messages. This communication system allows the computers to share resources including CPU time, memory capacity (storage space), or any kind of information. For the user, the distributed system appears as a single, integrated system. Computer systems participating in a distributed system are usually called 'nodes'[3] or in some contexts 'peers'.

Distributed systems can range from two standard PCs connected over some network link up to global networks such as the Internet. The design of distributed systems is driven by several objectives, including the following topics:

PARALLELIZATION In distributed systems, one large processing job is split and distributed among nodes, so that each node processes only a fraction of the original task. Finally, the results of each node are collected and combined into a result for the original job.

REDUNDANCY In the real world, computer systems do not work error-free for a number of reasons. Reliability can be increased because nodes can take over the tasks for a failing node. Fault-tolerance can be increased by processing the same task at different nodes and comparing the results, checking for differences.

LOAD BALANCING AND SCALABILITY Whereas a single node, even if equipped with considerable resources, may not be able to handle a large number of tasks, in a distributed system these tasks can be distributed among all available nodes, reducing the maximum load of each node.

TRANSPORT OF INFORMATION A distributed system may be used to transport all kinds of information between participating nodes. For practical purposes, this includes e-mails, web pages, or printer jobs.

---

3 Not to be confused with 'nodes' in graph-theoretical problems.

Although distributed systems provide several advantages for the user, there are several disadvantages to consider:

ADMINISTRATION & HETEROGENEITY From a practical perspective, the administration of a distributed system is considerably harder than single-location setups. Furthermore, participating nodes may belong to different administrative units, thus making global administration impossible. Having nodes with different properties (e. g. different hardware or software) may introduce additional sources of error.

GLOBAL VIEW From a theoretical perspective, it is impossible to achieve a global view on a distributed system. A global view on a distributed system includes the knowledge of each node's internal state and the state of the connections between nodes. A global view makes it very easy to solve several problems in a distributed system, including routing, membership, or global time.

SECURITY In distributed systems, two types of security problems can arise. Firstly, nodes may behave maliciously. This cannot be controlled if administrative control is not available. Malicious node behavior includes free riding and Byzantine faults [122]. Secondly, the transport of information on network links may get compromised, e. g. by man-in-the-middle attacks. Protection against such attacks can be provided by cryptographic protocols for authentication and encryption.

*Architectures*

The architectures of distributed systems range from centralized systems to completely decentralized peer-to-peer systems.

In centralized systems, a single node called the *server* provides all kinds of services to the other nodes (*clients*). Usually, the network topology is crafted as a star, where the clients are leaves and the server is the star's center. A global view can be achieved using a central server because the server is connected to each node. Furthermore, controlling the central server provides easy administration of the network. This central server, however, can be a single point of failure: the entire network's functionality depends on the server's error-free behavior. Even if the clients work without error, they can not communicate with each other if the network routes are disconnected. The importance of the central server makes it a prime target for network attacks.

The architecture in *peer-to-peer* (P2P) systems [155] is conceptually different. In ideal P2P systems, all nodes (called 'peers' in this context) perform the same tasks and no peer has a central role. All critical tasks such as network topology are solved in a self-organizing manner without central control. P2P systems have several advantages over client-server systems. By design, P2P systems are more robust against single node failures because another node takes over the function of the failed node. Networks are more dynamic, as nodes are allowed to enter or leave the system at any time. P2P systems scale better with the number of nodes, as no central server is a bottle neck for routing or administration. However, although P2P systems have many advantages, they also have disadvantages. Due to the lack of central control, fundamental problems of distributed systems such as routing or membership become harder to solve and require new approaches. Locating other nodes, available resources, or any information becomes considerably more expensive (in terms of number of messages or time).

Both central and P2P architectures can be combined in hybrid architectures. One example are the super-peer networks [207]. Here, some P2P nodes get elected (become *super-peers*) to provide special functions for some other peers, which a central server would provide in client-server systems. Super-peers are connected with each other in a dedicated overlay network which is used to forward messages of the normal peers assigned to them. Super-peer networks thus combine the advantages and disadvantages both of central systems and pure P2P systems. Unlike classical client-server systems, the role of distinguished nodes may change due to reorganizations in the P2P network. For example, if more and more nodes join the P2P systems, the load on peer nodes with special functions may increase so much that normal peers get 'promoted' to special peers, allowing the load to be balanced. If nodes leave, special peers become normal nodes again. Design issues with super-peer networks are in the strategies of promoting and demoting nodes and the development of algorithms that make use of such a topology.

Another hybrid architecture of strict client-server and pure P2P networks is the computational grid architecture [75, 72]. This architecture is inspired by the concept of power grids, which span whole continents and provide easy and cheap access to electrical power for each user. The grid architecture encapsulates the distributed and heterogeneity aspects of the distributed system, allowing transparent access to the available resources. Requirements for the introduction of grid architectures include both sufficient network connections (inexpensive and high bandwidth) and large amounts of available, as yet unused computational resources. Computational grids are designed to provide resources such as CPU time or storage space to users outside the provider's administrative domain. Unlike P2P systems, the usage is controlled, for example on a monetary basis, providing the user with a dependable service. As a design goal, potential users should be able to rent additional resources at short notice if necessary for a specific task and lease their own resources if they are not needed locally. The target audience is governments, businesses, and scientific communities with high demands on data throughput. Current research issues include the design of tools, libraries, and applications that efficiently use the grid, but the management of resources itself (including security and billing issues) is also of interest.

*Membership & Propagation of Information*

In distributed networks, participating nodes must have some knowledge of other nodes located in the same distributed system. This information may not be easily available, either due to the size of the distributed system (in number of nodes) or the dynamics of joining and leaving nodes. *Membership protocols* address this problem by maintaining a neighbor list which minimizes the impact of the list's incompleteness and outdatedness. Especially in networks, where memberships within a large group of nodes change regularly, no node can keep an up-to-date list of all nodes in the network. Rather, a node should only maintain a comparably small list of neighboring nodes that are used to forward messages to remote nodes. In the Chord system [189], for example, nodes get arranged in a logical ring (ordered by node id) and each node keeps a table of distance-node pairs, where distances (regarding node id) grow exponentially starting from the current position, keeping the list's size in $\mathcal{O}(\log|V|)$, where $V$ is the set of nodes in the graph. To route a message to a node with a target id, the sender forwards the message to the node from the table which matches the target id best (see Fig. 6). The closer the target node is, the better the forwarding becomes, resulting in a message complexity of $\mathcal{O}(\log|V|)$. The idea of routing messages by forwarding them to nodes with more similar ids has been used for Pastry [175], too. Here, a more complex routing table is used, consisting of a

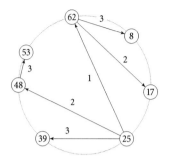

| $i$ | Theoretically | Actually |
|---|---|---|
| 0 | $25 + 2^0 = 26$ | 39 |
| 1 | $25 + 2^1 = 27$ | 39 |
| 2 | $25 + 2^2 = 29$ | 39 |
| 3 | $25 + 2^3 = 33$ | 39 |
| 4 | $25 + 2^4 = 41$ | 48 |
| 5 | $25 + 2^5 = 57$ | 62 |

Node table for node 25.

Figure 6: A Chord-like broadcast in a ring with $2^r = 64$ possible node ids and $n = 7$ actual nodes. Node 25 starts broadcasting a message. Arrows represent sent messages; arrow labels describe their chronological ordering. It is assumed that every node knows every other node.

leaf set (nodes in direct numerical neighborhood, for the last routing step), a routing table (two dimensional with node ids differing in at least one position from the current id), and a neighborhood set of 'backup' nodes located closely in the physical network. The complexity of routing a message to a node is $\mathcal{O}(\log |V|)$, too.

Both Chord and Pastry are examples of 'structured' approaches for propagating information in distributed systems and can even be used for broadcasts. Under conditions where the membership changes very often and both links and nodes fail regularly, these algorithms may fail to distribute their information. An 'unstructured' approach is taken with *epidemic algorithms* [57, 62, 109], where information is spread over a given network using the *gossip dissemination* paradigm. Inspired by biological epidemics, nodes in epidemic algorithms propagate incoming information to some (but not all) of the other nodes they stay in contact with. After the initial outspread phase, epidemics are much more resistant to obliteration than tree-based broadcast algorithms.

In epidemic algorithms, each node maintains an incomplete (and possibly outdated) list of nodes (including time stamps and other metadata) participating in the same P2P system. At regular intervals, each node contacts a randomly chosen neighboring node and exchanges information with this node. Exchanged information includes a limited number of messages received previously from other nodes and the sending node's neighbor list. Nodes store incoming messages for internal usage and future propagation. Given enough time, there is a high prob-

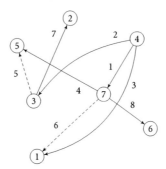

Figure 7: Distribution of information using an epidemic algorithm. Solid arrows show how a message passes through the network, starting from node 4. Dashed arrows represent information exchanges, where the receiving node already has this information. Labels next to arrows represent the time step in which the information was exchanged.

ability that every node will receive a given message (see Fig. 7). The received neighbor list is merged with the node's own list, with entries discarded based on a given criterion (e. g. age [61]) to limit the list's size, which is usually smaller than the number of nodes active in the P2P system. Initially, one neighbor must be provided to a node when joining the network. The neighbor list is updated later with node ids and time stamps of recent network communication events.

Epidemic algorithms can also be used for the purpose of maintaining *membership* in a distributed algorithm. A node is a member of an epidemic algorithm's network if it is in the neighbor list of at least one other node and is thus reachable. The information of new nodes entering the network is spread when the new nodes contact existing nodes (and is thus get included in the neighbor list). Nodes that have left the network are gradually removed from the other nodes' lists as the entries become too old. The design parameters of epidemic algorithms include the frequency of information exchanges and the size of message buffers and neighbor lists. The advantages of epidemic algorithms are resilience against obliteration and failures; disadvantages include constant message exchanges even in idle mode, and slow and undirected propagation of messages.

### 2.2.2 *Distributed Computation*

Distributed computation is best known for its use in public projects, where every Internet user can participate by donating computation time. Here, a software package is provided by the project maintainer and installed at the user's computer, connecting to a central server to receive a list of tasks to be processed. Once a task is finished, the result is sent back to the server and the peer receives the next task. Well-known projects of this type include 'SETI@home' [7], 'GIMPS' [204], and 'distributed.net' [36]. Newer versions of these projects are based on the 'Berkeley Open Infrastructure for Network Computing' (BOINC) [6]. Its design addresses typical problems in public-resource computing environments, including the often-changing availability of participants (e. g. turning off computers in the evening), the need for incentives to motivate potential participants, and the heterogeneity of participating computer systems. Cooperation or interaction between participating nodes, however, is not considered in this design.

Different toolkits with different features and target audiences are available for general high-performance computation tasks. A small selection is presented here:

GLOBUS TOOLKIT  is a system for high-performance distributed computations using abstractions from network resources [74, 73]. Development for Globus began in the late 1990s. In its current fourth version, Globus has grown into a grid community project where the focus has shifted to web technologies.

CONDOR  is a system providing infrastructure services for distributed computation [194]. Condor takes care of executing jobs that include resource allocation and scheduling (when and where to run), monitoring and error handling (e. g. check-pointing, job migration to other systems), and the abstraction of the distributed system, providing a sandbox that transparently encapsulates I/O operations (allowing remote data access without a network file system). Since its introduction in the mid-1980s, Condor has been enhanced to schedule jobs between different administrative domains or to integrate with the Globus project, for example.

MPI  is an environment for high-performance cluster computing in scientific environments [92]. Using the MPI framework, all nodes execute the same algorithm, differing only in the node id assigned by MPI. Independent processes synchronize during network send and receive operations. The major weakness in the design of MPI is its inflexibility, both regarding network structure and unpredictable communication operations.

DREAM  stands for 'Distributed Resource Evolutionary Algorithm Machine' and is a framework targeted primarily on evolutionary algorithms (EA) [17]. It allows the design of EAs using an island model [136], where each island is located on a different computer utilizing the spare CPU resources available on this system. The architecture of DREAM comprises five layers, allowing the user to interact with the system at different levels of complexity and abstraction. Different types of users (differing in their knowledge of EAs) can use the system. A graphical tool allows the development of EAs at the highest level, whereas direct access to the programming API, including the Distributed Resource Machine, is possible at the lowest level.

Distributed computations performed as part of this thesis focus on memetic algorithms. Here, an island model [136] is used, where each computational node (cluster node) holds one island with only one individual. Having only one individual per computing node allows the memetic algorithm instance on this node to optimize this individual, as in a non-distributed setup.

As the number of computational nodes is limited to the cluster nodes available to the Distributed Algorithms Group, none of the above distributed computing environments was suitable for the distributed memetic algorithms' needs. Operating in a controlled environment (full administrative control, single purpose hardware), advanced features such as redundancy were not needed. The requirements for the distribution setup, however, included the possibility for computing nodes to interact in an unpredictable manner (i. e. asynchronously). Furthermore, the effort to set up a distributed computation (both in developing programs and deploying the code) should be minimal. Eventually, small yet efficient distribution algorithms tailored to the needs of the distributed memetic algorithms presented in this thesis were developed.

For the TSP, which was the first combinatorial optimization problem to be addressed, a hypercube topology was used. Here, a dedicated central node 'arranged' nodes by providing appropriate neighbor lists. When exchanging individuals, nodes only considered neighbors they were connected to by hypercube edges. This setup is an example for a structured P2P approach, as the central node was only used for the initial setup phase and during the computation itself all nodes performed the same algorithm. Details on this approach will be presented in Sec. 3.3.1.

Whereas this hypercube approach is feasible, the use of a 'bootstrapping node' was seen to make this an imperfect design. Thus, an unstructured P2P network was used for combinatorial optimization problems to be addressed later. Here, an epidemic algorithm runs a membership protocol on the set of participating nodes. To exchange individuals between islands, a node sends its current solution to one of the nodes listed in the epidemic algorithm's neighbor list. An additional advantage of this approach compared to the hypercube approach (although not exploited in the experiments in this thesis) is the robustness against nodes leaving or joining in the middle of distributed computation.

*Alternative Approaches*

In preparation for the development of distribution algorithms for this thesis, other concepts of distributed computation were considered. For example, instead of using a decentralized algorithm, one node in a centralized component would initiate a computation by distributing computation jobs to participating nodes and collect the results at the end. As each of the collected results would have been found by each node independently, the initiator's job would be combine the results using some merging approach. The drawback of this approach is that computing nodes would not profit from the findings of other nodes and thus the search would not concentrate on promising search space regions. Furthermore, an effective merging operation would be required at the central node.

As a refinement of above concept, the job distribution could split the original problem into as many subproblems as there are participating nodes. Given that optimization objectives are designed on the problem instance as a whole, each subproblem instance must 'interface' with the other subproblems. For the TSP, for example, a problem instance would be split into subproblems by dividing the graph into several components. Within each component, a minimum-length Hamiltonian path has to be determined. However, it is not trivial to determine the start and endpoint of each path *a priori*.

In the approach discussed here, complete solutions are always exchanged between solutions. An alternative approach would have been to only exchange fragments of solutions. However, choosing the part of a solution to extract as a fragment for distribution and the integration of received fragments is not without problems. Although concepts of recombination operators can be reused, the effectiveness of this approach has to be challenged.

### 2.2.3    Arguments For and Against Distributed Algorithms

Using a distributed algorithm, as opposed to a non-distributed algorithm, has both advantages and disadvantages. They have to be evaluated during the design process of a distributed memetic algorithm.

There are several arguments against the distribution of an algorithm. Firstly, the computational effort to solve the problem instance at hand must justify the distribution. For small problem instances, the time required to initialize the computing nodes and setup the distribution infrastructure (e. g. the epidemic algorithms neighbor list) may have a significant impact on the total solving time. Furthermore, short running times require a tighter synchronization of computing nodes. Otherwise, nodes are in different stages of the search (e. g. close to the beginning or end) and thus can not cooperate efficiently. If the total CPU time is split among the participating nodes, the time available to each node may not be sufficient to solve the problem instance to a competitive solution even if solutions are exchanged among computing nodes. As observed in the experiments, an important factor is the availability of an efficient recombination operator allowing nodes to integrate incoming solutions into their local solutions. In the worst case, the distributed algorithm will revert to independently and parallel running iterated local search instances.

In favor of distributed algorithms is the argument that in a distributed environment with $k$ computing nodes, the absolute time is reduced by a factor of $k$ compared to a single node environment(theoretical case). Thus, large-scale computations can be performed that would be practically infeasible in non-distributed systems. In distributed evolutionary or memetic algorithms, each island maintains only a subpopulation (in the setups presented here only one individual). Consequently, the resource requirements per island are lower than the requirements of a single population, allowing larger problem instances to be solved in distributed setups. Whereas for small problem instances the distribution part requires a considerable fraction of time and system resources, this fraction becomes negligible with growing instance size. In a case where no 'good' recombination operator is available, replacement is an alternative if premature convergence towards a single or only a few different individuals is prevented by either mutation or other stochastical processes. A positive side effect of distributed algorithms with a message queue as employed in this thesis is the memory effect of this queue. Individuals in the queue may contain features that are extinct in the population; by reintegrating these features the algorithm may leave local optima. Beside algorithmic arguments, using desktop grids for an island model instead of a dedicated high-performance system with a single population may provide a cost benefit. In desktop grids, normal desktop PCs provide their available computational resources for a common computation project. Given that a large number of today's workstations provide more CPU performance than actually used by everyday software, desktop grids are platforms that are easily available for distributed computations.

## 2.3 EXPERIMENTAL ENVIRONMENT

Unless otherwise noted, experiments discussed in this thesis were conducted on a cluster system provided by the Distributed Algorithm Group at the University of Kaiserslautern. This cluster consisted of 15 nodes, each equipped with 3.0 GHz Pentium IV processors and 512 MB RAM running Linux (kernel 2.6). The cluster nodes were connected by a switched Gigabit Ethernet infrastructure. All time values refer to CPU time (not real time), unless otherwise noted.

# 3

## TRAVELLING SALESMAN PROBLEM

The *Travelling Salesman Problem* (TSP) is a well-known combinatorial optimization problem, which is about finding a minimum-length closed Hamiltonian cycle through a given set of $n$ cities with known inter-city distances, such that each city is visited exactly once.

Let $G = (V, E, d)$ be an edge-weighted, directed graph, where $V$ is the set of $n = |V|$ vertices (or nodes), $E \subseteq V \times V$ the set of (directed) edges (or arcs) and $d : E \rightarrow \mathbb{R}^+$ a *distance function* assigning each edge $e \in E$ a distance (or weight or length) $d(e)$. For simplicity, $d_{i,j}$ is written for $d(e)$ if $e = (i, j)$. Furthermore, in most applications the distance function is restricted to $d : E \rightarrow \mathbb{N}^+$.

The TSP's objective is to find a permutation $\pi$ on the set of vertices $V = \{1, \ldots, n\}$, minimizing the cost function

$$c(G, \pi) = \sum_{i=1}^{n-1} d_{\pi(i),\pi(i+1)} + d_{\pi(n),\pi(1)} \tag{3.1}$$

The resulting Hamiltonian cycle is called a *tour*. There are $\frac{(n-1)!}{2}$ different tours possible in a problem instance with $n$ nodes, as neither direction nor starting node are considered to differ between tours. For simplicity, $T$ represents a given tour and $c(T)$ the cost of this tour. An example for a TSP instance with its solution is given in Fig. 8.

Depending on the distance function $d$, a TSP instance may be either *symmetric* (STSP, for all $i, j \in V$ holds $d_{i,j} = d_{j,i}$) or *asymmetric* (ATSP, otherwise). Most benchmark problems are *Euclidean*, i. e. the vertices $V$ correspond to points in an Euclidean space, the distances are derived from Euclidean distances, and the triangle inequality is satisfied.

The TSP is related to the *Minimum Spanning Tree* problem (MST), as the TSP can be seen as a spanning tree plus one additional edge. Whereas efficient algorithms are known for the MST [33, 108, 121, 163, 154], the TSP is considerably harder due to its NP-completeness [82, ND22, p. 116f] (see also Sec. 2.1.1). The MST, however, can be used to determine lower bounds on the TSP (see Sec. 3.1.2).

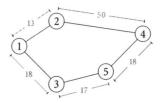

Figure 8: Example solution (permutation $\pi = \{1, 3, 5, 4, 2\}$) for a TSP instance with 5 nodes. For each tour edge, the edge length is given, resulting in a total tour length of $c(T) = 116$ units. Inter-node distances not used in the tour are omitted.

## 3.1    Literature

This section presents previous publications on the TSP. The literature overview is divided into three parts. The first part gives a historical overview of the TSP. The second part provides a short overview of exact algorithms and bounds (details given in the appendix). The third part presents heuristic approaches such as evolutionary or genetic algorithms. Table 1 gives a short overview on the publications.

### 3.1.1    Historical Background

The historical background of several combinatorial optimization problems, including the TSP, is given by Schrijver in [176]. Additional information is available through [10, 124, 15]. By referring to these sources, it is possible to summarize the historical development of the TSP.

Problems like the Travelling Salesman Problem were of interest before the 'discovery' of the TSP itself. Euler, for example, describes the problem of a *knight's tour*, where the knight piece in a game of chess has to visit each of the 64 squares and to return to its starting position using only knight moves. The earliest known reference to the TSP is from Voigt [197]. Within this book, the author describes five tours through cities in today's Germany and Switzerland. In [176], one tour with 45 cities is described with the tour proposed by the original author and an optimal tour based on geodesic distances. In the mid 19th century, Hamilton described the problem of finding a cycle in a graph, where the cycle visits each node exactly once. The TSP is a specialization of this problem: its objective is to find a Hamiltonian cycle of minimum length. The first mathematical formulation is from Menger [138], who defined

| Publication | Contribution |
|---|---|
| Exact Algorithms and Bounds | |
| DANTZIG *et al.* [52] (1954) | Cutting planes |
| APPLEGATE *et al.* [12] (2003) | Cutting planes for large problem instances |
| HELD and KARP [97, 98] (1970/71) | Branch and bound, lower bound |
| Practical/Heuristic Publications | |
| CROES [51] (1958) | 2-opt |
| LIN [128] (1965) | 3-opt |
| LIN and KERNIGHAN [129] (1973) | LK heuristic |
| BENTLEY [29] (1990) | Don't look bits |
| APPLEGATE *et al.* [13] (2003) | CLK |
| HELSGAUN [101, 102] (2000/06) | Advanced LK heuristic |
| JOHNSON and MCGEOCH [113] (2002) | Overview |
| MERZ and FREISLEBEN [143] (2001) | Memetic algorithm |
| REINELT [168] (1991) | Benchmark instances |

Table 1: Overview of literature on the TSP

a length function of a curve through a metric space. His discussion is restricted to Hamiltonian paths that only visit each set element (city) exactly once without returning to the first element. He also noted that a strategy of building a path by selecting the nearest neighbor to the partial path's current node does not necessarily lead to optimal solutions. Whereas MENGER did not require the path to be closed (thus a cycle), this concept was introduced in the 1930s by scientists such as WHITNEY, TUCKER, and FLOOD. In the 1940s, initial work was done to determine lower bounds for tours on instances with either Euclidean or Manhattan distances. This work led to the length estimations by BEARDWOOD *et al.* [28] (see also p. 49). The TSP gained larger public awareness in the later 1940s when the problem was addressed by members of the RAND Corporation [1], where the term 'travelling salesman problem' was coined. Even without the concept of NP-completeness, the TSP was recognized as a 'fundamentally complex' problem.

### 3.1.2  Exact Algorithms and Bounds

An important step in the TSP research was presented by DANTZIG, FULKERSON, and JOHNSON [52], which allowed a problem instance with 49 cities in the U. S. A.[1] to be solved using the simplex method applied on a linear programming (LP) formulation.

The following discussion uses the notation from [10]. In the LP formulation of the TSP, a vector $c$ of length $\frac{n(n-1)}{2}$ holds the edge weights in a fully connected graph and $x$ (also length $\frac{n(n-1)}{2}$) is the incidence vector, where a component $x_e$ equals 1 if the corresponding edge $e$ occurs in a tour and 0 otherwise). The TSP's objective is to minimize $c^T x$, where $x \in S$ and $S$ is the set of valid solutions (all nodes have degree 2, no subcycles).

The approach by DANTZIG *et al.* defines a relaxation of the original formulation, where $c^T x$ has to be minimized subject to $Ax \leq b$. Here, $Ax \leq b$ is a set of inequalities fulfilled by all solutions in $S$. Thus, any solution of the relaxation is a lower bound for the original problem and any solution of the original problem is feasible for the relaxation. The algorithm's idea is to iteratively insert additional inequalities (called *cutting planes* or *cuts*) to the system $Ax \leq b$, where all solutions in $S$ have to satisfy each new inequality. The algorithm stops once a solution

---

1  The problem instance was simplified to a 42-city problem by merging 7 east coast cities into one node.

is found for both the system $Ax \leq b$ and the original problem, i. e. all elements in $x$ are integer. Due to the lower bound property, this solution is optimal for the TSP.

Initially, two constraints are given:

$$0 \leq x_e \leq 1 \qquad \text{for all edges } e \in E \qquad (3.2)$$

$$\sum_{j \in V, i \neq j} x_{i,j} = 2 \qquad \text{for all nodes } i \in V \qquad (3.3)$$

Here, Eq. (3.2) defines the 'probability' of an edge $e$ in the relaxation's solution; Eq. (3.3) states that the degree of each node is exactly 2. This initial definition allows the appearance of subcycles so additional constraints (known as *subtour elimination constraints*) have to be added. Specifically, there must be at least two edges between each subset of nodes:

$$\sum_{i \in S, j \notin S} x_{i,j} \geq 2 \qquad \text{for all non-empty subsets } S \subsetneq V \qquad (3.4)$$

As the number of subsets $S$ increases exponentially with $|V|$, constraints of this type are added iteratively once they are required to 'guide' the search.

DANTZIG *et al.* specified 67 relations to find an integer solution for their 42 cities problem: 42 relations defined the node degree as specified in Eq. (3.3) and there were also 16 relations to limit multiple usage of edges, 5 rules to resolve subcycles as specified in Eq. (3.4), and 2 rules to maintain 2-connectivity. The final two inequalities were non-trivial and removed fractional solutions. The process of finding cuts can be automated, as first shown by GOMORY [89]. However, finding *good* cuts usually gets harder with the number of inequalities already added.

Instead of adding cuts that lead to integer solutions, a given problem instance can be *branched* into two smaller subproblems, which can be solved independently by adding cuts as described above [21]. Here, an edge $e$ is selected. In one subproblem this edge has to be included in all possible solutions ($x_e = 1$) and in the other subproblem this edge is forbidden to occur ($x_e = 0$). Knowing an upper bound for the TSP instance under consideration, branches can be removed (pruned from the search tree) if the cost of the relaxation of this branch's subproblem is above the upper bound. (This branch can not contain a better solution.)

APPLEGATE, BIXBY, CHVÁTAL, and COOK [12] discuss the issues arising from implementing and optimizing the original cutting-plane algorithm for large TSP instances (the authors' largest instance is the World

TSP instance [46]). They conclude that solving LP formulations is the single most expensive operation in the implementation (reported to consume 98 % for an instance of one million cities). The authors state that either replacing or improving the current simplex implementation is an important topic for future improvements.

*Lower Bound*

Evaluating the quality of a given solution for a TSP problem instance requires knowledge of the optimal solution to determine the excess in length. Especially for large problem instances, however, optimal solutions[2] are not known due to the prohibitive runtimes for exact algorithms. Therefore, lower bounds can be used instead to evaluate a given solution's quality.

There are several methods to determine lower bounds for the TSP. The most simple approach is to add the distances of the two nearest neighbors of each city and to divide the sum by 2. Better results can be expected from minimum spanning trees (MST), as each TSP tour is a spanning tree with maximum node degree 2, plus one additional edge.

The most-widely used lower bound algorithm is from HELD and KARP [97, 98]. The lower bound is determined by starting from a relaxed version of the TSP that requires a graph to span all nodes and to contain $n$ edges, but discards the requirement of node degree 2. The authors propose using a 1-tree as a graph, which fulfills these requirements. A 1-tree is defined in a graph as a tree spanning all nodes except for one node $v_1$, plus two edges connecting $v_1$ with the spanning tree. Therefore, a tour is a 1-tree with the additional constraint of a node degree of 2. Furthermore, a minimum 1-tree with node degree 2 is a minimum length tour for this graph, too. More details on this lower bound algorithm are provided in the appendix in Sec. A.1.1.

### 3.1.3   Practical Work

To find solutions for practical applications, it may not be necessary to find optimal solutions. Instead, good sub-optimal solutions found by heuristic algorithms are sufficient in many cases (therefore 'practical'). In this section, general techniques and selected algorithms to find local optima will be presented.

---

2 More precisely, the optimal solution itself may be known, but it may be unknown if it is indeed optimal.

*Representation*

Many heuristic algorithms perform a sequence of elementary moves on partial or complete solutions. Next, elementary moves are presented and implementation aspects are discussed. As a large number of these elementary operations are performed, it is crucial that efficient data structures and operators are used [76, 11]. For TSP solutions, the representation of a tour must handle information retrieval operations such as determining the successor (NEXT) or predecessor (PREV) of a node in the tour or the order of tree nodes in a tour (INBETWEEN) and, as a manipulation operation, flip a subsequence in a tour (FLIP), i. e. reverse the order of nodes in this segment.

The most simple representation is a set of two arrays, where the *tour array* contains the sequence of node indices as nodes occur in the tour and the *position array* maps the node indices to their position in the tour array. The NEXT and PREV functions can be implemented by looking up the node in the tour array using the position array; the desired nodes are the neighboring elements in the tour array. The INBETWEEN operation has to examine the positions provided by the position array only. The FLIP operation is performed by determining the location of both the segment's border nodes in the tour array and swapping corresponding nodes and updating the position array. This approach can be sped up by flipping the remaining tour instead of the segment to be flipped, if this segment is larger than the remaining tour. In this case, a *reversed* bit has to be maintained, which changes the semantics of the other tour operators.

Using a two-level data structure the FLIP can be performed with a low overhead, without introducing considerable additional cost to NEXT and PREV. Here, the tour is maintained as a sequence of segments imposed on a traditional array representation. Segments are connected in a linked list manner and there is no restriction on their size. For each segment, the segment's border nodes' positions and its current reversal status (boolean flag) are stored. Initially, a tour consists of one segment and the positions are 0 and $n - 1$ (where $n$ is the number of nodes). Whenever FLIP is performed, the segments of the flip's border nodes are determined and split so that the flip's border nodes become the border nodes of the new segments. All segments in the segment sequence between the new segments toggle their reversal flag. Operations such as NEXT and PREV have to consider the segment structure, as their semantic not only depends on the current node's segment reversal flag, but also on the status of the neighboring segments.

Using the segment data structure allows a Flip to be performed on a tentative base: if a local search operation decides to backtrack to a previous solution, only the flip operations on the segment data structure have to be undone; the underlying array structure is not affected. Once a sufficient solution has been found by the local search, the sequence of flip operations can be made permanent by applying the segment data structure's information on the tour array itself and resetting the segment sequence. The LK algorithm used in Sec. 3.2 implements such a data structure.

*Tour Construction*

An initial tour is required for many solving techniques for the TSP. Exact algorithms can use this initial tour's cost as an upper bound, for example in branch and bound algorithms. Local search algorithms (see below) start from an initial tour to perform a sequence of improvement steps. Different tour construction algorithms for the TSP have been proposed, each with different properties regarding computational cost, solution quality, or applicability in a larger solver framework. A small selection of construction heuristics includes:

Nearest Neighbor  The nearest neighbor heuristic is probably the best-known construction heuristic. Here, an initial node is chosen. Iteratively to the growing tour fragment, the shortest edge that does not connect to another node in the fragment is appended (otherwise this would introduce a subcycle), except for the last edge which finalizes the tour. This heuristic is known to insert good edges during early phases, but tends to include long edges towards the end of the construction. In practice, this heuristic has an excess of about 20–30 % [105].

Quick-Borůvka  This heuristic [113, p. 25] is a *greedy* heuristic. It is not a case of expanding one tour fragment; multiple fragments that exist as edges are chosen by some rule and inserted if no constraint is violated. Whereas a simple greedy heuristic would sort all edges by length and insert them until a tour is complete, the Quick-Borůvka heuristic (based on a similar MST algorithm [33]) sorts the nodes by some arbitrary criterion (e. g. coordinates) and iterates twice over all nodes. In each iteration, for each node with a degree < 2, the shortest edge whose insertion would not introduce a subcycle or let a node have a degree of > 2 is inserted into the partial tour. This heuristic is said to perform quite fast (faster than Nearest Neighbor, [113]) and to provide a good starting point for iterative local search algorithms.

CHRISTOFIDES  The Christofides heuristic [39, 113] is among the best performing heuristics guaranteeing a maximum excess factor of $3/2$ (given that the triangle inequality holds). The algorithm starts by building a minimum spanning tree (MST) on the TSP instance. For the set of nodes with an odd degree (including all leaves, the total number of odd degree nodes is even), a perfect matching is determined. The edges from the matching are inserted into the MST. Now, because each node has even degree, an Eulerian tour can be built which can be transformed into a tour by skipping already visited nodes when traversing the Eulerian tour. Its computational complexity is $\mathcal{O}(n^3)$. However, exploiting (geometric) instance properties, the complexity is reported to be $\mathcal{O}(n^{1.25})$ in practice [113, p. 36].

*Local Search*

Whereas construction heuristics are able to generate valid solutions for a TSP instance, the solution quality may not be satisfactory. Given that the construction heuristic contains stochastic elements, several tours can be constructed and the best one will be used for subsequent experiments. However, to significantly improve the solution quality, an heuristic improvement algorithm is required.

The most intuitive heuristic is the $k$-exchange local search [128, 51]. Here, in a local search step, $k$ edges are removed from the current solution and $k$ new edges are inserted to restore a feasible solution. In the context of this local search the neighborhood is defined as those solutions reachable from a given solution by one $k$-exchange step. A local optimum is reached once no $k$-exchange step can improve a given solution. It holds that for any tour that is $k$-optimal, this tour is $k'$-optimal, too, if $k' \leq k$, as $k'$-exchange moves are special cases of $k$-exchange moves where $k - k'$ edges were not touched. If $k = n$, then $k$-opt equals global optimality. Examining all possible candidates before performing an exchange move costs $\mathcal{O}(n^k)$ time. Thus, for practical reasons, $k \leq 3$ is used (for exceptions see [40]). For some cases such as

$k = 2$, one or several subtours have to be flipped (see p. 39) to regain a valid tour.

In a given tour, several alternative $k$-exchange moves are possible if the move can be selected by one of the following two strategies. The *best-improvement* strategy checks all possible moves and, in a greedy fashion, chooses the move with the best gain. The *first-improvement* strategy checks all candidate moves in a given (arbitrary) order and applies the first move with a positive gain. For the 2-exchange local search heuristic on the TSP, the effects of both strategies have been analyzed in [95]. It is argued that the first-improvement strategy results in better solutions compared to the best-improvement strategy if the first-improvement candidate edges are checked in non-decreasing order of their length.

To improve the speed of the $k$-exchange local search, the set of nodes to be involved in a possible exchange move has to be limited. Common approaches include fixed length (or fixed radius) neighbor lists, candidate lists, or *don't look bits* (DLB). In a fixed radius search, only edges to nodes within this radius are considered as new edges in an exchange move. For 2-exchange moves, the radius can be set to the maximum length of the two edges considered for removal in this move. Given that in an improving $k$-exchange move at least one new, shorter edge is introduced, this fixed radius search results in 2-optimal solutions. An alternative to a fixed radius search is using a list of nearest neighbors associated to each node. To limit the space requirements of these neighbor lists, their length is usually limited to value < 50. However, a 2-optimal solution is no longer guaranteed when restricting the search of nodes to such a neighbor list. Furthermore, the list of nearest neighbors may have some properties that limit the search. For example, in pathological problem instances such as clustered instances, the graph defined by the edges from the nearest neighbor list may not be connected, thus long inter-cluster edges will not be exchanged in any improvement step. Therefore, it may be favorable to include edges from special subgraphs guaranteeing connectivity. Examples of such subgraphs are (minimum) spanning trees, Gabriel graphs [80], Delaunay triangulations [56], or Yao graphs [208]. An alternative list of nodes associated to each node was proposed by HELSGAUN [101]. Here, a $\alpha$-nearest neighborhood is defined based on the edges with minimum $\alpha$-values. Based in the idea of 1-trees, the $\alpha$ value of an edge $(i, j)$ is defined as the difference in weight between a minimum 1-tree and a minimum 1-tree that is required to contain the edge $(i, j)$. Using this neighborhood, the optimal tour of problem instance att532 [157] is covered by an $\alpha$-neighborhood of size 5; using nearest neighbors, a neighborhood of size 22 is required.

To limit the number of evaluations performed in a $k$-exchange move, techniques such as *don't look bits* (DLB, [29, p. 95]) can be used to skip nodes that are assumed to be not involved in an improving exchange step. A node that has been a candidate for an exchange step that did not improve the current solution is unlikely to be involved in future improvement steps (unless the tour changes in its direct neighborhood). In this case, the node is marked with a DLB flag. However, once an exchange step has been performed, the DLB flags of involved nodes are cleared so that these nodes are considered again as future candidates. Experimental data suggests that DLBs speed up local search operations, but may degenerate the solution quality. Still, DLBs are standard techniques in many solvers and can be applied in a variety of algorithms, both for the TSP and other optimization problems.

The choice of $k$ for a $k$-exchange search is a trade-off between computation time and solution quality. This problem was addressed by LIN and KERNIGHAN [129] in keeping the $k$ variable performing a more complex search. Here, two disjoint sets of edges $X = \{x_1, \ldots, x_r\}$ and $Y = \{y_1, \ldots, y_r\}$ are built (with $r$ variable), holding that edges $X$ were contained in the original tour and can thus be removed and $Y$ are edges that are potential candidates to be inserted into the tour. Furthermore, for each $1 \le i < r$, it must hold that edges $x_i$ and $y_i$ and edges $y_i$ and $x_{i+1}$ share a common node. The LK algorithm is basically about the construction of both edge sets $X$ and $Y$. Note, that removing edges $X$ and inserting edges $Y$ does not yield a valid tour, as both sets grow when searching for additional edges. Still, it must hold that during the search process for each $Y = \{y_1, \ldots, y_i\}$ there is an alternative edge $y_i'$ for $y_i$ which restores a valid tour. Edges $Y' = \{y_1, \ldots, y_{r-1}, y_r'\}$ are only inserted to the partial tour to restore a valid tour once it is decided to stop the search. In each step $i$ the achieved gain $g_i = \sum_{j=1}^{i} d(y_j) - d(x_j)$ can be determined. The construction of $X$ and $Y$ stops once there is no edge available that would increase the gain and the changes from $X$ and $Y$ are made permanent to the current solution. Various modifications and variants are possible for the LK algorithm, such as allowing backtracking in the edge set building process (choosing alternative edges to be included in $X$ or $Y$) or limiting the search for edges to be included in $Y$. The LK algorithm can be parametrized to find 3-optimal solutions.

One of the best performing LK implementations is due to HELSGAUN [100, 101, 102]. This implementation ('LK-H') deviates from the original LK in several aspects:

- When searching for edges to be included in list $Y$, neighbors from the above-mentioned $\alpha$-nearest neighborhood are used.

- For the edge set $X$, modified rules of considering edges are used.

- Instead of using a sequential chain of edges to be removed or added (initially a 2-, 3- or sequential 4-exchange move followed by a sequence of 2-exchange moves), LK-H uses a sequential 5-exchange as its basic move. By using only a small candidate set here, the computational effort for this move can be limited.

- No backtracking is used, except for the first edge ($x_1$).

- Instead of testing for non-sequential 4-exchange moves after finding an improvement, infeasible solutions (containing subcycles) are generated and repaired.

- Initial tours are constructed using a nearest neighbor-like algorithm that prefers edges from the candidate set, low $\alpha$-values, or edges known to occur in good solutions.

A new version was released in 2007, but no publication is available yet.

*Iterated Local Search*

Although the above local search algorithms are able to find local optima, these local optima may not be of sufficient quality. To escape such local optima, metaheuristics (see Sec. 2.1.3) may be required to reach better local optima or even global optima. One example of such a metaheuristic is *iterated local search* (ILS, Sec. 2.1.3), where a local search algorithm (e. g. $k$-exchange) is combined with a perturbation operator. For the TSP, the most well-known perturbation operator is the non-sequential 4-exchange move called the *double-bridge move* (DBM) by MARTIN *et al.* (*Large-step Markov chains*, [134, 135]). Here, four edges are selected for removal, splitting the tour into four segments. These segments are reconnected with four new edges, restoring a valid tour without the requirement to flip any segment. A DBM cannot be easily undone by a $k$-exchange move usually. Different strategies can be used to choose the edges to be removed. Popular strategies are to randomly choose nodes or perform a limited random walk and variants have been discussed in [11, 13]. Variants of the ILS approach using an LK implementation for local search are called *Iterated Lin-Kernighan* (ILK, [111]) or *Chained Lin-Kernighan* (CLK, [13]). A publicly available implementation is included in the *Concorde* package [14].

A key aspect for population-based algorithms such as evolutionary or memetic algorithms is the recombination (or crossover) operator (Sec. 2.1.4). For the TSP, a number of recombination operators have been proposed with different properties or field of applications. For evolutionary algorithms lacking a local search, preservation of high-solution qualities in the offspring is of importance; for memetic algorithms (which include local search components), aspects such as maintaining diversity or introducing new features are more important. Examples of recombination operators used in conjunction with EAs include the following operators (each operating on two parent solutions):

The *Partially Mapped Crossover* (PMX) starts by setting two cut points in each parent tour, selecting two node sequences that are directly used in both offspring [88]. Where no conflict occurs in each offspring, add cities from the parent that is not the source of the sequence. For tour positions with conflict (a node is already used in the sequence), use the corresponding cities from the other sequence. The *Edge Assembly Crossover* (EAX) by NAGATA [152, 151] is a more advanced recombination operator using the concept of $AB$-cycles. In the multigraph created by merging both parent tours, an $AB$-cycle is a cycle consisting of edges that come alternately from both parents. Once the algorithm has constructed a set of $AB$-cycles, an intermediate offspring is generated by copying parent $A$ (or $B$), removing all $A$ (or $B$) edges from the cycles and adding the $AB$-cycles' $B$ (or $A$) edges. The intermediate solution consists of a set of subtours that are iteratively merged into a feasible tour.

Other recombination operators have been proposed for memetic algorithms with different design objectives:

The *Maximal Preservative Crossover* (MPX) by GORGES-SCHLEUTER [90] selects a sequence of nodes from one parent ($A$), which is directly used in the offspring. Two steps are then performed iteratively until a valid tour is constructed: Firstly, edges from the other parent ($B$) are added to this growing fragment until no more edges from $B$ can be added without violating a tour constraint. Secondly, edges from $A$ are added until including any other edge from $A$ would introduce subcycles. As no edge from any parent can be added, a new edge is introduced and the iteration continues.

The *Distance Preserving Crossover* (DPX) by Freisleben and Merz [78, 77] generates offspring that have the same distance (number of common edges) to both parents as the distance between both parents. In the first phase, edges common to both parents are copied into the offspring. In the second phase, these fragments in the offspring are connected by edges that are not part of any parent, but are found in a nearest neighbor search. Due to the constraints of inserting edges not employed in either parent, backtracking may become necessary in some cases.

The *Generic Greedy Recombination* (GX) by Merz [143, 141] consists of four phases. Firstly, the offspring tour is initialized by (a subset of) edges common to both parents. Secondly, short edges not contained in either parent are added to the offspring. Thirdly, feasible edges from any parent are included in the offspring, where shorter edges are preferred. Fourthly, additional edges are included (shorter edges are preferred) in the offspring to create a valid solution. The GX operator is controlled by three parameters (probabilities): 1. The *common inheritance rate* controls the probability of including edges common to the parents in the offspring. 2. The *new edge introduction rate* determines the proportion of required edges to be added in the second phase. 3. The *inheritance rate* controls the proportion of required edges to be added in the third phase. It is suggested in [143] that by choosing the right parameters, a memetic algorithm using this recombination operator can outperform similar setups using either MPX or DPX.

*Memetic Algorithms*

Memetic algorithms (see Sec. 2.1.5) are among the best performing algorithm classes for combinatorial optimization problems. A prominent example for a memetic algorithm for the TSP is from Merz and Freisleben [140, 143]. Certain aspects of this MA have been discussed above, but will be summarized here. Initial solutions are created in a two-phase algorithm. In the first phase, for $\frac{n}{4}$ of all nodes (randomly chosen), either the edge to the nearest neighbor (probability $\frac{2}{3}$) or the second nearest neighbor (probability $\frac{1}{3}$) is inserted. In the second phase, edges are inserted in a greedy manner, where all feasible edges are sorted by length and inserted into the partial tour until a valid tour is constructed. In both phases the tour constraints (node degree $\leq 2$, no subcycles of length $< n$) must be obeyed. As a mutation operation, a non-sequential 4-edge exchange (double bridge move) is performed.

Solutions are recombined using either the *distance preserving crossover* (DPX) or the *generic greedy recombination operator* (GX). The selection of parent individuals before performing a recombination is purely random. For local search, either a 2-exchange implementation or an LK implementation is used. To speed up the search, edges common to both parents in the offspring are marked as 'tabu' for the local search, i. e. by fixing these edges the local search may not replace them. Finally, the next generation's population is chosen by selecting the best individuals from both the previous generation and the set of offspring, where duplicates are avoided. If convergence is detected, either in the form of insufficient distance between population members or non-improving average fitness, a strong mutation followed by a local search is applied to all but the best population members. To speed up the algorithm, a large nearest neighbor list is built using a $k$d-tree and both local search algorithms use don't look bits. Distance computations are performed on-line due to memory restrictions on distance matrices, but a distance cache for common queries is used. To speed up backtracking, a tour representation using a segment tree data structure supporting tentative moves is used. This LK implementation was ported to Java and used in the experiments in Sec. 3.2.

The experimental analysis in [143] used benchmark instances from the TSPLIB [168] collection (see Sec. 3.1.4) with instance sizes of up to 3038 nodes and instance-dependent runtime bounds. Population sizes ranged from 10 to 100, depending on instance and setup. In the first batch of experiments, the recombination operators MPX, DPX, and GX are studied in a memetic algorithm using a 2-opt local search. To evaluate the effectiveness of these recombination operators, no mutation or restart was incorporated. These experiments showed that GX is able to outperform the other two recombinators and non-recombining setups given an instance-dependent parameter set. In the second batch of experiments, all features of the MA were activated as discussed. In a comparison between different recombining and non-recombining setups, both the DPX and GX setups performed best, with the GX setups achieving best results with a new edge introduction rate of 0.25. Compared to other approaches [91, 152, 147, 117], the MA by Merz and Freisleben is able to outperform these approaches for some or even all used problem instances. For most larger problem instances, solutions with an excess of < 1 % were achieved in less than one CPU hour.

### 3.1.4    *Benchmark Instances*

To compare various approaches for the Travelling Salesman Problem, sets of benchmark instances are available. Usually, numbers in instance names represent the number of nodes in this problem instance.

The most well-known instance collection is from Reinelt ('TSPLIB') [168, 169]. This library contains 111 instances for the symmetric TSP, 19 instances for the asymmetric TSP, and instances for different other problems related to the TSP. The number of cities contained in each instance ranges from 14 to 85 900. Most of the TSP instances, however, are rather small by today's standards and only the largest instances of this collection pose a challenge for modern solvers. Actually, all instances were solved to optimality by May 2007. For comparison reasons, because this library has been in use since 1991, it is still of importance for TSP research.

Two additional instance libraries have been published by Cook. The VLSI instance library [43], originally collected by Rohe, contains 102 data sets derived from VLSI design. The number of cities contained in each instance ranges from 131 to 744 710. Within this collection, only 40 instances were solved to optimality (as of May 2007), so the largest instances particularly are still open for future improvements. The national instance library [45] contains 25 instances, ranging from 29 to 71 009 cities. The data was derived from the U. S. National Geospatial-Intelligence Agency's Country Files database, which contains records for about $6.2 \cdot 10^6$ locations. Among these TSP instances, 14 are already solved to optimality (as of July 2007); solutions within 0.1% of the optimum are known for the remaining instances.

To test for special instance properties, instances can be created randomly. Usually, a given number of cities is placed within a square area, with the placing scheme controlling the structure of the instance. For Random Uniform Euclidean instances (RUE), coordinates of the cities are drawn with a uniform distribution from the interval of feasible coordinates. Inter-city distances are determined by the Euclidean distance based on the cities' coordinates. As clustered instances are usually harder to solve than instances with even distributions, Random Clustered Euclidean instances (RCE) may be of interest. Here, however, different approaches for the location of clusters and the exact distribution of cities are possible. Johnson *et al.* [113] suggest selecting $\frac{n}{100}$ cluster centers for instances between 1000 and 10 000 by randomly choosing coordinates within the unit square. For each city, one cluster center and two normally distributed variables (both scaled down by $\sqrt{n}$) are determined to set the city's coordinates relative to the corresponding center.

For RUE instances, it is known [28, 186] that $\lim_{n\to\infty} \frac{c(T)}{\sqrt{n}} = \beta$ holds within a unit square, where $T$ is a tour of optimal length, $n = |V|$, and $\beta$ is some finite constant. Thus, the expected length of a tour is $c(T) \approx \beta\sqrt{nR}$, where $R$ is the size of the square area ($R = 1$ for the unit square) and $\beta$ has be determined. Early approximations state $\beta \approx 0.53 \cdot \sqrt{2} \approx 0.75$ (BEARDWOOD *et al.* [28]) and $\beta \approx 0.765$ (STEIN [187]). Later publications estimated the constant to be smaller, e. g. $\beta \approx 0.7124 \pm 0.0002$ by JOHNSON [115].

## 3.2  FIXING EDGES IN TSP TOURS

Solving TSP instances with the help of computers started in the 1950s. During this first decade, the size of problem instances was rather small due to limited computational resources and the limited experience in developing algorithms for this problem by today's standards. Typical problem instances had a size of less than 100 nodes. DANTZIG *et al.*, for example considered a problem instance of 42 cities and CROES discussed an instance with 20 nodes. Today, significantly larger problem instances can be handled by both exact and heuristic solvers. The largest benchmark instance known to be solved to optimality is `pla85900` [9], whereas heuristic algorithms handle instances with several million nodes, such as the World TSP instance [46, 142].

However, solving large problem instances imposes considerable requirements on both computational and memory (RAM) resources. The problem of CPU time consumption can be approached, for example, by distributing the computation among a set of computers using distributed evolutionary algorithms (DEA, see Sec. 3.3) [65]. The high consumption of memory is due to data structures such as neighbor or candidate lists that have to be maintained in order to run a given TSP algorithm. This problem can be addressed by a fixing heuristic that marks certain features (e. g. edge sequences) of a problem instance or candidate solution as 'tabu', i. e. preventing any changes by mutation, recombination, or local search operators. The fixed problem instance is effectively a smaller problem instance with a smaller search space compared to the original problem instance. Thus, the general idea of solving large problem instances faster consists of three steps: (1) features of the original problem instance are fixed, resulting in a reduced problem instance (in an iterative process, this includes a reduced solution, too) (2) on the reduced problem instance, a TSP solver is applied (3) the reduced instance, including the found solution, is transformed back to a solution for the original problem instance. The effectiveness of the reducing and expanding step depends on the heuristic that selects the features to be fixed.

Different approaches can be taken to reduce a TSP instance's size using a fixing heuristic. Approaches to select features can be either node based or edge based. The latter can be divided further into whether they operate on a TSP instance or use an existing solution, respectively.

A *node-based approach* can work by merging subsets of nodes into meta-nodes (clusters), thus generating a smaller TSP instance. Within a meta-node a cost-effective path connecting all nodes (Hamiltonian path) has to be found. The path's end nodes will be connected to the edges connecting the meta-node to its neighbor nodes, building a tour through all meta-nodes. This approach can be problematic for a number of reasons: (i) how to group nodes into meta-nodes (ii) how to define distances between meta-nodes (and normal nodes) (iii) which two nodes of a cluster will have outbound edges. In an *edge-based approach*, edges are selected to be fixed. A sequence of fixed edges can be merged into a meta-edge, called a 'fixed path'. Subsequently, the inner edges and nodes are no longer visible and this meta-edge has to occur in every valid tour for this instance. Compared to the node-based approach, problems (ii) and (iii) do not apply, as the original node distances are still valid and a fixed path has exactly two nodes with outbound edges. So, the central problem is how to select the edges merged into a meta-edge. Examples for both node-based and edge-based problem reductions are shown in Fig. 9.

Edges selected for merging into meta-edges may be chosen based on instance information only or on a candidate tour's structure. From an instance with $n$ nodes, the former approach may select any of the $\frac{n(n-1)}{2}$ edges for a merging step; the latter approach reuses only edges from a given tour ($n$ edges). The *tour-based approach*'s advantage is a smaller search space and the reuse of an existing tour's inherent knowledge, as the tour edges may have been selected by some sophisticated heuristics. A disadvantage is that the restriction to tour edges will limit the fixing effect, especially in early stages of a local search when the tour quality is not sufficient.

Three examples for fixing heuristics in TSP solvers are presented here. In their original heuristic, LIN and KERNIGHAN [129] proposed

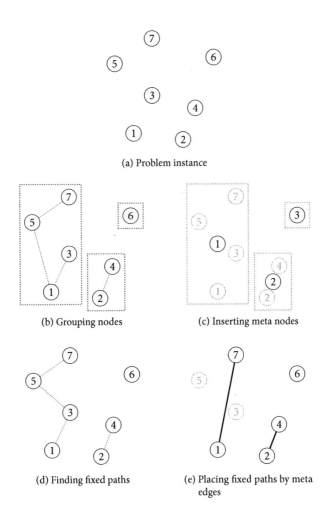

(a) Problem instance

(b) Grouping nodes

(c) Inserting meta nodes

(d) Finding fixed paths

(e) Placing fixed paths by meta edges

Figure 9: Examples of node-based and edge-based problem reductions. Starting from the original problem instance (a), the node-based approach assigns node sets to clusters and defines a Hamiltonian path within each cluster (b). Subsequently, in (c), only representatives of the clusters have to be considered (here arbitrarily located at each cluster's center). For the edge-based approach, edges to be fixed have to be selected (dotted lines in (d)). Subsequently, in (e), paths can be merged to single edges.

an edge fixing heuristic using a tour-based approach. Having found a small number of local optima, a set of 'good links' is determined containing edges common to all local optima. Subsequent search steps are not allowed to exchange edges from this set. The authors report that depending on the type and number of local optima, between 60–85 % of all edges are fixed. However, as this fixing may be too strong and edges not contained in an optimal solution get fixed, the fixing constraint is disabled in the initial phase of each search step (if $|X| < 4$). A speed up of factor 5 is reported in addition to the effect of directing the search towards more promising search space regions.

The primary related work to the fixation technique presented here, however, is the *multilevel approach* by Walshaw [200], which has been applied to several graph problems, including the TSP [199] and the RWA [68] (see also Sec. 4.7). In the first phase of a multilevel algorithm, a given graph is recursively coarsened by matching and merging node pairs, generating smaller graphs at each level. The coarsening stops with a minimum size of graph, for which an optimal solution can easily be found. In the second phase, the recursion backtracks, uncoarsening each intermediate graph and finally resulting in a valid solution of the original problem. In each uncoarsening step, the current solution is refined by some optimization algorithm. It has been reported that this strategy produces better solutions than applying the optimization algorithm to the original graph only. Furthermore, there is a hypothesis that the coarsening step smooths the search space, allowing the optimization algorithm to reach promising solution space regions. When uncoarsening again, the optimization algorithm can improve the current level's solution, based on an already good solution found in the previous level. Because the coarsening step defines the solution space of a recursion level, its strategy is crucial for the quality of the multilevel algorithm. In [199], the multilevel approach was applied to the TSP using a CLK algorithm [13] for optimization. Here, a multilevel variant (called $MLC^{N/10}LK$) of CLK gains better results than the unmodified CLK, as it is nearly 4 times faster. The coarsening heuristics applied to the TSP's graph matches node pairs by adding a fixed edge connecting both nodes. In each step, nodes are selected and matched with their nearest neighbor, if feasible. To speed-up the search for neighbors, a grid is put on top of the TSP graph. Neighbors for a node are only searched within the node's grid cell and the eight neighboring cells. Nodes involved in an (unsuccessful) matching may not be used in another matching at the same recursion level to prevent the generation of sub-tours. No neighbors may be available due to instance features, previous matchings, or the chosen grid width. As fewer free neighbors will be available at later recursion steps, the grid width gets adapted to the recursion level. It can be guaranteed that in each recursion step at least one match can be performed, but experimental results suggest node reduction rates of about 1.6. Recursion stops when only two nodes and one connecting edge are left.

An approach similar to WALSHAW's work but focusing on construction heuristics was presented by BOUHMALA [34]. Here, two different node matching methods for the coarsening phase are proposed. For an unmatched city, another city will be selected as a match either randomly or based on minimal inter-node distance. During the expansion phase, previously merged nodes at each level are expanded back to their original two nodes. An intermediate solution is constructed by using the previous level's tour and inserting the expanded nodes into this tour. Two strategies were proposed for the insertion: the 'simple insert' strategy inserts the two cities into the tour at the meta city's position where the ordering of the two nodes is chosen to cause the least increase in tour length; in the 'minimal insert' strategy, the two cities may be inserted at any position in the tour, which causes a minimum increase in tour length. Best results are achieved using the nearest neighbor matching and the minimal insert strategy, which allows the multilevel algorithm to find better solutions than those found by the Clarke-Wright Savings heuristic [112]. However, no computational costs are given to evaluate this approach and the minimal insert technique is basically an insertion construction heuristic that retains very little information of previous levels.

### 3.2.1 Edge Selection Heuristics

WALSHAW's multilevel TSP approach focuses on an edge-based approach considering the TSP instance only. LIN and KERNIGHAN's approach is edge-based, too, but requires several locally optimal solutions. Here, edge-based approaches will be discussed, too, but the discussion will focus on the following tour-based edge fixing heuristics:

MINIMUM SPANNING TREE (MST) Tour edges get fixed when they occur in a *minimum spanning tree* (MST) for the tour's instance. This can be motivated by the affinity between the TSP and the MST problem [121], as the latter can be used to establish a lower bound for the TSP. However, global instance knowledge in the form of an MST (complexity of $\mathcal{O}(m + n \log n)$ for $m$ edges using Fibonacci heaps) has to be available in advance.

Second Minimum Spanning Tree (MST2)    A second minimum spanning tree is built where edges from the previous MST are tabu. This edge selection uses edges contained in either spanning trees and thus guarantees that each node in the combined graph has at least two adjacent edges.

Nearest Neighbor (NN)  As already exploited by nearest neighbor tour construction heuristics, edges between a node and its nearest neighbor are likely to occur in optimal tours and are thus promising fixing candidates, too. Determining nearest neighbor lists may be computationally expensive (complexity of $\mathcal{O}(n^2 \log n)$), but the process can be sped up, for example using $k$d-trees [79, 185].

Second Nearest Neighbor (NN2)  This edge selection heuristic considers both edges to the nearest and the second nearest neighbors. The advantage of this selection is that a lower bound for TSP tours can be determined using the distances to the two nearest neighbors of each node.

Lighter than Median (<M)  Edges shorter than the median of the lengths of all edges in a tour are selected, as it is beneficial to keep short edges by fixing them and leave longer edges for further optimization. The most expensive operation of this approach is the necessary sorting of all tour edges (complexity of $\mathcal{O}(n \log n)$). There may be tours that have very few different edge lengths resulting in a small number of edges that are shorter than the median.

Lighter than or Equal to Median (≤M)  Similar to the previous strategy (<M), this also fixes edges with a length equal to the median length. It has the same complexity as the <M strategy.

Close Pairs (CP)  Here, a tour edge's length is compared to the lengths of the two neighboring edges. The edge will be fixed if and only if it is shorter than both neighboring edges and the edge's nodes therefore form a *close pair*. This approach considers only local knowledge (the edge and its two neighbor edges),

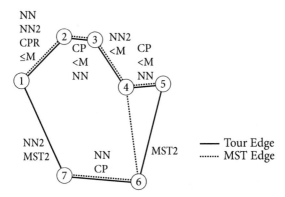

Figure 10: Example tour and minimum spanning tree with different edge properties highlighted. Tour and MST edges are drawn in different line styles. The properties of *second MST* (MST2), *nearest neighbor* (NN), *second nearest neighbor* (NN2), *lighter than median* (<M), *lighter than or equal to median* (≤M), *close pairs* (CP), and *relaxed close pairs* (CPR) are shown as markings on the edges.

allowing it to be applied even on large instances. It is expected to work well in graphs with both sparse and dense regions.

RELAXED CLOSE PAIRS (CPR)  Like the CP selection approach, an edge's length is compared to the edge's neighbor edges. Here, however, the edge under consideration will be selected if it is shorter than *either* of both neighboring edges.

The selection heuristics described above can be grouped into four pairs, with one heuristic of each pair representing a 'pure' approach (MST, NN, <M, CP) and the other heuristic representing a 'relaxed' approach (Second MST, Second NN, ≤M, Relaxed CP), which will select more edges than the edges selected from the pure approach. Thus, there is a choice of two strength levels for each concept of edge selection. The actual number of edges selected by one of the above heuristics during a fixing step depends on the current tour and the problem instance. The heuristics based on MST and NN can be expected to select more edges with better tours. For the lighter than median variant (<M) and the close pairs variant (CP) half of all edges may be selected, at most. This statement, however, does not hold for their respective counterparts ≤M and Relaxed CP. In the example in Fig. 10, solid lines represent tour

edges and dotted lines represent edges of the minimal spanning tree (MST). Out of 7 tour edges, 5 edges are also MST edges, 2 are MST2-only, 4 edges connect nearest neighbors (NN), 2 edges connect nodes with their second nearest neighbor (NN2), 3 edges connect close node pairs (CP) plus 1 edge as a relaxed close pair (CPR), and 3 edges are lighter than the edge weight median ($<M$) plus 1 edge which equals the median edge weight ($\leq M$).

For asymmetric TSP instances (ATSP), edge selection heuristics can be developed, too, but this is not pursued here. Applying the fixations heuristics presented here to ATSP instances poses new challenges, such as determining the direction when the fixation heuristics is based on undirected knowledge (e. g. from an MST).

### 3.2.2  *Analyzing Selection Heuristics*

Experiments have been conducted to estimate the effectiveness of the above edge selection heuristics to identify edges that are part of a (near-)optimal solution. Two types of probabilities were evaluated:

1.  the probability that a given tour edge is selected by the above heuristics

2.  the conditional probability that an edge in a given tour is part of a globally optimal tour, given that it is selected by the above heuristics.

For the analysis, six TSP instances were selected: Instances brd14051, d15112, and d18512 from the TSPLIB collection [168] and instances ja9847, it16862, and sw24978 from a collection of national TSPs [45]. These instances were selected because they are among the largest instances for which an optimal solution is known. For each TSP instance, 32 nearest-neighbor tours were constructed. From these initial solutions, different local optima were derived using the local search heuristics 2-opt, 3-opt, Lin-Kernighan (LK-opt), and LK-Helsgaun (LK-H), respectively. For Helsgaun's LK parameter, MAX_TRIALS was set to 100 (instead of number of cities) to limit the time consumption. In total, 960 tours were constructed to test the edge selection heuristics when applied to tours of different quality levels.

Each heuristic's selection scheme was applied to the set of 960 tours. Average values over each set of 32 tours with the same setup were taken and are summarized in Tables 2–4. Here, the first column details the instance under consideration. The 'Type' column determines in which local optimum the tours are located. Column 'OPT' shows the percentage of edges for a local optimal tour that also occur in the known global optimal tour. Columns 'MST', 'MST2', 'NN', 'NN2', '<M', '≤M', 'CP', and 'CPR' contain the probability that an edge from a local optimal tour matches the given property. Columns 'OPT|MST', 'OPT|MST2', 'OPT|NN', 'OPT|NN2', 'OPT|<M', 'OPT|≤M', 'OPT|CP', and 'OPT|CPR' contain conditional probabilities that an edge in a local optimal tour is part of the global optimal tour, given that it matches the properties MST, MST, NN, NN2, <M, ≤M, CP, or CPR, respectively.

Column 'OPT' shows the percentage of edges from a local optimal tour occurring in the global optimal tour. The better a tour construction or improvement heuristic works, the more edges the resulting tour has in common with the optimal tour. Whereas tours constructed by nearest neighbor construction heuristics share about 60–65 % of all edges with optimal tours (depending on the instance), tours found by subsequently applied local search algorithms are better, ranging from 65–70 % for 2-opt to more than 90 % for LK-H-opt tours.

As each edge selection strategy has different criteria for how to select edges, they differ in the proportion of optimal edges among the selected edges. The most edges are chosen by the MST2 strategy (column 'MST2'), selecting about 85–90 % of all edges in nearest neighbor tours (row 'NN') and about 94 % in LK-opt tours. Other strategies select fewer edges: from NN2 with 80–85% and CPR or MST with 70–75 % down to <M and CP with about 40–55% and 20–40% of all edges, respectively. For 'MST', 'MST2', 'NN', and 'NN2', the probability of selecting edges increases with tour quality, with the least proportion of edges from nearest neighbor tours and most edges from either 3-opt, LK-opt, or LK-H tours (depending on instance). Interestingly, for all instances, the number of selected edges decreases for high-quality tours such as 'LK-H' and optimal tours. For instance it16862, for example, using the NN selection strategy, the least number of edges are selected either from nearest neighbor or optimal tours; the most edges are selected from 3-opt and LK-opt tours. For '<M', '≤M', 'CP', and 'CPR', the probability of selection edges decreases with tour quality. So for problem instance d15112 and selection strategy CP, the probability of selection edges decreases from 39.6 % for nearest neighbor tours down to 31.3 % for optimal tours.

However, the quantity (number of edges selected for fixing) is not the only criterion for rating a selection strategy. Selected edges were

| | Tour Type | OPT | MST | OPT\|MST | MST2 | OPT\|MST2 | NN | OPT\|NN | NN2 | OPT\|NN2 | <M | OPT\|<M | ≤M | OPT\|≤M | CP | OPT\|CP | CPR | OPT\|CPR |
|---|---|---|---|---|---|---|---|---|---|---|---|---|---|---|---|---|---|---|
| ja9847 | NN | 64.9 | 75.7 | 75.9 | 88.3 | 71.7 | 61.9 | 77.5 | 83.3 | 72.3 | 46.0 | 74.2 | 57.0 | 74.1 | 34.5 | 75.7 | 72.0 | 71.3 |
| | 2-opt | 70.1 | 76.7 | 79.0 | 90.3 | 75.2 | 62.5 | 80.2 | 84.1 | 76.2 | 45.4 | 78.1 | 56.8 | 77.6 | 32.5 | 78.9 | 71.0 | 75.6 |
| | 3-opt | 74.8 | 78.4 | 81.5 | 92.2 | 78.4 | 64.3 | 82.3 | 85.4 | 79.7 | 45.9 | 80.9 | 57.7 | 80.5 | 31.3 | 81.8 | 69.9 | 79.4 |
| | LK-opt | 79.7 | 78.4 | 84.8 | 93.3 | 82.0 | 63.9 | 85.4 | 85.5 | 83.6 | 45.7 | 84.4 | 57.3 | 84.0 | 29.9 | 84.9 | 68.4 | 83.0 |
| | LK-H | 93.3 | 77.0 | 94.7 | 92.9 | 93.9 | 61.8 | 94.7 | 84.4 | 94.4 | 44.4 | 93.8 | 56.0 | 93.8 | 27.0 | 94.8 | 64.7 | 94.2 |
| | optimal | 100.0 | 75.9 | 100.0 | 92.5 | 100.0 | 60.3 | 100.0 | 83.7 | 100.0 | 43.7 | 100.0 | 55.2 | 100.0 | 25.9 | 100.0 | 63.1 | 100.0 |
| brd14051 | NN | 59.3 | 70.4 | 73.4 | 85.6 | 67.6 | 58.4 | 74.8 | 83.5 | 66.6 | 54.9 | 71.3 | 57.1 | 71.0 | 40.0 | 71.9 | 75.2 | 67.1 |
| | 2-opt | 65.3 | 73.7 | 75.9 | 89.8 | 70.8 | 60.3 | 77.4 | 84.7 | 71.6 | 53.4 | 75.0 | 55.6 | 74.7 | 38.4 | 75.7 | 74.6 | 72.2 |
| | 3-opt | 70.8 | 76.4 | 78.7 | 92.5 | 74.4 | 62.8 | 79.8 | 86.4 | 75.8 | 52.4 | 78.1 | 54.7 | 77.9 | 37.2 | 78.8 | 73.7 | 76.4 |
| | LK-opt | 77.2 | 77.5 | 82.7 | 94.4 | 79.2 | 62.9 | 83.6 | 86.9 | 81.2 | 52.2 | 82.5 | 54.6 | 82.3 | 35.2 | 83.1 | 71.9 | 81.0 |
| | LK-H | 92.6 | 76.8 | 94.0 | 93.0 | 94.5 | 61.1 | 94.1 | 86.5 | 93.8 | 48.6 | 93.7 | 51.2 | 93.7 | 31.7 | 93.9 | 68.2 | 93.4 |
| | optimal | 100.0 | 75.5 | 100.0 | 93.9 | 100.0 | 59.3 | 100.0 | 85.6 | 100.0 | 47.8 | 100.0 | 50.5 | 100.0 | 30.3 | 100.0 | 66.5 | 100.0 |

Table 2: Probabilities (in percent) for edges in a tour to match certain criteria. The data is grouped by TSP instance and tour type (part 1). The eight left-most columns contain the original and the conditional probabilities for the four edge fixation heuristics discussed in this thesis.

| Tour Type | OPT | MST | OPT\|MST | MST2 | OPT\|MST2 | NN | OPT\|NN | NN2 | OPT\|NN2 | <M | OPT\|<M | ≤M | OPT\|≤M | CP | OPT\|CP | CPR | OPT\|CPR |
|---|---|---|---|---|---|---|---|---|---|---|---|---|---|---|---|---|---|
| **d15112** | | | | | | | | | | | | | | | | | |
| NN | 61.4 | 71.3 | 74.3 | 86.9 | 69.0 | 59.1 | 76.1 | 83.5 | 68.8 | 54.6 | 72.1 | 55.4 | 72.0 | 39.6 | 73.5 | 75.6 | 68.5 |
| 2-opt | 66.1 | 73.6 | 76.1 | 90.2 | 71.3 | 60.5 | 77.8 | 84.6 | 72.4 | 54.1 | 74.7 | 54.9 | 74.6 | 38.6 | 76.1 | 75.3 | 72.4 |
| 3-opt | 71.0 | 76.1 | 78.6 | 92.5 | 74.6 | 63.0 | 79.9 | 86.3 | 76.1 | 53.6 | 77.7 | 54.4 | 77.6 | 37.7 | 79.1 | 74.7 | 76.3 |
| LK-opt | 76.9 | 77.1 | 82.2 | 94.3 | 78.8 | 63.2 | 83.3 | 86.8 | 81.0 | 52.4 | 81.7 | 53.3 | 81.7 | 35.9 | 82.7 | 73.2 | 80.6 |
| LK-H | 92.5 | 76.2 | 93.8 | 94.4 | 92.9 | 61.3 | 94.1 | 86.4 | 93.8 | 50.6 | 93.3 | 51.6 | 93.3 | 32.6 | 93.8 | 69.6 | 93.3 |
| optimal | 100.0 | 74.8 | 100.0 | 93.9 | 100.0 | 59.7 | 100.0 | 85.6 | 100.0 | 49.8 | 100.0 | 50.8 | 100.0 | 31.3 | 100.0 | 67.8 | 100.0 |
| **fl1662** | | | | | | | | | | | | | | | | | |
| NN | 61.4 | 72.4 | 74.4 | 86.9 | 68.9 | 60.1 | 76.1 | 82.9 | 69.2 | 52.6 | 73.4 | 64.0 | 70.6 | 32.8 | 73.5 | 70.5 | 68.9 |
| 2-opt | 66.9 | 74.8 | 76.7 | 89.9 | 72.1 | 62.0 | 78.1 | 84.2 | 73.2 | 53.8 | 76.3 | 64.3 | 74.5 | 30.6 | 76.4 | 69.3 | 73.2 |
| 3-opt | 71.9 | 77.0 | 79.3 | 92.1 | 75.5 | 64.2 | 80.4 | 85.8 | 77.0 | 54.6 | 79.2 | 54.9 | 79.1 | 29.1 | 79.3 | 67.7 | 77.2 |
| LK-opt | 77.3 | 77.6 | 82.6 | 93.6 | 79.4 | 64.2 | 83.6 | 86.1 | 81.4 | 53.5 | 82.7 | 53.9 | 82.6 | 27.4 | 82.9 | 65.6 | 81.1 |
| LK-H | 91.2 | 76.6 | 92.8 | 93.5 | 91.8 | 62.6 | 93.0 | 85.5 | 92.7 | 51.2 | 92.5 | 51.8 | 92.5 | 24.1 | 92.9 | 61.5 | 92.2 |
| optimal | 100.0 | 75.0 | 100.0 | 92.8 | 100.0 | 60.6 | 100.0 | 84.4 | 100.0 | 49.9 | 100.0 | 50.5 | 100.0 | 22.9 | 100.0 | 59.2 | 100.0 |

Table 3: Probabilities (in percent) for edges in a tour to match certain criteria. The data is grouped by TSP instance and tour type (part 2). The eight left-most columns contain the original and the conditional probabilities for the four edge fixation heuristics discussed in this thesis.

| | Tour Type | OPT | MST | OPT\|MST | MST2 | OPT\|MST2 | NN | OPT\|NN | NN2 | OPT\|NN2 | <M | OPT\|<M | ≤M | OPT\|≤M | CP | OPT\|CP | CPR | OPT\|CPR |
|---|---|---|---|---|---|---|---|---|---|---|---|---|---|---|---|---|---|---|
| d18512 | NN | 60.9 | 71.8 | 74.0 | 87.1 | 68.4 | 59.3 | 75.7 | 83.9 | 68.2 | 55.4 | 72.6 | 58.6 | 72.4 | 39.2 | 73.2 | 74.7 | 68.5 |
| | 2-opt | 65.8 | 74.2 | 76.0 | 90.4 | 70.9 | 60.7 | 77.6 | 84.8 | 72.1 | 53.9 | 75.3 | 55.8 | 75.1 | 38.1 | 76.1 | 74.3 | 72.5 |
| | 3-opt | 70.8 | 76.8 | 78.5 | 92.8 | 74.3 | 63.0 | 79.8 | 86.5 | 75.9 | 53.2 | 78.2 | 55.1 | 78.0 | 37.1 | 78.9 | 73.5 | 76.5 |
| | LK-opt | 77.2 | 77.7 | 82.5 | 94.6 | 79.1 | 62.9 | 83.6 | 86.8 | 81.2 | 53.0 | 82.4 | 54.9 | 82.2 | 35.3 | 82.9 | 71.7 | 81.0 |
| | LK-H | 92.7 | 76.8 | 94.1 | 94.7 | 93.2 | 61.1 | 94.2 | 86.4 | 94.0 | 50.0 | 93.8 | 51.8 | 93.8 | 31.7 | 94.1 | 67.8 | 93.5 |
| | optimal | 100.0 | 75.5 | 100.0 | 100.0 | 59.3 | 59.3 | 100.0 | 85.6 | 100.0 | 49.1 | 100.0 | 50.8 | 100.0 | 30.3 | 100.0 | 66.1 | 100.0 |
| sw24978 | NN | 65.5 | 76.2 | 75.3 | 88.6 | 72.1 | 65.6 | 75.8 | 85.3 | 71.9 | 42.6 | 74.5 | 58.3 | 74.3 | 24.9 | 74.9 | 66.0 | 71.1 |
| | 2-opt | 68.2 | 75.6 | 76.9 | 90.2 | 73.2 | 64.2 | 77.7 | 85.3 | 73.9 | 41.2 | 76.7 | 58.4 | 75.3 | 25.0 | 77.0 | 66.2 | 73.8 |
| | 3-opt | 72.3 | 77.0 | 79.1 | 92.1 | 75.8 | 65.5 | 79.6 | 86.3 | 76.9 | 41.8 | 78.9 | 59.6 | 77.6 | 24.3 | 79.2 | 65.2 | 77.1 |
| | LK-opt | 76.7 | 77.0 | 82.0 | 93.3 | 78.9 | 64.5 | 82.7 | 86.1 | 80.7 | 41.2 | 81.9 | 59.5 | 80.5 | 23.3 | 82.0 | 63.1 | 80.3 |
| | LK-H | 90.3 | 76.2 | 92.1 | 93.3 | 90.9 | 62.9 | 92.1 | 85.5 | 91.9 | 40.3 | 91.3 | 58.5 | 90.8 | 20.6 | 92.4 | 59.2 | 91.5 |
| | optimal | 100.0 | 74.6 | 100.0 | 100.0 | 92.6 | 60.9 | 100.0 | 84.5 | 100.0 | 39.2 | 100.0 | 57.5 | 100.0 | 19.4 | 100.0 | 57.1 | 100.0 |

Table 4: Probabilities (in percent) for edges in a tour to match certain criteria. The data is grouped by TSP instance and tour type (part 3). The eight left-most columns contain the original and the conditional probabilities for the four edge fixation heuristics discussed in this thesis.

checked to confirm whether they occur in the corresponding known optimal tour, too. When applying a fixing heuristic to a sub-optimal tour, a good heuristic should more likely select edges that also occur in the optimal tour, rather than edges that do not occur in the optimal tour. Therefore, the probability that a sub-optimal tour's edge selected by an edge selection strategy would actually be contained in an optimal tour ('true positive') rather than being a 'false positive' is of interest.

The quality of an edge selection strategy can be estimated by comparing its conditional probability (for example, the 'OPT|MST' column for the MST heuristic) with the probability of an edge to be part of an optimal tour (column 'OPT'). A selection strategy that randomly selects edges would have a conditional probability equal to 'OPT', whereas a purposeful strategy is expected to have higher probability values. This property holds for each of the discussed strategies. Furthermore, it can be observed that strategies with higher conditional probabilities select fewer edges for fixation compared to selection strategies with lower conditional probabilities. For example, for 2-opt tours of the instance d15112, the probability of an edge being part of an optimal tour is 66.1 %. For the edge selection strategy NN, 60.5 % of all edges would be selected, 77.8 % of which also occur in the optimal tour. By contrast, the edge selection strategy MST2 selects 90.2 % of the tour edges, but only 71.3 % of those edges are part of an optimal tour.

Generally, with an increasing number of edges from optimal solutions in a given solution, the probability of selecting such an edge increases for all selection strategies. For example, for problem instance sw24978, 'OPT|MST' increases in correspondence with 'OPT' from 75.3 % for nearest neighbor tours to 92.1 % for LK-H tours. Furthermore, relaxed versions of edge selection strategies have a lower probability of picking edges from optimal solutions than the more strict 'original' strategies. For problem instance d18512 and 2-opt tours, for example, the probability of having optimal tour edges among the selected edges is 76.1 % for the strict variant 'MST', but only 71.3 % for the relaxed variant 'MST2'. Thus, there is an obvious trade-off between two extrema in selecting edges: selecting too many edges increases the probability of including too many 'wrong' edges. If only few edges are selected, the probability of choosing 'good' ones is higher. The performance differences are only negligible between '<M' and '≤M', where very few edges are affected by the differences in the selection strategies. Among all edge selection strategies, the strategy with the highest probability of selecting edges from optimal tours is 'NN', except for two cases where the close pairs

strategy (CP) is more likely to find the right edges for LK-H tours. For instance brd14051 and 3-opt solutions, for example, the probability is 79.8 % for NN, but the corresponding values for all other selection strategies are ≤ 78.8 % (CP). The three worst-performing selection strategies here are MST2, NN2, and CPR, which all are relaxed variants of more strict selection strategies. However, the performance of these selection strategies improves with tour quality, so that for high-quality tours (LK-H), all selection strategies perform very similarly. For it16862 with LK-H tours, for example, the conditional probability ranges from 91.8 % to 93.0 %, whereas the probability values are less homogeneous for 2-opt tours (ranging from 72.1 % to 78.1 %).

### 3.2.3    Experimental Setup and Results

For the experimental evaluation, the fixing heuristics have been integrated into a simple TSP solver written in Java. The solver works as follows: each tour was reduced using one of the fixing heuristics and subsequently improved by an iterated local search (ILS) algorithm. In each iteration of the algorithm, the current tour was perturbed and locally optimized by an LK implementation (based on the one from [143]), enriched to handle fixed edges. For the perturbation, a variable-strength *double-bridge move* (DBM) was used, increasing the number of DBMs every two non-improving iterations. At the end of each iteration, the new tour was compared to the previous tour and discarded if no improvement was found. Otherwise it was kept for subsequent iterations. The iterations would stop after two non-improving iterations. Finally, the improved tour was expanded back to a solution for the original TSP instance. This reducing and expansion procedure was repeated 10 times on each solution. For comparison, all tours were optimized by the iterated local search algorithm without any reduction, too. This solver was not designed to compete with state-of-the-art solvers, but merely to evaluate the fixation heuristics. Each parameter setup was tested by applying it to the tours described in Sec. 3.2.1; average values were used for the following discussion.

Tables 5 to 10 show the results for the different setups applied to the ILS and are structured as follows: rows are grouped by instance (ja9847 to sw24978) and by starting tour for the ILS ('NN' to 'LK-H'). The instances are ordered by number of cities; the starting tours are ordered by strength of the heuristic used to generate these tours. Columns are grouped into blocks, where the first block summarizes an ILS setup

| Instance | Start Tour Type | No Fixing | | | | MST | | | | MST2 | | | | Nearest Neighbor | | | | NN2 | | | |
|---|---|---|---|---|---|---|---|---|---|---|---|---|---|---|---|---|---|---|---|---|---|
| | | Impr. [%] | CPU Time [s] | Free Edges [%] | Red. Size [%] | Impr. [%] | CPU Time [s] | Free Edges [%] | Red. Size [%] | Impr. [%] | CPU Time [s] | Free Edges [%] | Red. Size [%] | Impr. [%] | CPU Time [s] | Free Edges [%] | Red. Size [%] | Impr. [%] | CPU Time [s] | Free Edges [%] | Red. Size [%] |
| ja9847 | NN | 22.7 | 164.2 | – | – | 20.8 | 19.3 | 55.9 | 40.9 | 17.2 | 8.1 | 55.4 | 22.6 | 22.0 | 40.6 | 54.4 | 69.8 | 19.9 | 13.2 | 53.9 | 32.2 |
| | 2-opt | 13.6 | 171.3 | – | – | 11.9 | 18.7 | 55.3 | 41.9 | 9.2 | 7.0 | 53.5 | 21.1 | 13.1 | 41.2 | 54.4 | 70.3 | 11.0 | 13.1 | 53.1 | 31.6 |
| | 3-opt | 6.1 | 162.6 | – | – | 4.7 | 16.4 | 54.7 | 43.0 | 3.1 | 4.9 | 52.4 | 19.4 | 5.6 | 38.0 | 54.3 | 70.9 | 4.0 | 10.4 | 52.3 | 31.3 |
| | LK-opt | 1.0 | 139.1 | – | – | 1.1 | 13.2 | 54.7 | 45.3 | 0.9 | 3.0 | 52.1 | 16.8 | 0.9 | 32.4 | 55.1 | 73.0 | 1.0 | 7.6 | 52.2 | 30.9 |
| | LK-H | 0.0 | 77.0 | – | – | 0.0 | 7.7 | 54.1 | 44.5 | 0.0 | 1.6 | 51.7 | 15.0 | 0.0 | 19.5 | 54.8 | 72.4 | 0.0 | 4.2 | 51.7 | 28.6 |
| brd14051 | NN | 23.2 | 128.5 | – | – | 20.9 | 21.4 | 56.6 | 46.5 | 16.0 | 7.9 | 55.4 | 24.2 | 22.4 | 45.3 | 55.3 | 72.5 | 19.2 | 13.8 | 54.5 | 34.4 |
| | 2-opt | 12.5 | 135.6 | – | – | 9.9 | 21.5 | 55.6 | 46.6 | 6.2 | 6.0 | 53.0 | 22.2 | 11.6 | 46.9 | 54.9 | 72.5 | 8.5 | 12.3 | 53.2 | 33.7 |
| | 3-opt | 6.0 | 139.8 | – | – | 3.9 | 19.1 | 55.1 | 47.3 | 2.0 | 4.0 | 51.9 | 19.6 | 5.1 | 46.2 | 54.8 | 72.6 | 2.9 | 9.9 | 52.4 | 33.3 |
| | LK-opt | 0.4 | 122.1 | – | – | 0.1 | 12.7 | 55.0 | 48.9 | 0.0 | 1.5 | 51.5 | 14.5 | 0.2 | 33.6 | 55.8 | 75.1 | 0.0 | 5.4 | 52.0 | 30.7 |
| | LK-H | 0.0 | 56.7 | – | – | 0.0 | 7.7 | 54.3 | 45.4 | 0.0 | 1.0 | 50.9 | 11.8 | 0.0 | 20.4 | 55.1 | 73.8 | 0.0 | 2.9 | 51.5 | 25.6 |

Table 5: Result for ILS experiments with instances ja9847 and brd14051 using edge selection heuristics 'MST', 'MST2', 'NN', and 'NN2'. The rows are grouped by TSP instance and tour type. The columns are grouped into five blocks (for different selection heuristics) consisting of four columns each: achieved improvement from starting tour, utilized CPU time, fraction of tree edges after fixing, and size of the reduced instance (based on number of nodes).

| Instance | Start Tour Type | No Fixing | | | | <M | | | | ≤M | | | | Close Pairs | | | | CPR | | | |
|---|---|---|---|---|---|---|---|---|---|---|---|---|---|---|---|---|---|---|---|---|---|
| | | Impr. [%] | CPU Time [s] | Free Edges [%] | Red. Size [%] | Impr. [%] | CPU Time [s] | Free Edges [%] | Red. Size [%] | Impr. [%] | CPU Time [s] | Free Edges [%] | Red. Size [%] | Impr. [%] | CPU Time [s] | Free Edges [%] | Red. Size [%] | Impr. [%] | CPU Time [s] | Free Edges [%] | Red. Size [%] |
| ja9847 | NN | 22.7 | 164.2 | – | – | 22.2 | 59.7 | 76.5 | 73.3 | 21.8 | 42.9 | 71.6 | 63.2 | 22.3 | 110.5 | 73.2 | 100.0 | 20.8 | 42.6 | 51.6 | 68.0 |
| | 2-opt | 13.6 | 171.3 | – | – | 13.2 | 59.3 | 76.4 | 73.4 | 13.1 | 44.1 | 71.5 | 62.9 | 13.5 | 111.6 | 73.3 | 100.0 | 11.9 | 42.6 | 51.7 | 68.4 |
| | 3-opt | 6.1 | 162.6 | – | – | 5.9 | 55.9 | 76.4 | 73.4 | 5.7 | 40.6 | 71.4 | 62.7 | 6.2 | 107.8 | 73.4 | 100.0 | 5.0 | 36.8 | 51.9 | 69.1 |
| | LK-opt | 1.0 | 139.1 | – | – | 1.2 | 48.7 | 76.5 | 73.7 | 1.5 | 33.1 | 71.6 | 63.0 | 1.1 | 94.3 | 73.6 | 100.0 | 0.7 | 25.5 | 52.3 | 69.7 |
| | LK-H | 0.0 | 77.0 | – | – | 0.0 | 27.4 | 76.5 | 73.5 | 0.0 | 19.4 | 71.5 | 62.7 | 0.0 | 53.0 | 74.1 | 100.0 | 0.0 | 17.9 | 52.6 | 70.0 |
| brd14051 | NN | 23.2 | 128.5 | – | – | 21.7 | 50.1 | 73.7 | 68.7 | 21.6 | 47.6 | 72.7 | 66.6 | 23.1 | 105.3 | 68.9 | 100.0 | 20.9 | 48.8 | 50.4 | 64.4 |
| | 2-opt | 12.5 | 135.6 | – | – | 11.2 | 49.9 | 73.8 | 68.4 | 11.0 | 47.4 | 72.8 | 66.0 | 12.4 | 105.5 | 68.9 | 100.0 | 10.2 | 46.6 | 50.4 | 64.9 |
| | 3-opt | 6.0 | 139.8 | – | – | 5.1 | 49.2 | 74.2 | 68.6 | 5.0 | 43.8 | 72.9 | 65.8 | 5.9 | 109.4 | 68.9 | 100.0 | 4.2 | 38.9 | 50.5 | 65.6 |
| | LK-opt | 0.4 | 122.1 | – | – | 0.3 | 36.8 | 74.3 | 67.9 | 0.2 | 33.7 | 73.3 | 65.6 | 0.4 | 82.6 | 69.2 | 100.0 | 0.1 | 21.3 | 50.6 | 66.4 |
| | LK-H | 0.0 | 56.7 | – | – | 0.0 | 23.0 | 75.7 | 69.1 | 0.0 | 21.5 | 74.5 | 66.7 | 0.0 | 43.8 | 69.6 | 100.0 | 0.0 | 14.8 | 50.6 | 66.2 |

Table 6: Result for ILS experiments with instances ja9847 and brd14051 using edge selection heuristics '<M', '≤M', 'Close Pairs', and 'CPR'. The rows are grouped by TSP instance and tour type. The columns are grouped into five blocks (for different selection heuristics) consisting of four columns each: achieved improvement from starting tour, utilized CPU time, fraction of tree edges after fixing, and size of the reduced instance (based on number of nodes).

| Instance | Start Tour Type | No Fixing | | | | MST | | | | MST2 | | | | Nearest Neighbor | | | | NN2 | | | |
|---|---|---|---|---|---|---|---|---|---|---|---|---|---|---|---|---|---|---|---|---|---|
| | | Impr. [%] | CPU Time [s] | Free Edges [%] | Red. Size [%] | Impr. [%] | CPU Time [s] | Free Edges [%] | Red. Size [%] | Impr. [%] | CPU Time [s] | Free Edges [%] | Red. Size [%] | Impr. [%] | CPU Time [s] | Free Edges [%] | Red. Size [%] | Impr. [%] | CPU Time [s] | Free Edges [%] | Red. Size [%] |
| d15112 | NN | 21.7 | 163.7 | – | – | 19.0 | 22.9 | 57.0 | 46.4 | 14.3 | 7.8 | 55.6 | 23.9 | 20.7 | 49.1 | 55.5 | 71.4 | 17.2 | 12.8 | 54.5 | 33.4 |
| | 2-opt | 11.7 | 171.1 | – | – | 9.0 | 23.4 | 56.0 | 47.2 | 5.4 | 5.8 | 53.1 | 22.0 | 10.6 | 51.7 | 55.2 | 71.8 | 7.5 | 12.1 | 53.2 | 33.2 |
| | 3-opt | 5.8 | 179.0 | – | – | 3.5 | 21.2 | 55.3 | 48.1 | 1.8 | 3.7 | 52.2 | 19.7 | 4.8 | 51.6 | 55.0 | 72.0 | 2.6 | 9.5 | 52.5 | 32.6 |
| | LK-opt | 0.5 | 160.9 | – | – | 0.0 | 13.6 | 55.2 | 49.5 | 0.0 | 1.4 | 51.7 | 15.0 | 0.1 | 37.6 | 56.0 | 74.6 | 0.0 | 5.1 | 52.1 | 30.2 |
| | LK-H | 0.0 | 66.9 | – | – | 0.0 | 8.4 | 54.3 | 46.3 | 0.0 | 1.0 | 51.3 | 12.1 | 0.0 | 22.6 | 55.2 | 73.3 | 0.0 | 2.8 | 51.5 | 25.3 |
| d18512 | NN | 21.6 | 191.8 | – | – | 19.0 | 31.1 | 56.6 | 46.0 | 14.2 | 9.9 | 55.6 | 23.5 | 20.7 | 67.6 | 55.2 | 72.4 | 17.4 | 18.5 | 54.5 | 33.7 |
| | 2-opt | 11.4 | 202.0 | – | – | 8.8 | 30.8 | 55.7 | 46.8 | 5.1 | 7.4 | 53.0 | 21.9 | 10.5 | 72.0 | 55.0 | 72.7 | 7.4 | 17.5 | 53.2 | 33.6 |
| | 3-opt | 5.8 | 212.0 | – | – | 3.6 | 27.8 | 55.2 | 47.7 | 1.8 | 4.8 | 52.0 | 19.3 | 4.9 | 74.5 | 54.8 | 73.0 | 2.7 | 13.6 | 52.4 | 33.2 |
| | LK-opt | 0.4 | 187.9 | – | – | 0.0 | 18.8 | 55.0 | 49.0 | 0.0 | 1.8 | 51.5 | 14.4 | 0.1 | 51.5 | 55.8 | 75.4 | 0.0 | 7.5 | 52.0 | 30.7 |
| | LK-H | 0.0 | 85.4 | – | – | 0.0 | 11.3 | 54.1 | 45.3 | 0.0 | 1.2 | 51.1 | 11.4 | 0.0 | 31.3 | 55.1 | 73.8 | 0.0 | 4.0 | 51.5 | 25.5 |

Table 7: Result for ILS experiments with instances d15112 and d18512 using edge selection heuristics 'MST', 'MST2', 'NN', and 'NN2'. The rows are grouped by TSP instance and tour type. The columns are grouped into five blocks (for different selection heuristics) consisting of four columns each: achieved improvement from starting tour, utilized CPU time, fraction of tree edges after fixing, and size of the reduced instance (based on number of nodes).

| Instance | Start Tour Type | No Fixing | | | | $<M$ | | | | $\leq M$ | | | | Close Pairs | | | | CPR | | | |
|---|---|---|---|---|---|---|---|---|---|---|---|---|---|---|---|---|---|---|---|---|---|
| | | Impr. [%] | CPU Time [s] | Free Edges [%] | Red. Size [%] | Impr. [%] | CPU Time [s] | Free Edges [%] | Red. Size [%] | Impr. [%] | CPU Time [s] | Free Edges [%] | Red. Size [%] | Impr. [%] | CPU Time [s] | Free Edges [%] | Red. Size [%] | Impr. [%] | CPU Time [s] | Free Edges [%] | Red. Size [%] |
| d15112 | NN | 21.7 | 163.7 | – | – | 20.1 | 52.3 | 75.4 | 66.7 | 20.0 | 50.5 | 75.2 | 65.8 | 21.5 | 118.3 | 68.3 | 100.0 | 19.0 | 50.4 | 50.1 | 62.0 |
| | 2-opt | 11.7 | 171.1 | – | – | 10.3 | 53.4 | 75.4 | 66.8 | 10.2 | 51.6 | 75.1 | 65.8 | 11.5 | 128.6 | 68.3 | 100.0 | 9.0 | 47.9 | 50.1 | 62.6 |
| | 3-opt | 5.8 | 179.0 | – | – | 4.7 | 51.5 | 75.5 | 66.8 | 4.7 | 49.0 | 75.2 | 65.9 | 5.5 | 121.4 | 68.3 | 100.0 | 3.7 | 38.2 | 50.2 | 63.4 |
| | LK-opt | 0.5 | 160.9 | – | – | 0.2 | 37.6 | 75.8 | 66.4 | 0.2 | 35.7 | 75.5 | 65.5 | 0.3 | 97.3 | 68.5 | 100.0 | 0.0 | 21.0 | 50.2 | 64.1 |
| | LK-H | 0.0 | 66.9 | – | – | 0.0 | 22.2 | 76.3 | 65.9 | 0.0 | 21.5 | 76.0 | 64.9 | 0.0 | 49.3 | 68.9 | 100.0 | 0.0 | 15.4 | 50.2 | 63.8 |
| d18512 | NN | 21.6 | 191.8 | – | – | 20.2 | 77.8 | 73.0 | 70.1 | 20.0 | 71.7 | 71.7 | 67.4 | 21.5 | 162.1 | 68.9 | 100.0 | 19.3 | 75.4 | 50.5 | 64.9 |
| | 2-opt | 11.4 | 202.0 | – | – | 10.2 | 78.5 | 73.0 | 70.1 | 10.1 | 73.7 | 72.3 | 68.3 | 11.3 | 168.8 | 68.9 | 100.0 | 9.1 | 73.9 | 50.5 | 65.4 |
| | 3-opt | 5.8 | 212.0 | – | – | 4.9 | 74.7 | 73.1 | 69.9 | 4.8 | 72.4 | 72.4 | 68.1 | 5.6 | 166.7 | 68.9 | 100.0 | 4.0 | 59.9 | 50.5 | 66.2 |
| | LK-opt | 0.4 | 187.9 | – | – | 0.2 | 56.5 | 73.3 | 69.8 | 0.2 | 53.5 | 72.5 | 67.9 | 0.3 | 133.0 | 69.2 | 100.0 | 0.0 | 32.7 | 50.7 | 67.0 |
| | LK-H | 0.0 | 85.4 | – | – | 0.0 | 32.4 | 73.5 | 69.3 | 0.0 | 30.7 | 72.8 | 67.5 | 0.0 | 67.3 | 69.7 | 100.0 | 0.0 | 23.2 | 50.8 | 66.7 |

Table 8: Result for ILS experiments with instances d15112 and d18512 using edge selection heuristics '$<M$', '$\leq M$', 'Close Pairs', and 'CPR'. The rows are grouped by TSP instance and tour type. The columns are grouped into five blocks (for different selection heuristics) consisting of four columns each: achieved improvement from starting tour, utilized CPU time, fraction of tree edges after fixing, and size of the reduced instance (based on number of nodes).

| Instance | Start Tour Type | No Fixing | | | | MST | | | | MST2 | | | | Nearest Neighbor | | | | NN2 | | | |
|---|---|---|---|---|---|---|---|---|---|---|---|---|---|---|---|---|---|---|---|---|---|
| | | Impr. [%] | CPU Time [s] | Free Edges [%] | Red. Size [%] | Impr. [%] | CPU Time [s] | Free Edges [%] | Red. Size [%] | Impr. [%] | CPU Time [s] | Free Edges [%] | Red. Size [%] | Impr. [%] | CPU Time [s] | Free Edges [%] | Red. Size [%] | Impr. [%] | CPU Time [s] | Free Edges [%] | Red. Size [%] |
| it16862 | NN | 22.3 | 241.1 | – | – | 19.7 | 35.0 | 56.2 | 45.1 | 15.3 | 13.1 | 54.9 | 24.2 | 21.4 | 70.2 | 55.1 | 70.0 | 18.1 | 21.7 | 53.7 | 33.7 |
| | 2-opt | 12.4 | 249.3 | – | – | 9.8 | 33.7 | 55.4 | 45.7 | 6.4 | 10.6 | 53.0 | 22.5 | 11.5 | 73.0 | 54.9 | 70.3 | 8.5 | 20.1 | 52.8 | 33.3 |
| | 3-opt | 5.9 | 250.4 | – | – | 3.8 | 30.7 | 54.9 | 46.4 | 2.0 | 7.1 | 52.1 | 20.5 | 5.1 | 71.8 | 54.7 | 70.4 | 2.9 | 16.0 | 52.2 | 32.9 |
| | LK-opt | 0.7 | 223.7 | – | – | 0.2 | 21.8 | 55.0 | 48.5 | 0.1 | 3.4 | 51.6 | 16.7 | 0.4 | 57.8 | 55.4 | 72.9 | 0.1 | 9.8 | 51.9 | 31.6 |
| | LK-H | 0.0 | 96.6 | – | – | 0.0 | 11.7 | 54.4 | 46.0 | 0.0 | 1.8 | 51.3 | 14.2 | 0.0 | 30.9 | 55.0 | 71.8 | 0.0 | 5.0 | 51.5 | 27.7 |
| sw24978 | NN | 19.9 | 540.6 | – | – | 16.8 | 58.5 | 56.7 | 42.8 | 13.3 | 20.1 | 55.8 | 22.8 | 18.7 | 132.7 | 54.9 | 65.8 | 15.5 | 33.8 | 54.5 | 31.5 |
| | 2-opt | 11.6 | 588.5 | – | – | 9.0 | 65.5 | 55.9 | 45.0 | 6.1 | 16.6 | 53.4 | 21.9 | 10.5 | 147.8 | 54.9 | 67.5 | 7.9 | 35.5 | 53.2 | 32.4 |
| | 3-opt | 5.8 | 590.7 | – | – | 3.8 | 60.2 | 55.3 | 46.6 | 2.1 | 11.7 | 52.2 | 20.5 | 4.9 | 143.5 | 54.9 | 68.4 | 3.0 | 28.2 | 52.4 | 32.4 |
| | LK-opt | 0.5 | 474.0 | – | – | 0.1 | 39.3 | 55.3 | 49.2 | 0.0 | 5.0 | 51.8 | 17.4 | 0.3 | 103.7 | 55.9 | 71.7 | 0.1 | 16.2 | 52.1 | 31.7 |
| | LK-H | 0.0 | 196.3 | – | – | 0.0 | 22.2 | 54.6 | 47.0 | 0.0 | 2.9 | 51.4 | 14.7 | 0.0 | 54.5 | 55.3 | 70.8 | 0.0 | 8.3 | 51.5 | 28.0 |

Table 9: Result for ILS experiments with instances it16862 and sw24978 using edge selection heuristics 'MST', 'MST2', 'NN', and 'NN2'. The rows are grouped by TSP instance and tour type. The columns are grouped into five blocks (for different selection heuristics) consisting of four columns each: achieved improvement from starting tour, utilized CPU time, fraction of tree edges after fixing, and size of the reduced instance (based on number of nodes).

| Instance | Start Tour Type | No Fixing | | | | <M | | | | ≤M | | | | Close Pairs | | | | CPR | | | |
|---|---|---|---|---|---|---|---|---|---|---|---|---|---|---|---|---|---|---|---|---|---|
| | | Impr. [%] | CPU Time [s] | Free Edges [%] | Red. Size [%] | Impr. [%] | CPU Time [s] | Free Edges [%] | Red. Size [%] | Impr. [%] | CPU Time [s] | Free Edges [%] | Red. Size [%] | Impr. [%] | CPU Time [s] | Free Edges [%] | Red. Size [%] | Impr. [%] | CPU Time [s] | Free Edges [%] | Red. Size [%] |
| it16862 | NN | 22.3 | 241.1 | – | – | 21.3 | 89.4 | 71.5 | 70.7 | 19.5 | 55.0 | 67.7 | 55.6 | 22.3 | 190.9 | 75.9 | 100.0 | 20.4 | 93.5 | 52.6 | 72.1 |
| | 2-opt | 12.4 | 249.3 | – | – | 11.7 | 89.1 | 71.5 | 70.5 | 11.6 | 86.4 | 71.0 | 68.8 | 12.4 | 203.8 | 76.1 | 100.0 | 10.6 | 90.4 | 52.8 | 72.7 |
| | 3-opt | 5.9 | 250.4 | – | – | 5.4 | 85.8 | 71.6 | 70.7 | 5.3 | 85.6 | 71.4 | 69.7 | 5.9 | 198.2 | 76.2 | 100.0 | 4.6 | 80.8 | 53.1 | 73.6 |
| | LK-opt | 0.7 | 223.7 | – | – | 0.6 | 69.0 | 71.5 | 70.2 | 0.5 | 67.6 | 71.5 | 69.6 | 0.7 | 176.9 | 76.4 | 100.0 | 0.2 | 50.1 | 53.7 | 74.8 |
| | LK-H | 0.0 | 96.6 | – | – | 0.0 | 35.2 | 71.6 | 70.1 | 0.0 | 34.6 | 71.5 | 69.4 | 0.0 | 77.4 | 77.2 | 100.0 | 0.0 | 31.2 | 54.1 | 75.2 |
| sw24978 | NN | 19.9 | 540.6 | – | – | 19.2 | 219.7 | 77.4 | 77.3 | 18.5 | 128.9 | 71.4 | 61.7 | 19.9 | 462.8 | 79.8 | 100.0 | 18.2 | 213.0 | 54.1 | 74.5 |
| | 2-opt | 11.6 | 588.5 | – | – | 11.1 | 244.4 | 77.2 | 78.2 | 10.3 | 135.4 | 71.1 | 61.4 | 11.7 | 472.2 | 79.7 | 100.0 | 9.9 | 213.3 | 54.2 | 74.6 |
| | 3-opt | 5.8 | 590.7 | – | – | 5.4 | 234.0 | 77.0 | 78.5 | 4.8 | 126.3 | 71.0 | 61.2 | 5.9 | 481.3 | 79.8 | 100.0 | 4.6 | 176.3 | 54.5 | 75.5 |
| | LK-opt | 0.5 | 474.0 | – | – | 0.4 | 186.6 | 77.1 | 79.6 | 0.3 | 92.0 | 71.1 | 61.3 | 0.6 | 389.5 | 80.0 | 100.0 | 0.1 | 108.3 | 55.2 | 76.6 |
| | LK-H | 0.0 | 196.3 | – | – | 0.0 | 87.4 | 76.9 | 79.2 | 0.0 | 48.1 | 71.1 | 60.0 | 0.0 | 163.5 | 80.6 | 100.0 | 0.0 | 64.7 | 55.7 | 77.1 |

Table 10: Result for ILS experiments with instances it16862 and sw24978 using edge selection heuristics '<M', '≤M', 'Close Pairs', and 'CPR'. The rows are grouped by TSP instance and tour type. The columns are grouped into five blocks (for different selection heuristics) consisting of four columns each: achieved improvement from starting tour, utilized CPU time, fraction of tree edges after fixing, and size of the reduced instance (based on number of nodes).

without any fixation and the subsequent blocks summarize ILS setups with each fixation heuristic ('MST' to 'NN2' and '<M' to 'CPR'). Each column block consists of four columns: improvement in percent found when applying the ILS, required CPU time until termination, fraction of edges that are fixed (tabu for any ILS operation), and size of the reduced instance (normalized).

For every instance and each fixing heuristic (including no fixing), it holds that the better the starting tour, the smaller the improvements found by the ILS. Applying our TSP solver to nearest neighbor tours (rows with start tour type 'NN'), for example, results in improvements of about 20 % for setups without fixing ('Impr. [%]' columns). For better starting tours, less improvement is achieved, down to improvements of 0 % for tours provided by LK-H. Computation times are lowest when starting from very good initial solutions, such as those generated by the LK-opt and LK-H algorithms. Given only minimal potential to improve these solutions, our ILK terminates as soon as the maximum of non-improving iterations is reached quickly. For instance sw24978 in setups with no reduction, for example, starting from LK-H and LK-opt tours it takes 196.3 s and 474.0 s to converge, respectively, but more than 540 s for all other start tour types.

Each fixing ILS setup can be compared with the corresponding ILS setup without fixing in terms of the improvement on the given start tour and the required CPU time. The following observations can be made from Tables 5 to 10:

- For non-fixing setups, the CPU time is always higher compared to fixing setups, as the effective problem size is larger for the non-fixing setup. However, time consumption does not directly map to better tour quality.

- The Close Pairs (CP) fixing heuristic yields improvements as good as those for the non-fixing ILS, but requires considerably less time to reach these quality levels. For instance brd14051 starting with 3-opt tours, for example, both the non-fixing ILS and the CP fixing ILS improve the start tour by about 6 %, but the CP variant requires only 109.4 s, whereas the non-fixing ILS requires 139.8 s.

- Both '<M', '≤M', and 'Nearest Neighbor' perform nearly as well as 'Close Pairs' but again require considerably less time. For the above example, the improvements are 5.1 %, 5.0 %, and 5.1 %,

respectively, at a cost of 49.2 s, 43.8 s, and 46.2 s in CPU time, respectively.

- Selection strategies 'CPR', 'MST', and 'NN2' follow with decreasing improvements and lower CPU time consumption. For the above example, the improvements are 4.2 %, 3.9 %, and 2.9 %, respectively, requiring CPU times of 38.9 s, 19.1 s, and 9.9 s.

- Among all fixation-based ILS setups, the 'MST2' heuristic results in both the smallest improvements and lowest running times compared to the other fixation heuristics. For the example used, the MST2 heuristic results in an improvement of only 2.0 %, consuming 4.0 s.

This categorization can be visualized as in Fig. 11. Here, for each of the six instances, both improvement and CPU time consumption have been normalized by the results from the corresponding ILS runs without any fixing. Figure **??** compares the improvements for each fixing heuristic applied to 2-opt tours; Fig. **??** compares the results when starting from 3-opt tours. From both plots, the following conclusions can be drawn:

1. The 'expensive', but good Close Pairs heuristic reaches improvements as good as the non-fixing ILS, requiring only 3/4 of the time.

2. The 'medium' heuristics Relaxed Close Pairs, NN, MST, $\leq$M and <M have normalized improvement above 75 % and normalized time of less than 50 %.

3. The 'cheap', but not so good heuristics (Second MST and Second NN) each have a normalized time of less than 25 % (quarter of the CPU time) and a normalized improvement of < 70 % for 2-opt starting tours and < 55 % for 3-opt starting tours. The exception here is instance ja9847, which performs considerably better than the other five TSP instances.

Relaxed Close Pairs and MST have to be considered as border cases between 'medium' and 'cheap' heuristics.

For all fixing heuristics, the size of the original instance was compared to the corresponding reduced instance size (number of nodes in percent, relative to the original instance, shown in columns 'Red. Size [%]' in Tables 5 to 10) and the number of free edges within the reduced instance (in percent, in columns 'Free Edges [%]').

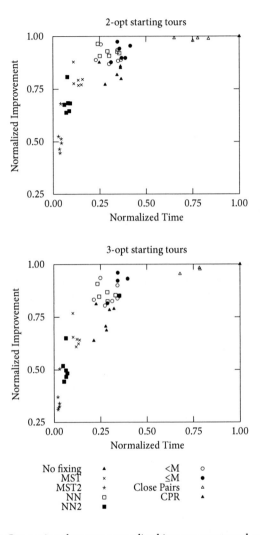

Figure 11: Comparison between normalized improvements and normalized CPU time for ILS setups with different fixation strategies (MST, Second MST, NN, Second NN, <M, ≤M, CP, and Relaxed CP) normalized on ILS runs without fixation. Each of the six dots of the same type represents one of the problem instances considered here.

- Most edge selection heuristics are very stable in the number of free edges available in reduced instances, independent of the initial solution type under consideration. For <M, ≤M, 'Close Pairs', and 'CPR', the percentages differ only marginally for setups with the same problem instance, but differ between problem instances. For example, for it16862 and <M, the proportion of free edges is 71.5 ± 0.1 %, but for sw24978 it is 77.2 ± 0.3 %.

- For 'MST' and 'NN', the number of free edges available in reduced instances is independent of the TSP instance: for fixing heuristic 'MST', the percentage of free edges ranges between 54.1 % and 57.0 % only; for 'NN' it is only 50 ± 1 %.

- For fixing heuristics 'MST2' and 'NN2', the size of the reduced instance decreases with increasing quality of the tours. For example, for 'MST2' and instance brd14051, the number of free edges decreases from 55.4 % for nearest neighbor initial solutions down to 50.9 % for LK-H solutions.

- For all combinations of instance and start tour, the MST2 fixing heuristic is the most progressive one, resulting in the smallest instances. Fixed instances have, on average, less than a quarter of the number of cities than the original instances. For example, for instance d15112 and 3-opt tours, only 19.7 % of the original nodes are left, whereas comparable heuristics such as NN2 and MST keep 32.6 % and 48.1 % of the nodes, respectively. Furthermore, the size of the reduced instance decreases with increasing quality of the tours. For instance it16862, for example, the size of the reduced instance decreases from 24.2 % for nearest neighbor initial solutions down to 14.2 % for LK-H solutions.

- The Nearest Neighbor heuristic reduces most instance types to about the same level (to 70–75 % of the original size) with the exception of instance sw24978, which has a relative size of 65.8 % to 71.7 %. Similar observations can be made for the 'MST' heuristic, which reduces most instances to a size of 45–50 % regardless of start tour type; the only exception is ja9847, where the size is reduced to 40–45 %.

- As for the proportion of free edges for both fixing heuristics <M and ≤M, the size of the reduced instance is nearly constant within a problem instance regardless of the starting tour, but

differs between problem instances. For example, for it16862 and <M, the reduced instance's size is 71.4 ± 0.3 % of the original instance's size.

- For Close Pairs (CP) fixations, it holds that the reduced instance's size always equals the original instance's size, as fixed edges can not have neighboring edges that are fixed, too, thus there is no path of fixed edges to be joined and no nodes are redundant. For 'CPR', the size of the reduced instance is about 65–75 %, where the two largest problem instances (it16862 and sw24978) are reduced the least (≥ 72.1 %), whereas the smaller instances are reduced more (< 70.0 %).

### 3.2.4  Summary

The proposed edge selection heuristics offer a range of choices for reducing the search space and thus affecting the expected solution quality. When selecting one of the proposed fixing heuristics, there has to be a trade-off between expected solution quality and computation time. Furthermore, preprocessing steps such as building minimum spanning trees have to be considered in the decision-making process.

Selection heuristics which are very progressive (MST2, NN2, and MST) may considerably reduce the computation time to find a local optimum but this greediness will notably reduce the gain of the local search. Other heuristics that are more selective fix fewer edges and thus allow the local search to exploit a larger search space, which still requires less time compared to a local search in the original instance. Furthermore, the Close Pairs strategy can be used if no global knowledge is available, but too few edges get fixed here to decrease an instance's size considerably. As a compromise in terms of time and quality, either the Nearest Neighbor (NN), the Lighter or equal to Median (≤M), or the Lighter than Median (<M) heuristics can be applied.

It has been shown that using problem reduction techniques as presented here allow a saving of considerable amounts of time when a minor decrease in solution quality is acceptable. The only drawback is that the reduction strengths of the proposed fixing strategies depend on the problem instance only. Edges cannot be fixed with user-defined strength, nor can the strategies be applied several times to the same instance to multiply the fixing effects.

## 3.3    DISTRIBUTED CHAINED LIN-KERNIGHAN ALGORITHM

In the previous section, the reduction of instance sizes was proposed to solve large problem instances. This section presents an alternative approach using a distributed algorithm for the TSP. Unlike the edge selection algorithm, which strives to reduce the computation time, the distributed algorithm's objective is to parallelize the computation among several computers. In the latter case, the total computation time is about the same as for a non-distributed setup (indeed, may be even larger due to the parallelization's overhead), but the absolute time (the real-world time between start and end of an experimental run) may be considerably lower.

The distributed algorithm presented here resembles a distributed evolutionary algorithm (DEA) with an island model. Each island executes a well-known TSP solver (CLK, due to APPLEGATE *et al.* [14, 49]) to locally optimize the island's current solution. The DEA framework takes care of evolutionary operations and the actual distribution.

### 3.3.1    *System Architecture*

The distributed evolutionary algorithm uses an island model for its computation, where each participating computer equals one island. Each island holds only a single individual, which is iteratively either modified (mutation and local search) or sent to a neighboring island for recombination. The inner structure of an island consists of two layers, as explained below.

The lower layer is the CLK by APPLEGATE *et al.* [14], as provided in the Concorde package [49]. Its implementation provides two functions: firstly, an initial solution can be constructed using Quick-Borůvka tour construction heuristics (see Sec. 3.1.3); secondly, a given solution can be optimized to a local optimum using the internal LK implementation and perturbation. For the experiments conducted here, the CLK implementation was treated as a black box. The CLK implementation was configured to use double-bridge moves (DBM, see Sec. 3.1.3), based on a random walk. Using a random walk to select the four cities for a DBM is the default configuration for CLK and it has been shown in preliminary experiments [64] to be the most successful node selection strategy compared to other strategies provided by CLK. For this strategy, the first of four relevant cities for the double-bridge move is chosen randomly. Starting there, three independent random walks of a given length $k$ are performed on a neighborhood structure, terminating at the remaining three nodes required for DBM. The neighborhood structure for each city includes the three closest cities in each of the four geometric quadrants relative to the current city. Shorter random walks make the DBM local, for large $k$ the DBM becomes similar to a completely random 4-exchange. By default, CLK sets $k = 50$.

The upper layer consists of the evolutionary framework and the network management and communication part. Incorporating this network communication part and the functions provided by CLK, the evolutionary framework builds a distributed evolutionary algorithm (structure in Fig. 12 and pseudocode in Fig. 13). Components of an evolutionary algorithm used in this framework include a variable-strength perturbation and a simple recombination operator.

The *variable-strength perturbation* (VSP) is a mutation mechanism independent from the perturbation within the CLK implementation. It is meant to lead the algorithm to different search space regions once a node's current individual gets stuck in a local optimum. The strength of the mutation depends on the success of previous mutation/optimization iterations and increases with the number of non-improving iterations. This strength value corresponds to the number of random double-bridge moves applied to the current solution. Given that the CLK's internal DBM is more local in nature, this perturbation allows larger steps in the search space. The strength of a perturbation operation has to be chosen carefully. A perturbation that is too weak might not be able to leave the current local optimum, whereas one that is too strong might damage the tour heavily, causing a loss of quality. Here, the mutation strength $\sigma$ of the VSP is adapted as follows:

$$\sigma = \left\lfloor \frac{i_{\text{non-impr}}}{c_v} \right\rfloor + 1 \tag{3.5}$$

where $i_{\text{non-impr}}$ is the number of non-improving iterations and $c_v$ is a setup parameter set to 64 for the experiments. Using this strategy, a weak perturbation is performed while finding improvements on a regular basis and once no better solutions are found, increasingly larger steps are necessary to find better search space regions. If the variable-strength mutation strategy is not successful, a restart may be necessary. This restart is performed once no improvement has been found within $c_r$ non-improving iterations. Here, the setup parameter $c_r$ is set to $c_r = 256$.

The recombination simply selects the best solution from the set of solutions, consisting of the current and previous iteration's solutions

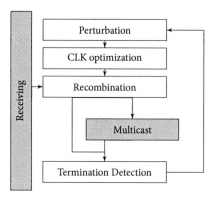

Figure 12: Flow diagram for the distributed algorithm.

and all solutions received since the last recombination operation. If the resulting solution is the one found by the local CLK function call, this solution is sent to all neighboring islands. The termination criterion as represented by the function TERMINATIONDETECTED is triggered when a node's solution quality equals an already known optimum (if available) or when a given instance-dependent time bound is hit. The notification of the occurrence of an optimal solution is propagated through the network terminating all nodes.

A structured network with a hypercube topology is used to connect islands in a distributed evolutionary algorithm. A perfect hypercube consists of $2^k$ nodes, each connected to $k$ other nodes and the shortest path between any two nodes in this hypercube has a maximum hop length $k$. During an initial setup phase, the nodes connect to a dedicated bootstrapping node $B$ (called 'hub') which constructs the structure (see Fig. 14) by supplying neighborhood lists to each node. As the whole communication is based on TCP/IP, the nodes are supplied with hostname and port number of the hub at the beginning. Initially, the nodes only know how to connect to the hub, which is contacted for a list of neighbors. The hub determines the node's position within the hypercube and assembles the node's neighbor list based on nodes that are already known to the hub. The neighborhood relationship between nodes resembles the edges of a hypercube, thus the name. The first nodes receive a sparse list of neighbors; to build the connected hypercube, a node contacts each neighbor after receiving the list. If the contacting

**function** DISTRIBUTEDEVOLUTIONARYALGORITHM
   $s \leftarrow$ INITIATETOUR
   $s \leftarrow$ CHAINEDLINKERNIGHAN$(s)$
   **while** $\neg$TERMINATIONDETECTED **do**
      **if** $i_{\text{non-impr}} > c_r$ **then**
         $i_{\text{non-impr}} \leftarrow 0$
         $s' \leftarrow$ INITIATETOUR
      **else**
         $\sigma \leftarrow \left\lfloor \frac{i_{\text{non-impr}}}{c_v} \right\rfloor + 1$
         $s' \leftarrow$ PERTURBETOUR$(s, \sigma)$
      **end if**
      $s'' \leftarrow$ CHAINEDLINKERNIGHAN$(s')$
      $S_{\text{recv}} \leftarrow$ ALLRECEIVEDTOURS
      $s^* \leftarrow$ SELECTBESTTOUR$(S_{\text{recv}} \cup \{s\} \cup \{s''\})$
      **if** $s^* \geq s$ **then**
         $i_{\text{non-impr}} \leftarrow i_{\text{non-impr}} + 1$
      **else**
         $i_{\text{non-impr}} \leftarrow 0$
      **end if**
      **if** $s^* = s''$ **then**        ▷ Best solution was found locally
         MULTICASTTONEIGHBORS$(s^*)$
      **end if**
      $s \leftarrow s^*$
   **end while**
   **return** $s$
**end function**

Figure 13: Pseudocode for the distributed evolutionary algorithm.

node is unknown to the contacted node, the contacting node is added to the contacted node's neighbor list. The topology is static; after the initialization nodes are not allowed to leave or enter the system.

As the nodes communicate directly and hence constitute a structured peer-to-peer network (P2P), the hub is the only central component in the network and is only used during initialization. For systems with a small network size, this approach appears to be feasible, as the focus is put on the effects of distributed (population-based) optimization, which is independent of the utilization of centralized or decentralized protocols for network setup.

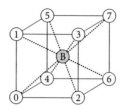

Figure 14: Hypercube topology with 8 regular nodes and a dedicated bootstrapping node $B$.

### Recombination

In related experiments, recombination operators other than replacement have been evaluated for distributed computations. As any sophisticated recombination operation requires more time than the replacement operation, the application of the recombination operator must be justified by the gain in solution quality (either directly due to recombination or indirectly by allowing the local search to enter better search space regions).

In [142], the recombination operator QBX was introduced based on the Quick-Borůvka tour construction heuristic (QB-C, see p. 40). The QBX operator constructs an offspring tour by inheriting edges common to both parents and inserting the missing edges by using QB-C. Compared to a simple replacement operator, the QBX operator shows a slow start. Even for small problem instances QBX requires a considerable amount of time before outperforming the replacement operator. For larger instances, its time consumptions negate its practical application.

Given our experience with TSP recombination operators in distributed setups, we discard the concept of sophisticated recombination operators for experiments conducted for this thesis.

### 3.3.2   Experimental Setup

For the analysis, a set of instances from well-known sources were selected, with instance sizes ranging from 1000 to 85 900 cities (Tab. 11).

- From REINELT's TSPLIB [168] the following instances were taken: fl1577, fl3795 (both clustered instances), pr2392, pcb3038 (both drilling problems), fnl4461 (map of East Germany), usa-

| Instance | $|V|$ | Optimum* | Reference |
|----------|-------|----------|-----------|
| C1k.1 | 1000 | 11 376 735 | |
| E1k.1 | 1000 | 22 985 695 | |
| fl1577 | 1577 | 22 249 | |
| pr2392 | 2392 | 378 032 | |
| pcb3038 | 3038 | 137 694 | |
| fl3795 | 3795 | 28 772 | |
| fnl4461 | 4461 | 182 566 | |
| fi10639 | 10 639 | 520 383* | [47] |
| usa13509 | 13 509 | 19 982 859 | [8] |
| sw24978 | 24 978 | 855 597 | [44] |
| pla33810 | 33 810 | 66 005 185* | [140] |
| pla85900 | 85 900 | 142 382 641 | [16] |

Solutions marked with '*' represent lower bounds only.

Table 11: Selected TSP testbed instances. Instances marked with a star are not yet solved to optimum; values represent the best-known lower bound.

13509 (map of the U. S. A.), pla33810 and pla85900 (both programmed logic array).

- From the 8th DIMACS challenge [110], the random instances C1k.1 and E1k.1 were used. In both instances 1000, cities are arranged in a square using Euclidean distances. For instance E1k.1, the cities are randomly uniform distributed. For instance C1k.1, the cities are normally distributed around one of 10 cluster centers. For details on the construction, see [113].

- From the collection of national TSPs [45], fi10639 (map of Finland) and sw24978 (map of Sweden) were chosen. No optimal solutions for instance fi10639 is currently known.

Each simulation setup was performed 10 times, from which the average values were used for discussion. For the experiments on a distributed setup, a hypercube consisting of $2^3 = 8$ computing nodes was used. For setups using the original CLK or distributed setups with only one node (resembling non-distributed setups), the time limit was set to $10^4$ CPU seconds for instances with less than $10^4$ cities and $10^5$ CPU seconds for larger instances. For distributed setups, the time limit was set to $10^3$ CPU seconds per computing node for instances with less than $10^4$ cities and $10^4$ CPU seconds for larger instances. For the evaluation of distributed setups, the total CPU time spent was considered, i. e. the elapsed time was multiplied by the number of nodes (unless otherwise noted). The solution of the distributed algorithm at a given point in time is the best solution known to any participating node in the distributed algorithm. This way, the distributed and non-distributed setups are comparable in terms of CPU time and quality. The number of iterations within the CLK implementation was set to the number of nodes for distributed setups (after that, the resulting tour would be handed over to the distributed evolutionary framework). For the comparison studies, the number of iterations was set to infinity in the CLK, leaving the above time bounds as the only termination criteria (except for known optima, where applicable).

### 3.3.3   *Experimental Results*

In the first set of experiments, the distributed CLK variant was compared to the unmodified CLK implementation using the variable-strength perturbation running on 8 nodes, .

In an initial evaluation, the number of runs in which either algorithm found the known optimal solutions for a given problem instance (Tab. 12) was compared. For instances with more than 3000 cities, the original CLK could not find an optimal solution in any run within the given time limit. Optimal solutions were only found for three problem instances (C1k.1, E1k.1, and pr2392). The distributed algorithm (abbreviated 'DistCLK') found the optimal solution for all problem instances up to fnl4461 in at least one run. It can handle problem instances (e. g. fl3795) very well (successful in most runs) while the unmodified CLK failed to solve every time, even given more CPU time.

In a more detailed evaluation, it was observed that the approximation towards the optimum is faster with the distributed algorithm than the original algorithm. As shown for several problem instances in Figures 15–16, the distributed version is better than CLK for these instances.

Problem instance C1k.1 is easy to solve for both the original and the distributed CLK. The distributed variant finds the optimal solution in all 10 runs (after 283.3 CPU seconds, at most); the original CLK in 9 runs (the 10th run has an excess of 0.018 %). As for C1k.1, for instance E1k.1

| Instance | CLK | DistCLK |
|----------|-----|---------|
| C1k.1    | 9/10  | **10/10** |
| E1k.1    | 3/10  | **10/10** |
| fl1577   | 0/10  | **8/10**  |
| pr2392   | 4/10  | **10/10** |
| pcb3038  | 0/10  | **7/10**  |
| fl3795   | 0/10  | **10/10** |
| fnl4461  | 0/10  | **1/10**  |

Table 12: Number of CLK and DistCLK runs reaching the optimum within the given time bound. Larger instances were omitted as neither algorithms found optimal solutions here.

the distributed CLK finds optimal solutions in all runs (after 2718 CPU seconds at most). The original CLK finds the optimal solution in only 3 runs, resulting in a final average excess of 0.016 %. For instance fl1577 (Fig. 15a), CLK gets stuck after about 150 seconds in local optima (9 runs in 22 395, 1 run in 22 256) that it can not escape within the time bound. The distributed variant, however, finds the optimum in 8 out of 10 runs in less than 2400 CPU seconds; the other two runs need about 8000 CPU seconds. The unmodified CLK was able to find optimal solutions in 4 out of 10 runs, with an average excess of 0.093 %. In the 6 unsuccessful runs, 5 different local optima with an excess of 0.11 % to 0.25 % were found. The distributed algorithm finds optimal solutions in all 10 runs after 2098 CPU seconds at most.

Out of 10 runs, the unmodified CLK algorithm reaches 9 different local optima for problem instance pcb3038 (Fig. 15b). The excess for these local optima ranges from $2.9 \cdot 10^3$ % to 0.134 %, with an average excess of 0.06 %. The distributed algorithm, however, finds optimal solutions in 7 out of 10 runs. In the remaining three runs, two different local optima costing 137 698 (excess $2.9 \cdot 10^3$ %) and 137 749 (excess 0.04 %) were found. The overall average excess was 0.004 % and the original CLK's average excess was reached already after 164 CPU seconds. The distributed CLK found optimal solutions for instance fl3795 in all 10 runs, whereas the original CLK fails to find an optimal solution in any run. Instead, two different local optima with cost 28 935 (excess 0.57 %, 9 runs) and 28 813 (excess 0.14 %, 1 run) are found. Thus, the average excess is 0.52 %, which is reached by the distributed CLK after 627.5 CPU seconds. Instance fnl4461 is the largest instance where any algorithm presented here was able to find an optimal solution. The distributed algorithm finds this optimal solution in one single run after 4133 CPU seconds, resulting in an average excess of $2.8 \cdot 10^3$ %. The original CLK's average excess is only 0.041 %, which is reached by the distributed variant after 665.6 CPU seconds.

No setup reached an optimal solution for instance fil10639 within the given time bound. Using the unmodified CLK algorithm, the average solution quality is 0.084 % above the optimum and the best solution has an excess of 0.034 %. Better average solutions were found with the distributed algorithm, which reached an average solution quality of 0.05 %, where the best solution has an excess of only 0.036 %. Whereas the minima of both algorithms are about the same, the distributed variant has a better average value and reaches the CLK's average solution after just 4142 seconds. For problem instance usa13509 (Fig. 16a), the distributed algorithm results in solutions with an excess of 0.021 % (best is 19 984 419 with excess 0.008 %) above the lower bound. The original CLK, however, achieves only an average excess of 0.090 % and a minimum excess of 0.071 % above the lower bound. The original CLK's final average solution quality is reached by the distributed variant after spending only about $\frac{1}{30}$ of the CPU time. For instance sw24978 (Fig. 16b), the distributed algorithm has an average tour quality of 0.050 % over the optimum after reaching its time bound (best is 0.033 %), whereas CLK has an average tour quality of 0.088 % (best is 0.064 %). The CLK algorithm's final average tour length is reached after just 19 020 CPU seconds by the distributed algorithm. Thus, the original CLK requires about 5 times more CPU time to reach this tour quality level than the distributed algorithm.

For problem instance pla33810 (Fig. 17a), the distributed and original CLK find solutions with an average excess of 0.149 % and 0.221 % above the lower bound, respectively. Minima for both algorithms have an excess of 0.118 % and 0.139 %, respectively. The original CLK's average final solution quality is achieved by the distributed CLK after spending only 5361 CPU seconds in total. Finally, for instance pla85900 (Fig. 17b), the original CLK has a final solution quality level of 0.079 % (minimum is 0.065 %) above the optimum, whereas the distributed variant has an average excess of 0.074 (minimum 0.062 %). Thus, for this instance, both algorithms perform very similarly (reaching the CLK's average

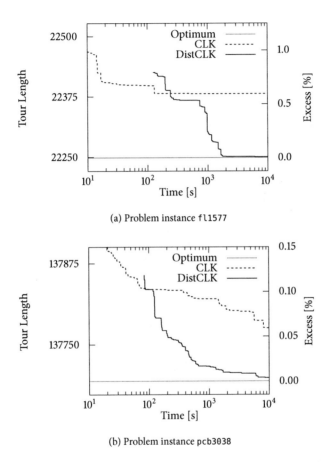

(a) Problem instance fl1577

(b) Problem instance pcb3038

Figure 15: Tour length versus CPU time for the distributed Chained Lin-Kernighan algorithm ('DistCLK'), compared to the original CLK for instances fl1577 and pcb3038. See also Figs. 16 and 17.

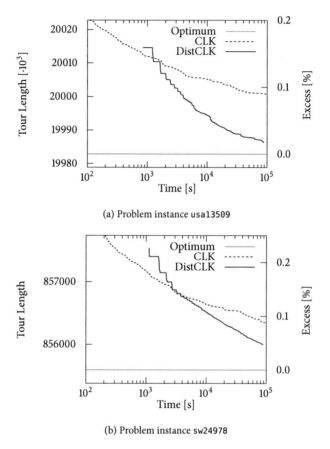

(a) Problem instance usa13509

(b) Problem instance sw24978

Figure 16: Tour length versus CPU time for the distributed Chained Lin-Kernighan algorithm ('DistCLK'), compared to the original CLK for instances usa13509 and sw24978. See also Figs. 15 and 17.

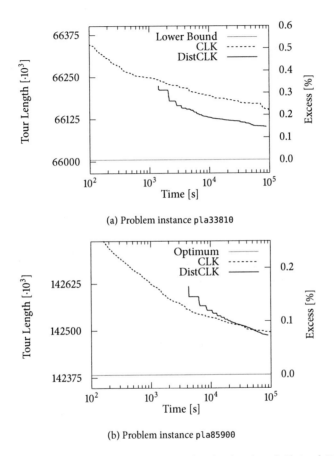

(a) Problem instance pla33810

(b) Problem instance pla85900

Figure 17: Tour length versus CPU time for the distributed Chained Lin-Kernighan algorithm ('DistCLK') compared to the original CLK for instances pla33810 and pla85900. See also Figs. 15 and 16.

| Algorithm ▶ | CLK | | DistCLK | |
| Instance ▼ | 100 s | $10^4$ s | 10 s | $10^3$ s |
|---|---|---|---|---|
| E1k.1 | 0.005 | 0.002 | OPT | OPT |
| C1k.1 | 0.024 | 0.016 | – | OPT |
| fl1577 | 0.670 | 0.594 | – | 0.006 |
| pr2392 | 0.237 | 0.093 | 0.152 | OPT |
| pcb3038 | 0.103 | 0.060 | – | 0.004 |
| fl3795 | 0.643 | 0.524 | – | OPT |
| fnl4461 | 0.098 | 0.041 | – | 0.013 |
| fi10639* | 0.217 | 0.106 | – | 0.116 |
| usa13509 | 0.204 | 0.112 | – | 0.062 |
| sw24978 | 0.307 | 0.122 | – | 0.116 |
| pla33810* | 0.519 | 0.287 | – | 0.126 |
| pla85900 | 0.334 | 0.160 | – | 0.182 |

Table 13: Excess above the optimum (lower bound) of the average tour length compared to known optimum (best known lower bound if not available, marked with '*') after 100 and $10^4$ (for CLK) and 10 and 1000 CPU seconds per node (for DistCLK), respectively. No data is available for cells marked '–', as the algorithm had not yet found an intermediate solution.

result after 59 589 s), although the distributed algorithm still has an advantage, given the same CPU time.

*Effects of Parallelization*

To compare the effects of parallelization, a subset of the instances was run in setups with both 1 and 8 nodes, while keeping other setup parameters constant. In the case of the 8-node variant the locally improved tours were exchanged between neighboring nodes. Simulation results show that the distributed algorithm scales well with the number of nodes.

In Tables **??–??** and Fig. **??**, a comparison between the original Chained LK and the distributed algorithm running on 1 or 8 nodes, respectively, is shown. For all three instances, both variants of the distributed CLK perform better than the original CLK, either by reaching a given

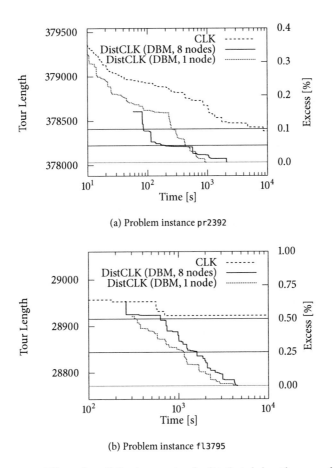

(a) Problem instance pr2392

(b) Problem instance fl3795

Figure 18: Effects of parallelization running the distributed algorithms on a different number of nodes and optional variable strength perturbation (VSP) for problem instances pr2392 and fl3795. Additional horizontal lines represent solution quality levels used for comparison; see also Fig. 19 and Tab. 14.

| Instance | Total CPU time [s] | | |
|----------|------|---------|---------|
| Excess | CLK | 1 node | 8 nodes |
| Instance pr2392 | | | |
| 0.10 % | 8518.7 | 246.2 | 85.2 |
| 0.05 % | – | 421.2 | 193.9 |
| 0.00 % | – | 937.1 | 2097.6 |
| Instance fl3795 | | | |
| 0.50 % | – | 336.9 | 627.5 |
| 0.25 % | – | 1153.3 | 1598.1 |
| 0.00 % | – | 4223.7 | 4552.4 |
| Instance fi10639 | | | |
| 0.12 % | 3912.6 | 1183.4 | 1496.4 |
| 0.10 % | 15183.4 | 2671.7 | 2805.0 |
| 0.08 % | – | 6960.5 | 5784.4 |

Table 14: Total CPU time spent on average by different algorithms/setup to reach a given solution quality level (excess above optimum/lower bound) for selected problem instances. Cells without value (marked by '–') represent setups that were not able to achieve results with the corresponding average solution quality levels. Solution quality levels are depicted as horizontal lines in Fig. ??.

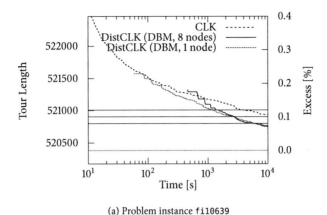

(a) Problem instance fi10639

Figure 19: Effects of parallelization running the distributed algorithms on a different number of nodes and optional variable strength perturbation (VSP) for problem instance fi10639. Additional horizontal lines represent solution quality levels used for comparison; see also Fig. 18 and Tab. 14.

level of solution quality in much less time or by reaching solution quality levels that can not be reached by the original CLK.

For problem instance pr2392 (Fig. 18a), the variant with 8 nodes is considerably faster than the 1-node variant when reaching the average solution quality of 0.10 % and 0.05 % excess. The former bound is reached after 246.2 s by the single-node variant and after just 85.2 s by the 8-node variant. The same holds for the latter bound, which is reached after 421.2 s and 193.9 s, respectively. After about 64 s, there is a turning point and the 8-node variant falls behind the 1-node variant. The optimal solution is reached after 937.1 s (1 node) and 2097.6 s (8 nodes). This behavior depends on three runs in the 8-node variant needing more than 920 CPU seconds, whereas the other 7 runs require less than 270 s. The median for the 8-node variant is only 238.9 s, but 361.1 s for the single-node variant.

With problem instance fl3795 (Fig. 18b), the approximation to the optimum over time is smoother than for pr2392. Again, three different quality levels were selected for evaluation. To find a tour that is 0.5 % above the optimum, the single-node variant requires 336.9 CPU seconds, whereas the parallel variant requires 627.5 CPU seconds. Although the single node variant is about twice as fast in reaching this level of quality, the difference in performance diminishes closer to the optimum. For an average excess of 0.25 %, the required CPU seconds are 1153.3 versus 1598.1, respectively, leaving the single-node variant with an advantage factor of about 1.4 only. Only one out of 10 runs with the original CLK was able to reach this quality level. To reach the optimal solution, the single-node variant requires 4223.7 CPU seconds on average, whereas the 8-node variant requires 4552.4. Given this minimal difference in required time, both setups can be considered equal.

As for instance fi10639 (Fig. 19a), no optimal solution is known; the lower bound [47] was used to measure tour qualities. The first distance level of 0.12 % above the lower bound for this instance was reached after 1183.4 CPU seconds in the single-node variant, while the 8-node variant required 1496.4 seconds. The original CLK required 3912.6 s on average to reach a solution with this level of quality. The tour quality of 0.10 % is reached on average after 2671.7 s (1 node) versus 2805.0 s (8 nodes) versus 15 183.4 s (original CLK). Finally, the quality level of 0.08 % required a computation time of 6960.5 seconds for the single-node variant and 5784.4 seconds for the 8-node variant, resulting in an increase in speed of about 17 %. The original CLK only reaches a solution at this quality level in four out of 10 runs.

*Variator Strength and Restarts*

The perturbation and restarting strategy can effectively help the CLK to leave local optima. Out of 10 runs, three example runs of the distributed algorithm (8 nodes) applied on instance fi10639 were selected for a detailed discussion. CPU times given here are per node and thus limited to $10^4$ s. Improvements in tour quality propagate very quickly through the hypercube and thus events such as changing the variable-strength mutation's strength occur at all nodes within a small time frame. To simplify the discussion, these events are assumed to occur simultaneously in all nodes.

For run $A$ (Fig. 20a), only a weak perturbation was required to find better tours. During the first 4952 CPU seconds, 51 improvements were found by the nodes. As after about 6600 seconds no new improvements were made, within a small time frame all eight nodes increased $\sigma$ to 2. Before requiring any further increase, a better tour was found (7858 seconds) by a node. As this tour was multicast in the net and improved the local best tours, the local $i_{\text{non-impr}}$ variables were reset, too. After about 9500 seconds $\sigma$ increased again as no new tour was found in the meantime. Finally, the best tour's length was 520 627 (excess 0.047 %), which was found after 7858 seconds.

Run *B* (Fig. 20b) showed that strong perturbations can be necessary. For the first 3396 CPU seconds, 45 improvements were found by the nodes. Hereafter, $\sigma$ was increased sequentially: after about 5020 seconds to level 2, after about 6700 seconds to level 3 and after 8370 seconds to level 4. A better tour was found by a node after 9337 seconds, preventing a further increase of $\sigma$. This tour was improved four more times, resulting in a final tour of length 520 584 (0.039 % excess).

In contrast, for run *C* (Fig. 20c) a strong perturbation was applied during simulation, but the tour quality was not thereby improved. During the first 2503 CPU seconds, 48 improving tours were found by the nodes. Here, the nodes exchanged their tours often enough not to require to increase their variation level or even to restart. As no better tours were found, the perturbation strength $\sigma$ increased to 2 on all nodes after about 4140 seconds, to strength level 3 after 5830 seconds, and to level 4 after about 7500 seconds. Perturbation strength level 5 was reached, too, but superseded soon after (about 9400 seconds) by restarts with new tours on every node. Within the remaining time, no better tour had been found and the tour found after a quarter of the given time was finally the best tour of all. This final tour's length was 520 662, which is 0.054 % above the lower bound.

Tour qualities in all runs with the same parameters were between 520 563 (0.035 %) and 521 002 (0.119 %).

*Comparison with Related Work*

For a comparison with other TSP solvers, the running times of selected instances have been normalized to a 500 MHz Alpha processor, as standardized for the 8th DIMACS Implementation Challenge for the TSP [113, 110]. The normalization factor was calculated by comparing the running times of a greedy algorithm to the known values for the Alpha machine. For problem instances with sizes not covered by the testbed, the normalization factor was interpolated from surrounding instance sizes. The computational data of other TSP solvers for the following comparison has been taken from the DIMACS challenge website [110]. Different excess values are due to the fact that different pairs of tour quality and CPU times were available for each algorithm.

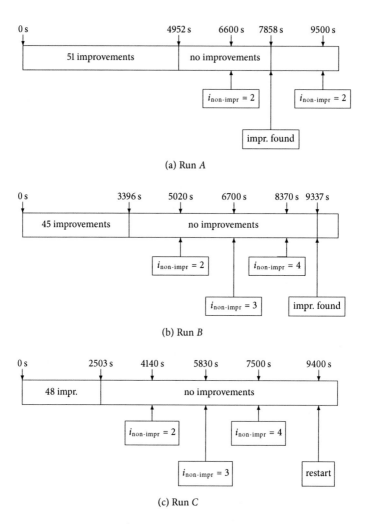

(a) Run $A$

(b) Run $B$

(c) Run $C$

Figure 20: Occurrences of improvement and perturbation events over time for three selected example runs.

HELSGAUN's LK is an LK-based algorithm[3] (LK-H, [100, 101]) modifying the original LK algorithm. JOHNSON and MCGEOCH report [113] that LK-H finds better tours than their own LK implementation (LK-JM) for most instances in their testbed, but LK-H requires significantly more time to reach these tour qualities. Due to its long running times and good tour qualities, LK-H is an adequate choice for comparison with the distributed algorithm presented in this thesis. For the data used here, LK-H's MAX_TRIALS parameter was set to 1.

WALSHAW's Multi-Level LK [199] is a multi-level approach to solving TSP problems that also embeds the Chained Lin-Kernighan algorithm, which is the reason for including it into the following comparison. For the data used here, the number of iterations of the CLK algorithm was set to $N$ (MLC$^N$LK or MLCLK-N), were $N$ is the number of cities in the instance.

COOK and SEYMOUR improve in their *Tour Merging* algorithm [48] results from independent runs of an underlying TSP solver (such as CLK or LK-H) by merging the edges into a new graph and finding tours in this new graph. In an example using instance rl5934 and LK-H, 10 runs of LK-H result in an average tour quality of 0.089% above the optimum and a best tour length of 0.006% above. The union of all 10 tours contains the optimal tour which is found by COOK and SEYMOUR's algorithm within a very short period of time (compared to the time required for the LK-H runs).

As this algorithm features both long running times (it is the sum of several independent TSP solvers) and good tour qualities, it has been chosen for comparison with the distributed algorithm.

For the data used here, the average over 5 runs of tour-merging using a branch decomposition with 10 CLK tours (12 quadrant neighbors, Don't-Look-Bits, $N$ iterations and Geometric kicking strategy) was used. It is not clear if the reported times include the time to find the CLK tours.

In their comparison of ILK algorithms, JOHNSON and MCGEOCH [113] use their own algorithm [112] as reference. In this thesis, the data of a variant with $10N$ iterations, 20 quadrant neighbors, don't-look bits and maximum depth of 50 is compared to the results of the distributed algorithm. This variant from the DIMACS challenge [110] is the one with the longest running time and the best tour qualities over all ILK variants by JOHNSON and MCGEOCH.

To compare the results of the heuristics, the results of the exact TSP solver from the *Concorde* [49] package were included in Tab. 16.

---

3  For the comparison, version 1.3 dated July 2002 has been used.

The computation time presented for the distributed algorithm (columns marked with 'DistCLK' in Tables 15–16) are the average CPU times (summarized over all nodes) normalized to a 500 MHz Alpha processor. The DistCLK algorithm provides first values comparatively late in the search process, as result values were determined only once all repetitions had found at least an initial solution.

For all but the two largest instances, the distributed algorithm takes longer to find its initial solutions in comparison with the total running times for HELSGAUN's LK (LK-H). The solution quality of the distributed algorithm, however, is considerably better than the result provided for LK-H. For example, for problem instance pr2392, LK-H finds a solution of cost 378 923 after 0.24 s, whereas the first intermediate solution of the DistCLK algorithm is found after 205.4 s (normalized) with cost 378 606.9 on average. The ratio between the computation times for both algorithms shifts towards the distributed algorithm for increasing instances size: it grows from 0.13 for instance fnl4461 and 0.50 for usa13509 to 2.87 (instance pla33810) and 4.46 for instance pla85900. For the last instance, LK-H requires more than 13 hours to find a solution with an excess of 0.84 %, whereas the DistCLK algorithm finds a solution with excess 0.16 % after about 2.5 hours.

WALSHAW's Multi-level ($MLC^N LK$) approach's final tour qualities are worse compared to the tour qualities of the first iteration within the distributed algorithm, except for one case, but $MLC^N LK$ requires significantly less time for its first iteration than the distributed algorithm . For one comparable case (instance fl3795), $MLC^N LK$ requires only 26 normalized CPU seconds to find a tour whose quality is 0.54 % above the optimum. The distributed variant, however, requires 938 seconds.

The tour merging (TM-CLK) by COOK and SEYMOUR finds very good tour qualities for the instances that are used for comparison here. To reach this tour quality, TM-CLK requires more time than the two heuristics above, but is still significantly faster than the distributed algorithm. For example, for problem instance pr2392, TM-CLK requires only 93 s to find an optimal tour, whereas the distributed algorithm requires 7465 s. For the tour merging algorithm, only data for instances with < 6000 cities is available, as the algorithm fails for larger problem instances. The distributed algorithm may perform better for larger instances when compared to the tour merging algorithm.

Compared to JOHNSON & MCGEOCH's Iterated LK (ILK-JM), the distributed algorithm performs better for most instances. Except for instances pr2392 and E1k.1, the distributed algorithm requires signifi-

cantly less time, up to the factor of 4.5 for instance pla33810. No data
is provided for problem instance pla85900.

The exact tour lengths and the required computation times from
Concorde are only available for the six smallest instances of this testbed.
However, the DistCLK algorithm found optimal solutions in only four
of these six instances in all 10 runs, requiring more time than the exact
algorithm. The advantage of Concorde ranges from the factor 1.8 (instance Clk.1) to 63.9 for instance pr2392. These instance sizes are still
quite small, but this approach becomes computationally prohibitive for
large instances.

Finally, the last block of Tab. 16 contains the distributed algorithm's
best results out of 10 runs and the normalized CPU time until the first
occurrence of this result. For instances where the known optimal tour
quality was not found, the algorithm continued its search, so the CPU
time until termination may be higher in some cases.

### 3.3.4 *Summary*

The proposed distributed algorithm improves the quality and performance of the original CLK algorithm in different ways. By exchanging
tours between nodes, nodes with worse tours can leave the current
search space region to enter more promising areas. To increase the effectiveness of the distributed algorithm even further, a perturbation
move with variable strength was introduced. The approach presented
here therefore converges faster towards good solutions and finds better
tours within a given time bound (sum over all nodes), compared to the
original CLK algorithm. In the experiments, the distributed algorithm
finds optimal solutions for instances pr2392 and fl3795, where the
plain CLK algorithm fails to find optimal solutions.

Experiments show that distributed computation of TSP instances is,
in fact, possible. The approach presented here reuses established concepts of non-distributed evolutionary and memetic algorithms. Due
to its modular design, components can be exchanged, so that instead
of CLK, for example, another solver could be used. A major drawback
for distributed TSP solvers is the lack of a fast and efficient recombination operator. Using a replacement operator for recombination implies
wasting CPU time on some nodes (if the local solution is discarded in
favor of a received solution), but for the island setup as a whole, better solutions are found compared to setups where each node operates
independently with the exchange of information.

| Instance | Helsgaun LK | | | Walshaw Multi-Level CLK | | | Cook & Seymour Tour Merging | | |
|---|---|---|---|---|---|---|---|---|---|
| | Excess [%] | LK-H [s] | Dist-CLK [s] | Excess [%] | $MLC^N$ LK [s] | Dist-CLK [s] | Excess [%] | TM-CLK [s] | Dist-CLK [s] |
| C1k.1 | 0.12 | 8.89 | <944.43 | 0.03 | 11.96 | <944.43 | 0.00 | 105.06 | 944.42 |
| E1k.1 | 0.08 | 9.78 | <9059.94 | 0.20 | 4.35 | <9059.94 | 0.01 | 31.02 | <9059.94 |
| fl1577 | 5.56 | 14.86 | <438.16 | 0.11 | 8.65 | 5203.27 | 0.02 | 161.70 | 5993.88 |
| pr2392 | 0.24 | 34.87 | <205.37 | 0.52 | 8.29 | <205.37 | 0.00 | 92.50 | 7465.24 |
| pcb3038 | 0.16 | 55.85 | <308.82 | 0.30 | 11.62 | <308.82 | 0.01 | 682.58 | 1663.77 |
| fl3795 | 6.73 | 74.06 | <9059.94 | 0.54 | 26.03 | 937.62 | 0.06 | 509.69 | 16402.12 |
| fnl4461 | 0.07 | 129.23 | 978.12 | 0.20 | 22.38 | <584.41 | | | |
| usa13509 | 0.21 | 1133.81 | <2272.18 | 0.19 | 148.49 | <2272.18 | | | |
| pla33810 | 0.96 | 7982.09 | <2785.89 | 1.08 | 294.81 | <2785.89 | | | |
| pla85900 | 0.84 | 48173.84 | <9350.55 | 0.75 | 1092.51 | <9350.55 | | | |

Table 15: Normalized computation time compared with other algorithms (part 1). "Excess" is the excess above the optimum or lower bound (for instances fi10639, pla33810, and pla85900) as listed for the corresponding instance in the DIMACS challenge [110]. The two columns next to the excess are the CPU times for the two algorithms mentioned in the columns' headers. For cells marked with "<", the distributed algorithm's intermediate results only included tours of better quality, so the value given is the point of time when all repetitions of the experiments reported values for the first time.

| Instance | Johnson & McGeoch ILK | | | Exact Concorde | | | Best of 10 runs | |
|---|---|---|---|---|---|---|---|---|
| | Excess [%] | ILK-JM [s] | Dist-CLK [s] | Excess [%] | Exact [s] | Dist-CLK [s] | Excess [%] | DistCLK [s] |
| C1k.1 | 0.00 | 1292.40 | 944.43 | 0.00 | 533.64 | 944.43 | 0.00 | 198.29 |
| E1k.1 | 0.05 | 65.14 | <9059.94 | 0.00 | 854.50 | 9059.94 | 0.00 | 65.07 |
| fl1577 | 0.02 | 3845.32 | 5993.88 | 0.00 | 6704.04 | – | 0.00 | 4157.02 |
| pr2392 | 0.05 | 220.54 | 681.95 | 0.00 | 116.86 | 7465.24 | 0.00 | 575.90 |
| pcb3038 | 0.10 | 383.84 | 442.81 | 0.00 | 80828.87 | – | 0.00 | 1826.03 |
| fl3795 | 0.00 | 20597.78 | 16402.12 | 0.00 | 6986.48 | 16402.12 | 0.00 | 4283.36 |
| fnl4461 | 0.11 | 722.42 | 674.93 | | | | 0.00 | 14536.58 |
| usa13509 | 0.11 | 8640.36 | 5418.11 | | | | 0.01 | 179213.99 |
| pla33810 | 0.68 | 47599.30 | 10662.38 | | | | 0.56 | 171839.09 |
| pla85900 | | | | | | | 0.47 | 189023.53 |

Table 16: Normalized computation time compared with other algorithms (part 2). "Excess" is the excess above the optimum or lower bound (for instances fl10639, pla33810, and pla85900) as listed for the corresponding instance in the DIMACS challenge [110]. The two columns next to the excess are the CPU times for the two algorithms mentioned in the columns' headers. For cells marked with "<", the distributed algorithm's intermediate results only included tours of better quality, so the value given is the point of time when all repetitions of the experiments reported values for the first time.

## 3.4 SUMMARY

This chapter has addressed two different approaches to solving large TSP instances. The content can be summarized as follows:

- In the section on literature on the TSP, the main focus was on heuristic algorithms. For this problem, a large number of heuristic algorithms exists, only a small selection of which was presented here. This selection included construction heuristics, advanced local search algorithms, recombination operators, and memetic algorithms.

- The first algorithm contributed by this thesis was an edge selection and fixing algorithm. As an introduction to this topic, different concepts of fixing solution and instance components were discussed. Examples were presented and put into relation with related work.

- For the edge fixing algorithm, different edge selection algorithms were proposed and motivating factors for the applications at hand were given. The intention is to select edges that are supposed to occur in optimal solutions and put a tabu on those edges that prevent any changes. The edge selection heuristics come from four different origins, with two different variants available for each type (either strict or relaxed). An analysis of these heuristics showed that they differ in the number of selected edges and the quality of their choice. Selection heuristics based on the nearest neighbor or the close pairs concepts (strict variants) had the highest probability of selecting optimal tour edges, whereas relaxed variants of the MST, nearest neighbor and close pairs concepts had the lowest probabilities.

- The selection heuristics were integrated into a ILS framework, where edges chosen by the selection heuristics were made tabu for the following LK algorithm, effectively reducing the problem instance size. In comparison to a reference experiment without edge fixation, the degeneration in solution quality is negligible using the close pairs edge selection heuristic, yet it only takes $3/4$ of the time to converge. Edge selection heuristics based on relaxed variants of the MST or nearest neighbor strategy fix the largest amount of edges (including false positives). This requires less than $1/5$ of the reference time but results in the least improvement. Most setups require less than $1/2$ of the time of the reference setup without fixing, but find improvements that are not more than 25 % worse.

- For the distributed algorithm, an island model was used where the participating nodes were arranged in a hypercube topology. The distributed memetic algorithm was realized using an existing TSP solver as the improvement component on each island. On each island, the algorithm iterates on the only individual, only interrupted by variable strength perturbation or the exchange of individuals between islands.

- The completely random variable strength perturbation (VSP) was designed to be complementary to the more local perturbation of the CLK (both based on DBMs). The VSP allowed the CLK to find better solutions on average compared to an unmodified CLK, even in non-distributed setups.

- Corresponding non-distributed setups and distributed setups perform similarly in terms of solution quality, given the same total computational resources. As the computation is distributed among eight nodes in the experiments conducted here, the absolute time is about eight times smaller for distributed setups than for non-distributed setups.

- The lack of a recombination operator that is as efficient as a local search operation in terms of the invested time and the gain of solution quality is the largest issue for the distributed algorithm presented here. A replace recombinator was used as a compromise due to its minimal computational complexity.

The edge fixing heuristic and the distributed CLK are conceptionally different approaches for solving large TSP instances. Whereas the edge fixing heuristic tries to reduce the computational effort required to find a local optimum in a local search, the distributed algorithm keeps the total computational effort at about the same level but parallelizes it among a number of computing nodes. With both approaches, the actual TSP solver can be treated as a black box requiring only minimal adaption (e. g. honoring fixed edges).

Compared to unmodified implementations of the used TSP solver, larger problem instances can be handled using the problem reduction approach. Sequences of fixed edges (called 'fixed paths') can be replaced by a single fixed edge in the reduced instance. Auxiliary data structures (e. g. nearest neighbor tables) do not have to be maintained for inner nodes of the fixed paths.

# 4

# ROUTING AND WAVELENGTH ASSIGNMENT PROBLEM

The *Routing and Wavelength Assignment* problem (RWA) is a graph-theoretical optimization problem, where communication requests between nodes in a network have to be fulfilled by allocating routes on optical fiber links with a given capacity. On these optical fiber links, *wavelength-division multiplexing* (WDM) is used to send multiple optical carrier signals (laser light) with different wavelengths (colors) on the same physical link. In [93, 2, 150], physical properties and practical issues of wavelength-division multiplexing and fiber optics are presented. Here, the RWA is addressed as an abstract optimization problem; physical aspects of optical networks such as dispersion or loss in signal quality are simplified or discarded.

The problem is defined as follows: given is a graph $G = (V, E, W)$ with nodes $V$ (defining $n = |V|$), a set of edges $E$, and a set of wavelengths $W$. An edge $e \in E$ is an optical fiber link in the physical network, where each wavelength $\lambda \in W$ is eligible. A set of requests $R$ is given, where a request $(v_r^s, v_r^t, d_r) = r \in R$ connects nodes $v_r^s$ and $v_r^t$ with a demand of $d_r \in \mathbb{N}^+$. The sum of demands of all requests is defined as $D = \sum_{r \in R} d_r$. A lightpath between the request's endpoints has to be established for each unit of demand. A *lightpath* is an optical path between two nodes created by the allocation of the same wavelength throughout the path of optical fiber links providing a 'circuit-switched' interconnection. Lightpaths have to fulfill two constraints: the *wavelength conflict constraint* (or *wavelength clash constraint*) states that each wavelength on a physical link is used by at most one lightpath at the same time; The *wavelength continuity constraint* requires a lightpath to use the same wavelength on each link. There are problem variants relaxing these constraints. The first constraint can be relaxed by *multiple-fiber links* [206, 133]; the latter constraint can be relaxed by introducing *wavelength converters* [38] that change the wavelength of a lightpath at selected nodes. Wavelength converters reduce the RWA to a flow minimization problem, unless additional constraints such as converter usage costs or limited availability are considered.

A solution $s$ can be represented by a mapping from requests $R$ to sets of wavelength-path combinations

$$s : R \rightarrow \left( W \times 2^E \right)^{\mathbb{N}^+} \tag{4.1}$$

where $2^E$ represents the set of all possible paths in $G$. Different cost functions are available for the RWA, depending on the specific problem definition. The RWA can be defined as either static or dynamic. In the *static case*, requests are known *a priori* including their demand volume. The objective is to minimize the total number of wavelengths used to route all requests in a given network. Alternatively, the number of wavelengths is limited and as many requests as possible have to be routed (subject to a gain function on requests). In the *dynamic case*, communication requests turn up over time (either with limited or infinite duration) and an algorithm has to decide whether (and how) it routes an incoming request or discards it, in an on-line fashion without knowledge on future requests. Again, there is a gain function associated with each routed request. Furthermore, a *blocking probability* may be considered, where the probability that potential future requests will be blocked is considered. For setups with a limited number of wavelengths and without wavelength conversion, blocking may arise for two reasons. A request is blocked due to *capacity blocking* if there is a cut in the network between both endpoints, where the cut edges are all edges with no capacity left. If there is capacity left between both endpoints but no continuous wavelength on any path, it is called *wavelength blocking*.

The RWA can be defined based on an undirected or directed graph. In a directed graph, requests require a directed path from source to target nodes. In this case, edges are either directed (can be used only in one direction) or bidirectional (can be used independently in both directions). There may be two different requests where source and target nodes are exchanged. In undirected graphs, some amount of bandwidth between two nodes has to be established without classifying nodes as source or target nodes. Furthermore, edges are undirected and thus can be used in any direction, but each wavelength is only available once.

Requests can be modeled with two equivalent formulations: (a) a request has a demand of $\geq 1$ but only one request between each node pair is allowed (b) each request has a demand of $= 1$ but multiple requests between each node pair are allowed. Depending on the algorithm to be discussed, the model that is most convenient will be chosen.

In this thesis, the static case of the RWA in undirected graphs is used, where the number of wavelengths has to be minimized, but is not lim-

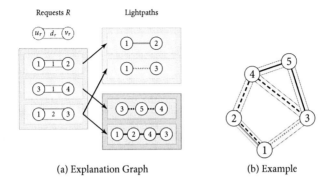

(a) Explanation Graph                    (b) Example

Figure 21: Example instance for the RWA, using two wavelengths (black, gray) to route requests $\{(1,3,2),(1,2,1),(3,4,1)\}$. The first request uses the gray dotted lightpath $\langle 1,3 \rangle$ and black dashed path $\langle 1,2,4,3 \rangle$; the second request the gray solid path $\langle 1,2 \rangle$. The last request uses the black solid path $\langle 3,5,4 \rangle$. Physical links are shaded in gray.

ited. A distributed multilevel memetic algorithm (ML-DMA) that is able to handle large problem instances will be introduced. The main components of this algorithm consist of the construction heuristics (Sec. 4.4), an iterated local search (Sec. 4.5), a (distributed) memetic algorithm including recombination (Sec. 4.6), and the multilevel approach (ML, Sec. 4.7).

## 4.1 RELATED WORK

In the 1990s, the Routing and Wavelength Assignment problem emerged when optical networks with full-optical switching at nodes became available. Routing in these optical networks has been proven to be NP-complete [37] and thus is a challenging optimization problem of practical relevance. A number of papers have tackled this problem using a wide range of optimization techniques. However, comparing results among different publications is barely possible since both optimization criterion and exact problem definitions vary considerably among these publications and no public benchmark library exists.

In the literature, there are two different kinds of approaches for solving the static RWA. The RWA is either divided into its subproblems or

| Publication | Routing | Wavelength Assignment |
|---|---|---|
| Chlamtac and Ganz [37] (1992) | – | Bin Packing |
| Nagatsu, Hamazumi and Sato [153] (1995) | Heuristic for MCF | Bin Packing |
| Varela and Sinclar [196] (1999) | ACO | Bin Packing |
| Baroni and Bayvel [26] (1997) | Heuristic for MCF | Bin Packing |
| Banerjee and Mukherjee [22] (1996) | fractional MCF & rand. rounding | GC |
| Hyytiä and Virtamo [107] (1998) | SP & ILS | GC |
| Banerjee and Sharan [23] (2004) | $k$-SP with GA | GC |
| Li and Simha [125] (2000) | $k$-SP | generalized GC (PCP) |
| De Noronha and Ribeiro [54] (2004) | $k$-EDP | generalized GC (PCP) |

Table 17: Overview of literature splitting the RWA into its two subproblems.

it is addressed as an integral problem. In the remainder of this section, related work to both approaches will be presented.

### 4.1.1   Solving the Subproblems of the RWA Independently

The majority of publications address the two subproblems separately. For the routing subproblem, most approaches use some kind of shortest path (SP) algorithm for path assignments. The wavelength assignment subproblem is either solved by bin packing inspired heuristics or, due to its equivalence to the graph (node) coloring problem (GC, [82, GT4]), it is solved as such a problem instance. Table 17 gives an overview of the methods used; the corresponding papers are presented in detail below.

In one of the earliest publications on the RWA, Chlamtac and Ganz introduced the *Lightpath Establishment Problem* [37], which is equivalent to the RWA's wavelength assignment subproblem. Beside a lower bound formulation (see Sec. 4.2) and the proof of NP-completeness for this subproblem, a bin packing inspired heuristic for the wavelength assignment part was presented. This heuristic sorts the given paths decreasingly by length; the set of allocated wavelengths is empty. As long as there are paths without assigned wavelengths, a new wavelength is allocated iteratively. Each path is routed according to the ordering, if it does not violate the wavelength conflict constraint. The routing subproblem was not addressed here at all.

NAGATSU, HAMAZUMI and SATO [153] presented heuristic algorithms for the static RWA, with or without wavelength conversion enabled. The authors designated lightpaths without wavelength conversion *wavelength path* (WP) and lightpaths with wavelength conversion *virtual wavelength path* (VWP). For setups with wavelength conversion, the objective of minimizing the number of used wavelengths can be achieved by minimizing the maximum load on any edge.

For the routing subproblem, NAGATSU *et al.* proposed an iterative algorithm. Sorting the requests in a priority queue, the paths are initialized by shortest paths using DIJKSTRA's algorithm, where a link's weight equals the number of paths already routed on this link. Once all initial paths have been established, the paths get refined: requests with paths traversing links with maximum load are iteratively rerouted on links with lower loads or on paths that traverse fewer links with maximum load. Whereas the above algorithm (number of required wavelengths equals the maximum link load) is sufficient for setups with wavelength converters, wavelengths have to be assigned to each path obeying the wavelength conflict constraint for setups with no wavelength converters. The proposed wavelength assignment algorithm starts by allocating the first wavelength and checking all unassigned paths (in no specific order) to see if the wavelength can be assigned to this path without conflict. When all paths have been checked and there are unassigned paths left, the number of wavelengths is increased iteratively and an attempt is made to assign the remaining paths to this new wavelength. In the experiments conducted here, it was observed that on grid structures, setups without wavelength conversion required at least 2 % more wavelengths than setups with wavelength conversion. For irregular structures, at least 5 % more wavelengths were required.

VARELA and SINCLAIR [196] described an ant colony optimization (ACO, see Sec. 2.1.4) algorithm for the routing subproblem and solved the wavelength assignment subproblem by a bin packing inspired algorithm (trivial when given wavelength conversion). Unlike normal ACO algorithms where ants are attracted by pheromone trails, the authors let ants be repelled by higher levels of pheromone. The ACO follows the structure of well-researched ACOs for the TSP, but introduces additional constraints for finding paths for the RWA: when searching for a path between two nodes, ants may visit a node at most once (to avoid cycles) and thus must be allowed to backtrack, given that the network is not fully connected (dead ends possible). The authors stated that their ACO could not compete with problem-specific heuristics in terms of runtime or solution quality.

BARONI and BAYVEL [26] used a similar approach to NAGATSU *et al.* for the routing subproblem and a bin packing approach for the wavelength assignment.

For the routing subproblem, the shortest path between both endpoints is assigned initially to each request, regardless of link usage by other requests. In an iterative improvement phase that runs until a local optimum is reached, a path is replaced by an alternative path if the highest load on any link in the alternative paths is lower than the highest load on any link in the old path. Wavelength assignments are done by a bin packing approach where the paths are sorted non-increasingly by hop count. The authors assume that between each node pair in the physical graph a request of demand = 1 exists.

For the experiments, three types of problem instances were considered: (a) networks based on real world network topologies with up to 21 nodes and 39 edges (b) random graphs with additional constraints to avoid degenerated or unconnected networks (c) regular graphs based, for example, on de Bruijn graphs. Observations suggested that for randomly connected graphs, the number of wavelengths is independent on the network size but depends on the physical connectivity $\alpha$, which describes the fraction of edges in a fully connected graph actually used in a given graph: graphs with smaller $\alpha$ required more wavelengths to fulfill all requests than graphs with larger $\alpha$. Furthermore, the authors stated that the minimum number of wavelengths for such problem instances is $\overline{H}/\alpha$, where $\overline{H}$ is the average over the shortest path lengths between any node pair. The authors discussed using multi-fiber links (wavelengths are available multiple times per link) on heavily loaded edges, which decreases the number of wavelengths required to fulfill all requests.

BANERJEE and MUKHERJEE [22] presented a heuristic where the routing subproblem is solved by stating an LP formulation where wavelength conversion is allowed, resulting in a fractional multi-commodity flow (MCF) formulation. The actual MCF formulation is similar to the one used for lower bounds (see Sec. 4.2). From the set of edges used in the fractional flow, a set of paths for each request is extracted and one path is randomly selected, where the probability of each path corresponds to its fractional weight (*randomized rounding*).

The wavelength assignment subproblem was solved by presenting the problem as a graph coloring problem instance. For each path in the RWA instance, a node is created in the GC graph. Nodes in the GC graph are connected if the corresponding RWA paths share a common link. The coloring of GC graph nodes represents assigning a wavelength to a path. The GC graph is colored using the *sequential graph coloring* algorithm that adds nodes sequentially to the GC graph, keeping the number of colors minimal. As the result depends on the order in which the nodes are inserted, the authors proposed a *smallest-last* ordering of $\langle v_1, \ldots, v_D \rangle$, where $v_D$ is the node with minimum degree in the graph, and all other nodes $v_i$ have minimum degree in the graph induced by $V \smallsetminus \{v_{i+1}, \ldots, v_D\}$.

HYYTIÄ and VIRTAMO [107] interpreted the wavelength assignment subproblem as a graph coloring problem instance and discussed several algorithms:

1. A greedy algorithm that sorts nodes in the GC problem non-increasingly by their degree and iteratively colors each node with the lowest-indexed feasible color (wavelength).

2. An exhaustive search algorithm where two non-connected GC nodes are either merged into one node or connected by a new edge (branching) in each step; the algorithm prunes subtrees if the subtree's lower bound is above the best-known solution and terminates once a perfect graph is obtained.

3. A simulated annealing (SA, Sec. 2.1.3) approach where a modification step is changing a single node's color to another feasible assignment.

4. A genetic algorithm (GA) using only recombination but no mutation, optimizing a vector determining the node order for a greedy algorithm.

5. A tabu search (TS, Sec. 2.1.3) algorithm that represents the GC as a decision problem and divides nodes into sets sharing the same color; a search step moves a node from one set to another set.

The above algorithms were integrated into an RWA algorithm, where the routing subproblem was solved by a simple iterative local search (ILS). In this ILS, random path changes were performed on an existing solution and a new solution was kept if it reduced the number of wavelengths. Experimental results suggested that the choice on the wavelength assignment algorithm has no effect as the underlying graph coloring problem is very easy to solve. The authors stated that the solution found for the larger of the two instances they considered could be improved further ('[...] if just few connections could be handled with other colors the total number of colors would be significantly smaller.').

BANERJEE and SHARAN [23] presented an evolutionary algorithm for the routing subproblem. Individuals are represented as a sequence of genes, where each gene corresponds to a request (demand = 1) and points to one path in a set of predetermined shortest paths between the request's endpoints. The cost function for an individual is the sum of all the edges' costs, where an edge's cost grows exponentially with its usage by other paths. The EA's crossover operator is an $n$-point crossover on the genome creating one new offspring. The next generation is selected using a $(\mu + \lambda)$ operator. The mutation changes the path assignment in a gene with probability $1/k$, where $k$ is the number of genes (number of requests). Few details were given on the wavelength assignment subproblem. Experimental results on four instances with up to five different demand matrices suggested that this EA found better solutions (in number of used wavelengths) compared to a simple first-fit construction heuristic. This advantage increased both with network size and total demand.

The sizes of problem instances considered here are rather small: the same problem graphs were used both in [23] and in [26], but although the latter is several years older, larger demand matrices were used and solved to (near-)optimality.

LI and SIMHA [125] used a generalized graph coloring problem definition to solve the wavelength assignment subproblem. Firstly, instead of a single path per request (assuming its demand = 1), a set of paths (such as the $k$-shortest paths) is determined for each request in the routing subproblem. In the wavelength assignment subproblem, the graph coloring problem has to be modified to the *partition coloring problem* (PCP) to select one path out of several available paths for each request. Each path is still represented by one node in the graph coloring graph, but the nodes $V$ get divided into disjoint subsets $V_1, \ldots, V_a$. A feasible subset $V^P \subseteq V$ guarantees $|V^P \cap V_i| = 1$ and induces a new graph $G^P = (V^P, E^P)$ where $(i, j) = e \in E^P$ if $e \in E$ and $i, j \in V^P$. The partition coloring problem's objective is to find a node set $V^P$ so that the chromatic number $\chi(G^P)$ is minimized. For the experiments, both a regular mesh network (100 nodes) and a real-world instance with 14 nodes have been used. For the former instance, several rectangular paths were considered; for the latter, the $k$-shortest paths (where $k \leq 3$) were considered. Experimental results suggested that only increasing the number of candidate paths for requests does not always improve the solution quality (number of used wavelengths): for the real-world instance, increasing $k$ from 2 to 3 yielded no significant improvement, but increased the computation time.

DE NORONHA and RIBEIRO [54] presented an algorithm that follows the idea of generalized graph coloring in LI *et al.* [125]. For the routing subproblem, for each node pair with positive demand, a set of candidate paths is computed using a $k$-EDP algorithm (*maximum edge disjoint paths*). In this $k$-EDP algorithm, the maximum edge disjoint path algorithm from [132] is executed $k$ times with different request orderings and the sets of paths found in each repetition are combined for each node pair.

For the wavelength assignment subproblem, a tabu search algorithm (TS-PCP) for the partition coloring problem is presented. Here, a feasible initial solution is constructed using an algorithm from [125]. Iteratively, nodes with the highest-indexed color are randomly recolored in another color and all emerging conflicts are subsequently resolved using a repairing local search. The algorithm returns the solution, where decreasing the number of colors further resulted in infeasible solutions due to unresolvable conflicts.

Comparing both LI's PCP algorithm ([125], used for initialization here) and the TS-PCP, the latter algorithm found solutions with about 20 % fewer colors than the former algorithm, when applied to a set of graph coloring benchmark instances. Combining both $k$-EDP ($k = 2$) and TS-PCP resulted in an algorithm for the static RWA that produced results the same as or better than the greedy EDP algorithm from [132] when applied on a set of four networks. Furthermore, it was claimed that the authors' approach had a more stable time-to-solution behavior than the greedy EDP algorithm.

### 4.1.2 *Solving the RWA as an Integral Problem*

Whereas splitting the RWA into two subproblems allows the use of existing algorithms, for example for path finding or graph coloring, good solutions for each (independent) subproblem do not necessarily

| Publication | Construction | Improvement |
|---|---|---|
| BANERJEE and CHEN [25] (1996) | SP + load reduction + Bin Packing | – |
| MANOHAR, MANJUNATH, and SHEVGAONKAR [132] (2002) | EDP + Bin Packing | – |
| YOON, KIM, CHUNG, LEE, and CHOO [209] (2006) | EDP + generalized GC | – |
| SKORIN-KAPOV [181] (2007) | SP + Bin Packing | – |
| TAN and SINCLAIR [191] (1995) | Random Bit Vector | GA |
| SINCLAIR [180] (1998) | – | GA + LS |
| WAUTERS and DEMEESTER [203] (1996) | $k$-SP, WL? | ILS |
| WANG, CHENG, and LIM [201] (2005) | $k$-SP + random WA (infeasible!) | Tabu Search |

Table 18: Overview of literature using integral approaches for construction or improvement.

lead to good solutions for the full RWA problem. Therefore, a number of algorithms address the RWA as an integral problem. Construction algorithms usually iterate over all requests, use a path finding algorithm (e. g. shortest path) and assign a wavelength to each path considering previous iterations' assignments in a bin packing inspired manner. Improvement algorithms operate on feasible solutions and iteratively try to improve the solution's objective value by rerouting paths and assigning different wavelengths to requests. A selection of papers on these topics is presented in the remainder of this section and an overview is given in Tab. 18.

BANERJEE and CHEN [25] proposed a constructive heuristic algorithm called *coloring adaptive path-graph* (CAP), which can be used both to reduce the blocking probability and minimize the number of used wavelengths. The algorithm uses a graph coloring approach (called a *path graph* in the paper), which is initialized by using the shortest paths in the physical graph to route all requests; no wavelengths are assigned. For each physical link, the set of routed paths and the set of used wavelengths is maintained. Starting an iteration with the coloring and rerouting step, a path with maximum *color degree* (number of distinct colors used by neighbors in the GC graph) or maximum node degree in the GC graph (secondary criterion) is chosen. If both degrees are equal to the degrees of the path chosen in the previous iteration, the 'smallest' possible wavelength is assigned to this iteration's path. Otherwise, an alternate route is determined that minimizes the number of other paths with different wavelengths sharing at least one link with the alternate route. A secondary criterion is to minimize the number of paths without assigned wavelengths sharing at least one link. Using the alternate route, the GC graph is updated and another path in the physical graph is chosen for rerouting. The iteration stops once wavelengths have been assigned to all paths. Wavelength assignments are not changed once they are set.

Experiments conducted on both the CAP algorithm and the algorithm using shortest paths only showed that the CAP algorithm required fewer wavelengths to route a set of requests than the SP algorithm. This effect was strongest for high-degree networks, but diminished with an increasing number of requests. For finding a path to route a request, the authors concluded that an adaptive approach is superior to approaches using only a fixed set of alternatives (e. g. only shortest paths).

MANOHAR, MANJUNATH, and SHEVGAONKAR [132] addressed the problem of finding paths by solving the maximum edge disjoint paths (EDP) problem. The idea is motivated by the fact that the same wavelength can be assigned to lightpaths that share no common edge (thus, are edge disjoint) without violating any constraint. As the EDP itself is an NP-complete problem, the authors use the *bounded greedy algorithm* (BGA) from [119]: each time a new path subset has to be determined, requests are randomly drawn from the set of unassigned requests and the shortest path in $G$ is determined for each request. If this path is available and shorter (in terms of hop count) than $\max\left\{\mathrm{diam}(G), \sqrt{|E|}\right\}$, the path is added to the subset and its edges are temporarily blocked in $G$. Once all unassigned requests have been inspected, the subset is complete and the BGA returns this path set. The next available wavelength is assigned to the paths in this set and the temporary block on edges in $G$ is lifted. A new set of EDPs is determined as long as there are requests without paths and wavelength assignments.

Experiments were conducted with the two objectives of minimizing the number of used wavelengths and minimizing the blocking probability given a limited number of wavelengths. For the former objective, competitive results in less time were reported compared to the results from BANERJEE and MUKHERJEE [22]. The instances under consideration were very, requiring less than a second to be solved.

YOON, KIM, CHUNG, LEE, and CHOO [209] presented a combination of edge disjoint paths (EDP) as used in [132] and *path conflict graphs*, which are related to partition coloring graphs [125]. In a preprocessing step, a set of paths in $G$ between each node pair with positive demand is determined. Whereas LI *et al.* [125] use $k$-shortest paths, here the EDP algorithm from [132] is called $k$ times and the set of paths for each request is stored. Using these paths, a *path conflict graph* is constructed by creating nodes for each EDP and partitioning these nodes by their corresponding requests. Edges between nodes in the path conflict graph are introduced between two nodes if the corresponding paths share a common edge in the RWA graph. EDPs are stored in a priority queue, where the sorting criteria are path length (non-decreasing) and node degree in the conflict graph (non-decreasing). One wavelength is available initially. Iteratively, the queue's head element (node in conflict graph, path in RWA graph) is taken, colored with the current wavelength and the path is used to route the request in the RWA graph. In the conflict graph, edges adjacent to the nodes in the partition of the request just routed are removed. When all edges have been removed, a new wavelength is introduced and the conflict graph's edges and the priority queue are reinitialized for all uncolored partitions. The iteration stops once all requests have been colored, as a valid RWA solution has been constructed.

Results suggested that this approach is superior to the EDP algorithm presented in [132] in terms of minimization of the number of wavelengths used for both random and real-world networks using different randomly generated request matrices.

TAN and SINCLAIR [191] described a genetic algorithm (GA) to solve a static RWA instance with 11 nodes using real-world data where available. The authors considered setups with wavelength converters (but may impose a penalty per conversion) and the objective is to minimize the number of used wavelengths. As a secondary criterion to differentiate between solutions with the same wavelength, usage solutions with fewer links utilizing this usage were preferred.

Individuals in the GA are represented by one of four bit string encodings, depending on how routes are assigned to a request and whether assigned wavelengths are stored for each path. The initial population's individuals are randomly created. Until some termination criterion (not exactly specified) is reached, the GA iterates over the population and performs mutation, recombination, and selection operations. Mutation simply toggles bits in the genotype, whereas recombination performs a crossover on two parent individuals. The individual's fitness is determined by decoding the genotypes into phenotypes; if wavelengths are not encoded in the bit string, they are assigned heuristically to the paths. The next generation's individuals are chosen probabilistically considering the fitness of both parents and offsprings.

The authors provided several solutions depending on the used bit string encoding, but even for increased penalty on wavelength converters, no solution without wavelength conversion was found.

SINCLAIR [180] described a hybrid algorithm combining GA operators with local search. The problem formulation differs from other publications in two points: (a) the author allowed multi-fiber links which allows the same wavelength to be assigned multiple times to an edge (b) usage of an intricate complex cost function that considers link capacity, node distance, node costs, and other criteria.

The GA features standard operators such as mutation, recombination, and two local search operators. Each operator is applied with varying probabilities depending on success in previous generations. The mutation operator reroutes a given request on a path randomly chosen from the set of $k$-shortest paths ($k = 8$) between both endpoints using the first available wavelength. The recombination operator performs a crossover where the set of requests is divided and each of the two offspring contains both path and wavelength assignments from one half and only the paths from the other half requiring a new wavelength assignment for these paths. The first local search tries to reroute a request in a wavelength with a high index in a lower-indexed wavelength using one of the $k$-shortest paths. The second local search operates similarly, but here a target wavelength is chosen first and all conflicting paths are routed before rerouting the path from the high-index wavelength. No information on the selection operator is given.

Given that the algorithm used problem-specific operators and representation, the large population size (500) together with the vast number of generations (100 000) call its efficiency into question.

WAUTERS and DEMEESTER [203] presented an heuristic algorithm called HRWA that minimizes the number of used wavelengths. In a preparatory step, all shortest paths between any node pair are determined and the shortest routes to minimize the number of wavelengths are selected. Iteratively, until no more improvement is possible, two possible local search steps are evaluated: (a) a path in the highest-indexed wavelength is rerouted in a lower-indexed wavelength (b) a lower-indexed wavelength is selected and all requests in this wavelength that have a common link with a path in the highest-indexed wavelengths are rerouted, and the highest-indexed wavelength path is routed in this lower-index wavelength. This heuristic algorithm was evaluated in a comparative study with another heuristic algorithm called 'Dijkstra' and an integer linear programming (ILP) formulation on two problem instances (with different demand matrices). The ILP formulated by the authors maximizes the throughput as an objective function while minimizing the path length. To reduce the ILP's computation time, the path set was restricted to the 25-shortest paths.

Results suggested that the usage of wavelength converters has no influence on the solution quality, as the ILP found equally good solutions for setups with and without converters. However, in the network under consideration, 6 out of 19 nodes had a degree of only 2. Requests ending at those nodes increased the number of required wavelengths to fulfill the wavelength conflict constraint (cf. Sec. 4.4). Regarding the wavelength minimization objective, the HRWA found solutions with the same quality as the ILP, but in less time by two orders of magnitudes. Finally, link failures where paths have to be rerouted in different links (and possibly different wavelengths) were handled equally well for cases with and without wavelength conversion.

WANG, CHENG, and LIM [201] presented a tabu search (TS) algorithm which proceeds as follows: starting from an initial number of available wavelengths (determined by the algorithm from BANERJEE and SHARAN in [23]), the number of available wavelengths is decreased by 1 iteratively. The TS's objective is to find a feasible solution for the RWA with a limited number of wavelengths starting from an initial infeasible solution where paths are chosen from the set of $k$-shortest paths and wavelengths are randomly assigned. The TS stops once no feasible solution can be found for a given decreasing step and the previous step's (feasible) solution is the final solution. In each iteration, requests are ordered non-increasingly by the number of conflicts they are involved in and put in a priority queue called the *conflict request list*. A new path and a wavelength are assigned to the queue's head element to reduce the number of conflicts and are appended to a tabu list. Elements in the queue are processed until a feasible solution is found or a given limit of non-improving changes (depending on the number of requests) is reached.

The TS was compared to an ILP, where both algorithms were applied to two problem instances with either 14 or 50 nodes, respectively. Experiments with different request sets were evaluated. The TS achieved optimal or near-optimal results in most setups while requiring less time than the ILP of one order of magnitude.

SKORIN-KAPOV [181] presented construction heuristics based on four bin packing algorithms. These heuristics are explained in detail in Sec. 4.4.

## 4.2   LOWER BOUNDS

To evaluate the quality of heuristic algorithms, *lower bounds* can be used (see also Sec. 2.1.6). For the RWA, two different lower bound algorithms are presented from the literature, followed by a lower bound developed with the participation of the author of this thesis. The lower bound algorithms differ in their complexity and quality (closeness to the actual optimum).

Based on the problem instance's properties, RAMASWAMI and SIVARA-JAN [166, Sect. IV] presented a lower bound for the RWA variant which minimizes the network congestion. This bound was adapted by SKORIN-KAPOV [181] for the static RWA variant. The lower bound consists of two components, each assuming that a request has demand = 1. Firstly, the number of requests where a given node is the endpoint in relation to the number of adjacent edges to this node is used (node degree $\delta$). Secondly, the sum of the hop count of each request's shortest path divided by the number of edges available in the graph determines a lower bound. As both components result in lower bounds but may differ, the maximum of both is used to determine the final lower bound:

$$\text{LB}_{\text{SK}} = \max \left\{ \max_{v \in V} \left\lceil \frac{|\{r \in R | v = v^t \wedge v = v^s\}|}{\delta(v)} \right\rceil , \right.$$
$$\left. \left\lceil \frac{\sum_{r \in R} |\text{SP}_G(r)|}{|E|} \right\rceil \right\} \quad (4.2)$$

BARONI and BAYVEL [26] introduced a lower bound for the RWA by relaxing and translating the problem to a maximum cut problem instance: disregarding the wavelength continuity constraint, the minimum number of wavelengths required to route all requests is the maximum cut in the graph where the size of a cut is defined as the number of requests connecting any two nodes from both components, divided by the number of available wavelengths and links on this cut. Assuming that the node set is divided into $S$ and $\overline{S}$ where $S \cup \overline{S} = V$,

$R' = \{r \in R | (u^r, v^r) \in (S \times \overline{S} \cup \overline{S} \times S)\}$, and a cut is defined by its link set $C$, the lower bound is

$$\text{LB}_{\text{BB}} = \max_{C} \left\lceil \frac{\sum_{r \in R'} d^r}{|C| \cdot |W|} \right\rceil \tag{4.3}$$

This lower bound is tight, as BARONI and BAYVEL find optimal solutions for three out of four of their problem instances. A generalization and more formal approach was given in [178].

In [27], a lower bound algorithm for the RWA was provided by relaxing the wavelength continuity constraint. Thus, the RWA becomes a multi-commodity flow problem, where each request represents a unique commodity, which has to be routed by means of flow through the problem instance's network $G$. This flow is maintained by defining a mass balance property $b_v^r$ (see Eq. (4.8)) for each request $r = (v_r^s, v_r^t, d_r)$ and each node $v$ in $G$. Furthermore, let variable $x_{(i,j)}^r$ indicate the amount of flow of request $r$ sent over edge $(i, j) \in E$. Minimizing the maximum flow sent over an edge can be stated by the following ILP:

$$\text{minimize} \quad \max_{(u,v) \in E} \sum_{r \in R} x_{(u,v)}^r + \sum_{r \in R} x_{(v,u)}^r \tag{4.4}$$

subject to

$$\sum_{u \in V:(u,v) \in E} x_{(u,v)}^r - \sum_{u \in V:(v,u) \in E} x_{(v,u)}^r = b_v^r \quad \text{for all } v \in V, r \in R \tag{4.5}$$

$$x_{(u,v)}^r + x_{(v,u)}^r \leq b_v^r \quad \text{for all } r \in R, (i, j) \in E \tag{4.6}$$

$$x_{(u,v)}^r \in \mathbb{N} \quad \text{for all } r \in R, (u, v) \in E \tag{4.7}$$

$$b_v^r = \begin{cases} -d_r & v = v_r^s \\ d_r & v = v_r^t \\ 0 & \text{otherwise} \end{cases} \tag{4.8}$$

The load of an edge equals the number of paths routed over this edge in this relaxed RWA formulation, which corresponds to an RWA definition with wavelength converters. Thus, the objective is to minimize the maximum load over all edges as stated in Eq. (4.4). This minimization is subject to the flow-conservation constraints in Eq. (4.5) so that each request's demand is fulfilled. Equation (4.6) states that an edge may only be used in one direction by each request. Finally, no fractional flows

| Instance | $LB_{SK}$ | $LB_{MCF}$ | UB |
|---|---|---|---|
| 10.50.deg4 | 158 | 225 | 225 |
| 15.50.deg8 | 363 | 363 | 366 |
| 15.50.deg8 | 120 | 258 | 258 |
| 20.50.deg4 | 375 | 432 | 438 |
| atlanta▼[20] | 1147 | 1256 | 1256 |
| germany50 | 147 | 147 | 147 |
| janos-us-ca▼[200] | 886 | 1288 | 1288 |
| nobel-us | 646 | 670 | 670 |
| norway | 325 | 543 | 543 |
| polska | 1178 | 1682 | 1682 |
| zib54 | 457 | 705 | 705 |

Table 19: Lower bound as described in [181] compared to lower bounds found by our MCF-based algorithm and upper bounds found by our algorithms for selected problem instances (Sec. 4.3).

are allowed in Eq. (4.7). This lower bound algorithm was implemented using CPLEX 9.1.2 and AMPL.

For an evaluation, the lower bound presented by SKORIN-KAPOV ('$LB_{SK}$') was compared with the lower bound presented here ('$LB_{MCF}$') and the best-known solution ('UB') for a selection of problem instances as listed in Tab. 20. The results of this comparison are shown in Tab. 19. Due to its simplicity, the lower bound $LB_{SK}$ is easily available. The quality obtained, however, strongly depends on the instance. This lower bound formulation only yields bounds close or equal to the optimum for problem instances that display 'pathological' behavior (see Sec. 4.3). For other instances this bound can be considerably worse. For problem instance zib54 (Sec. 4.3), for example, the simple lower bound is 35.2 % below the MCF-based lower bound as presented here. Experimental results indicate that $LB_{MCF}$ is indeed tight: for several non-pathological problem instances, feasible solutions are found with the heuristic algorithms from this thesis that require exactly the same number of wavelengths as predicted by the lower bound. However, this sophisticated lower bound is not available for large instances due to prohibitive computation times and the simple lower bounds algorithm is disregard as the results are too erratic for meaningful solution quality evaluations.

## 4.3  BENCHMARK INSTANCES

The selection of public RWA benchmark instances is rather limited: either problem instances are randomly generated and thus not reproducible or known small graphs are used in conjunction with self-defined demand matrices. These demand matrices are either randomly generated [125, 24] (same problem as above) or too small for sophisticated algorithms [26, 54] (e. g. demand = 1 for each node pair). Additionally, in most publications only very few instances are used to demonstrate the presented algorithm's capability.

Randomly generated instances as used in [25, 132, 181, 55] are variants of the Erdős-Rényi random graph model $G(n, p)$ [60, 32]. Each possible edge $(i, j)$ is chosen with probability $p = \frac{\delta}{n-1}$ independently from all other edges (where $n = |V|$ and $\delta$ is the expected node degree) and only connected graphs are accepted. Preliminary experiments with this type of instance indicated that the underlying graph is 'pathological' in most cases. A graph is called pathological if it is only 1-edge connected (see Fig. 23a), i. e. it contains at least one bridge[1]. To illustrate the high probability of getting a pathological graph by the Erdős-Rényi random graph model, consider a graph $G(100, \delta=3)$ with $n = 100$ nodes. Here it is rather improbable that a graph with a connectivity of degree > 1 will be generated. The probability of one special node being a leaf is already as high as

$$\left(1 - \frac{\delta}{n-1}\right)^{n-2} \cdot \left(\frac{\delta}{n-1}\right)^{1} \cdot (n-1)$$

$$= \left(1 - \frac{3}{99}\right)^{98} \cdot \left(\frac{3}{99}\right)^{1} \cdot 99 = 0.147 \quad (4.9)$$

indicating that the probability of an at least 2-edge connected graph is very small. Every request depending on such a bridge automatically requires an additional wavelength, which increases the total number of wavelengths, although previously allocated wavelengths still have a lot of free links.

Realizing the problem with random instances, we started to build an instance collection for the RWA based on SND problems. The *survivable*

---

1  A bridge is an edge whose removal disconnects the graph.

*fixed telecommunication network design* problem (SND) [188] describes
a class of network problems that consider fulfilling a set of communication requests between nodes. Based on a given set of planning data (e. g.
network topology, demands, link capacities, cost function) and a model
(e. g. survivability concept, direction of edges, splitting of demands),
the total link cost has to be minimized. It is thus strongly related to the
RWA, which can be seen as a special case of the SND (e. g. survivability is missing, no fixed costs per link). RWA problem instances were
created using SND problem instances from two different sources: the
first set of instances is based on problem instances found in the SNDlib
collection [156], the second set is due to ATAMTÜRK and RAJAN [18].
These instances have been used in a number of publications including
[27, 68, 67].

Instances from SNDlib [156] are derived from an industrial and research background. As these instances are based on realistic network
design problems, they are of higher relevance than purely randomly
generated instances and are not pathological. An example of how to
convert an instance from SNDlib to a problem instance for the RWA
is shown in Sec. A.3.1. The SNDlib collection consists of 22 networks,
of which 14 networks have been chosen in this thesis as the other instances are either uninteresting for sophisticated algorithms or exceed
the available system capacities. Very large problem instances can still
be used by 'scaling down' the demand matrix. Here, scaling down refers
to dividing each request's demand (each demand matrix element) by
some constant factor (rounding to the closest natural number). Due
to this scaling, the problem instance's total demand decreases by the
same factor and the instance becomes easier as less paths have to be
routed. Whereas the scaling of problem instances described here can
be seen as part of the problem instance generation, a similar scaling
approach was pursued in a multilevel approach (Sec. 4.7) to handle large
instances. To include some large instances and to broaden the selection
of problem instance, the demand matrices of instances atlanta, france,
ta1, and ta2 were scaled down by a factor of 20, 10, 100, and 100, respectively. Problem instance janos-us-ca was used with two different
scaling factors of 10 and 200, respectively, labeled as janos-us-ca$^{\blacktriangledown 10}$
and janos-us-ca$^{\blacktriangledown 200}$. Furthermore, a smaller instance (nobel-us) was
scaled up by a factor of 50. The properties of these instances are summarized in the upper half of Tab. 20. The graph of instance nobel-us
corresponds to the well-known NSF network with 14 nodes and 21 links

(e. g. used in [26, 125, 23]). Instance germany50 is depicted in Fig. 23b (p. 124).

Another set of RWA problem instances was derived from SND instances by Atamtürk and Rajan [18]. These instances are available in different sizes (number of nodes), where three networks with different properties are available for each instance size: (a) average node degree 4, (b) average node degree 8, and (c) 75 % of a complete graph's edges are included. As the authors use fractional demands in their data, each request's demand has been multiplied by 100 to get values in $\mathbb{N}^+$. Using the concept of undirected edges, the demands with different directions between the same nodes were added up. The properties of these instances are summarized in the lower half of Tab. 20.

In the discussion, instances with $D < 10\,000$ will be referred to as 'small', instances with $D < 40\,000$ as 'medium-sized', and the remaining instances as 'large'. This categorization matches the application of the multilevel approach (see Sec. 4.7), where instances are either not scaled down (small instances), scaled down once (medium-sized instances), or scaled down multiple times (large instances).

## 4.4   Construction Algorithms

Skorin-Kapov [181] proposed four construction heuristics based on bin packing algorithms. The four bin packing construction algorithms assign items to bins either online or offline. In the online case, items are processed in an arbitrary order; in the offline case all items are known *a priori* and sorted non-increasingly by size (algorithms marked with suffix 'D' for 'decreasing'). An item is packed either into the first feasible bin (first-fit, 'FF') or in the bin which leaves the least free space after insertion of the item (best-fit, 'BF').

The same concepts can be used for the static RWA, where the requests (each with demand = 1) represent items and each wavelength represents a bin. For the offline cases 'FFD' and 'BFD', the requests are sorted non-increasingly by the length (hop count) of the shortest paths between both endpoints during a preprocessing step. It can be argued that it is favorable to route longer paths first. Initially, one wavelength is allocated. Then, iteratively for each request (either in arbitrary order or sorted), each already allocated wavelength is checked to see if the request can be routed in this wavelength. For both first-fit algorithm variants, the first feasible wavelength is used for the request. For the best-fit algorithm variants, all wavelengths are checked and the best wavelength is used

| Instance | $\|V\|$ | $\|E\|$ | Pairs | $D$ | LB | UB | Time | Setup |
|---|---|---|---|---|---|---|---|---|
| atlanta | 15 | 22 | 210 | 136726 | $-^\dagger$ | 25138 | 3600 | D |
| atlanta▼20 | 15 | 22 | 210 | 6840 | 1256 | 1256 | 300 | A – D |
| france | 25 | 45 | 300 | 99830 | $-^\dagger$ | 10572 | 3600 | D |
| france▼10 | 25 | 45 | 300 | 10008 | 1060 | 1060 | 1800 | A, B |
| germany50 | 50 | 88 | 662 | 2365 | 147 | 147 | 120 | A, B |
| janos-us-ca▼10 | 39 | 122 | 1482 | 203222 | $-^\dagger$ | 25750 | 21600 | D |
| janos-us-ca▼200 | 39 | 122 | 1482 | 10173 | 1288 | 1288 | 1800 | A – D |
| nobel-eu | 28 | 41 | 378 | 1898 | 304 | 304 | 60 | A |
| nobel-germany | 17 | 26 | 121 | 660 | 85 | 85 | 120 | A, B |
| nobel-us | 14 | 21 | 91 | 5420 | 670 | 670 | 600 | A – C |
| nobel-us▲50 | 14 | 21 | 91 | 271000 | $-^\dagger$ | 33580 | 21600 | D |
| norway | 27 | 51 | 702 | 5348 | 543 | 543 | 300 | A, B |
| pdh | 11 | 34 | 24 | 4621 | 214 | 214 | 300 | A, B |
| polska | 12 | 18 | 66 | 9943 | 1682 | 1682 | 600 | A, B |
| ta1▼100 | 24 | 51 | 163 | 101271 | $-^\dagger$ | 5967 | 3600 | D |
| ta2▼100 | 65 | 108 | 807 | 314207 | $-^\dagger$ | 18749 | 21600 | D |
| zib54 | 54 | 81 | 1501 | 12230 | 705 | 705 | 1800 | A – D |
| 10.50.75 | 10 | 36 | 30 | 3410 | 155 | 155 | 300 | A – C |
| 10.50.deg4 | 10 | 31 | 30 | 3410 | 225 | 225 | 300 | A – C |
| 10.50.deg8 | 10 | 68 | 72 | 3410 | 120 | 120 | 300 | A – C |
| 15.50.75 | 15 | 90 | 72 | 9500 | 152 | 155 | 1500 | A – C |
| 15.50.deg4 | 15 | 48 | 72 | 9500 | 363 | 366 | 450 | A – C |
| 15.50.deg8 | 15 | 68 | 72 | 9500 | 258 | 258 | 450 | A – C |
| 20.50.75 | 20 | 150 | 137 | 18210 | 188 | 188 | 3000 | C, D |
| 20.50.deg4 | 20 | 82 | 137 | 18210 | 432 | 438 | 1000 | C, D |
| 20.50.deg8 | 20 | 106 | 137 | 18210 | 283 | 294 | 2000 | C, D |

$^\dagger$ No lower bounds available due to extensive computation time requirements.

Table 20: Properties of benchmark instances. 'Pairs' is the number of communicating node pairs; $D$ the demand volume. Lower bounds were determined as in Sec. 4.2. Upper bounds are the best results found in this thesis. Time limits are CPU seconds. 'Setup' refers to either Construction (A), ILS (B), Recombination (C), or Multilevel (D).

(the wavelength with the shortest feasible path for this request). If no wavelength can accommodate the request or all shortest paths are longer than a given bound, a new wavelength is allocated and the request is routed there.

Experimental results in [181] suggested that the number of wavelengths used is significantly lower than the greedy EDP algorithm [132]. Among all four variants, the BFD variant performed best in nearly all setups.

The construction heuristics used here are based on the BFD variant ('BFD_RWA'), too, but differ from this in one aspect: Both in SKORIN-KAPOV's algorithm and in [132], the shortest path inserted into a partial solution is limited by length $\max \left\{ \mathrm{diam}(G), \sqrt{|E|} \right\}$ (number of hops). This limit was originally proposed by KLEINBERG [119] for maximum edge disjoint paths (EDP) used in his bounded greedy algorithm. Neither SKORIN-KAPOV [181] nor MANOHAR et al. [132] document the influence of this restriction on their RWA algorithms. This path length limit has been evalutated in preliminary experiments, but no significant advantage was found in using this parameter (see Fig. 22). As the path length limitation introduces additional complexity to the algorithm but no gain in quality, this feature has been omitted in the experiments.

Preliminary experiments indicated that the structure of the graph is not the only limiting factor for the solution quality. Additional problems arise if the requests' load is not homogeneously distributed among the node pairs. Given a node with degree $\delta$, this node can handle at most $\delta$ requests in each wavelength, especially requests starting or ending in this node. In instance germany50 (Fig. 23b), the highlighted node has a node degree of 2 and 43 requests start here with a summarized demand of 293. This leads to the lower bound $\left\lceil \frac{293}{2} \right\rceil = 147$, which equals the solution found by the iterated local search (Sec. 4.5) and the lower bound given by the multi-commodity flow solution (Tab. 20 and Sec. 4.2).

Depending on overloaded edges, requests are classified as 'evil' requests. The influence of evil requests can best be observed for instances where an unfavorable combination of graph and request set leads to some heavily overloaded edges. These observations motivate a new request sorting strategy class, where these evil requests are routed before non-evil requests. For the experiments, the following sorting strategies were considered:

LEN    Requests are ordered non-increasingly by the length of their shortest path, equals BFD_RWA.

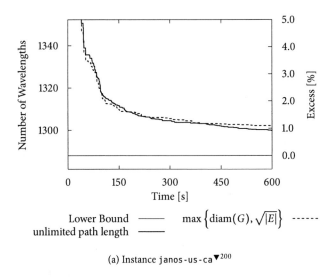

(a) Instance janos-us-ca▼$^{200}$

Figure 22: Preliminary experiments for the influence of limited shortest path lengths during solution construction on the iterated local search algorithm (Sec. 4.5). The plot shows the average performance over 30 repetitions and same set of random seeds for each setup.

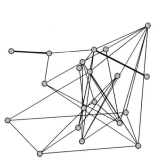

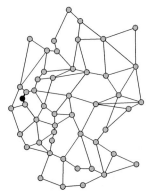

(a) Random graph with 20 nodes and 40 edges (average node degree $\delta$ = 4). Bridges are highlighted as bold edges. This problem instance was not used in the experiments.

(b) Instance germany50 based on 50 cities in Germany. The node and its two edges causing the pathological behavior is highlighted.

Figure 23: Examples of problem instances, special features are highlighted.

ANTIEVIL  Evil requests are routed first, otherwise using a random sorting.

LENANTIEVIL  Requests are first sorted by Len and then by AntiEvil within each set of requests with equal shortest path length.

ANTIEVILLEN  Requests are first sorted by AntiEvil and then by Len within the evil and non-evil requests, respectively.

SHUFFLE  Requests are ordered in a random fashion.

Other combinations of the components Len, Anti and Evil are also possible but will not be considered further.

To locate evil requests for a given graph and set of requests, the following method is proposed. In the first step, an initial solution is constructed with the standard BFD_RWA algorithm. The edge set $E'$ is determined to contain all edges that are used by lightpaths in wavelengths that are used only marginally by other lightpaths. 'Marginally used wavelengths' are defined as wavelengths whose usage lies below $u$, which is the average path length in $s$ multiplied by a factor $k$; $k$ = 3 has been chosen. In the second step, requests are marked as evil requests

1: **function** FINDEVILREQUESTS(Graph $G$, Requests $R$, $k \in \mathbb{R}$)
2:     $s \leftarrow \text{BFD\_RWA}(G, R)$
3:     $u \leftarrow \left\lceil k \cdot \text{avg}_{r \in R} |p_{G,s}(r)| \right\rceil$
4:     $E \leftarrow \varnothing$                          ▷ Set of possibly overloaded edges
5:     $W' \leftarrow \{\lambda \in W : \text{LOAD}(s, \lambda) < u\}$
6:     **for all** $e \in E$ **do**
7:         **if** $\text{USAGE}(s, W', e) > |W'| - 2$ **then**
8:             $E' \leftarrow E' \cup \{e\}$              ▷ store overloaded edge
9:         **end if**
10:     **end for**
11:     **return** $\{r \in R : \neg\text{ROUTABLE}(G \smallsetminus E', r)\}$
12: **end function**

Figure 24: Algorithm to determine evil requests in RWA problem instances.

if they can not be routed in $G \smallsetminus E'$. Function FINDEVILREQUESTS in Fig. 24 explains this in detail. Here, $\text{LOAD}(s, \lambda)$ calculates the actual load of wavelength $\lambda$ (number of used physical links), $\text{USAGE}(s, W', e)$ describes how often edge $e$ is used in solution $s$ restricted to wavelengths $W'$, and $\text{ROUTABLE}(G, r)$ checks if request $r$ is physically routable in $G$.

### 4.4.1 Results

All problem instances from Tab. 20 marked with 'A' were solved by the construction heuristics Len, LenAntiEvil, AntiEvil, AntiEvilLen, and Shuffle. Each experiment was repeated 50 times with different seeds; the results (minimum and average, each with excess above lower bound) are summarized in Tables 21–22. The data found in the experiments leads to the following conclusions:

- There is no significant difference (99 % confidence intervals) between sorting strategies Len and LenAntiEvil, except for instances janos-us-ca[▼200], nobel-us, and polska.

- AntiEvil and AntiEvilLen, however, are much more often significantly different. The differences between both sorting strategies are only insignificant for atlanta[▼20], france[▼10], pdh, polska, all 10.50s and 15.50.75.

| Instance | $W_{LB}$ | Len | | | LenAntiEvil | | | AntiEvil | | | AntiEvilLen | | | Shuffle | | |
|---|---|---|---|---|---|---|---|---|---|---|---|---|---|---|---|---|
| | | $t$ [s] | $W_{min}$ | $W_{avg}$ | $t$ [s] | $W_{min}$ | $W_{avg}$ | $t$ [s] | $W_{min}$ | $W_{avg}$ | $t$ [s] | $W_{min}$ | $W_{avg}$ | $t$ [s] | $W_{min}$ | $W_{avg}$ |
| 10.50.75 | 155 | 0.9 | 188 (21.29) | 201.7 (30.13) | 1.7 | 187 (20.65) | 201.5 (30.00) | 1.7 | 189 (21.94) | 206.2 (33.03) | 1.7 | 186 (20.00) | 200.0 (29.03) | 0.9 | 188 (21.29) | 206.0 (32.90) |
| 10.50.deg4 | 225 | 1.0 | 242 (7.56) | 263.7 (17.20) | 2.0 | 245 (8.89) | 262.5 (16.67) | 1.9 | 243 (8.00) | 271.3 (20.58) | 2.0 | 249 (10.67) | 264.2 (17.42) | 1.0 | 254 (12.89) | 274.8 (22.13) |
| 10.50.deg8 | 120 | 0.8 | 155 (29.17) | 165.7 (38.08) | 1.6 | 148 (23.33) | 164.0 (36.67) | 1.5 | 153 (27.50) | 164.6 (37.17) | 1.5 | 151 (25.83) | 165.8 (38.17) | 0.8 | 155 (29.17) | 165.1 (37.58) |
| 15.50.75 | 152 | 4.6 | 207 (36.18) | 219.5 (44.41) | 9.3 | 205 (34.87) | 219.6 (44.47) | 9.5 | 210 (38.16) | 225.5 (48.36) | 9.3 | 208 (36.84) | 220.3 (44.93) | 4.9 | 213 (40.13) | 226.7 (49.14) |
| 15.50.deg4 | 363 | 7.4 | 422 (16.25) | 462.0 (27.27) | 14.6 | 430 (18.46) | 462.2 (27.33) | 14.4 | 425 (17.08) | 498.9 (37.44) | 14.7 | 412 (13.50) | 456.1 (25.65) | 6.9 | 452 (24.52) | 491.6 (35.43) |
| 15.50.deg8 | 258 | 6.7 | 280 (8.53) | 300.5 (16.47) | 13.5 | 284 (10.08) | 302.6 (17.29) | 13.2 | 292 (13.18) | 326.4 (26.51) | 13.3 | 281 (8.91) | 302.4 (17.21) | 6.4 | 302 (17.05) | 328.5 (27.33) |
| atlanta▼[20] | 1256 | 6.0 | 1413 (12.50) | 1468.8 (16.94) | 12.2 | 1422 (13.22) | 1470.0 (17.04) | 12.6 | 1477 (17.60) | 1555.6 (23.85) | 12.6 | 1427 (13.61) | 1519.1 (20.95) | 5.4 | 1430 (13.85) | 1528.7 (21.71) |
| france▼[10] | 1060 | 14.2 | 1098 (3.58) | 1119.0 (5.57) | 28.1 | 1104 (4.15) | 1124.6 (6.09) | 28.2 | 1125 (6.13) | 1168.0 (10.19) | 29.7 | 1106 (4.34) | 1138.0 (7.36) | 12.4 | 1130 (6.60) | 1161.6 (9.58) |

Table 21: Results for solution construction experiments for different instances and sorting strategies (part 1). Here, 'LB' denotes an instance's lower bound, '$t$' the computation time in seconds, 'min' the best found solution, and 'avg' the average solution quality (both in number of wavelengths). The small numbers below minimum and average values denote the excess in percent above the lower bound. See also Tab. 22.

| Instance | $W_{LB}$ | Len | | | LenAntiEvil | | | AntiEvil | | | AntiEvilLen | | | Shuffle | | |
|---|---|---|---|---|---|---|---|---|---|---|---|---|---|---|---|---|
| | | $t$ [s] | $W_{min}$ | $W_{avg}$ | $t$ [s] | $W_{min}$ | $W_{avg}$ | $t$ [s] | $W_{min}$ | $W_{avg}$ | $t$ [s] | $W_{min}$ | $W_{avg}$ | $t$ [s] | $W_{min}$ | $W_{avg}$ |
| germany50 | 147 | 0.7 | 186 (26.53) | 193.1 (31.36) | 1.5 | 186 (26.53) | 193.1 (31.36) | 2.4 | 161 (9.52) | 191.4 (30.20) | 2.6 | 165 (12.24) | 165.1 (12.31) | 0.8 | 164 (11.56) | 173.3 (17.89) |
| j-us-ca ▼200 | 1288 | 23.5 | 1734 (34.63) | 1767.9 (37.26) | 47.9 | 1704 (32.30) | 1767.9 (37.26) | 69.3 | 1491 (15.76) | 1745.2 (35.50) | 67.8 | 1483 (15.14) | 1523.5 (18.28) | 32.3 | 1500 (16.46) | 1563.7 (21.41) |
| nobel-eu | 304 | 0.7 | 304 (0.00) | 304.1 (0.03) | 1.4 | 304 (0.00) | 304.1 (0.03) | 1.7 | 304 (0.00) | 304.0 (0.00) | 1.7 | 304 (0.00) | 306.1 (0.69) | 0.6 | 305 (0.33) | 311.1 (2.34) |
| n-germany | 85 | 0.1 | 90 (5.88) | 93.4 (9.88) | 0.2 | 91 (7.06) | 93.4 (9.88) | 0.2 | 92 (8.24) | 93.6 (10.12) | 0.2 | 90 (5.88) | 98.6 (16.00) | 0.1 | 91 (7.06) | 98.2 (15.53) |
| nobel-us | 670 | 3.0 | 853 (27.31) | 903.3 (34.82) | 6.2 | 817 (21.94) | 903.3 (34.82) | 7.7 | 792 (18.21) | 876.3 (30.79) | 7.5 | 835 (24.63) | 852.2 (27.19) | 3.0 | 847 (26.42) | 914.9 (36.55) |
| norway | 543 | 3.5 | 561 (3.31) | 566.5 (4.33) | 7.1 | 557 (2.58) | 566.5 (4.33) | 6.4 | 578 (6.45) | 566.7 (4.36) | 7.2 | 561 (3.31) | 591.8 (8.99) | 2.8 | 576 (6.08) | 590.4 (8.73) |
| pdh | 214 | 1.5 | 267 (24.77) | 296.8 (38.69) | 3.1 | 261 (21.96) | 296.8 (38.69) | 3.1 | 263 (22.90) | 293.3 (37.06) | 3.1 | 262 (22.43) | 291.7 (36.31) | 1.5 | 268 (25.23) | 290.5 (35.75) |
| polska | 1682 | 11.2 | 1776 (5.59) | 1835.7 (9.14) | 23.0 | 1802 (7.13) | 1835.7 (9.14) | 23.7 | 1782 (5.95) | 1871.4 (11.26) | 24.4 | 1780 (5.83) | 2024.9 (20.39) | 10.1 | 1761 (4.70) | 1955.9 (16.28) |
| zib54 | 705 | 25.5 | 835 (18.44) | 898.6 (27.46) | 51.1 | 811 (15.04) | 898.6 (27.46) | 48.2 | 834 (18.30) | 901.6 (27.89) | 51.9 | 836 (18.58) | 945.0 (34.04) | 21.2 | 853 (20.99) | 977.5 (38.65) |

Table 22: Results for solution construction experiments for different instances and sorting strategies (part 2). Here, 'LB' denotes an instance's lower bound, '$t$' the computation time in seconds, 'min' the best found solution, and 'avg' the average solution quality (both in number of wavelengths). The small numbers below minimum and average values denote the excess in percent above the lower bound. See also Tab. 21.

- Instances germany50, janos-us-ca$^{\blacktriangledown 200}$, nobel-us, and pdh perform better with sorting strategy AntiEvil than with Len or LenAntiEvil on average, but there is only a significant difference for germany50 and janos-us-ca$^{\blacktriangledown 200}$. For example, the best solution for germany50 using AntiEvil is 13 % better than using Len or LenAntiEvil (186 vs. 161). It has been observed that for these instances the least used wavelength in solutions built using Len contain only a few similar paths indicating that the underlying request matrix is unbalanced and thus yields some heavy overloaded edges. For example, for one selected solution for germany50 with wavelength usage 186, a request with a demand of 76 uses 31 wavelengths used by no other request to route 61 lightpaths.

- As long as there are no evil requests, AntiEvilLen matches the sorting strategy Len and LenAntiEvil and thus has a similar performance. In instance 15.50.deg8, for example, no evil requests were found and thus the average initial wavelength usage is 300.5 for Len, 303.2 for AntiEvilLen, and 302.6 for LenAntiEvil.

- The Shuffle sorting strategy is the fastest strategy, but results on average in the worst results for both best found solution and average solution. It only finds the best solution (1761, excess 4.7 %) for polska. The average solution quality is superseded for each problem instance by a 'sorting' strategy.

- Every construction heuristic that determines evil requests is considerably more expensive in terms of computation time than to Shuffle (no sorting) or Len (simple search). Finding evil requests doubles the computation times for all instances: For 15.50.deg4, for example, initialization and construction using the Len sorting strategy takes 7.4 s on average, but sorting requests with AntiEvilLen takes 14.7 s.

For the instances where AntiEvil performs well, no clear preference can be made between AntiEvil and AntiEvilLen. Thus, for unknown instances, the experiments indicate the merit of trying both strategies Len and AntiEvil first and then, depending on which strategy performs better, constructing the final solutions either with Len/LenAntiEvil or with AntiEvil/AntiEvilLen, respectively. However, there may be a large variance between different solutions from the same construction heuristic. For nobel-us, for example, the deviation on the number of wavelengths for different strategies ranges between 19.6 and 43.3 (not shown in Tables 21–22). This suggests the construction of several solutions to confirm the decision for the best construction heuristic. For the problem instances considered here, however, the Len sorting strategy performs best; it finds best average solutions for nine out of 20 instances and competitive solutions for several other.

Problem instance nobel-eu is trivial, as most construction heuristics find solutions which equal the lower bound and thus are optimal. This instance has been excluded from subsequent experiments.

## 4.5   ITERATED LOCAL SEARCH

Although there is a large variety in solution quality among different request sorting strategies, in most cases the results are considerably worse than the lower bounds, motivating a sophisticated approach such as iterated local search (ILS). For germany50, for example, the best performing sorting strategy is 12.3 % above the lower bound on average and the minimum excess is 9.5 %.

In this section, the focus is on the iterated local search (ILS, see also Sec. 2.1.3), where a local search algorithm and a mutation operator is defined. Starting from an initial solution, the ILS first performs a mutation in each iteration step and then applies the local search algorithm to the permutated solution. Within the ILS, a new solution is accepted after mutation and local search if it is better than the previous best solution, otherwise the previous best solution is restored. Since comparing two RWA solutions is non-trivial, a more sophisticated comparator is used, as described below. Iterated local search has no inherent termination criterion; a termination strategy is therefore applied as discussed in Sec. 4.5.

### Length-Lex Ordering Objective Function

Using the number of wavelengths (optimization objective) as the only criterion for comparing two solutions is not sufficient, as two solutions may allocate the same number of wavelengths, but employ different routes to their requests. Furthermore, it may take a large number of iterations until a gain in wavelength usage is found. Therefore, a secondary criterion is introduced to honor improvement steps within the same wavelength usage level. The secondary criterion considers the usage of each wavelength. Given that two solutions require the same number of wavelengths, a solution that uses some wavelengths on very many links but other wavelengths only on few links is to be preferred over a solution that has more homogeneous load on all allocated wavelengths. Use of this criterion is motivated by the fact that the former solution is more compact, i. e. uses wavelengths more efficiently.

Both criteria are combined by determining the usage of each wavelength and storing this information in a vector that is sorted non-increasingly. The vectors of two solutions are compared using a *length-lex ordering* (to be minimized), where shorter vectors are preferred over longer vectors (first criterion) and, if the lengths are equal, the vectors are compared lexicographically and the vector with the first component with higher usage 'wins'. As an example, it holds that $(3, 3, 1) < (3, 2, 1) < (3, 1, 1, 1)$: The first comparison holds, as both vectors have the same length but the second components differ ($3 > 2$); the second comparison holds as the right vector is the longest of all three. In Fig. 26a, the solution's length-lex vector is $(3, 2)$, whereas in Fig. 26c the vector is $(6, 1)$. According to the definition above, the local search improved the solution.

*Termination Detection*

Several termination detection criteria were discussed in Sec. 2.1.7. Depending on the instance (see Tab. 20), a time limit was used for the RWA in order to compare different algorithms and setups. The time limits were chosen based on the expected time required to converge towards a (near-)optimal solution.

Furthermore, an alternative termination criterion was proposed for the algorithms that does not depend on *a priori* setup parameters. An algorithm terminates after iteration $k$ if it has not found a better solution (in number of used wavelengths) within the last $k/2$ iterations. Whereas the choice of $k/2$ is still arbitrary, it is applicable for a large set of problem instances. In the experiments, the events involved in reaching this 'soft' termination criterion were recorded, but the algorithms were only stopped for the 'hard' time criterion above.

### 4.5.1   Local Search

The general idea of this local search is to shift requests from less used wavelengths to more often used wavelengths. By 'cleaning up' sparse

```
 1: function LOCALSEARCH(Solution s, Requests R)
 2:     repeat
 3:         for all r ∈ R do
 4:             W' ← {λ ∈ W | SP_{G,s}(r, λ) ≠ ∅}
 5:             λ ← arg max_{λ∈W'} USAGE(s, λ)
 6:             if USAGE(s, λ) > USAGE(s, λ_s(r)) then
 7:                 λ_s(r) ← λ
 8:                 p_{G,s}(r) ← SP_{G,s}(r, λ)
 9:             end if
10:         end for
11:     until ¬LOCALOPTIMUMREACHED
12:     return s
13: end function
```

Figure 25: Local search algorithm moving paths to wavelengths with higher usage.

wavelengths, the local search strives to remove all requests routed in these wavelengths, eventually decreasing the number of used wavelengths. Note that even when using indices to address wavelengths, wavelengths are basically unordered and interchangeable; gaps in the numbering of wavelengths do not influence the solution's quality. For simplicity, each request's demand is limited to 1, but multiple requests between the same node pair are allowed.

The local search algorithm (Fig. 25) operates on a solution $s$ and the set of requests $R$. Until a local optimum is reached, the algorithm iterates over all requests in $R$ and performs the following steps. Firstly, $W' \subseteq W$ contains all wavelengths where a feasible path between the endnodes of the current request $r$ exists (Fig. 25:4). Among all wavelengths in $W'$, the wavelength $\lambda$ with highest usage is chosen (Fig. 25:5). If the usage for $\lambda$ is larger than the usage for the request's current wavelength, then the request's wavelength is set to $\lambda$ and the request's path is updated with the shortest available path in $\lambda$. The request's path in the new wavelength can be longer than the path in the old wavelength. Function $SP_{G,s}(r, \lambda)$ calculates the shortest path in $G$ for request $r$ routed in $\lambda$. If no such path exists, it is defined $SP_{G,s}(r, \lambda) = \emptyset$. For each wavelength $\lambda$ in solution $s$, a usage function $USAGE(s, \lambda)$ is defined, counting the number of physical links on which the wavelength is currently in use. This value can range from 0 (not used at all) to $|E|$ (used on every link).

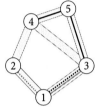

(a) Initial state. There are four requests using two wavelengths. The usage of the black wavelength is 3; the gray wavelength's usage is 2.

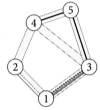

(b) The request routed in the gray wavelength between nodes 1 and 3 (drawn bold) is selected for a local search step.

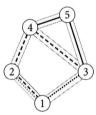

(c) The selected request between nodes 1 and 3 is routed on path $\langle 1, 2, 4, 3 \rangle$ (dashed line) in the black wavelength.

Figure 26: Example for a local search step.

```
 1: procedure MUTATE(Solution s, Requests R, strength)
 2:     for i = 1 . . . strength do
 3:         (λ₁, λ₂) ← RANDOMWAVELENGTHS
 4:         if USAGE(s, λ₁) < USAGE(s, λ₂) then
 5:             SWAP(λ₁, λ₂)
 6:         end if
 7:         r ← RINWL(s, λ₂, R)
 8:         p ← p_{G,s}(r)
 9:         R' ← REMOVE(s, λ₁, p)          ▷ remove conflicting requests
10:         p_{G,s}(r) ← p
11:         λ_s(r) ← λ₁
12:         for all r ∈ R' do
13:             λ_s(r) ← arg min_{λ∈W} SP_{G,s}(r, λ) ≠ ∅
14:             p_{G,s}(r) ← SP_{G,s}(r, λ)              ▷ re-route request
15:         end for
16:     end for
17: end procedure
```

Figure 27: Mutation algorithm shifting path between wavelengths.

### 4.5.2  Mutation

The mutation operator is similar to the local search operator as it reroutes single requests in a different wavelength with a new path. It differs from the LS operator as it moves away other requests routed on the shortest path in the target wavelength for the selected request. Thus, it 'spreads' requests among the set of wavelengths counteracting the local search and allowing with these 'jumps' to escape local optima.

In each mutation step, two wavelengths $\lambda_1$ and $\lambda_2$ are randomly chosen and an arbitrary request is taken whose path $p$ is routed in the wavelength with lower usage (here, $\lambda_2$) (Fig. 28a); this action is performed by function $\text{RINWL}(s, \lambda_2, R)$. Paths preventing $p$ from being routed in wavelength $\lambda_1$ are removed from the solution (Fig. 28c) and $p$ is routed in $\lambda_1$ (Fig. 28d). The function $\text{REMOVE}(s, \lambda_1, p)$ determines the paths to be removed and stores the paths' requests in $R'$. To restore a valid solution, each request in $R'$ is rerouted in the first feasible wavelength which has a lower usage value than $\lambda_1$. The found wavelength may correspond to a previously unused wavelength thus an additional wavelength was allocated.

The strength of the mutation can be controlled by the number of applications. It is reasonable to make the number of applications dependent on the total number of paths (total sum of the requests' demand $D$). In the experiments, different mutation strategies were applied to the ILS, where the strength is defined by a percentage of the number of paths. Mutation strategies were either constant (1 %, 5 %, and 25 %) or variable, where the mutation strength started with an initial high mutation rate of 25 % and decreased linearly in each iteration (step width 2 %) until reaching a strength of 1 % and keeping this mutation rate until termination (designated as '25 %$\downarrow_{2\%}$'). The variable mutation rate was designed to combine the advantages of both strong and weak constant mutation strengths.

### 4.5.3    Experimental Setup & Results

To evaluate the iterated local search, experiments with different mutation strategies were performed. Each experiment was repeated 30 times; best and average values are used for discussion.

The experiments were restricted to three different sorting strategies: (a) Len, which finds best average initial solutions for most instances (b) AntiEvil as a representative for all AntiEvil sorting strategies (c) Shuffle, as the simplest strategy which performs no sorting at all. The results, however, suggest that the choice of the initial sorting strategy has little to no influence on the final result for each problem instance considered here. For instance 15.50.deg4, for example, the average number of used wavelengths when reaching the termination criterion (values omitted in Tables 23–24) ranges between 392.0 (AntiEvil) and 392.2 (Len) for mutation strength 1 %, whereas for mutation strength 25 %, the number of wavelengths ranges between 400.0 (AntiEvil) and 402.1 (Len). Thus, all later experiments are restricted to one strategy. Len was chosen as it was already used in [181] and is faster than any strategy with an AntiEvil component.

In the experiments with static mutation strength, it is observed that strong mutation (25 %, sometimes 5 %) allows the ILS to initially improve solution quality very quickly, but most often the ILS converges to suboptimal results. A weak mutation rate (1 %) on the other side, leads to a slower convergence rate (later 'soft' termination, see below), eventually reaching better solutions than strong mutations. For nobel-us, for example, the ILS would terminate due to convergence after 12.4 s with an average solution quality of 707.6 (699.0 after 300 s) when using

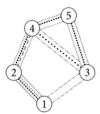

(a) The request between nodes 1 and 2 in the gray wavelength is selected.

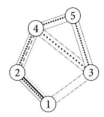

(b) The selected request is moved to the black wavelength and keeps its previous path ⟨1, 2⟩.

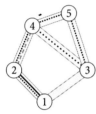

(c) The request routed on path ⟨1, 2, 4, 5, 3⟩ conflicts with the moved request, as both requests use the black wavelength on link ⟨1, 2⟩.

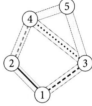

(d) The conflicting request is rerouted on path ⟨1, 3⟩ in the black wavelength (dashed line).

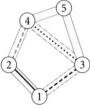

(e) Now a local search step is performed: the request in gray wavelength on path ⟨2, 4⟩ is selected.

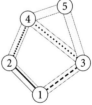

(f) The selected request is rerouted in the black wavelength on the same path.

Figure 28: Example of a mutation step followed by a local search step.

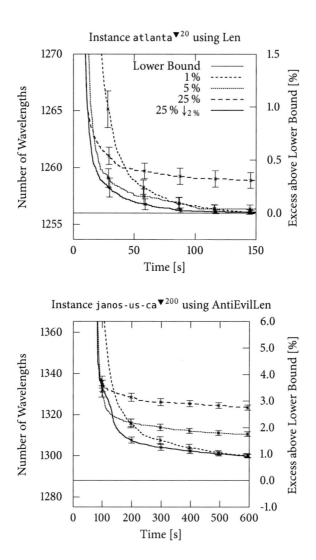

Figure 29: Performance plots (initial phase) for two ILS setups using different mutation strategies.

mutation strength 25 %. With mutation strength 1 % however, convergence is detected after 207.7 s, with an average solution quality of 683.0 (677.9 after 300 s). However, this pattern does not hold for trivial instances that are easy to solve (such asnobel-germany), as here other factors such as the computational effort of the permutation and local search influence the performance. The initial behavior of representative problem instances for these two patterns is depicted in Fig. 29.

Combining the advantages of both patterns, a variable mutation operator called $25\%\downarrow_{2\%}$ was designed as described above. Saving time by using this mutation strength strategy does not have a detrimental impact on the final solution's quality. For example, the average excess for janos-us-ca$^{\blacktriangledown 200}$ is 1.1 % with $25\%\downarrow_{2\%}$ compared to an excess of 1.1 % to 3.1 % for the static mutation strengths at the 'soft' termination criterion using Len as the sorting strategy. Furthermore, the mutation strategy is considerably faster than the constant mutation strength 1 %, since the 'soft' convergence criterion triggers 400 s earlier with the same solution quality for this setup.

In the experiments, both a 'soft' and a 'hard' termination criterion was used. For most of the setups, the 'soft' criterion based on convergence triggered considerably earlier than the fixed time limit set *a priori*. For france$^{\blacktriangledown 10}$, for example, convergence was reached after 317.5 s at most, but had a high variety among different mutation strategies. For the above example (AntiEvil and mutation strength 1 %), minimum and maximum over 30 repetitions on the time to reach the 'soft' termination criterion were 110.9 s and 961.4 s, respectively, which justifies the generous fixed time limit of 1800 s for this problem instance. For 'easy' instances, where the lower bound can be reached by any proper algorithm, the excess is < 1.0 % for most setups. For germany50, for example, convergence is reached after < 20.0 s and the average solutions are less than 3 wavelengths above the lower bound. For larger instances, the termination criterion is a chosen compromise between invested computation time and solution quality.

Instances atlanta$^{\blacktriangledown 20}$, france$^{\blacktriangledown 10}$, germany50, nobel-germany, norway, pdh, polska, and 10.50.deg4 have been solved to optimality and thus are not interesting for further experiments with more advanced algorithms. However, atlanta$^{\blacktriangledown 20}$ was kept as a representative in the benchmark set in order to show that new features in the algorithm do not have a degenerative effect on the performance for 'easy' instances.

| Instance | LB | $t_{max}$ | Len | | | | AntiEvil | | | | Shuffle | | | |
|---|---|---|---|---|---|---|---|---|---|---|---|---|---|---|
| | | | $t_{conv}$ | $W_{t_{conv}}$ | $W_{t_{max}}$ | $W_{min}$ | $t_{conv}$ | $W_{t_{conv}}$ | $W_{t_{max}}$ | $W_{min}$ | $t_{conv}$ | $W_{t_{conv}}$ | $W_{t_{max}}$ | $W_{min}$ |
| 10.50.75 | 155 | 300 | 1.8 (30) | 159.5 2.90 | 157.6 1.68 | 156 0.65 | 2.6 (30) | 159.5 2.90 | 157.6 1.68 | 157 1.29 | 1.8 (30) | 159.6 2.97 | 157.8 1.81 | 157 1.29 |
| 10.50.deg4 | 225 | 300 | 2.3 (30) | 227.0 0.89 | 225.3 0.13 | 225 0.00 | 3.2 (30) | 227.1 0.93 | 225.3 0.13 | 225 0.00 | 2.2 (30) | 227.1 0.93 | 225.5 0.22 | 225 0.00 |
| 10.50.deg8 | 120 | 300 | 1.6 (30) | 125.8 4.83 | 123.1 2.58 | 122 1.67 | 2.4 (32) | 132.1 10.08 | 122.7 2.25 | 122 1.67 | 1.6 (33) | 135.1 12.58 | 123.0 2.50 | 121 0.83 |
| 15.50.75 | 152 | 1500 | 8.7 (30) | 171.4 12.76 | 169.4 11.45 | 168 10.53 | 13.5 (30) | 171.6 12.89 | 169.3 11.38 | 168 10.53 | 9.0 (30) | 171.6 12.89 | 169.5 11.51 | 168 10.53 |
| 15.50.deg4 | 363 | 450 | 27.4 (30) | 391.7 7.91 | 386.9 6.58 | 385 6.06 | 40.4 (30) | 390.6 7.60 | 386.8 6.56 | 385 6.06 | 23.4 (30) | 392.7 8.18 | 386.7 6.53 | 384 5.79 |
| 15.50.deg8 | 258 | 450 | 16.1 (30) | 268.5 4.07 | 263.2 2.02 | 262 1.55 | 22.4 (30) | 268.5 4.07 | 263.3 2.05 | 261 1.16 | 14.1 (30) | 269.1 4.30 | 263.3 2.05 | 262 1.55 |
| atlanta▼20 | 1256 | 300 | 23.7 (30) | 1259.4 0.27 | 1256.0 0.00 | 1256 0.00 | 36.8 (30) | 1258.9 0.23 | 1256.0 0.00 | 1256 0.00 | 27.5 (30) | 1259.1 0.25 | 1256.0 0.00 | 1256 0.00 |
| france▼10 | 1060 | 1800 | 80.5 (30) | 1063.8 0.36 | 1060.0 0.00 | 1060 0.00 | 76.6 (30) | 1064.3 0.41 | 1060.1 0.01 | 1060 0.00 | 73.4 (30) | 1064.1 0.39 | 1060.0 0.00 | 1060 0.00 |

Table 23: Results for ILS experiments for different instances and sorting strategies using mutation strategy 25%↓2% (part 1). Here, 'LB' denotes the lower bound, '$t_{max}$' the hard time limit, '$t_{conv}$' the average time to converge ('soft' termination criterion), '$W_{t_{conv}}$' the solution quality when terminating due to convergence, and '$W_{min}$' is the best found solution when reaching the time limit. Small numbers below convergence time values denote the number of repetitions converging within the hard time limit, small numbers below the number of wavelength values denote the excess in percent above the lower bound.

| Instance | LB | $t_{max}$ | Len $t_{conv}$ | Len $W_{t_{conv}}$ | Len $W_{t_{max}}$ | Len $W_{min}$ | AntiEvil $t_{conv}$ | AntiEvil $W_{t_{conv}}$ | AntiEvil $W_{t_{max}}$ | AntiEvil $W_{min}$ | Shuffle $t_{conv}$ | Shuffle $W_{t_{conv}}$ | Shuffle $W_{t_{max}}$ | Shuffle $W_{min}$ |
|---|---|---|---|---|---|---|---|---|---|---|---|---|---|---|
| germany50 | 147 | 120 | 7.0 (30) | 148.3 (0.88) | 147.0 (0.00) | 147 (0.00) | 7.9 (30) | 148.4 (0.95) | 147.0 (0.00) | 147 (0.00) | 7.5 (30) | 147.7 (0.48) | 147.0 (0.00) | 147 (0.00) |
| j-us-ca ▼200 | 1288 | 1800 | 609.8 (25) | 1302.4 (1.12) | 1295.4 (0.57) | 1291 (0.23) | 643.9 (28) | 1298.1 (0.78) | 1292.4 (0.34) | 1289 (0.08) | 532.3 (24) | 1301.3 (1.03) | 1293.1 (0.40) | 1290 (0.16) |
| n-germany | 85 | 120 | 0.6 (30) | 86.5 (1.76) | 85.0 (0.00) | 85 (0.00) | 0.6 (30) | 86.6 (1.88) | 85.0 (0.00) | 85 (0.00) | 0.5 (30) | 86.9 (2.24) | 85.0 (0.00) | 85 (0.00) |
| nobel-us | 670 | 600 | 62.8 (30) | 687.4 (2.60) | 678.1 (1.21) | 675 (0.75) | 73.6 (30) | 685.1 (2.25) | 678.1 (1.21) | 674 (0.60) | 76.2 (30) | 685.4 (2.30) | 676.8 (1.01) | 674 (0.60) |
| norway | 543 | 300 | 23.7 (30) | 543.7 (0.13) | 543.0 (0.00) | 543 (0.00) | 24.0 (30) | 543.6 (0.11) | 543.0 (0.00) | 543 (0.00) | 19.5 (30) | 543.5 (0.09) | 543.0 (0.00) | 543 (0.00) |
| pdh | 214 | 300 | 3.4 (30) | 218.0 (1.87) | 214.5 (0.23) | 214 (0.00) | 4.7 (30) | 217.7 (1.73) | 214.2 (0.09) | 214 (0.00) | 3.2 (30) | 218.2 (1.96) | 214.5 (0.23) | 214 (0.00) |
| polska | 1682 | 600 | 30.2 (30) | 1682.4 (0.02) | 1682.0 (0.00) | 1682 (0.00) | 42.5 (30) | 1682.5 (0.03) | 1682.0 (0.00) | 1682 (0.00) | 29.4 (30) | 1682.3 (0.02) | 1682.0 (0.00) | 1682 (0.00) |
| zib54 | 705 | 1800 | 81.9 (30) | 712.0 (0.99) | 707.5 (0.35) | 706 (0.14) | 101.3 (30) | 710.4 (0.77) | 706.6 (0.23) | 706 (0.14) | 83.3 (30) | 710.3 (0.75) | 706.6 (0.23) | 705 (0.00) |

Table 24: Results for ILS experiments for different instances and sorting strategies using mutation strategy 25 %↓2% (part 2). Here, 'LB' denotes the lower bound, '$t_{max}$' the hard time limit, '$t_{conv}$' the average time to converge ('soft' termination criterion), '$W_{t_{conv}}$', the solution quality when terminating due to convergence, and '$W_{min}$' is the best found solution when reaching the time limit. Small numbers below convergence time values denote the number of repetitions converging within the hard time limit, small numbers below the number of wavelength values denote the excess in percent above the lower bound.

| Instance | LB | $t_{max}$ | Mut | Len | | | | AntiEvil | | | | Shuffle | | | |
|---|---|---|---|---|---|---|---|---|---|---|---|---|---|---|---|
| | | | | $t_{conv}$ | $W_{t_{conv}}$ | $W_{max}$ | $W_{min}$ | $t_{conv}$ | $W_{t_{conv}}$ | $W_{max}$ | $W_{min}$ | $t_{conv}$ | $W_{t_{conv}}$ | $W_{max}$ | $W_{min}$ |
| atlanta▼20 | 1256 | 300 | 1 % | 150.0 (30) | 1256.5 0.04 | 1256.0 0.00 | 1256 0.00 | 156.8 (27) | 1256.3 0.02 | 1256.0 0.00 | 1256 0.00 | 148.3 (29) | 1256.6 0.05 | 1256.0 0.00 | 1256 0.00 |
| | | | 5 % | 62.4 (29) | 1257.6 0.13 | 1256.1 0.01 | 1256 0.00 | 64.2 (29) | 1258.0 0.16 | 1256.1 0.01 | 1256 0.00 | 57.6 (30) | 1258.2 0.18 | 1256.1 0.01 | 1256 0.00 |
| | | | 25 % | 44.4 (30) | 1260.8 0.38 | 1258.4 0.19 | 1257 0.08 | 37.4 (14) | 1259.8 0.30 | 1258.0 0.16 | 1257 0.08 | 37.7 (30) | 1260.4 0.35 | 1258.3 0.18 | 1256 0.00 |
| | | | 25 %↓2% | 23.7 (30) | 1259.4 0.27 | 1256.0 0.00 | 1256 0.00 | 36.8 (30) | 1258.9 0.23 | 1256.0 0.00 | 1256 0.00 | 27.5 (30) | 1259.1 0.25 | 1256.0 0.00 | 1256 0.00 |
| nobel-us | 670 | 600 | 1 % | 207.7 (25) | 683.0 1.94 | 677.7 1.15 | 674 0.60 | 162.7 (24) | 685.1 2.25 | 679.0 1.34 | 674 0.60 | 189.2 (21) | 684.2 2.12 | 677.1 1.06 | 674 0.60 |
| | | | 5 % | 49.9 (30) | 694.8 3.70 | 686.5 2.46 | 683 1.94 | 52.3 (30) | 696.8 4.00 | 686.6 2.48 | 682 1.79 | 27.2 (30) | 693.0 3.43 | 684.9 2.22 | 681 1.64 |
| | | | 25 % | 12.4 (30) | 707.6 5.61 | 699.0 4.33 | 692 3.28 | 21.1 (30) | 710.3 6.01 | 701.1 4.64 | 694 3.58 | 15.7 (30) | 704.9 5.21 | 697.5 4.10 | 693 3.43 |
| | | | 25 %↓2% | 62.8 (30) | 687.4 2.60 | 678.1 1.21 | 675 0.75 | 73.6 (30) | 685.1 2.25 | 678.1 1.21 | 674 0.60 | 76.2 (30) | 685.4 2.30 | 676.8 1.01 | 674 0.60 |

Table 25: Results for ILS experiments with instances atlanta▼20 and nobel-us and sorting strategies using mutation strategies as described in the text. Here, 'LB' denotes the lower bound, '$t_{max}$' the hard time limit, '$t_{conv}$' the average time to converge ('soft' termination criterion), '$W_{conv}$' the solution quality when terminating due to convergence, and '$W_{min}$' is the best found solution when reaching the time limit. Small numbers below convergence time values denote the number of repetitions converging within the hard time limit, small numbers below the number of wavelength values denote the excess in percent above the lower bound.

## 4.6    MEMETIC ALGORITHM

Solutions found by independent ILS runs have a considerable set of paths in common (not considering wavelength assignments). This observation suggests that these common paths are an essential part of (near-)optimal solutions and further improvement steps should concentrate on the remaining path assignments. Such a concept can be pursued in population-based approaches using sophisticated recombination (see Sec. 2.1.4).

A recombination operator was introduced by the author in [67] that employs both intensification, since it keeps common features of both parents, and diversification, as it introduces new features on a random base (details below). According to the definition of RADCLIFFE and SURRY [165] (see also Sec. 2.1.4) the recombination operator presented here is assorting but not respectful. Combining the ILS and recombination in a population-based framework results in a *memetic algorithm* (MA, see Sec. 2.1).

The ILS (Sec. 4.5) is expanded to a population-based MA. Initialization and termination correspond to the ILS. The population is initialized by using the construction heuristic from Sec. 4.4, using the Len sorting strategy for each individual. Although this heuristic orders requests by the length of their shortest path, requests are inserted in random order within each subset of equal shortest path lengths, thus resulting in different solutions.

In each iteration of the MA, the same steps are performed for each individual. Firstly, with given probabilities, either a recombination or a mutation step is performed. Another individual from the current population is then chosen uniformly at random for the recombination. Thus, in each generation each individual of the population will participate at least once in a recombination. As the recombination is expected to perform larger jumps in the search space, especially during the first iterations, a somewhat weaker strength for the mutation $10\%\downarrow_{2\%}$ instead of $25\%\downarrow_{2\%}$ from Sec. 4.5.2 is chosen initially. Once a provisional offspring has been created, this individual is improved by the local search (see Sec. 2.1.2).

For each individual of the next generation, offspring and parent are compared. If the offspring is better than its parent, the offspring replaces its parent, otherwise the offspring is discarded. Thus, the only interaction between individuals of the same generation is the recombination operator.

Two parameters determine the performance of the memetic algorithm: population size and recombination probability. In general, too small a population size may lead to a low diversity in the population, whereas a population that is too large requires considerable computation time. As a sophisticated local search, mutation, and recombination operators are used, the memetic algorithm can operate on considerably smaller populations compared to pure GAs, which only use $n$-crossover as recombination and no local search.

Choosing the recombination rate is also not trivial, since mutation and recombination pursue different search strategies. Setting the recombination probability to 0.0, the memetic algorithm equals as many independent ILS runs as there are individuals in the population, allowing a comparison of the memetic algorithm with the ILS by adjusting this probability. For the experiments, static recombination rates from 0.2 to 1.0 in steps of 0.2 are used, which are set as part of the experimental setup and stay constant during the run of the algorithm. As the choice of this parameter depends on the problem instance and may not be trivial, an adaptive recombination operator is used, too. The adaptive operator starts with a recombination rate of 0.5. After each generation it adapts the rate depending on the success of the recombination or mutation operations in the current generation. A successful recombination increases the rate by $\Delta$; a successful mutation decreases the rate by $\Delta$ set to $\Delta = 1/20 \cdot |S|$, where $|S|$ is the population size. The recombination rate was limited to the interval $[0.2, 0.8]$ to keep a minimum probability for both operations.

Termination criterion (see Sec. 4.5) is adapted for the population-based MA by simply using the best individual from the population to check for convergence.

### 4.6.1   Recombination

The recombination operator allows the combination of common features (here, paths) of two parent individuals to one offspring. For the operator, it is assumed that all requests have a demand of 1, corresponding to the definition on p. 102. To determine the set of paths common to both parents, a matching problem between paths from both parents has to be solved. Two paths can be matched if they use the same set of links regardless of the wavelengths assigned to the paths. Each request that is not routed on the same paths in both parents has to be added to the offspring in the recombinator's second phase using an approach similar to a construction heuristic.

Details of the recombination operator are given in Fig. 31. W. l. o. g. parent solution $a$ is better than $b$ with regard to the length-lex ordering (Sec. 4.5). The offspring solution $s$ is initialized as a copy of $a$. To determine a matching between paths from $a$ and $b$, $b$'s set of paths is stored in the multiset $P_b$. In the recombination's first phase, the algorithm iterates on the set of wavelengths sorted non-increasingly by usage. For each request using the current wavelength, a check is made on whether the request's path $p_{G,s}(r)$ is an element of $P_b$. If the test holds, a match has been found and the path is removed from $P_b$ to prevent future matchings. Otherwise, the request is removed from $s$ (removed requests are collected in $R'$). Sorting wavelengths ensures that paths in already highly used wavelengths are more likely be kept than paths in less-often used wavelengths. It can be argued that wavelengths with high load are efficiently used (fewer gaps) and thus the path assignments in these wavelengths should not be changed if possible. For wavelengths with low load, gaps are more likely to be exploited by the local search.

At the end of the recombination, removed requests $R'$ have to be reinserted into $s$ using an approach similar to a construction heuristic, with the request routed in the first wavelength where a feasible path connecting both endpoints is available. New wavelengths may be allocated, if necessary.

### 4.6.2  *Distribution*

Distributed computation (see Sec. 2.2.2) is an active field of research, as it offers the possibility of finding solutions in less absolute time than computations on a single machine. With this in mind, the memetic algorithm as presented here has been enhanced to create a distributed memetic algorithm (DMA). Whereas the MA uses a single population of $n$ individuals in one algorithm instance, the distributed MA uses $n$ independently operating algorithm instances with one individual each.

To resemble the recombination in the non-distributed memetic algorithm, algorithm instances (called 'islands', see Sec. 2.2.2) are allowed to exchange individuals regularly. Here, a simple epidemic algorithm (see Sec. 2.2.1) is used both to run a membership protocol on the islands participating in the computation and to send solutions for recombination from one island to another island. In the membership protocol, each island maintains a list of neighboring islands. In the experiments, the epidemic algorithm's membership protocol settled the neighbor list for each node in less than 5 s, providing a stable neighbor list in each case.

The distributed memetic algorithm, shown in detail in Fig. 33, is similar to the MA (Fig. 30). The main differences are (a) the DMA operates on a single individual per algorithm instance (b) the exchange and recombination between algorithm instances is managed differently. To exchange solutions between islands, the following approach is used. Each island has a receiving queue $Q$, where incoming individuals are stored temporarily (implemented by using an asynchronous thread). At the beginning of each MA iteration a check is run on whether the queue contains at least one element. If the test holds, the queue's top element is removed and used in a recombination operation. Otherwise, the MA operates like the ILS and mutates its current solution.

After the obligatory local search and selection, with a given probability the current solution is sent to one randomly selected neighboring island, regardless of whether recombination or mutation was performed or an improvement was found. The probability for sending an individual equals the recombination probability in the non-distributed MA. Due to the asynchronous nature of the DMA and the queuing effects, the queue acts as a memory in the distributed setup and the actual recombination rate may differ from the set value. The queue was limited to 16 elements (twice the largest population size) and any solution received at a node with a full queue was discarded.

Termination detection in a distributed system is more complicated than it is in the non-distributed setups discussed before. Here, nodes are either in the state 'terminated' or 'not terminated'. Nodes are 'not terminated' initially, until the previously used termination criterion is triggered because of convergence. However, even in state 'terminated', nodes continue to participate in the distributed MA (until the 'hard' time limit is reached). Thus, nodes are reset to 'not terminated' if a better solution is found either by mutation or by recombination (both followed by local search step) and switch back to 'terminated' if the convergence criterion is triggered again. A global termination holds if all nodes are in the state 'terminated' at the same time, which is easily detected by standard termination detection algorithms [137] at negligible costs. The hard time limit is enforced by granting each of the $|S|$ islands only $1/|S|$ of the instance-specific time limit. It has to be noted that the distributed convergence criterion is stricter than the non-distributed criterion: in the distributed case, all islands must agree on termination; in the non-distributed case, global view termination detection is much simpler.

### 4.6.3    *Results*

Experiments were performed on instances that had not been solved to optimality by the ILS. Each experiment was repeated 15 times; best and average values are used for discussion. For the experiments, population sizes of either 2, 4, or 8, respectively, were used. Recombination rates were either static or adaptive, as described above. The resulting data is summarized in two tables: tables 26 and 27 contain data for all instances, but are restricted to population size 4 and adaptive recombination; tables 28 and 29 are restricted to instance nobel-us (chosen as an example), but contain data for all used population sizes and recombination strategies. For a more detailed discussion, the average solution quality for three different events is compared: detecting convergence and triggering the 'soft' termination criterion (columns '$t_{conv}$' and '$W_{t_{conv}}$'), having spent half of the time granted by the 'hard' termination criterion (columns '$W_{t_{max}/2}$'), and reaching the time limit (columns '$W_{t_{max}/2}$').

From the experiments, the following conclusions can be drawn:

- Of the different population sizes, population size 2 leads to worse final results, especially for the non-distributed case. Population sizes 4 and 8 result in comparable solutions, but population size 8 requires more time to converge and thus longer running times. Thus, for the experiments to follow and the remaining discussion of results, the setups are restricted to population size 4.

- Using recombination only (rate 1.0), results are worst among all recombination rate strategies, both for the distributed and the non-distributed case. For nobel-us and population size 4, for example, the best solution found for this rate cost 708 (non-distributed), whereas the average solution quality for all other rate strategies is < 678 when the 'soft' termination criterion is triggered. Thus, recombination alone can not compete with setups that use both recombination and mutation.

- In a direct comparison between corresponding distributed and non-distributed MA setups, the distributed algorithm performs better than the non-distributed algorithm, as it finds better solutions both after half the time limit and when reaching the time limit. This holds for all problem instances except for zib54 and janos-us-ca$^{\blacktriangledown 200}$. For 15.50.deg4, for example, the non-distributed algorithm finds solutions with 376.4 (3.7 % excess) and 376.1 (3.6 %) wavelengths at both time points, respectively, whereas the distributed algorithm finds solutions with 370.3 (2.0 %) and 368.3 (1.5 %) wavelengths, respectively.

- For 'soft' termination criterion in the memetic algorithm, the adaptive recombination rate is among the top performing recombination strategies for most setups in terms of solution quality. For zib54, for example, the adaptive recombination rate converges at a cost 707.4 (0.34 % excess) and the static recombination rates (except 1.0) range between 708.4 (0.47 %) and 709.3 (0.61 %). For the constant recombination rates, a common trend for non-distributed setups is to perform better lower recombination rates. For 15.50.75 not shown in table) the quality of the best-found solution increases from 158 to 166 for rates 0.2 to 1.0 (adaptive recombination has a quality of 159). For the DMA, this trend is far less evident than for the MA, as the distribution seems to reduce the influence of the recombination rate on the solution quality. For the above instance, the solution qualities are either 156 or 157 for all recombination rates, except for rate 1.0 (quality 158) and adaptive (155).

- The convergence termination criterion ('soft' criterion) did not trigger for all repetitions in all setups. This happens if (minor) improvements are found late (with reference to the time limit) during a run. In the non-distributed MA, three out of 12 instances converged in less than 13 out of 15 repetitions (which can be seen as the minimum number to draw conclusions); in the distributed MA, four instances did not converge. Termination times increase with problem instance size (number of nodes and edges, demand): the smallest instances (10.50.*) require about 10 s and 65 s (non-distributed and distributed, respectively) to converge; larger instances such as janos-us-ca$^{\blacktriangledown 200}$ and 20.50.* converge after 10 min to 30 min.

- For the distributed MA, the convergence criterion triggers termination later than the non-distributed MA. Due to the later convergence and better performance of the DMA, the results are considerably better: for setups with a sufficient number of converging repetitions (see above), the excess above the lower bound is either < 0.6 % or less than 2 wavelengths.

- The memetic algorithm, both in its non-distributed and distributed variant, is able to find optimal solutions for several instances where the original ILS failed. Optimal solutions were found for the instances janos-us-ca$^{\blacktriangledown 200}$, nobel-us, 10.50.75, 15.50.deg8, and zib54. Not only were more optima found, but the average solution quality also improved. For 15.50.deg4, for example, the ILS's best-found solution in any setup is 384 (excess 5.79 %), whereas the memetic algorithm's average results for all setups (except for population size 2 in non-distributed setups), both after half the time limit and when reaching the time limit, is always < 4.5 %. The best solutions' excesses are < 1 % in some cases.

## 4.7 Multi-Level

Approaches presented in previous sections were able to solve small and medium-sized instances to (near-)optimality in reasonable time. So for problem instance janos-us-ca$^{\blacktriangledown 200}$, an instance with 39 nodes, 122 edges, and a total demand of 10 173, solutions can be found with 1 % excess within about 5 minutes. For large instances, however, even constructing an initial solution is extremely expensive computationally. For janos-us-ca$^{\blacktriangledown 10}$ (total demand of 203 222), for example, solution construction alone takes more than 2.5 hours. This magnitude of computation time was the reason for omitting these large instances so far.

The above numbers motivate an estimation of the algorithms' complexity. Let $n = |V|$ and $D = \sum_{r \in R} d_r$. In this section, furthermore, the requests have a demand of $\geq 1$ and no two requests have the same endpoints (see also p. 102). The number of wavelengths is obviously limited by $D$, as each unit of demand is routed in its own wavelength in the worst case. The following complexity estimations can be made for each component:

- Searching a *shortest path* takes $\mathcal{O}(n^2)$, assuming $\mathcal{O}(n^2)$ many edges.

- The bin packing-like *construction* costs $\mathcal{O}(D^2 n^2)$, performing a shortest path search for each unit of demand in each available wavelength.

|  | | | Non-distributed MA | | | | | Distributed MA | | | | |
|---|---|---|---|---|---|---|---|---|---|---|---|---|
| Instance | $W_{LB}$ | $t_{max}$ | $t_{conv}$ | $W_{conv}$ | $W_{tmax/2}$ | $W_{tmax}$ | $W_{min}$ | $t_{conv}$ | $W_{conv}$ | $W_{tmax/2}$ | $W_{tmax}$ | $W_{min}$ |
| 10.50.75 | 155 | 300 | 11.4 (15) | 158.1 2.00 | 157.2 1.42 | 157.1 1.35 | 156 0.65 | 81.8 (15) | 156.7 1.10 | 155.5 0.32 | 155.4 0.26 | 155 0.00 |
| 10.50.deg4 | 225 | 300 | 10.1 (13) | 226.1 0.49 | 225.1 0.04 | 225.1 0.04 | 225 0.00 | 67.6 (15) | 225.7 0.31 | 225.0 0.00 | 225.0 0.00 | 225 0.00 |
| 10.50.deg8 | 120 | 300 | 10.7 (15) | 125.7 4.75 | 125.0 4.17 | 124.8 4.00 | 122 1.67 | 50.7 (15) | 121.9 1.58 | 121.7 1.42 | 121.6 1.33 | 121 0.83 |
| 15.50.75 | 152 | 1500 | 184.5 (15) | 162.3 6.78 | 161.7 6.38 | 161.6 6.32 | 159 4.61 | 812.1 (9) | 157.2 3.42 | 156.9 3.22 | 156.7 3.09 | 155 1.97 |
| 15.50.deg4 | 363 | 450 | 148.6 (15) | 377.3 3.94 | 377.2 3.69 | 376.1 3.61 | 373 2.75 | 407.9 (1) | 371.0 2.20 | 370.3 2.01 | 368.3 1.46 | 367 1.10 |
| 15.50.deg8 | 258 | 450 | 79.1 (15) | 261.3 1.28 | 259.9 0.74 | 259.9 0.74 | 259 0.39 | 239.9 (15) | 258.8 0.31 | 258.5 0.19 | 258.3 0.12 | 258 0.00 |

Table 26: Results for experiments on both the non-distributed and distributed MA. Data is restricted to setups with population size 4 and adaptive recombination (part 1). Here, 'LB' denotes an instance's lower bound, '$t_{max}$' hard time limit per instance, '$t_{conv}$' the average time to converge ('soft' termination criterion), '$W_{conv}$' the average wavelength when terminating due to convergence, '$W_{tmax}/2$' and '$W_{tmax}$' the average wavelength after half the time limit and when reaching the time limit, and '$W_{min}$' is the best found solution when reaching the time limit. Small numbers below convergence time values denote the number of repetitions converging within the hard time limit, small numbers below the number of wavelength values denote the excess in percent above the lower bound. See also Tab. 27.

| Instance | $W_{LB}$ | $t_{max}$ | Non-distributed MA | | | | | | Distributed MA | | | | |
| --- | --- | --- | --- | --- | --- | --- | --- | --- | --- | --- | --- | --- | --- |
| | | | $t_{conv}$ | $W_{t_{conv}}$ | $W_{t_{max}/2}$ | $W_{t_{max}}$ | $W_{min}$ | | $t_{conv}$ | $W_{t_{conv}}$ | $W_{t_{max}/2}$ | $W_{t_{max}}$ | $W_{min}$ |
| 20.50.75 | 188 | 3000 | 933.6 (14) | 190.6 1.38 | 189.7 0.90 | 189.1 0.59 | 188 0.00 | | 1928.8 (14) | 188.1 0.05 | 188.1 0.05 | 188.0 0.00 | 188 0.00 |
| 20.50.deg4 | 432 | 1000 | 703.8 (4) | 444.5 2.89 | 445.1 3.03 | 443.1 2.57 | 441 2.08 | | – (0) | – | 447.7 3.63 | 443.3 2.62 | 442 2.31 |
| 20.50.deg8 | 283 | 2000 | 1362.6 (12) | 297.9 5.27 | 298.0 5.30 | 296.9 4.91 | 294 3.89 | | – (0) | – | 299.1 5.69 | 296.5 4.77 | 294 3.89 |
| atlanta▼[20] | 1256 | 300 | 205.9 (1) | 1258.0 0.16 | 1257.6 0.13 | 1256.2 0.02 | 1256 0.00 | | 249.8 (7) | 1256.0 0.00 | 1256.7 0.06 | 1256.0 0.00 | 1256 0.00 |
| nobel-us | 670 | 600 | 166.4 (12) | 684.6 2.18 | 675.7 0.85 | 673.3 0.49 | 670 0.00 | | 298.0 (15) | 670.1 0.01 | 670.1 0.01 | 670.0 0.00 | 670 0.00 |
| j-us-ca▼[200] | 1288 | 1800 | 984.9 (14) | 1293.6 0.43 | 1293.4 0.42 | 1292.7 0.36 | 1289 0.08 | | 1465.4 (3) | 1300.7 0.99 | 1300.1 0.94 | 1296.6 0.67 | 1288 0.00 |
| zib54 | 705 | 1800 | 438.0 (14) | 707.4 0.34 | 706.1 0.16 | 705.7 0.10 | 705 0.00 | | 916.9 (13) | 709.0 0.57 | 708.7 0.52 | 707.9 0.41 | 705 0.00 |

Table 27: Results for experiments on both the non-distributed and distributed MA. Data is restricted to setups with population size 4 and adaptive recombination (part 2). Here, 'LB' denotes an instance's lower bound, '$t_{max}$' hard time limit per instance, '$t_{conv}$' the average time to converge ('soft' termination criterion), '$W_{t_{conv}}$' the average wavelength when terminating due to convergence, '$W_{t_{max}/2}$' and '$W_{t_{max}}$' the average wavelength after half the time limit and when reaching the time limit, and '$W_{min}$' is the best found solution when reaching the hard time limit. Small numbers below convergence time values denote the number of repetitions converging within the hard time limit, small numbers below the number of wavelength values denote the excess in percent above the lower bound. See also Tab. 26.

| Instance | $W_{LB}$ | $t_{max}$ | $|S|$ | $P_{rec}$ | Non-distributed MA | | | | | Distributed MA | | | | |
|---|---|---|---|---|---|---|---|---|---|---|---|---|---|---|
| | | | | | $t_{conv}$ | $W_{conv}$ | $W_{fmax}/2$ | $W_{fmax}$ | $W_{min}$ | $t_{conv}$ | $W_{conv}$ | $W_{fmax}/2$ | $W_{fmax}$ | $W_{min}$ |
| nobel-us | 670 | 600 | 2 | 0.2 | 144.3 | 677.3 | 673.7 | 672.5 | 670 | 255.5 | 670.4 | 670.0 | 670.0 | 670 |
| | | | | | (13) | 1.09 | 0.55 | 0.37 | 0.00 | (14) | 0.06 | 0.00 | 0.00 | 0.00 |
| | | | | 0.4 | 130.5 | 680.8 | 676.9 | 674.9 | 671 | 223.8 | 670.1 | 670.0 | 670.0 | 670 |
| | | | | | (14) | 1.61 | 1.03 | 0.73 | 0.15 | (14) | 0.01 | 0.00 | 0.00 | 0.00 |
| | | | | 0.6 | 115.1 | 686.2 | 677.1 | 674.9 | 672 | 199.5 | 670.1 | 670.0 | 670.0 | 670 |
| | | | | | (14) | 2.42 | 1.06 | 0.73 | 0.30 | (14) | 0.01 | 0.00 | 0.00 | 0.00 |
| | | | | 1.0 | 11.2 | 786.3 | 786.3 | 786.3 | 752 | 122.7 | 690.8 | 679.9 | 673.5 | 670 |
| | | | | | (15) | 17.36 | 17.36 | 17.36 | 12.24 | (12) | 3.10 | 1.48 | 0.52 | 0.00 |
| | | | | dyn | 98.7 | 689.9 | 679.1 | 676.7 | 674 | 245.8 | 670.0 | 670.0 | 670.0 | 670 |
| | | | | | (12) | 2.97 | 1.36 | 1.00 | 0.60 | (14) | 0.00 | 0.00 | 0.00 | 0.00 |

Table 28: Results for experiments on both the non-distributed and distributed MA. Data is restricted to nobel-us (part 1) with all population sizes and all recombination rates except for 0.8 (due to space restrictions). Here, 'LB' denotes an instance's lower bound, '$|S|$' is the population size, 'P[recomb]' is the recombination rate, '$t_{max}$' the hard time limit per instance, '$t_{conv}$' the average time to converge ('soft' termination criterion), '$W_{conv}$' the average wavelength when terminating due to convergence, '$W_{fmax}/2$' and '$W_{fmax}$' the average wavelength after half the time limit and when reaching the time limit, and '$W_{min}$' is the best found solution when reaching the hard time limit. Small numbers below convergence time values denote the number of repetitions converging within the hard time limit; small numbers below the number of wavelength values denote the excess in percent above the lower bound. See also Tables 29–30.

| Instance | $W_{LB}$ | $t_{max}$ | $|S|$ | $p_{rec}$ | Non-distributed MA | | | | Distributed MA | | | | |
|---|---|---|---|---|---|---|---|---|---|---|---|---|---|
| | | | | | $t_{conv}$ | $W_{t_{conv}}$ | $W_{t_{max}/2}$ | $W_{t_{max}}$ | $W_{min}$ | $t_{conv}$ | $W_{t_{conv}}$ | $W_{t_{max}/2}$ | $W_{t_{max}}$ | $W_{min}$ |
| nobel-us | 670 | 600 | 4 | 0.2 | 224.4 (9) | 673.2 / 0.48 | 671.3 / 0.19 | 670.3 / 0.04 | 670 / 0.00 | 372.3 (12) | 670.0 / 0.00 | 670.2 / 0.03 | 670.0 / 0.00 | 670 / 0.00 |
| | | | | 0.4 | 211.1 (9) | 676.7 / 1.00 | 671.9 / 0.28 | 670.9 / 0.13 | 670 / 0.00 | 290.5 (15) | 670.0 / 0.00 | 670.0 / 0.00 | 670.0 / 0.00 | 670 / 0.00 |
| | | | | 0.6 | 248.3 (12) | 677.9 / 1.18 | 673.6 / 0.54 | 671.9 / 0.28 | 670 / 0.00 | 230.9 (15) | 670.0 / 0.00 | 670.0 / 0.00 | 670.0 / 0.00 | 670 / 0.00 |
| | | | | 1.0 | 35.1 (15) | 731.1 / 9.12 | 730.8 / 9.07 | 730.8 / 9.07 | 708 / 5.67 | 501.7 (4) | 670.5 / 0.07 | 672.0 / 0.30 | 670.3 / 0.04 | 670 / 0.00 |
| | | | | dyn | 166.4 (12) | 684.6 / 2.18 | 675.7 / 0.85 | 673.3 / 0.49 | 670 / 0.00 | 298.0 (15) | 670.1 / 0.01 | 670.1 / 0.01 | 670.0 / 0.00 | 670 / 0.00 |

Table 29: Results for experiments on both the non-distributed and distributed MA. Data is restricted to nobel-us (part 2) with all population sizes and all recombination rates except for 0.8 (due to space restrictions). Here, 'LB' denotes an instance's lower bound, '$|S|$' is the population size, 'P[recomb]' is the recombination rate, '$t_{max}$' the hard time limit per instance, '$t_{conv}$' the average time to converge ('soft' termination criterion), '$W_{t_{conv}}$' the average wavelength when terminating due to convergence, '$W_{t_{max}/2}$' and '$W_{t_{max}}$' the average wavelength after half the time limit and when reaching the time limit, and '$W_{min}$' is the best found solution when reaching the hard time limit. Small numbers below convergence time values denote the number of repetitions converging within the hard time limit; small numbers below the number of wavelength values denote the excess in percent above the lower bound. See also Tabs. 28 and 30.

| Instance | $W_{LB}$ | $t_{max}$ | $|S|$ | $P_{rec}$ | Non-distributed MA | | | | | Distributed MA | | | | |
|---|---|---|---|---|---|---|---|---|---|---|---|---|---|---|
| | | | | | $t_{conv}$ | $W_{t_{conv}}$ | $W_{t_{max}/2}$ | $W_{t_{max}}$ | $W_{min}$ | $t_{conv}$ | $W_{t_{conv}}$ | $W_{t_{max}/2}$ | $W_{t_{max}}$ | $W_{min}$ |
| nobel-us | 670 | 600 | 8 | 0.2 | 420.6 | 671.0 | 670.9 | 670.2 | 670 | 534.6 | 670.0 | 670.1 | 670.0 | 670 |
| | | | | | (8) | 0.15 | 0.13 | 0.03 | 0.00 | (7) | 0.00 | 0.01 | 0.00 | 0.00 |
| | | | | 0.4 | 345.4 | 672.5 | 671.8 | 670.3 | 670 | 424.3 | 670.0 | 670.0 | 670.0 | 670 |
| | | | | | (10) | 0.37 | 0.27 | 0.04 | 0.00 | (14) | 0.00 | 0.00 | 0.00 | 0.00 |
| | | | | 0.6 | 174.3 | 677.9 | 672.5 | 670.5 | 670 | 429.4 | 670.0 | 670.0 | 670.0 | 670 |
| | | | | | (9) | 1.18 | 0.37 | 0.07 | 0.00 | (15) | 0.00 | 0.00 | 0.00 | 0.00 |
| | | | | 1.0 | 76.2 | 701.1 | 700.1 | 700.1 | 690 | 564.7 | 670.0 | 670.9 | 670.0 | 670 |
| | | | | | (15) | 4.64 | 4.49 | 4.49 | 2.99 | (4) | 0.00 | 0.13 | 0.00 | 0.00 |
| | | | | dyn | 248.1 | 677.5 | 673.7 | 671.2 | 670 | 420.3 | 670.0 | 670.0 | 670.0 | 670 |
| | | | | | (11) | 1.12 | 0.55 | 0.18 | 0.00 | (14) | 0.00 | 0.00 | 0.00 | 0.00 |

Table 30: Results for experiments on both the non-distributed and distributed MA. Data is restricted to nobel-us (part 3) with all population sizes and all recombination rates except for 0.8 (due to space restrictions). Here, 'LB' denotes an instance's lower bound, '$|S|$' is the population size, 'P[recomb]' is the recombination rate, '$t_{max}$' the hard time limit per instance, '$t_{conv}$' the average time to converge ('soft' termination criterion), '$W_{t_{conv}}$' the average wavelength when terminating due to convergence, '$W_{t_{max}/2}$' and '$W_{t_{max}}$' the average wavelength after half the time limit and when reaching the time limit, and '$W_{min}$' is the best found solution when reaching the time limit. Small numbers below convergence time values denote the number of repetitions converging within the hard time limit; small numbers below the number of wavelength values denote the excess in percent above the lower bound. See also Tables 28–29.

- In a single *local search* step, a shortest path is determined resulting in a time complexity of $\mathcal{O}(D^2 n^2)$ for each unit of demand and each wavelength.

- Each single *mutation* step has complexity $\mathcal{O}(Dn^3)$, as it reallocates $\mathcal{O}(n)$ paths requiring to search a shortest path in each wavelength. As a mutation operation depends linearly on $D$, the total complexity becomes $\mathcal{O}(D^2 n^3)$.

- *Recombination* has a complexity of $\mathcal{O}(D^2 n^2)$, as finding matches between paths from each parent costs $\mathcal{O}(D^2 n)$ and routing the remaining requests costs $\mathcal{O}(D^2 n^2)$ (essentially like construction).

The impact of $D$ on the time complexity of all the above algorithms provokes a divide & conquer approach for the RWA on the requests' demands. Scaling demand has already been successfully exploited in reducing the size of SNDlib derived instances.

Here, a multilevel approach is used to realize the divide & conquer paradigm. The multilevel approach as promoted by WALSHAW [200] builds a hierarchy of approximations to the original problem instance. A multilevel algorithm starts by coarsening a given problem instance by removing or merging instance features. This coarsening is done stepwise: in each step, a limited set of features is removed until the resulting problem instance is easy to solve. Once a solution for the coarsened instance has been determined, the coarsening is reversed stepwise and in each of those expansion steps a valid solution for the intermediate solution is built using the previous step's solution and the features removed earlier. The intermediate solution is improved further by a problem-specific heuristic. Although solutions get harder to solve in each expansion step due to their increasing size, the improvement heuristic's search is boosted by the good solution constructed from previous levels. Reaching the original problem instance again, it is easier to find a good solution based on the multilevel algorithm's history. Furthermore, because much optimization work has been done on simpler instances, computation times are lower than when operating only on the original problem instance.

The original multilevel algorithm structure is simplified by performing only one large coarsening step by dividing the demand of each request by the same scaling factor. Expanding a solution of the coarsened instance, the set of paths for each demand in the coarsened instance's solution is copied multiple times (determined by the scaling factor) in the expanded instance. The strength of the scaling operation is motivated by the experimental findings for the ILS: for small instances with $D < 10^4$, the ILS was able to produce (near-)optimal solutions in a short time. Therefore, the scaling constructor (SC) and the multilevel (ML) approach discussed below will scale down a problem instance by a factor of $a^k$ so that the sum of the problem instance's demand is below this threshold. The multilevel approach performs $k$ expansion operations, each multiplying the demand with $a \in \mathbb{N}$, whereas the SC expands back to the original instance directly. Scaling step $a$ has to be supplied ($a = 4$ here), whereas $k = \left\lceil \log_a \frac{D}{10\,000} \right\rceil$ will be derived from the experimental setup. Both approaches are expected to considerably reduce the runtime due to the smaller $D$ in reduced instances.

### 4.7.1   Scaling Constructor

The scaling constructor (SC, Fig. 39:1–7) is a simplified multilevel algorithm, as no refinement is applied to the intermediate solution and only one expansion step is performed. The algorithm starts by scaling the demand of the original instance's requests $R_{\text{orig}}$ down to $R_{\text{scaled}}$ using a scaling factor $f = a^k$ to get $D < 10^4$ (Fig. 39:2). For the scaled instance, an initial solution is constructed using an arbitrary construction heuristic (here, the standard construction algorithm is used). When expanding the scaled instance's solution $s_{\text{scaled}}$ to a solution for the original instance (Fig. 38:1–11), paths from $s_{\text{scaled}}$ are copied multiple times to the original instance's solution $s_{\text{orig}}$, but a conflict-free wavelength has to be assigned to each path copy. Here, a rather straightforward approach is used, leaving the search for better assignments to an improvement algorithm applied later. Assuming the number of used wavelengths in $s_{\text{scaled}}$ is $|W(s_{\text{scaled}})|$ and for a given request $r$ the $j$-th path's wavelength is $\lambda(s_{\text{scaled}}, r, j)$, the wavelength $\lambda'$ assigned to the $i$-th copy for this path in $s_{\text{orig}}$ is

$$\lambda' = i \cdot |W(s_{\text{scaled}})| + \lambda(s_{\text{scaled}}, r, j) \tag{4.10}$$

For each unit of demand $1 \leq d \leq d_{\text{orig}}^r$ quotient and remainder of $d_{\text{scaled}}^r/d$ determine the copy's number $i$ and path index $j$, respectively (Fig. 38:6). ScaleRequests guarantees that there is at least one path in $s_{\text{scaled}}$ for each $r \in R_{\text{orig}}$, i. e. for each request $r$ with $d_{\text{orig}}^r > 0$, it holds that $d_{\text{scaled}}^r > 0$. An example of the multiplication of paths is given in Fig. 36.

### 4.7.2 *Multilevel Approach*

Compared to the scaling constructor, the multilevel approach is more sophisticated as it performs several steps of expanding, each refining its intermediate population using the memetic algorithm. Initially, one large coarsening step is performed, scaling the original instance (dividing by $a^k$) to an instance with $D < 10^4$. Starting from the deepest coarsening step, the multilevel algorithms iterates (Fig. 40:4–20) through the expansion steps until the original instance is restored. In each iteration $0 \leq i \leq k$, the original requests $R_{orig}$ are scaled down to $R_{new}$ by the iteration's scaling factor $f = a^{k-i}$ (Fig. 40:7). In the deepest coarsening step, the population is initialized using the standard construction algorithm (Fig. 40:9); all later steps create a new population based on a scaled version of the previous step's population members (Fig. 40:11–13). Then, the memetic algorithm is applied to the population until no improvement can be found for $c_{ML}$ iterations (ML-specific convergence criterion) or a global time limit $t$ is reached (Fig. 40:16). For the last iteration (Fig. 40:18) operating on the original instance only, the global time limit $t$ is used (see Sec. 4.5). The memetic algorithm is limited for all but the last iteration, as optimal solutions for the scaled instances are of no interest. Instead, acceptable solutions for later expansion steps in a short time are preferred, i. e. it is more efficient to undertake refinement steps on these, only as long as improvements in a short time can be achieved that are still significant.

The multilevel approach can be used both for non-distributed and distributed setups. In Fig. 40, the distributed variant is depicted; to run a non-distributed variant, DISTMA has to be replaced by MEMETIC-ALGORITHM only.

The most important issue arising in the distributed multilevel memetic algorithm (ML-DMA) is that the islands change their local scaling factor independently. Thus, individuals in the receiving queue $Q$ may be scaled by different factors than those in the current solution (either too small or too large). This problem can be solved by scaling the incoming solution to the current solution's level using function SCALESOLUTION (Fig. 38).

```
1: function INITIALIZEPOPULATION(Graph G, Requests R)
2:     S ← ∅
3:     for i ← 1, ..., n do
4:         s ← INITIALIZEINDIVIDUAL(G, R)
5:         S ← S ∪ {s}
6:     end for
7:     return S
8: end function
```

```
1: function MEMETICALGORITHM(Graph G, Requests R, Population
   S, TerminationCriterion T)
2:     while ¬T do
3:         S' ← ∅
4:         for all s ∈ S do
5:             if RANDOM≤P[recomb] then
6:                 s̄ ← CHOOSEINDIVIDUAL(S, s)
7:                 s' ← RECOMBINATOR(G, s, s̄, R)
8:             else
9:                 s' ← MUTATE(s, R, strength)
10:            end if
11:            s'' ← LOCALSEARCH(s', R)
12:            if s'' < s then
13:                S' ← S' ∪ {s''}
14:            else
15:                S' ← S' ∪ {s}
16:            end if
17:        end for
18:        S ← S'
19:    end while
20:    return S
21: end function
```

Figure 30: Memetic algorithm for the RWA.

1: **function** RECOMBINATOR(Graph $G$, Solution $a$, Solution $b$, Requests $R$)
2:    $s \leftarrow a$
3:    $R' \leftarrow \varnothing$
4:    $P_b \leftarrow \bigcup_{r \in R} p_{G,b}(r)$
5:    **for** $\lambda \in \{\lambda_1, \ldots, \lambda_{|W|} : \text{USAGE}(a, \lambda_i) \geq \text{USAGE}(a, \lambda_{i+1})\}$ **do**
6:        **for** $r \in R : \lambda_s(r) = \lambda$ **do**
7:            **if** $p_{G,s}(r) \in P_b$ **then**
8:                $P_b \leftarrow P_b \setminus \{p_{G,s}(r)\}$
9:            **else**
10:                $s \leftarrow s \setminus r$
11:                $R' \leftarrow R' \cup \{r\}$
12:            **end if**
13:        **end for**
14:    **end for**

15:    **for all** $r \in R'$ **do**
16:        $\lambda_s(r) \leftarrow \arg\min_{\lambda \in W} \text{SP}_{G,s}(r, \lambda) \neq \varnothing$
17:        $p_{G,s}(r) \leftarrow \text{SP}_{G,s}(r, \lambda_s)$
18:    **end for**
19:    **return** $s$
20: **end function**

Figure 31: Recombination operator for the RWA.

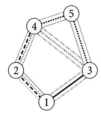

(a) The better of two parents. The length-lex vector on wavelength usage is $(5, 3)$.

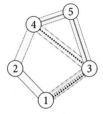

(b) The worse of two parents. The length-lex vector on wavelength usage is $(3, 2, 1)$.

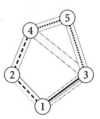

(c) Offspring when recombining both parents on the left. The length-lex vector on wavelength usage is $(5, 1)$.

Figure 32: Example for a recombination step. Paths common to both parents and kept in the offspring are paths $\langle 4, 5, 3 \rangle$ (dotted, black) and $\langle 1, 3 \rangle$ (solid, black). Requests between nodes pairs $\{1, 4\}$ and $\{1, 3\}$ are routed on new paths in the offspring.

1:  **function** DISTMA(Graph $G$, Requests $R$, Solution $s$, Termination-Criterion $T$)
2:      **while** $\neg T$ **do**
3:          **if** $\{q_1, \ldots, q_k\} = Q \neq \varnothing$ **then**
4:              $\bar{s} \leftarrow q_1, \quad Q \leftarrow \{q_2, \ldots, q_k\}$
5:              $s' \leftarrow$ RECOMBINATOR$(G, s, \bar{s}, R)$
6:          **else**
7:              $s' \leftarrow$ MUTATE$(s, R, \text{strength})$
8:          **end if**
9:          $s'' \leftarrow$ LOCALSEARCH$(s', R)$
10:         **if** $s'' < s$ **then**
11:             $s \leftarrow s''$
12:         **end if**
13:         **if** RANDOM$\leq$P[recomb] **then**
14:             SENDTORANDOMNEIGHBOR$(s)$
15:         **end if**
16:     **end while**
17:     **return** $s$
18: **end function**

Figure 33: Distributed memetic algorithm for the RWA.

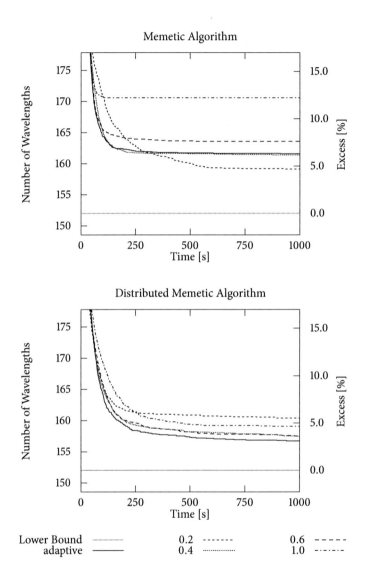

Figure 34: Performance plots for problem instances 15.50.75 with population size 4 each. The upper plot depict non-distributed MA setups, the lower plot depict distributed MA setups.

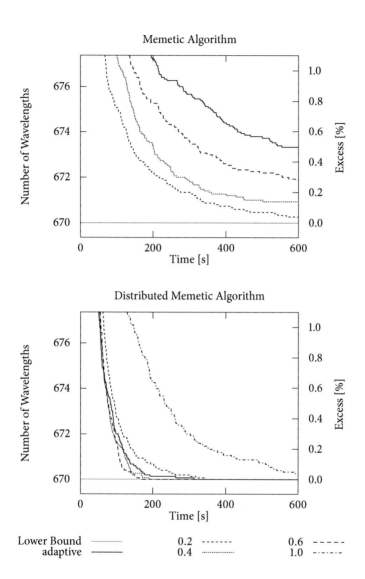

Figure 35: Performance plots for problem instances nobel-us with population size 4 each. The upper plot depicts non-distributed MA setups; the lower plot depicts distributed MA setups.

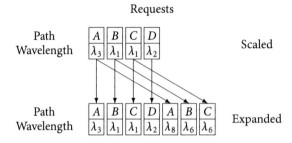

Figure 36: Example for the multiplication of paths for a single request during an expansion step. In this example, $d^r_{\text{scaled}} = 4$, $d^r_{\text{expanded}} = 7$, and $|W(s_{\text{scaled}})| = 5$.

1: **function** SCALEREQUESTS(Requests $R$, scaling factor $f$)
2:     $R_{\text{scaled}} = R$
3:     **for all** $r \in R$ **do**
4:         $d^r_{\text{scaled}} \leftarrow \left\lceil \frac{d^r}{f} \right\rceil$
5:     **end for**
6:     **return** $R_{\text{scaled}}$
7: **end function**

Figure 37: Algorithm to scale requests in a problem instance.

1: **function** SCALESOLUTION(Solution $s_{\text{old}}$, Requests $R_{\text{old}}$, $R_{\text{new}}$)
2:     $s_{\text{new}} \leftarrow \varnothing$
3:     **for all** $r \in R_{\text{new}}$ **do**
4:         **for** $d \leftarrow 1, \ldots, d^r_{\text{new}}$ **do**
5:             $p \leftarrow \text{PATH}(s_{\text{old}}, r, d \mod d^r_{\text{old}})$
6:             $\lambda \leftarrow \left\lfloor \frac{d}{d^r_{\text{old}}} \right\rfloor \cdot |W(s_{\text{old}})| + \lambda(s_{\text{old}}, r, d \mod d^r_{\text{old}})$
7:             $\text{ADDPATH}(s_{\text{new}}, r, d, p, \lambda)$
8:         **end for**
9:     **end for**
10:     **return** $s_{\text{new}}$
11: **end function**

Figure 38: Algorithm to scale a solution. Note that $R_{\text{old}} = \{(u^r, v^r, d^r_{\text{old}})\}$ and $R_{\text{new}} = \{(u^r, v^r, d^r_{\text{new}})\}$.

```
1: function SCALINGCONSTRUCTOR(Graph G, Requests R_orig, Scaling a)
```

2:    $k \leftarrow \left\lceil \log_a \frac{\sum_{r \in R} d^r_{\text{orig}}}{10\,000} \right\rceil$

3:    $f \leftarrow a^k$

4:    $R_{\text{scaled}} \leftarrow$ SCALEREQUESTS$(R_{\text{orig}}, f)$

5:    $s_{\text{scaled}} \leftarrow$ INITIALIZEINDIVIDUAL$(G, R_{\text{scaled}})$

6:    **return** SCALESOLUTION$(s_{\text{old}}, R_{\text{scaled}}, R_{\text{orig}})$

7: **end function**

Figure 39: Algorithm to construct solutions for large problem instances. Note that $R_{\text{orig}} = \{(u^r, v^r, d^r_{\text{orig}})\}$.

1: **function** MULTILEVEL(Graph $G$, Requests $R_{\text{orig}}$, Scaling $a$, Time $t$)

2:    $\{S, R_{\text{new}}, R_{\text{old}}\} \leftarrow \varnothing$

3:    $k \leftarrow \left\lceil \log_a \frac{\sum_{r \in R} d^r_{\text{orig}}}{10\,000} \right\rceil$

4:    **for** $i \leftarrow 0, 1, \ldots, k-1, k$ **do**

5:        $f \leftarrow a^{k-i}$

6:        $R_{\text{old}} \leftarrow R_{\text{new}}$

7:        $R_{\text{new}} \leftarrow$ SCALEREQUESTS$(R_{\text{orig}}, f)$

8:        **if** $i = 0$ **then**                    ▷ First Iteration, strongest scaling

9:            $S \leftarrow$ INITIALIZEPOPULATION$(G, R_{\text{new}})$

10:        **else**

11:            **for all** $s \in S$ **do**

12:                $s \leftarrow$ SCALESOLUTION$(s, R_{\text{old}}, R_{\text{new}})$

13:            **end for**

14:        **end if**

15:        **if** $i < k$ **then**                   ▷ MA on scaled instance

16:            $S \leftarrow$ DISTMA$(G, R_{\text{new}}, S, \text{TIME}(t) \vee \text{CONV}(c_{\text{ML}}))$

17:        **else**                                ▷ MA on original instance

18:            $S \leftarrow$ DISTMA$(G, R_{\text{new}}, S, \text{TIME}(t))$

19:        **end if**

20:    **end for**

21:    **return** $S$

22: **end function**

Figure 40: Multilevel algorithm for the RWA. Note that $R_{\text{orig}} = \{(u^r, v^r, d^r_{\text{orig}})\}$.

### 4.7.3   Results

All setups were repeated 15 times and average values were used for the following discussion. Two groups of experiments were conducted: the first group analyzes the influence of the ML approach on the 'pure' ILS; the second group combines the DMA with the multilevel approach to build a high-performance solver for the static RWA. Due to the prohibitive computation times to acquire lower bounds for large instances, best-known solutions (upper bound, Tab. 20) are used to determine the solution excess instead.

In the first group of experiments, neither population nor distribution was used to study the influence of multilevel scaling on the ILS directly. The findings are summarized as follows:

- As seen in Tab. 31 and 32, constructing an initial solution using the construction heuristic Len (Sec. 4.4) takes considerable time (rows 'ILS', column '$t_{\text{init}}$') for large instances. Even for the 'fastest' large instance ($\text{ta1}^{\blacktriangledown 100}$), building an initial solution takes 1020.6 s; for $\text{ta2}^{\blacktriangledown 100}$ no solution was built within the given time limit of 21 600 s. Therefore, conventional construction heuristics are not applicable for population-based algorithms.

- The above problem is addressed by both the scaling constructor and the multilevel approach (rows 'SC-ILS' and 'ML-ILS'), as both algorithms require significantly less time to construct solutions. Whereas is takes 2200.4 s (average 2365.7 s) to find an initial solution in the best case using the original constructor applied to instance atlanta, the scaling constructor requires only 10.5 s on average to find an initial solution. This solution's quality is worse than the original constructor's quality (29 420 vs. 29 317, 17.0 % vs. 16.6 % excess), but investing the saved time in any improvement heuristic will result in better solutions. For example, using the ILS to improve the scaling constructor's solution for the above example, the average solution quality is already 25 805.8 (2.7 % excess) at the point where the original constructor finishes (average 2365.7 s). These results are superseded by the multilevel approach, which finds solutions of quality 25 222.0 (excess 0.3 %) for the above example.

- For medium-sized instances (20.50.*, $\text{atlanta}^{\blacktriangledown 20}$, janos-us-$\text{ca}^{\blacktriangledown 200}$, zib54) which can be solved to good suboptimal solutions

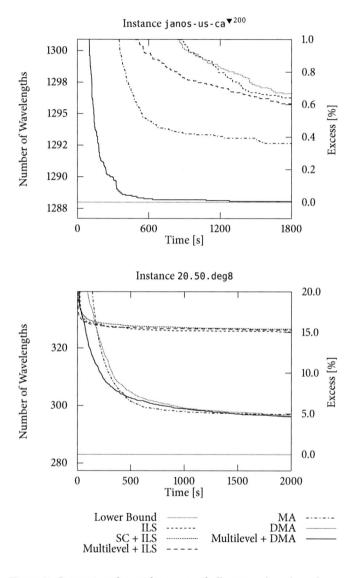

Figure 41: Comparing the performance of all major algorithms for two medium-sized problem instances.

even without multilevel approaches, both SC-ILS and ML-ILS find results comparable or slightly better than the 'pure' ILS. This effect is due to the time saved during construction, which allows more time to be spent on optimization. For instance 20.50.75, for example, the solutions are 200.9, 200.4, 200.9 (excess either 6.6 %, 6.6 %, or 6.9 %) for ILS, SC-ILS, and ML-ILS, respectively when reaching the time limit ($t_{max}$).

- When comparing convergence times (column '$t_{conv}$') between ILS, SC-ILS, and ML-ILS, it can be observed that ML-ILS converges fastest in all but one cases. ML-ILS's solution quality is still comparable to the other two algorithms' solutions. For 20.50.deg8, for example, when ILS (62.7 s), SC-ILS (60.6 s), and ML-ILS (12.2 s) terminate, their average solution quality is 331.2 (17.0 %), 332.8 (17.6 %), and 332.1 (17.4 %), respectively.

The second group of experiments combines all the RWA algorithms described before into a multilevel distributed MA (ML-DMA). The experimental results for the ML-DMA are as follows:

- The ML-DMA outperforms ILS, SC-ILS, and ML-ILS in comparable experiments. For instance 20.50.75, for example, the DMA finds optimal solutions (cost 188.0).

- For large instances, convergence can only be observed for a few repetitions in any setup, as the time limits are too short to trigger this termination criterion. The soft termination criterion is only triggered if no improvement was found in generation $k$ for the last $k/2$ generations. For large instances, even relatively small improvements may decrease the wavelength usage of a solution by several wavelengths. For instance atlanta, for example, the final solution for setups with ML-DMA requires 25 205 wavelengths, but even with an excess of only 0.21 %, this gap spans 38 wavelengths. To find an improvement of only one wavelength just before reaching the time limit would require twice the time limit to trigger the convergence criterion and produce an improvement of only 0.004 %.

- As shown above, constructing solutions takes considerable time and both SC-ILS and ML-ILS can find better solutions before reaching the point in time where the ILS finishes building its initial solution. This trend is even stronger when using ML-DMA, which finds even better solutions when reaching this point in time. For instance tal$^{\blacktriangledown 100}$, for example, ILS, SC-ILS, and ML-ILS find solutions with wavelength usage of 7645.8 (excess 26.5 %), 6132.0 (2.8 %), and 6087, 3 (2.0 %), respectively, at time $t_{init}$ = 1020.6. The multilevel distributed MA finds solutions with average wavelength usage of 5996.9 (0.5 % excess).

- Similar results can be observed when reaching the time limit $t_{max}$ = 3600. Here, the wavelength usages are 6097.6 (2.2 %), 6050.0 (1.4 %), 6065.8 (1.7 %), and finally 5983.7 (0.3 %), respectively, for the above algorithms. Although this problem instance is an example where the ML-ILS results in final solutions that are slightly worse than the SC-ILS, for all other large instances, ML-ILS performs better than SC-ILS.

- Regarding the solutions found, the ML-DMA finds the best solutions for each large instance, thus setting the best-known solutions for the experimental evaluation.

The results discussed here and in Sec. 4.6 are summarized in the plots in Fig. 41 and 42. ML-DMA outperforms both DMA and ML for all large instances (Fig. 42) and for janos-us-ca$^{\blacktriangledown 200}$ (Fig. ??). For instance 20.50.deg8 (Fig. ??), all recombination setups (MA, DMA, ML-DMA) find solutions that are on average 5 % above the lower bound, whereas all variants with ILS converge at solutions with an excess of about 15 %. Figures ?? and ?? contain the same setups as Tab. 31 and 32 showing the superiority of the ML-DMA compared to setups without recombination and distribution. There are no setups with ILS only in Fig. 32 as no valid solutions were constructed within the given time limit.

In summary, the ML-DMA is the best RWA solver presented in this thesis. For small instances, it performs as well as the ILS; most medium-sized instances are solved to better solutions than using either ILS or DMA, and for large instances, ML-DMA outperforms ML-ILS.

## 4.8 ANALYZING THE SEARCH SPACE

In this section, the properties of instances solved to optimality by the algorithms presented here are analyzed. Both in cases where the RWA is either divided into two independent subproblems or solved as an integral problem, finding 'good' paths is a major issue. As discussed in

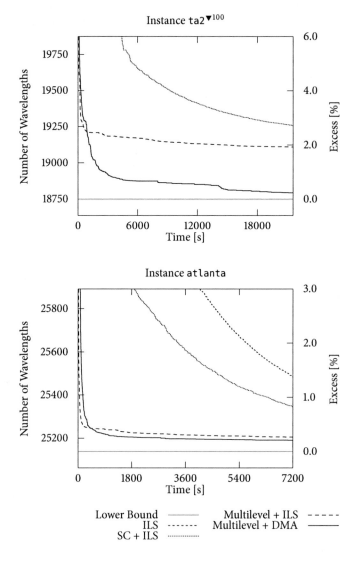

Figure 42: Comparing the performance of various algorithms for two large
problem instances.

| Instance | Type | $t_{\text{init}}$ | $W_{t_{\text{init}}}$ | $t_{\text{conv}}$ | $W_{t_{\text{conv}}}$ | $W_{t_{\text{max}}}$ | $W_{\text{min}}$ |
|---|---|---|---|---|---|---|---|
| 20.50.75 | ILS | 15.0 | 267.3 / 42.18 | 127.3 (15) | 205.9 / 9.52 | 200.9 / 6.86 | 200 / 6.38 |
| | SC-ILS | | 210.1 / 11.76 | 60.8 (15) | 206.9 / 10.05 | 200.4 / 6.60 | 198 / 5.32 |
| | ML-ILS | | 207.2 / 10.21 | 9.8 (15) | 209.0 / 11.17 | 200.9 / 6.86 | 200 / 6.38 |
| | ML-DMA | | 213.9 / 13.78 | 1619.1 (15) | 188.1 / 0.05 | 188.0 / 0.00 | 188 / 0.00 |
| 20.50.deg4 | ILS | 21.3 | 570.2 / 31.99 | 91.9 (15) | 477.3 / 10.49 | 471.1 / 9.05 | 469 / 8.56 |
| | SC-ILS | | 480.3 / 11.18 | 172.1 (15) | 477.1 / 10.44 | 471.2 / 9.07 | 469 / 8.56 |
| | ML-ILS | | 476.1 / 10.21 | 13.4 (15) | 477.7 / 10.58 | 470.9 / 9.00 | 469 / 8.56 |
| | ML-DMA | | 482.2 / 11.62 | – (0) | – | 442.1 / 2.34 | 441 / 2.08 |

[†] Best known solution where no LB known (cf Tab. 20).

Table 31: Results for the scaling constructor and multilevel approach in comparison with the original ILS for instances 20.50.75 and 20.50.deg4. Column '$t_{\text{init}}$' denotes the average time required for the original ILS to construct an initial solution; '$W_{t_{\text{init}}}$' is the average solution quality at this point in time. Columns '$t_{\text{conv}}$' and '$W_{t_{\text{conv}}}$' describe the time of convergence and the number of wavelengths at this point in time, respectively. Column '$W_{t_{\text{max}}}$' holds the solution quality when reaching the time limit. Small values denote the excess. See also Tables 32–36.

| Instance | Type | $t_{init}$ | $W_{init}$ | $t_{conv}$ | $W_{conv}$ | $W_{max}$ | $W_{min}$ |
|---|---|---|---|---|---|---|---|
| 20.50.deg8 | ILS | 19.1 | 393.4 | 62.7 | 331.2 | 325.7 | 324 |
| | | | 39.01 | (15) | 17.03 | 15.09 | 14.49 |
| | SC-ILS | | 334.5 | 60.6 | 332.8 | 326.6 | 324 |
| | | | 18.20 | (15) | 17.60 | 15.41 | 14.49 |
| | ML-ILS | | 331.2 | 12.2 | 332.1 | 326.2 | 325 |
| | | | 17.03 | (15) | 17.35 | 15.27 | 14.84 |
| | ML-DMA | | 336.1 | — | — | 296.1 | 295 |
| | | | 18.76 | (0) | — | 4.63 | 4.24 |
| atlanta▼20 | ILS | 6.0 | 1465.1 | 62.7 | 1258.0 | 1256.0 | 1256 |
| | | | 16.65 | (3) | 0.16 | 0.00 | 0.00 |
| | SC-ILS | | — | 74.7 | 1259.0 | 1256.0 | 1256 |
| | | | | (3) | 0.24 | 0.00 | 0.00 |
| | ML-ILS | | — | 64.7 | 1258.0 | 1256.0 | 1256 |
| | | | | (3) | 0.16 | 0.00 | 0.00 |
| | ML-DMA | | —— | 258.0 | 1256.0 | 1256.0 | 1256 |
| | | | | (11) | 0.00 | 0.00 | 0.00 |

[†] Best known solution where no LB known (cf Tab. 20).

Table 32: Results for the scaling constructor and multilevel approach in comparison with the original ILS for instances 20.50.deg8 and atlanta▼20. Column '$t_{init}$' denotes the average time required for the original ILS to construct an initial solution; '$W_{init}$' is the average solution quality at this point in time. Columns '$t_{conv}$' and '$W_{conv}$' describe the time of convergence and the number of wavelengths at this point in time, respectively. Column '$W_{max}$' holds the solution quality when reaching the time limit. Small values denote the excess. See also Tabs. 31, 33–36.

4.8 Analyzing the Search Space 171

| Instance | Type | $t_{\text{init}}$ | $W_{t_{\text{init}}}$ | $t_{\text{conv}}$ | $W_{t_{\text{conv}}}$ | $W_{t_{\text{max}}}$ | $W_{\text{min}}$ |
|---|---|---|---|---|---|---|---|
| j-us-ca▼200 | ILS | 23.3 | 1772.5 <br> 37.62 | 396.7 <br> (11) | 1313.1 <br> 1.95 | 1296.3 <br> 0.64 | 1291 <br> 0.23 |
| | SC-ILS | | 1344.1 <br> 4.36 | 379.3 <br> (9) | 1319.3 <br> 2.43 | 1304.4 <br> 1.27 | 1298 <br> 0.78 |
| | ML-ILS | | 1326.5 <br> 2.99 | 257.6 <br> (15) | 1307.7 <br> 1.53 | 1295.8 <br> 0.61 | 1293 <br> 0.39 |
| | ML-DMA | | 1401.9 <br> 8.84 | 970.9 <br> (14) | 1288.2 <br> 0.02 | 1288.1 <br> 0.01 | 1288 <br> 0.00 |
| zib54 | ILS | 25.5 | 894.0 <br> 26.81 | 197.5 <br> (15) | 712.7 <br> 1.09 | 707.9 <br> 0.41 | 707 <br> 0.28 |
| | SC-ILS | | 718.3 <br> 1.89 | 198.5 <br> (15) | 710.5 <br> 0.78 | 706.7 <br> 0.24 | 705 <br> 0.00 |
| | ML-ILS | | 715.2 <br> 1.45 | 67.9 <br> (15) | 713.0 <br> 1.13 | 707.7 <br> 0.38 | 707 <br> 0.28 |
| | ML-DMA | | 820.5 <br> 16.38 | 991.0 <br> (12) | 705.8 <br> 0.11 | 705.7 <br> 0.10 | 705 <br> 0.00 |

† Best known solution where no LB known (cf Tab. 20).

Table 33: Results for the scaling constructor and multilevel approach in comparison with the original ILS for instances j anos-us-ca ▼200 and zib54. Column '$t_{\text{init}}$' denotes the average time required for the original ILS to construct an initial solution; '$W_{t_{\text{init}}}$' is the average solution quality at this point in time. Columns '$t_{\text{conv}}$' and '$W_{t_{\text{conv}}}$' describe the time of convergence and the number of wavelengths at this point in time, respectively. Column '$W_{t_{\text{max}}}$' holds the solution quality when reaching the time limit. Small values denote the excess. See also Tables 31–32, 34–36.

| Instance | Type | $t_{init}$ | $W_{init}$ | $t_{conv}$ | $W_{conv}$ | $W_{t_{max}}$ | $W_{min}$ |
|---|---|---|---|---|---|---|---|
| atlanta | ILS | 2365.7 | 29317.3 / 16.63 | – (0) | – | 25482.1 / 1.37 | 25393 / 1.01 |
| | SC-ILS | | 25805.8 / 2.66 | – (0) | – | 25346.6 / 0.83 | 25304 / 0.66 |
| | ML-ILS | | 25222.0 / 0.33 | 4605.1 (3) | 25199.0 / 0.24 | 25205.0 / 0.27 | 25167 / 0.12 |
| | ML-DMA | | 25203.2 / 0.26 | – (0) | – | 25190.7 / 0.21 | 25138 / 0.00 |
| france | ILS | 1426.2 | 11184.9 / 5.80 | – (0) | – | 10623.2 / 0.21 | 10620 / 0.45 |
| | SC-ILS | | 10663.5 / 0.87 | – (0) | – | 10617.0 / 0.43 | 10610 / 0.36 |
| | ML-ILS | | 10636.6 / 0.61 | – | – | 10615.1 / 0.41 | 10610 / 0.36 |
| | ML-DMA | | 10597.8 / 0.24 | 6919.1 (1) | 10574.0 / 0.02 | 10573.3 / 0.01 | 10572 / 0.00 |

† Best known solution where no LB known (cf. Tab. 20).

Table 34: Results for the scaling constructor and multilevel approach in comparison with the original ILS for instances atlanta and france. Column '$t_{init}$' denotes the average time required for the original ILS to construct an initial solution; '$W_{init}$' is the average solution quality at this point in time. Columns '$t_{conv}$' and '$W_{conv}$' describe the time of convergence and the number of wavelengths at this point in time, respectively. Column '$W_{t_{max}}$' holds the solution quality when reaching the time limit. Small values denote the excess. See also Tables 31–33, 35–36.

| Instance | Type | $t_{init}$ | $W_{t_{init}}$ | $t_{conv}$ | $W_{t_{conv}}$ | $W_{t_{max}}$ | $W_{min}$ |
|---|---|---|---|---|---|---|---|
| j-us-ca▼[10] | ILS | 9473.5 | 35693.5 | – | – | 26485.6 | 26414 |
| | | | 38.62 | (0) | | 2.86 | 2.58 |
| | SC-ILS | | 26673.7 | – | – | 26519.8 | 26480 |
| | | | 3.59 | (0) | | 2.99 | 2.83 |
| | ML-ILS | | 26270.8 | 15936.3 | 26257.2 | 26257.4 | 26181 |
| | | | 2.02 | (10) | 1.97 | 1.97 | 1.67 |
| | ML-DMA | | 25776.3 | – | – | 25757.0 | 25750 |
| | | | 0.10 | (0) | | 0.03 | 0.00 |
| nobel-us▲[50] | ILS | 7228.2 | 45516.9 | – | – | 35799.0 | 35270 |
| | | | 35.55 | (0) | | 6.61 | 5.03 |
| | SC-ILS | | 36219.3 | – | – | 35125.1 | 34993 |
| | | | 7.86 | (0) | | 4.60 | 4.21 |
| | ML-ILS | | 34929.5 | 14840.4 | 34916.6 | 34924.9 | 34680 |
| | | | 4.02 | (11) | 3.98 | 4.01 | 3.28 |
| | ML-DMA | | 33840.1 | – | – | 33810.0 | 33580 |
| | | | 0.77 | (0) | | 0.68 | 0.00 |

† Best known solution where no LB known (cf Tab. 20).

Table 35: Results for the scaling constructor and multilevel approach in comparison with the original ILS for instances janos-us-ca▼[10] and nobel-us▲[50]. Column '$t_{init}$' denotes the average time required for the original ILS to construct an initial solution; '$W_{t_{init}}$' is the average solution quality at this point in time. Columns '$t_{conv}$' and '$W_{t_{conv}}$' describe the time of convergence and the number of wavelengths at this point in time, respectively. Column '$W_{t_{max}}$' holds the solution quality when reaching the time limit. Small values denote the excess. See also Tables 31–34, 36.

| Instance | Type | $t_{init}$ | $W_{init}$ | $t_{conv}$ | $W_{conv}$ | $W_{max}$ | $W_{min}$ |
|---|---|---|---|---|---|---|---|
| ta1▼100 | ILS | 1020.6 | 7545.8 26.46 | – (0) | – | 6097.6 2.19 | 6062 1.59 |
| | SC-ILS | | 6132.0 2.77 | – (0) | – | 6050.0 1.39 | 6017 0.84 |
| | ML-ILS | | 6087.3 2.02 | 1618.0 (2) | 6060.5 1.57 | 6065.8 1.66 | 6040 1.22 |
| | ML-DMA | | 5996.9 0.50 | – (0) | – | 5983.7 0.28 | 5967 0.00 |
| ta2▼100 | ILS | – | – | – (0) | – | – | – |
| | SC-ILS | | – | – (0) | – | 19256.5 2.71 | 19214 2.48 |
| | ML-ILS | | – | – (0) | – | 19110.1 1.93 | 19054 1.63 |
| | ML-DMA | | –– | – (0) | – | 18793.1 0.24 | 18749 0.00 |

† Best known solution where no LB known (cf Tab. 20).

Table 36: Results for the scaling constructor and multilevel approach in comparison with the original ILS for instances ta1▼100 and ta2▼100. Column '$t_{init}$' denotes the average time required for the original ILS to construct an initial solution; '$W_{init}$' is the average solution quality at this point in time. Columns '$t_{conv}$' and '$W_{conv}$' describe the time of convergence and the number of wavelengths at this point in time, respectively. Column '$W_{max}$' holds the solution quality when reaching the time limit. Small values denote the excess. See also Tables 31–35.

| | Paths [%] | | | | | | |
|---|---|---|---|---|---|---|---|
| Hop Count Excess | 0 | 1 | 2 | 3 | 4 | 5 | ≥6 |
| janos-us-ca▼[200] | 76.3 | 9.9 | 6.6 | 4.3 | 1.0 | 1.3 | 0.7 |
| atlanta▼[20] | 72.9 | 12.3 | 7.4 | 3.4 | 0.9 | 1.4 | 1.6 |
| 20.50.75 | 77.1 | 19.9 | 2.0 | 0.7 | 0.2 | >0.0 | >0.0 |

Table 37: Distribution of hop count excess above shortest paths length in optimal solutions for instances janos-us-ca▼[200] (541 optimal solutions), atlanta▼[20] (3086 solutions), and 20.50.75 (756 solutions).

the related work section (Sec. 4.1), different strategies to determine paths exist, where the most popular choice is to use some kind of shortest path algorithm. Using shortest paths in a pure greedy fashion, however, may lead to worse solutions, as longer paths are necessary to reduce the number of wavelengths used. As shown in Tab. 37, for janos-us-ca▼[200] about a quarter of all paths in an optimal solution are at least one hop longer than the shortest paths between the paths' end nodes. Thus, as choosing the 'right' paths is important, the analysis is focused on the set of paths in different types of solutions, including the path set found when determining the lower bound for each instance. Wavelengths assigned to paths, however, are not considered.

In this analysis, two types of path sets are compared with path sets found in optimal solutions:

- 250 random solutions $s_{rand}$ for each problem instance listed in Tables 38–39 were created. To create unbiased but not degenerated solutions, the general construction approach is modified in the following aspects:

  1. Instead of determining the shortest path between two nodes, a depth first search is performed (with backtracking), where ties are broken randomly.

  2. Assuming each request has demand = 1 and multiple requests between the same node pair are allowed, a path is constructed independent of the link usage and wavelength availability for each request. The resulting set of paths is processed in random order as follows: all allocated wavelengths are checked in random order and the path is routed in the first feasible wavelength; if the path can not

be routed in any wavelength, a new wavelength is allocated and the path is inserted in this wavelength.

- The random solutions were optimized by applying *local search* (Sec. 2.1.2) until a local optimum was reached.

Using the minimization of wavelength usage as the objective function, a large number of different optimal solutions exist. For example, for instance germany50, the lower bound is determined by the requests routed to one node over its two adjacent links; the remaining requests are basically free in their choice of path and wavelength. Thus, the set $P$ of paths common to all optimal solutions found in the experiments is determined for each problem instance and used as a reference for the comparison. The number of optimal solutions evaluated per instance depended on the experiments in which the instance was used and the 'success' of each algorithm applied to this instance (note that in a population-based approach, every individual representing an optimal solution is considered). Here, the number of optima per instance ranged between 76 (10.50.deg8, all unique regarding used paths) and 3168 (10.50.deg4, 3079 unique solutions); the average and median were 1157.6 and 992.5, respectively. The set of common paths is later used in a fitness distance analysis when using the number of common paths included in a given solution as a distance measure. It should be noted that non-optimal solutions may contain all paths of the common paths set, too.

When analyzing the size of the set of common paths for each instance, the fraction of common paths compared to the demand is smaller for pathological instances than for more challenging instances. As mentioned above, for germany50, many optimal solutions exist and thus only 20.0 % of all paths are common in all optima. For harder instances such as nobel-us, 75.5 % of a solution's paths are already shared among all the optimal solutions found. Interestingly, the set of common paths is quite large considering that up to 3079 unique solutions have been found.

For both the random instances and the local optima, the following values were determined: (a) average distances between any two solutions, (b) average distance between a solution and the paths common to all known optima, and (c) the fitness distance correlation (FDC). Additionally, the average distance between each random solution and the local optimum derived from this solution was evaluated.

| Instance | $D$ | $|P|$ | $d_{Rnd,LS}$ | Random | | | Local | | |
|---|---|---|---|---|---|---|---|---|---|
| | | | | $\overline{d}_{Rnd}$ | $d_{Rnd,opt}$ | $\rho$ | $\overline{d}_{LS}$ | $d_{LS,opt}$ | $\rho$ |
| 10.50.75 | 3410 | 2091 | 1353.3 | 2515.9 | 1461.3 | 0.426 | 1872.6 | 794.1 | 0.701 |
| | | 61.3 | 39.7 | 26.2 | 30.1 | | 45.1 | 62.0 | |
| 10.50.deg4 | 3410 | 1302 | 1255.4 | 2344.6 | 719.5 | 0.431 | 1790.4 | 242.8 | 0.307 |
| | | 38.2 | 36.8 | 31.2 | 44.7 | | 47.5 | 81.4 | |
| 10.50.deg8 | 3410 | 2442 | 1427.8 | 2633.3 | 1860.6 | 0.466 | 1996.0 | 1228.2 | 0.649 |
| | | 71.6 | 41.9 | 22.8 | 23.8 | | 41.5 | 49.7 | |
| 15.50.deg8 | 9500 | 6060 | 5478.5 | 8332.0 | 5034.3 | 0.341 | 6064.8 | 2920.8 | 0.549 |
| | | 63.8 | 57.7 | 12.3 | 16.9 | | 36.2 | 51.8 | |
| atlanta▼20 | 6840 | 4423 | 2304.0 | 1861.1 | 2804.0 | 0.457 | 1650.0 | 1608.6 | −0.088 |
| | | 64.7 | 33.7 | 72.8 | 36.6 | | 75.9 | 63.6 | |
| france▼10 | 10008 | 3549 | 4843.1 | 6767.0 | 2452.0 | 0.161 | 5230.5 | 963.0 | 0.416 |
| | | 35.5 | 48.4 | 32.4 | 30.9 | | 47.7 | 72.9 | |
| germany50 | 2365 | 472 | 1641.2 | 2075.4 | 250.8 | 0.302 | 1364.4 | 42.5 | 0.287 |
| | | 20.0 | 69.4 | 12.2 | 46.9 | | 42.3 | 91.0 | |
| j-us-ca▼200 | 10173 | 5986 | 54489.1 | 6840.8 | 3996.1 | 0.421 | 4419.7 | 1633.6 | −0.024 |
| | | 58.8 | 54.0 | 32.8 | 33.2 | | 56.6 | 72.7 | |

Table 38: Properties of random solutions $s_{rand}$ and associated local optima (part 1). Column '$|P|$' denotes the size of the set of common paths (small number the percentage on the total number of paths). Both '$\overline{d}_{Rnd}$' and '$\overline{d}_{LS}$' describe the average distance between two solutions of each group (small numbers the fraction on the total number of paths). '$d_{Rnd,opt}$' and '$d_{LS,opt}$' denote the distance between solutions of each group to the set of paths common to all known optima (small numbers the relative distance in percent, where 0 means no common path and 100 means that the path set is included completely in such a solution). Columns '$\rho$' denote the fitness distance correlation value, column '$d_{Rnd,LS}$' the average distance between a random solution and its corresponding local optimum (small number the fraction of paths in common).

| Instance | D | |P| | Random | | | | Local | | |
|---|---|---|---|---|---|---|---|---|---|
| | | | $d_{Rnd,LS}$ | $\bar{d}_{Rnd}$ | $d_{Rnd,opt}$ | $\rho$ | $\bar{d}_{LS}$ | $d_{LS,opt}$ | $\rho$ |
| newyork | 1774 | 368 | 1088.0 | 1578.1 | 227.0 | 0.393 | 1147.4 | 30.0 | 0.214 |
| | | 20.7 | 61.3 | 11.0 | 38.3 | | 35.3 | 91.8 | |
| nobel-eu | 1898 | 321 | 995.3 | 1555.2 | 157.5 | 0.280 | 1022.7 | 12.7 | 0.084 |
| | | 16.9 | 52.4 | 18.1 | 50.9 | | 46.1 | 96.0 | |
| n-germany | 660 | 144 | 297.6 | 465.5 | 70.8 | 0.348 | 347.1 | 13.3 | 0.204 |
| | | 21.8 | 45.1 | 29.5 | 50.8 | | 47.4 | 90.8 | |
| nobel-us | 5420 | 4094 | 1909.9 | 2067.5 | 2775.7 | 0.550 | 1531.0 | 1266.4 | 0.568 |
| | | 75.5 | 35.2 | 61.9 | 32.2 | | 71.8 | 69.1 | |
| norway | 5348 | 956 | 3265.7 | 4671.4 | 577.2 | 0.313 | 3286.7 | 75.7 | 0.257 |
| | | 17.9 | 61.1 | 12.7 | 39.6 | | 38.5 | 92.1 | |
| pdh | 4621 | 3172 | 1727.6 | 2816.1 | 2186.2 | 0.451 | 1987.4 | 1194.3 | 0.708 |
| | | 68.6 | 37.4 | 39.1 | 31.1 | | 57.0 | 62.3 | |
| polska | 9943 | 6850 | 3178.8 | 2257.6 | 4453.0 | 0.585 | 1930.6 | 1806.7 | 0.556 |
| | | 68.9 | 32.0 | 77.3 | 35.0 | | 80.6 | 73.6 | |
| zib54 | 12230 | 7500 | 6737.4 | 7357.3 | 4846.9 | 0.400 | 4185.6 | 2314.2 | 0.537 |
| | | 61.3 | 55.1 | 39.8 | 35.4 | | 65.8 | 69.1 | |

Table 39: Properties of random solutions $s_{rand}$ and associated local optima (part 2). Column '$|P|$' denotes the size of the set of common paths (small number the percentage on the total number of paths). Both '$\bar{d}_{Rnd}$' and '$\bar{d}_{LS}$' describe the average distance between two solutions of each group (small numbers the fraction on the total number of paths). '$d_{Rnd,opt}$' and '$d_{LS,opt}$' denote the distance between solutions of each group to the set of paths common to all known optima (small numbers the relative distance between solutions of each group to the set of paths common to all known optima (small numbers the fraction of paths in such a solution). Columns '$\rho$' denote the fitness distance correlation value, column '$d_{Rnd,LS}$' the average distance between a random solution in percent, where 0 means no common path and 100 means that the path set is included completely in such a solution). and its corresponding local optimum (small number the fraction of paths in common).

The average distance among the random solutions ($\overline{d}_{Rnd}$) depends on the instance's average node degree. For high degree instances (*.50-.deg8, newyork with degree 6.1), the distance between random solutions is considerably larger (> 60 % paths different) than instances with lower node degrees, such as atlanta▼[20] (degree 2.9) or polska (degree 3.0), where less than 30 % of all paths are different. This effect is simply due to the fact that fewer different paths can be exploited by the randomized DFS in graphs with small node degrees. The distance between local optima, however, is considerably smaller and the node degree has less influence.

Regarding the distance between random solutions and the corresponding instance's common paths set, random solutions contain at most half of the paths from the set of common paths (maximum is 50.9 % with nobel-eu); other instances contain down to 16.9 % of the paths (15.50.deg8). Locally optimal solutions share a larger portion of paths with the set of common paths: even in the worst cases (10.50-.deg8 and 15.50.deg8) about half of the optimal solution's common paths are included in the local optima. In some cases, more than 90 % of those paths are included (e. g. norway). Again, this effect can be interpreted as the solutions' convergence towards the set of common paths.

The fitness distance correlation (FDC) analysis [116] is a common approach to describe the difficulty of the search space for heuristic algorithms. Given a set of solutions $S$, for each solution $s \in S$ the fitness $f_s$ and distance $d_s$ is determined. Furthermore, both average values $\overline{d}$ and $\overline{f}$ and standard deviations $\sigma_d$ and $\sigma_f$ are determined for all $\{d_s : s \in S\}$ and $\{f_s : s \in S\}$, respectively. The covariance on fitness and distance and the correlation coefficient $\rho$ are determined as follows:

$$C_{FD} = \frac{1}{n} \sum_{s \in S} \left(f_s - \overline{f}\right) \cdot \left(d_s - \overline{d}\right) \qquad \rho = \frac{C_{FD}}{\sigma_f \cdot \sigma_d} \qquad (4.11)$$

As the static RWA is a minimization problem by the definition used here, $\rho \to 1$ is preferred as this implies that solutions that have better objective values have more paths in common with optimal solutions, too. If $\rho \to -1$, solutions have better objective values with less common paths and for $\rho \approx 0$ no correlation between fitness and distance is observed. For randomly generated solutions in all instances, a positive $\rho$ can be observed for the FDC value, where the two smallest values 0.161 (france▼[10]) and 0.280 (nobel-eu) refer to instances that are easy to solve by the algorithms presented here. For all other problem instances,

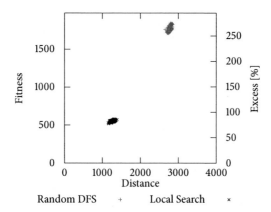

Figure 43: Fitness distance correlation plot for instance nobel-us. The x-axis'
range (distance) matches the number of paths common to all known
optima.

it holds that $\rho > 0.3$, which suggests that the static RWA is accessible
for heuristic search algorithms. For local optima, these correlation coefficients either decrease or increase compared to their random solution
counterpart and even become negative for instances atlanta▼20 and
janos-us-ca▼200. Therefore, no conclusions can be drawn from the
FDC values.

To visualize the correlation between fitness and distance, plots for all
instances from Tables 38–39 have been created, but all show the same
behavior as instance nobel-us depicted in Fig. 43. Interestingly, both
random solutions and the derived local optima form dense clusters. In
each case, local optima are closer to the plot's origin (global optima) for
both fitness and distance.

In summary, it can be concluded that optimal solutions for the RWA
share a considerable amount of common paths. Starting from the random solution, the fraction of paths common to all optima included in a
solution increases when applying the local search, thus the LS performs
a directed walk in the search space towards (near-)optimal solutions.

4.9 SUMMARY

The Routing and Wavelength Assignment problem (RWA) is relevant for long range telecommunication, for example, where traffic patterns have to be assigned to available resources given by optical networks. In this chapter the static variant of the RWA was addressed.

- Existing algorithmic approaches were summarized, both historic and state of the art.

- Different ideas for lower bounds were presented and a lower bound formulation based on the multi-commodity flow problem was proposed. In the benchmark instance set, lower bounds are know for 20 out of 26 instances. For 16 out of those 20 instances the algorithms presented find optimal solutions; for the remaining 4 instances, the largest gap between lower bound and best found solution is 3.9 %. For the largest 6 instances, no lower bounds are available due to excessive computation time requirements.

- No public benchmark library for the RWA existed previously and random instances were generated instead. It has been observed that the random instances generated by the Erdős-Rényi random graph model are often pathological due to the high probability of having a low connectivity. Therefore, as the SND problem is related to the RWA benchmark, instances for the RWA were derived from publicly available SND problem instances.

- Moving on from construction heuristics in the literature, construction heuristics were presented which are capable of dealing with 'evil' requests, where evil requests are defined as requests depending on highly overloaded edges (depending both on network and request matrix).

- As a foundation for the algorithms presented in this thesis, a local search was developed and integrated into an iterated environment. Starting from feasible initial solutions, this iterated local search is able to find (near-)optimal results for many small and medium-sized problem instances.

- By expanding the ILS with the features of population and recombination, a memetic algorithm was developed. Using an island approach in an epidemic network, the MA was enhanced to become a distributed MA. Both the non-distributed and the distributed MA are able to improve the ILS's results significantly. Here, the distributed version performs more robustly in terms of perameter choice.

- A multilevel approach was proposed to address large problem instances. It can either be integrated into the ILS or used as a simple but very fast construction heuristic.

- Finally, both the distributed MA and the multilevel approach were combined, resulting in a multilevel distributed memetic algorithm (ML-DMA) capable both of handling large instances and finding optimal solutions for small and medium-sized instances. Given that a wide range of techniques such as problem-specific algorithms (local search, mutation, recombination), multilevel scaling, and distributed computation using epidemic algorithms was used, the ML-DMA can be considered the most sophisticated heuristic algorithm for the static RWA problem.

- A search space analysis focusing on paths in different types of solutions was conducted. Results suggest that optimal solutions share a large proportion of paths. Furthermore, about one quarter of all the paths in an optimal solution are at least one hop longer than the shortest paths between the same endpoints.

Despite a focus on the static RWA, the research presented in this thesis provides a basis for dynamic RWA algorithms. The dimensioning of the network in dynamic setups can be determined by solving a static RWA with an estimated request matrix. In online algorithms, ad-hoc decisions on whether and how to route incoming requests have to be made, based on the current state and without knowledge of the future. Furthermore, requests can not be rerouted after being set once. Using the solution of the static RWA for the network dimensioning problem above, a set of predetermined path and wavelength assignment is obtained for each request. Based on this predetermined set, an online decision algorithm either assigns the incoming requests to one of these path and wavelength assignments or rejects the incoming request.

This thesis focused on the static RWA with undirected edges and requests. Other variants of the RWA consider directed edges and requests that influence the algorithms' core components, such as path finding in problem instances and internal representation. High-level concepts such as local search, mutation, or even the multilevel approach, however, are unaffected by this change.

The ML-DMA is one of the most powerful tools for static RWA computation. Benchmark instances several magnitudes larger than previously considered are solved by this algorithm, still finding (near-)optimal solutions. This thesis is thus an important contribution to current research on the RWA.

# 5

## OPTIMUM COMMUNICATION SPANNING TREE PROBLEM

The *Optimum Communication Spanning Tree* problem (OCST) describes a cost minimizing spanning tree, where the cost depends on the communication volume between each pair of nodes routed over the tree. The problem is also known as the *Optimal Communication Spanning Tree* problem or *Minimum Communication Spanning Tree* problem (MCST).

The OCST is defined as follows: given is an undirected graph $G = (V, E, d, r)$ with a distance function $d$ and a requirement function $r$. The *distance function* $d : E \rightarrow \mathbb{R}^+$ assigns a distance (or weight or length) $d(e)$ to each edge $e \in E$; the *requirement function* (or demand function) $r : V \times V \rightarrow \mathbb{R}^+$ assigns a communication volume to each node pair. The set of unique node pairs is defined as $n = |V|$, $m = |E|$, $Q = \{(i, j) \in V \times V : i \neq j\}$, and a tree $T = (V, E', d, r) \subseteq G$ to be an acyclic subgraph spanning all nodes holding $E' \subseteq E$ and $|E'| = n - 1$. The OCST's objective is to find a tree $T$ that minimizes the following cost function:

$$c(T) = \sum_{(i,j) \in Q} r_{i,j} \cdot c(p_{i,j}^T) \tag{5.1}$$

where $c(p_{i,j}^T)$ is the length of the unique path $p_{i,j}^T$ from node $i$ to node $j$ in $T$. It is defined $r_{i,i} = 0$ for all $i \in V$. In the common case, both $d$ and $r$ are symmetric, each value is an integer and the distances do not need to satisfy the triangle inequality. It is equivalent to represent $d$ and $r$ either as functions or matrices.

Computing the cost function requires time $\mathcal{O}(n^2)$. An equivalent formulation determines the 'flow' over each edge in a tree. The flow over an edge is defined as the sum of all requirements between node pairs where the nodes are located on different sides of the edge. The total cost is determined by the sum of each edge's flow multiplied by the edge's length.

An example solution for an OCST problem instance with 9 nodes is given in Fig. 44. Next to each edge, the distance between both adjacent nodes is printed in gray. To determine the path length between two nodes, the lengths of each edge on the unique path have to be added.

$$c(T) = r_{1,2} \cdot c(p_{1,2}^T) + \ldots$$
$$+ r_{8,9} \cdot c(p_{8,9}^T)$$
$$= 6 \cdot (211 + \ldots + 251) + \ldots$$
$$+ 53 \cdot (276 + \ldots + 239)$$
$$= 358\,131$$

Figure 44: Example for an OCST problem instance with 9 nodes.

In this chapter, a *memetic algorithm* (MA, see Sec. 2.1.5) is presented for the OCST. In the following sections, the MA's building blocks will be discussed in detail. Several construction heuristics known from literature are evaluated in their applicability for different types of problem instances (e. g. types of distance matrices). The local search, which is a significant improvement of an existing algorithm, is used to improve these initial solutions. Enhancing this algorithm to a population-based MA, recombination operators differing in complexity are introduced. Finally, a distributed variant of the MA is proposed that allows finding solutions for the OCST using multiple computing nodes in parallel.

## 5.1    LITERATURE

In this section, previous publications on the OCST are presented. The literature overview is divided into two parts. An overview of theoretical approaches, including approximation algorithms, is given initially, followed by a presentation of heuristic approaches, such as local search, evolutionary or genetic algorithms. Table 40 gives a short overview of the publications.

### 5.1.1    *Theoretical Works*

The Optimum Communication Spanning Tree problem was defined by HU [106]. The motivation for the problem is the objective to design a cost-effective communication network, where the nodes represent cities and the requirement matrix describes the number of telephone calls between two cities. The network's cost is thus defined by the length of the land lines and the communication volume routed over each line.

Whereas HU defines the OCST, his main contribution is focused on special cases of the OCST. In the first case, called *Optimum Requirement*

| Publication | Contribution |
|---|---|
| Theoretical Works | |
| Hu [106] (1974) | Problem definition, focusing on special cases, properties are analyzed |
| JOHNSON *et al.* [114] (1978) | Proof of NP-completeness |
| GAREY and JOHNSON [82] (1979) | Listed as problem ND7 |
| AHUJA and MURTY [4] (1987) | Lower bounds |
| AHUJA and MURTY [3] (1987) | Exact algorithm |
| PELEG and RESHEF [161, 162] (1998) | Deterministic polylog approximation algorithm |
| Practical Works | |
| AHUJA and MURTY [3] (1987) | Heuristic algorithm |
| PALMER and KERSHENBAUM [159, 158, 160] (1994/95) | Heuristic algorithm and GA |
| BERRY *et al.* [30] (1995) | GA and two benchmark instances (Berry6 and Berry35) |
| LI and BOUCHEBABA [126] (1999) | GA |
| ROTHLAUF *et al.* [174] (2003) | Analyzing solutions for an EA |
| ROTHLAUF and HEINZL [172] (2004) | EA |
| ROTHLAUF [171] (2006) | Benchmark instances |
| SHARMA (2006) | Local search algorithms |
| SOAK [182] (2006) | EA |

Table 40: Overview of literature on the OCST.

*Spanning Tree* (ORST), the distance matrix is constant, i. e. $d(i, j) = 1$ for all $(i, j) \in E$. The second case is called *Optimum Distance Spanning Tree* (a. k. a. *Minimum Routing Cost Spanning Tree*, MRCST) and defines $r_{i,j} = 1$ for all $(i, j) \in Q$.

A problem instance for the ORST can be solved to optimality by constructing a *cut-tree* in $\mathcal{O}(n^4)$ time. A cut-tree is a spanning tree with two special properties. Firstly, each tree edge has a special value corresponding to the size of a cut in the original graph. Removing a tree edge divides the tree into two components (node sets). The cut associated with a tree edge is the one that divides the graph according to these two components. Secondly, the maximum flow between any two nodes in the graph equals the least value of an edge in the unique path in the tree. The proof that a cut-tree is an optimal solutions is argued in three steps: (1) A spanning tree equals a unique set of $n - 1$ non-crossing cuts, (2) The capacity of each cut equals the communication volume routed on the corresponding tree edge, and (3) The sum of capacities in a cut-tree is minimal among all possible sets of $n - 1$ non-crossing cuts.

For the MRCST, it can be shown that, if all distances are equal, the optimal solution is a star where any node may be the root node. HU showed that a star is an optimal solution to this problem, even if the constraint of equality on distances is relaxed. Given any three edges in a graph ($|V| > 3$) forming a triangle where the tree edge lengths are $a$, $b$, and $c$ with $a \leq b \leq c$ and the following constraint holds, the solution of any MRCST problem on this graph is a star (root yet to be determined).

$$\frac{n - 2}{2n - 2} \geq \frac{c - a}{b} \tag{5.2}$$

This formulation is indeed a relaxation of the edge-lengths equality constraint, as the equation's right side would always be 0 in this case. The inequality in Eq. (5.2) is derived by determining the requirements on node distances so that a stepwise transformation of an arbitrary tree into a star does not increase the cost of the tree. If the node distances hold for a given graph, the optimal solution must be a star. If there were to be a non-star tree with less cost than any star, this tree could be transformed into a star, but then its cost would increase, contradicting the assumption. The root is determined by finding the minimum-cost star among all $|V|$ stars.

A proof for the NP-completeness of the OCST was provided by JOHNSON, LENSTRA, and RINNOOY KAN in [114]. The proof is shown in Sec. A.2.1. The idea is to reduce the *Exact 3-Cover* to the OCST (thus, the exact 3-cover problem is a special case of the OCST). To be exact, a special case of the decision variant of the OCST called *simple network design problem* (SNDP) is used. The proof gives an algorithm to construct a SNDP problem instance from an arbitrary exact 3-cover problem instance and shows that a solution for the SNDP instance is a solution for the exact 3-cover instance.

A simple lower bound for the OCST can be determined by lifting the tree constraint. In this case, communication requests are routed on the shortest path in $G$ between each two communication nodes. The lower bound is thus

$$\text{LB}_{\text{simple}} = \sum_{(i,j)\in Q} r_{i,j} \cdot c(p^G_{i,j}) \qquad (5.3)$$

where $p^G_{i,j}$ is the shortest path in $G$ between nodes $i$ and $j$.

More sophisticated lower bounds for the OCST can be determined by modifying existing algorithms for the *Network Design Problem* (NDP), for which several lower bound algorithms are known [103, 81, 4] as explained in Sec. A.2.1. The general approach here is to start from a connected graph and remove edges (although the graph has to stay connected). Depending on the edges to be removed, the cost of solutions increases as longer paths have to be used. The choice of the removed edges differs among lower bound algorithms.

*Exact Algorithm*

In [3], AHUJA and MURTY propose a branch and bound algorithm for the OCST. This algorithm finds exact solutions by recursively partitioning the solution space. The algorithm starts by initializing three disjunctive edge sets $I$, $U$, and $D$, for which it holds that $I \cup U \cup D = E$. Edge set $I$ contains those edges to be included in the resulting tree, $D$ contains edges that will not be included, and $U$ contains those edges for which no decision has yet been made. For a valid solution, $I$ contains exactly those edges that span the graph. The node set spanned by the edges in $I$ and $Q^I = \{(i,j) \in Q : i,j \in V^I\}$ is defined as $V^I$. Thus, the lower bound will restrict the search for paths to $I \cup \tilde{U}$, where $\tilde{U} = \{(i,j) \in U : i \notin V^I \vee j \notin V^I\}$ (edges in $U \setminus \tilde{U}$ would introduce a cycle). For simplicity, $\tilde{E} = I \cup \tilde{U}$ is used.

During the process of finding an optimal solution, the lower bound can be improved by using the unique path consisting of edges from $I$ for each node pair in $Q^I$ and the shortest path in $I \cup U$ for any other node pair in $Q$. The original lower bound function as stated in Eq. (5.3) is modified to the following definition:

$$\text{LB}_{Q^I} = \sum_{(i,j)\in Q^I} r_{i,j} \cdot c(p^I_{i,j}) + \sum_{(i,j)\in Q\setminus Q^I} r_{i,j}c(p^{\tilde{E}}_{i,j}) \tag{5.4}$$

When starting the branch and bound algorithm, all edges $E$ of the problem graph are assigned to $U$ and both $I$ and $D$ are empty. This initial configuration is put as the first element on the stack of subproblems. The upper bound used from pruning subproblems is initialized by a solution found by a heuristic algorithm (see Sec. 5.1.2).

As long as there are configurations on the stack, the top element is removed and used as the current subproblem. In the first step, the lower bound of this subproblem is determined and checked if it is above the best-known upper bound $Z^\star$. If the subproblem's lower bound is above the upper bound, this branch cannot contain an optimal solution and subsequently gets pruned.

Otherwise the subproblem is split into two new subproblems by selecting, and edge $e_s \in F$ where $F = \{(i,j) = e \in U : i \in V^I \wedge j \notin V^I\}$ is a set of undecided edges that allow $I$ to grow while not violating the tree constraint. Although any edge in $F$ is feasible, for best results

$$e_s = \arg\max_{(i,j)=e\in F} \sum_{(i,j)\in Q} r_{i,j}c(p^{\tilde{E}}_{i,j}) \tag{5.5}$$

is chosen. Two subproblems are created by removing edge $e_s$ from $U$ and adding to $I$ in one subproblem and adding it to $D$ in the other subproblem. Both subproblems are pushed on the stack.

The stack of subproblems is maintained so that the algorithm resembles a depth-first search of subproblems with edge inclusions first. Ahuja and Murty report that this approach improves the algorithm's performance on memory consumption and convergence.

### Approximation Algorithm

Peleg and Reshef present a deterministic polylog approximation algorithm [161, 162] for the OCST in complete graphs. Based on the close relation between the OCST and the *minimum average stretch spanning tree* (MAST), such an algorithm is derived with a ratio of $\mathcal{O}(\log^3 n)$ above a simple lower bound[1].

---

1 The abstract of [161] contains a misprint on the complexity, which is corrected in [162].

```
 1: function ExactOCST(G = (V, E), Q ⊂ V × V, Z*)
 2:     T* ← ∅
 3:     StackPush(∅, ∅, E)
 4:     while ¬StackEmpty do
 5:         (I, D, U) ← StackPop
 6:         Ẽ ← I ∪ {(i, j) ∈ U : i ∉ V^I ∨ j ∉ V^I}
 7:         if LowerBoundLP1(Ẽ) ≤ Z* then
 8:             if |I| = |V| − 1 ∧ c(I) < c(T*) then
 9:                 T* ← I
10:                 Z* ← c(T*)
11:             end if
12:             if U ≠ ∅ then
13:                 F = {(i, j) = e ∈ U : i_k ∈ V^I ∧ j_k ∉ V^I}
14:                 e_s = arg max_{e∈F} ∑_{(i,j)∈Q} r_{i,j} c(p^Ẽ_{i,j})
15:                 StackPush(I ∪ {e_s}, D, U ∖ {e_s})
16:                 StackPush(I, D ∪ {e_s}, U ∖ {e_s})
17:             end if
18:         end if
19:     end whilereturn T*
20: end function
```

Figure 45: Exact algorithm for the OCST.

The average stretch of a spanning tree within a multigraph is defined as follows: Given is a connected graph $G = (V, E, d, m)$ with nodes $V$, edges $E$, an edge weight function $d : E \to \mathbb{R}^+$ and an *edge multiplicity* function $m : E \to \mathbb{R}^+$. Let $\mathcal{M} = \sum_{e \in E} m(e)$. The *stretch* of a node pair $i, j \in V$ in a tree $T = (V, E')$ with $E' \subseteq E$ is defined as

$$\frac{c(p^T_{i,j})}{d_{i,j}} \tag{5.6}$$

and the *average stretch* of $T$ as

$$\bar{S}(T) = \frac{1}{\mathcal{M}} \sum_{(i,j)=e \in E} m(e) \cdot \frac{c(p^T_{i,j})}{d_{i,j}} \tag{5.7}$$

The objective of the MAST is to find a tree $T$ with minimum average stretch. Any instance of the OCST can be transformed into an MAST instance by keeping the graph $G$ and setting the multiplicity to $m(e) =$

$r_{i,j} \cdot c(p_{i,j}^G)$ for each edge $(i, j) = e \in E$ (see [170, p. 39]). Transforming a MAST problem instance into an OCST problem instance is similar, where the requirements are set to

$$r_{i,j} = \frac{m(e)}{c(p_{i,j}^G)} \tag{5.8}$$

for each edge $(i, j) = e \in E$.

Using the approximation algorithm below, it is possible to construct trees in polynomial time for any given OCST problem instance, where the solution's cost is $\mathcal{O}(\log^3 n)$ times the lower bound, as defined in Eq. (5.3). Such a tree is found by solving a MAST problem instance in which solution $T$ has a stretch of $\overline{S}(T) = \mathcal{O}(\log^3 n)$. This complexity is due to the fact that the constructive algorithm in [161] is designed for Euclidean graphs only. To handle non-Euclidean problem instances, the use of a polynomial time algorithm for embedding the non-Euclidean graph into an $\mathcal{O}(\log n)$-dimensional Euclidean space which introduces an $\mathcal{O}(\log n)$ distortion on the edge weights [130] is suggested. Finding an approximation for $d$-dimensional Euclidean networks is a generalization of the case for 2-dimensional Euclidean networks. This special case is solved by first showing that a separated partition (fulfilling some constraints) of an arbitrary graph $G$ allows recursive construction of a tree with an average stretch of $\mathcal{O}(\alpha \log n)$. Secondly, an algorithm constructs a tree with an average stretch of $\mathcal{O}(\log n)$, partitioning any 2-dimensional Euclidean graph, holding the partitioning constraints and granting $\alpha = \mathcal{O}(1)$.

Details on this algorithm are shown in Sec. A.2.3.

### 5.1.2    Practical Approaches

In this section, practical approaches to the OCST will be presented.

AHUJA and MURTY present both an exact and a heuristic algorithm in [3]. The heuristic algorithm consists of a construction phase and an improvement phase and is inspired by an algorithm presented in [35] for the OCST's special case PROCT (optimal product-requirement communication spanning tree problem). The heuristic algorithm's result is used as an upper bound for the branch and bound algorithm; lower bounds are determined as described by the same authors in [4]. These algorithms will be presented in detail, as they are the starting points for the algorithms presented in this thesis.

The *construction heuristic* (see Fig. 47) builds a tree by determining a seeding node and iteratively adding edges to the growing non-cyclic fragment. The algorithm is based on the idea that all requests are routed on the shortest path in $G$ initially. Now, when edges in $G$ are selected to be part of the growing fragment, all requests between nodes spanned by the fragment must be routed on the unique path in the fragment. Using the tree fragment for routing instead of shortest paths, increases the total routing cost. Thus edges appended to the fragment have to be chosen carefully. The algorithm terminates once the fragment has become a spanning tree.

The algorithm can be implemented as follows: during an initialization phase, all-pairs shortest paths in $G$ are determined and stored in the path set $p^G$. The fragment which will grow into the resulting tree is called $T$ and is initially empty and this contains no paths ($p^T$ is therefore empty, too). Nodes in $T$ are called $S \subseteq V$; the complementary set of nodes not in $T$ is designated as $\overline{S} = V \setminus S$. Node set $S$ is initialized by a randomly selected node $s$. The algorithm iteratively adds a node to $S$ until $S = V$ and $T$ is a spanning tree on $V$. In each iteration, two auxiliary data structures are determined. For each node $i \in V$, $w_i$ is the sum of requirements that node $i$ has with nodes in the complementary node set.

$$
w_i = \begin{cases} \sum_{j \in \overline{S}} r_{i,j} & \text{if } i \in S \\ \sum_{j \in S} r_{i,j} & \text{if } i \in \overline{S} \end{cases} \tag{5.9}
$$

The edge to be added to the fragment is a bridge between node sets $S$ and $\overline{S}$ and thus all traffic has to be routed on this bridge. Function $h_i$ describes the partial cost within $i$'s component arising when routing traffic from any node in $i$'s component to the other component, given that the edge to be added is adjacent to $i$

$$
h_i = \begin{cases} \sum_{j \in S} w_j \cdot c(p_{i,j}^S) & \text{if } i \in S \\ \sum_{j \in \overline{S}} w_j \cdot c(p_{i,j}^{\overline{S}}) & \text{if } i \in \overline{S} \end{cases} \tag{5.10}
$$

Here, it holds that $p^S = p^T$ and $p^{\overline{S}} = p^G$. Given both $w$ and $h$, the impact $\alpha_{i,j}$ of adding an edge $(i, j) \in (S \times \overline{S}) \cap E$ can be determined. Routing costs increase, as traffic between $j$ and all nodes in $S$ will be no longer use the shortest paths in $G$, but the unique paths in $T$. For the inclusion into $T$, the edge $(p, q)$ with minimum impact will be chosen.

$$W = \sum_{i \in S} w_i \tag{5.11}$$

$$\alpha_{i,j} = h_i + W \cdot d_{i,j} + h_j \tag{5.12}$$

$$(p, q) = \underset{(i,j) \in (S \times \bar{S}) \cap E}{\arg\min} \alpha_{i,j} \tag{5.13}$$

At the iteration's end, adding $(p, q)$ to $T$ (and thus $S$ becomes $S \cup \{q\}$) increases the total cost by

$$\Delta_{\text{cost}} = \sum_{i \in S} r_{i,q} c(p^T_{i,q}) - \sum_{i \in S} r_{i,q} c(p^G_{i,q}) \tag{5.14}$$

The construction algorithm's time complexity is determined by the computation of the all-pairs shortest paths during the initialization costing time $\mathcal{O}(n^3)$. At most, $n$ iterations will be performed, each costing $\mathcal{O}(n^2)$ time.

The *improvement heuristic* (Fig. 48) is structured similarly to the construction algorithm. The heuristic performs a sequence of first-improvement 1-exchange steps, each removing an edge from the tree (thus splitting the tree in two components) and inserting a new edge that connects both components again. To restore a valid tree, one of the $\mathcal{O}(n^2)$ many candidate edges is inserted, connecting both components. The chosen edge has to result in a tree with minimum cost among all alternatives. Computing the cost of an OCST solution is $\mathcal{O}(n^2)$ time. Thus, following a simple approach, evaluating $\mathcal{O}(n^2)$ many alternatives would cost $\mathcal{O}(n^4)$ time. Using auxiliary data structures $w$ and $h$ as defined in Eqs. 5.9 and 5.10 reduces the computation time down to $\mathcal{O}(n^2)$ but increases the space requirement by $\mathcal{O}(n)$. Building the auxiliary data structures costs $\mathcal{O}(n^2)$ time and thus does not increase the total time complexity. The algorithm stops once a local optimum has been reached, i. e. no exchange step yields an improvement.

The implementation of both the construction and the improvement heuristic can rely on a common subroutine ALPHA (Fig. 46). This function requires four arguments: the first two parameters contain the disjunctive node sets $S$ and $\bar{S}$ in which the graph is divided; the last two parameters contain the path functions (or sets of paths) $p^S$ and $p^{\bar{S}}$ to be used for cost computation in either node set. For the construction heuristic, $S$ is the growing fragment, $\bar{S}$ is the set of nodes not yet included

```
 1: function ALPHA(Node sets S, S̄, path sets pˢ, pˢ̄)
 2:     for all i ∈ S do
 3:         wᵢ ← ∑ⱼ∈S̄ rᵢ,ⱼ
 4:     end for
 5:     for all i ∈ S̄ do
 6:         wᵢ ← ∑ⱼ∈S rᵢ,ⱼ
 7:     end for
 8:     for all i ∈ S do
 9:         hᵢ ← ∑ⱼ∈S wⱼ · c(pˢᵢ,ⱼ)
10:     end for
11:     for all i ∈ S̄ do
12:         hᵢ ← ∑ⱼ∈S̄ wⱼ · c(pˢ̄ᵢ,ⱼ)
13:     end for
14:     W ← ∑ᵢ∈S wᵢ
15:     for all i ∈ S, j ∈ S̄ do
16:         αᵢ,ⱼ ← hᵢ + dᵢ,ⱼ · W + hⱼ
17:     end for
18:     return α
19: end function
```

$$1:\ \textbf{function}\ \text{ALPHA}(\text{Node sets}\ S, \overline{S},\ \text{path sets}\ p^S, p^{\overline{S}})$$
$$3:\quad w_i \leftarrow \sum_{j\in\overline{S}} r_{i,j}$$
$$6:\quad w_i \leftarrow \sum_{j\in S} r_{i,j}$$
$$9:\quad h_i \leftarrow \sum_{j\in S} w_j \cdot c(p^S_{i,j})$$
$$12:\quad h_i \leftarrow \sum_{j\in\overline{S}} w_j \cdot c(p^{\overline{S}}_{i,j})$$
$$14:\quad W \leftarrow \sum_{i\in S} w_i$$
$$16:\quad \alpha_{i,j} \leftarrow h_i + d_{i,j} \cdot W + h_j$$

Figure 46: Common subroutine ALPHA for the construction and improvement algorithms by AHUJA and MURTY [3].

in the fragment, $p^S$ equals the unique paths in the fragment, and $p^{\overline{S}}$ the shortest paths in $G$. For the improvement heuristic, $p^S$ and $p^{\overline{S}}$ are the unique paths in either component as defined by node sets $S$ and $\overline{S}$. The construction heuristic's pseudo code is depicted in Fig. 47; the improvement heuristic is shown in Fig. 48.

*Other Evolutionary and Heuristic Algorithms*

In a series of publications [158, 159, 160], PALMER and KERSHENBAUM present both a heuristic and a genetic algorithm. The heuristic algorithm consists both of two construction and one improvement algorithms. The genetic algorithm features a 'link and node bias' encoding to represent solutions, which will be explained in detail below.

For the *heuristic algorithm*, PALMER and KERSHENBAUM favor stars as good solutions for the OCST and thus propose either constructing a star only (no improvement heuristic applied) or starting from an MST and iteratively moving edges towards the tree's median node. Solutions for

```
 1: function TREEBUILDING(Graph G(V, E))
 2:     p^G ← ALLPAIRSSHORTESTPATH(G)
 3:     T ← ∅                                          ▷ Empty tree
 4:     c(p^T) ← 0                                      ▷ No paths in empty tree
 5:     s ← SEED(G)                                     ▷ Select seeding node
 6:     S ← {s}
 7:     S̄ ← V \ S
 8:     while |S| < |V| do
 9:         α ← ALPHA(S, S̄, p^T_{i,j}, p^G_{i,j})
10:         (p, q) ← arg min_{(p,q)∈(S×S̄)} {α_{p,q}}
11:         for each i ∈ S do
12:             c(p^T_{i,q}) ← c(p^T_{i,p}) + d(p, q)   ▷ Update path costs
13:         end for
14:         S ← S ∪ {q}                                 ▷ Update components
15:         S̄ ← S̄ \ {q}
16:     end while
17:     return T
18: end function
```

Figure 47: Tree construction heuristic according to AHUJA and MURTY [3] called 'AM-C'.

an OCST problem instance are close to a star if all edge weight values are very similar. Furthermore, HU proved that, given a stronger triangle inequality, a star is an optimal solution (see Sec. 5.1.1, p. 188). Testing all possible stars for a given problem instance can be done in $\mathcal{O}(n^2)$ by a two-step algorithm. Firstly, for each node $j$ its requirements to all other nodes are summed up in $W_j$:

$$W_j = \sum_{i \in V} r_{i,j} \quad \text{for all } j \in V \tag{5.15}$$

Secondly, the cost for each star with node $i \in V$ as center is evaluated (stored in $S_i$) and the star with minimum cost is the resulting tree.

$$S_i = \sum_{j \in V} d_{i,j} W_j \quad \text{for all } i \in V \tag{5.16}$$

If a star with a single center does not provide a sufficient solution quality, a modified star with $k$ centering nodes (and $n - k$ leaves) can be considered. Constructing such a tree, however, has cost $\mathcal{O}(n^{k+1})$.

```
1: function TreeImprovement(Graph G(V, E), Tree T)
2:     c' ← ∞
3:     while c(T) < c' do
4:         c' ← c(T)
5:         Q ← E
6:         while not every edge in Q visited do
7:             e = Pull(Q)                          ▷ Fetch edge from queue
8:             (S, S̄) ← CutTree(T*, e)                      ▷ Cut T*
9:             α ← Alpha(S, S̄, p^T, p^{T*})
10:            (p, q) ← arg min_{(p,q)∈(S×S̄)}{α_{p,q}}
11:            if α_{p,q} < α_e then
12:                T* ← T* ∖ {e} ∪ {(p, q)}          ▷ Update tree T*
13:            end if
14:        end while
15:        Q ← E                               ▷ Restart search on edge set
16:    end while
17:    return T*                               ▷ Return best solution
18: end function
```

Figure 48: Tree improvement heuristic according to Ahuja and Murty [3] called 'AM-H'.

As an alternative to constructing a star directly, the authors propose constructing an MST as initial solution and performing a sequence of local exchange moves which moves subtrees 'upwards' towards a median node. It is suggested that the center of the best star found with the construction heuristic above is used as the median node. The improvement heuristic applied to the MST checks each node that is not the median node or already attached to the median node to see if moving the node's subtree to its 'grandparent' does decrease the trees total cost. If a decrease can be achieved, the move is made permanent and the possibility of moving the node even further upwards is considered. Although not stated explicitly, the algorithm terminates once a local optimum is reached.

As a preparatory step to their *genetic algorithm*, the authors compare several approaches with regard to representations of trees in genetic algorithms. According to the authors, a good representation must be complete (represent all possible trees), unbiased (not favoring special types of trees), valid (no non-tree structures should be represented), easily convertible between genotype and phenotype, and possess locality (small changes in representation equal small changes in phenotype). A number of representations was considered, including characteristic vectors (bit vector showing if an edge in $E$ is in the tree or not), predecessor vectors (only the parent node is stored for each node), and Prüfer numbers (encodes each tree uniquely into a vector of length $n - 2$). As none of these representations fulfills the requirements as stated above, the authors propose their own alternative representation called *link and node bias* encoding (LNB). This encoding maintains two vectors for biases on each node (vector length $n$) and each edge (vector length $\frac{n(n-1)}{2}$). These biases are used to modify an edge's cost $d_{i,j}$ to become a new cost $d'_{i,j}$:

$$d'_{i,j} = d_{i,j} + b_{(i,j)}P_1 d_{\max} + (b_i + b_j)P_2 d_{\max} \qquad (5.17)$$

where $b_i$ is the bias for node $i$ and $b_{(i,j)}$ is the bias for edge $(i, j)$. The influence of the biases is controlled by two parameters $P_1$ and $P_2$ and scaled by the maximum distance $d_{\max}$ between any two nodes. Using the modified edge weights, an MST is constructed using PRIM's algorithm [163]. It is noted that if link bases are disabled (set to 0), not every feasible tree can be constructed. However, the authors claim that link biases are not relevant for finding solutions for the OCST. Little to no details are given on the other aspects of the GA (mutation or recombination), except for parameters such as mutation or recombination rates and population size. For the experiments, parameters were set to $P_1 = 0$ and $P_2 = 1$. On average, the GA was able to find better solutions for the four largest out of five benchmark instances than their heuristic algorithm above. Furthermore, both the heuristic and the GA were applied to a modified problem with 'regional distribution centers': the GA was able to adapt to this new problem, whereas the heuristic failed to find competitive results.

BERRY, MURTAGH, SUDGEN, and McMAHON [30] also present a genetic algorithm. The main difference to the algorithm from PALMER and KERSHENBAUM (see above) is the representation of individuals. Whereas the PALMER *et al.* discard a predecessor vector encoding as it allows non-tree representations and therefore introduce the LNB encoding, the BERRY *et al.* design their GA so that no operation (for example, mutation or recombination) generates a predecessor vector which does not represent a tree. During a mutation step, a leaf node is moved to another parent node. This change can be easily mapped to the predecessor encoding, as only the leaf node's element has to be changed and any other node is a feasible new predecessor. For recombination, the authors propose an operator where an offspring is constructed by making a copy of one parent and replacing a desired number of edges with edges from the other parent. As removing an edge from the tree splits it into two subtrees, the edge from the second parent has to be chosen such that it reconnects both components and does not introduce a cycle. For initialization, either stars, MSTs or randomly generated trees are proposed. Three new benchmark instances with 6 or 35 nodes are introduced and designated as Berry6, Berry35, and Berry35u in this thesis.

Li and Bouchebaba [126] present a GA that is said to be unconcerned with the representation of trees, as all GA operations are performed on the tree directly. For initialization, a modified Prim algorithm is used where, contrary to the original algorithm, a node outside the fragment is chosen and edges from this node to the fragment are considered for inclusion into the fragment. Both mutation and recombination perform quite similarly and are either path based or tree based. For the recombination, either $k$ paths or subtrees, respectively, are copied between both parent trees. For the mutation, paths and subtrees are randomly drawn from a complete graph. As cycles arise during the copy operation, edges that were not introduced by this operation are deleted from the graph to restore a valid tree. Experiments were conducted on both of Berry's instances ([30], the 35 node instance with two distance matrices) and the two smallest instances from Palmer [160]. Results show that the author's GA finds better solutions for three out of five instances. However, only the best values out of 10 repetitions are given, the population size is larger than in Berry's and Palmer's experiments, and no computation times for a direct comparison are presented.

Rothlauf, Gerstacker, and Heinzl [174] analyze the properties of solutions for the OCST. Firstly, known benchmark instances from Palmer [159], Raidl [94], Berry et al. [30], and Rothlauf et al. [171] are analyzed, then random instances with different sizes (number of nodes) and distance metrices (either random or Euclidean) are generated. Best known solutions for the instances from literature are compared to both MSTs and stars. Experimental results suggest that solutions for these problem instances have a bias towards MSTs, as the distance (number of different edges) between MSTs and best-known solutions is always smaller than the distance between MSTs and random trees. For stars, however, no such relationship could be observed, as stars have about the same distance to both best-known solutions as random trees.

Next, a set of random instances with sizes ranging from 8 to 26 nodes were created and optimized using a GA. As representation, each edge in the graph is associated with a number in $[0;1]$ and this genotype is transferred into a phenotype by sorting edges non-increasing by their number and iteratively using edges for the tree (skipping edges that introduce cycles) until the tree is complete. Notably, the authors restart their GA with a population of twice the size until no better results are found by the GA. The final result is claimed to be optimal, although no proof is given. For instances with random distances, the distance between local optima and MSTs is much smaller than the distance between MSTs and random trees. For instances with Euclidean distances, however, this relation between MSTs and local optima is much weaker.

ROTHLAUF and HEINZL [172] develop both a genetic algorithm and a simulated annealing algorithm to solve benchmark instances as already used by the same authors in [174]. The authors discuss several representations for trees in genetic algorithms including the link and node biased encoding (LNB), characteristic vectors (CV), and direct representations. Eventually, it is argued that the link biased encoding (LB) is the best choice as MSTs are overrepresented in this encoding. Motivated by [174], MSTs are expected to be good approximations allowing the algorithm find good solutions. In the link biased encoding, a vector $b$ of floating values is maintained, where each of the $|E|$ many vector elements is assigned to one edge in the graph. The distance of an edge $(i, j)$ is modified to

$$d'_{i,j} = d_{i,j} + b_{(i,j)} P_1 d_{\max} \tag{5.18}$$

where $d_{i,j}$ is the original distance, $P_1$ is a global parameter controlling the influence of the edge-dependent bias value $b_{(i,j)}$, which is scaled by the largest inter-node distance $d_{\max}$. Given the modified distance matrix, a minimum spanning tree is constructed using PRIM's algorithm. If $P_1 = 0$, the resulting tree represents an MST for the original graph. Increasing $P_1$, the resulting trees become less similar to MSTs and more similar to random trees. For their experiments the authors used $P_1 = 1$, as here any tree can be generated and the bias towards MSTs still exists.

In the experiments, for each problem instance and setup the percentage of runs reaching a given quality bound within 200 generations was determined. In the first group of experiments, known benchmark instances were solved by the GA using different genotype encodings and

$n$-point crossover only. Results suggest than using an LB encoding and $0.5 \leq P_1 \leq 2$ performs better than LB encoding with smaller or larger values for $P_1$ and other encodings such as CV, Prüfer, or NetKeys [173]. The second group of experiments introduced random instances, where the inter-node distances were either randomly generated within a given interval or Euclidean by placing nodes in 2-dimensional plane. The GA was modified to perform both recombination and mutation (with low probability, however). For comparison, a simple SA was designed performing mutation only, accepting generated solutions according to a standard cooling scheme, and terminating after 5000 iterations. Results suggest that both GA perform somewhat better than the SA for both Euclidean and non-Euclidean instances. Both algorithms, however, do not scale with instance size and a decrease in solution quality can already be observed with small graphs of size 20. Furthermore, the success probabilities are generally lower for Euclidean instances compared to non-Euclidean instances, given the same graph size.

SOAK, CORNE, and AHN [183] present an evolutionary algorithm with a special modification operator called *adaptive link adjustment algorithm* (ALA). Here, an individual in the population is represented by a vector of length $|E|$. Such a genotype is transformed into a phenotype by ordering the edges non-decreasingly by the value of the corresponding vector element and iteratively adding each edge into a growing fragment until a tree is built (skipping edges that would introduce cycles). The modification operator changes the values in the above vector by either 'punishing' edges occurring in the found tree by increasing their value by a given amount $\alpha$ or randomly selecting a given portion of edges to be 'rewarded' by a given amount $\beta$. The performance of the EA with ALA is compared to EAs using an LNB, NetKeys, or edge window encoding [184]. Results suggest that the ALA's performance is average only, but it finds the best solution for one out of nine benchmark instances.

SHARMA [179] presents two local search algorithms based on 1-exchange moves. Both local search algorithms are based on the idea that simplifying an OCST instance allows the construction of optimal solutions. Then, the problem instance is iteratively transformed back to its original state while the local search algorithms make local adjustments on the tree.

The first local search starts by resetting the distance matrix's values to a small constant value. As long as there is an edge $(i, j)$ for which the distance has not yet been restored, the components, as defined by a possible removal of $(i, j)$, are used to perform a 1-exchange move.

In this move, an edge $(s, t)$ for insertion between both components and an edge $(p, q)$ for removal (repair of the cycle) are searched, which minimize the cost of the resulting tree. After the move, the distance of edge $(i, j)$ is increased by a fraction of the achieved gain. The cost of this local search is $\mathcal{O}(Mn^4)$, where $M = \max_{i,j \in V} d_{i,j}$. This complexity is due to the cost of $\mathcal{O}(d_{i,j}n^3)$ for checking a single edge $(i, j)$ with a weight below its original value.

The second local search is based on Hu's statement that if a relaxed triangle inequality holds for an instance, the optimal solution is a star. This local search's concept is similar to the first one, but here the requirement matrix's elements are reset to a constant minimum value. A star is constructed where the center is the node with the minimum summed distance to all other nodes. Requirement values for node pairs that represent edges in the constructed tree are reset to their original values, whereas the other node pairs' requirement values are adapted by the following procedure: as long as there are node pairs with a requirement below its original value, one of these node pairs is selected. For each edge on the path in the tree between both nodes, find an 1-exchange move (removing this edge, inserting a new edge) that results in the largest cost decrease. Increase the requirement value for the above node pair by a value depending on the gain. If the node pair's requirement value did not reach its original value, perform the exchange as determined, otherwise discard this change. This local search's complexity is $\mathcal{O}(n^3 m)$, since there are $\mathcal{O}(m)$ non-tree edges and checking for an exchange move costs $\mathcal{O}(n^3)$ time.

Although both local search algorithms are highly sophisticated, they are very complex, too. Furthermore, no experimental results are given that show the feasibility of the algorithms.

SOAK [182] presents an EA for the OCST that employs both a new type of representation (encoding) and a new recombination operator called *adjacent node crossover* (ANX). The new encoding represents individuals as a vector of $2 \cdot (|V| - 1)$ numbers, where each vector element corresponds to a node in $G$. Such a vector is transferred into an individual using a special routing called CB-TCR. Here, each two subsequent vector elements are treated as an edge and included into a growing fragment until a tree is constructed. If a cycle is introduced in an intermediate step, the cycle's edges are checked and the longest edge is removed. The authors prove that any vector containing each node at least once yields a valid tree when encoded in CB-TCR and that any spanning tree can be represented by such a vector.

The recombinator ANX builds an offspring by performing a walk through the node sets built from both parent's vector representation. Starting to walk from a random node, a neighboring node in either parent's vector is chosen (nodes occurring as neighbor in both parents are preferred). If there is no unvisited neighboring node, an unused node is chosen at random. The chosen node (either neighbor or random) is set to be the new current node. The process terminates once $2 \cdot (|V|-1)$ nodes have been selected. ANX, however, may generate invalid representations as some nodes may not be included, requiring an additional repair function. Experimental results suggest that the EA is actually effective. For two benchmark instances with 35 (Berry35) and 50 (Raidl50) new best known solutions are found. For smaller instances, this EA performs competitively compared to other representations, including LNB and NetKeys. Finally, some analysis on the performance of the proposed EA and alternative EAs with different representations is undertaken. The authors claim that other encodings do not perform as well as they lose diversity, either due to fast convergence (into local optima) or high locality of their mutation operator.

## 5.2 PROBLEM INSTANCES

For the OCST, no 'official' instance collection exists, but there are a number of problem instances available used by several authors. Most of these instances are rather small ($\leq$ 100 nodes) and thus are only included for comparison. For the experiments, random instances with up to 2000 nodes were created either with Euclidean or random inter-node distances. Details of all used problem instances are summarized in Tab. 42.

### 5.2.1  Benchmark Instances

The first benchmark instances for the OCST were created by PALMER and KERSHENBAUM [159]. These five instances contained between 6 and 98 nodes based on cities in the U. S. A., where the requirements between two cities are inversely proportional to the inter-node distances and the link cost equals real communication costs. The best found solutions for each of these five instances are summarized in Tab. 41. More recent literature [171] describing these instances suggests different objective values for instances Palmer6, Palmer12, and Palmer24. As the

| Instance | Cost | Instance | Cost |
|----------|------|----------|------|
| Palmer6 | 1 386 360 | Palmer98 | 711 287 300 |
| Palmer12 | 6 857 020 | Berry6 | 534 |
| Palmer24 | 36 029 600 | Berry35 | 30 467 |
| Palmer47 | 143 949 400 | Berry35u | 16 915 |

Table 41: Best solutions found by PALMER and KERSHENBAUM for their benchmark instances as given in [159], and best solutions found by BERRY et al. for their benchmark instances as given in [30].

old problem instances including Palmer47 and Palmer98 are said to be no longer available, the new instance variants will be used here.

BERRY et al. introduced three new instances in [30] with either 6 or 35 nodes. The instance with 6 nodes is used for testing purposes, only, whereas both problem instances with 35 nodes are considered benchmark instances. Both instances with 35 nodes differ only in their distance matrix: the original instance with inter-node distances $\geq 1$ is designated Berry35, whereas the instance with unit distances ($d_{i,j} = 1$ for all $i, j \in V$) is designated Berry35u. The solutions provided by BERRY et al. are shown in Tab. 41.

RAIDL provides six problem instances ranging from 10 to 100 nodes. These instances were used in a diploma thesis supervised by RAIDL [94]. Both distance and requirement matrices are generated randomly and uniformly.

For problem instances Palmer6, Palmer12, Palmer24, Raidl10, Raidl20, Raidl50, Berry6, Berry35, and Berry35u both distance and demand matrices are given in the appendix of [171].

### 5.2.2    Randomly Generated Instances

For the generation of random instances, the same construction specification was used as in [174]. Random instances were set to have either random inter-node distances or Euclidean instances. For instances with non-Euclidean distances, the distance between each node pair was a natural number generated randomly and uniformly distributed within the interval $[0, 100]$. For instances with Euclidean distances, nodes were embedded into a 2-dimensional plane on a $1000 \times 1000$ grid and distances were computed using the Euclidean norm and rounded to the closest natural number:

$$d_{i,j} = \left\lfloor \sqrt{(x_i - x_j)^2 + (y_i - y_j)^2} + \frac{1}{2} \right\rfloor \qquad (5.19)$$

Here, $x_i$ and $y_i$ denote the randomly chosen position of a node $i \in V$ in the grid above. For both instance types, requirements between each node pair were natural numbers, also randomly generated and uniformly distributed within the interval $[0, 100]$.

Instances with a size (number of nodes) of 100 to 2000 were generated. The instances are designated with an R as prefix, followed by a number denoting the number of nodes in the instance. For instances with Euclidean distances, the suffix -E is appended. Detailed information on these instances is given in the lower half of Tab. 42.

### 5.2.3  *Lower Bounds*

The lower bound algorithm described in Sec. A.2.2 was implemented to evaluate results from the experiments. This lower bound, however, turned out to be unreliable: the found lower bound is only tight for two instances, Palmer24 and Berry35. For other instances, this bound is considerably lower. For example, for Berry35u, the found lower bound is 13 106 which is 23.4 % below the best known solution with cost 16 167. Furthermore, the gap between lower bound and upper bound (best known solution) increases with instance size. For instances from the Raidl series the gap grows from 2.3 % for Raidl10 to 21.4 % for Raidl50.

This lower bound was therefore not used to compute the excess of the algorithms' results. The best known solution of each solution is used instead.

### 5.3  CONSTRUCTION HEURISTICS

The objective of a construction heuristic is to build a valid solution for a given problem instance. This initial solution may be refined with an improvement heuristic, such as a local search algorithm. Properties of construction heuristics include complexity (running time), solution quality, randomness, and applicability to improvement heuristics. As there is a trade-off when choosing a construction heuristic for a given

| Instance | $\lvert V \rvert$ | Distances | Requirements | UB |
|----------|------|-----------|--------------|-----|
| Palmer6 | 6 | – | – | 693 180 |
| Palmer12 | 12 | – | – | 3 428 509 |
| Palmer24 | 24 | – | – | 1 086 656 |
| Berry6 | 6 | – | – | 534 |
| Berry35 | 35 | – | – | 16 915 |
| Berry35u | 35 | – | – | 16 167 |
| Raidl10 | 10 | R/U | R/U | 53 674 |
| Raidl20 | 20 | R/U | R/U | 157 570 |
| Raidl35 | 35 | R/U | R/U | 412 167 |
| Raidl50 | 50 | R/U | R/U | 806 864 |
| Raidl75 | 75 | R/U | R/U | 1 717 491 |
| Raidl100 | 100 | R/U | R/U | 2 561 543 |
| R100 | 100 | R/U | R/U | 2 427 890 |
| R100-E | 100 | E | R/U | $183.832 \cdot 10^6$ |
| R300 | 300 | R/U | R/U | $15.331 \cdot 10^6$ |
| R300-E | 300 | E | R/U | $1.611 \cdot 10^9$ |
| R500 | 500 | R/U | R/U | $37.744 \cdot 10^6$ |
| R500-E | 500 | E | R/U | $4.476 \cdot 10^9$ |
| R750 | 750 | R/U | R/U | $79.704 \cdot 10^6$ |
| R750-E | 750 | E | R/U | $10.303 \cdot 10^9$ |
| R1000 | 1000 | R/U | R/U | $136.225 \cdot 10^6$ |
| R1000-E | 1000 | E | R/U | $17.915 \cdot 10^9$ |
| R2000 | 2000 | R/U | R/U | $508.728 \cdot 10^6$ |
| R2000-E | 2000 | E | R/U | $72.506 \cdot 10^9$ |

Table 42: Problem instances for the Optimum Communication Spanning Tree problem as used in this thesis. 'R/U' means 'random uniform', 'E' means 'Euclidean', 'UB' designates the best known solution's cost. For instance with '–' for distance and requirements, no information on the generation process is available.

setup, several construction heuristics are presented and categorized as either random, structured, or problem-specific.

*Random Trees*

The simplest tree construction heuristic is to use a random tree. Two slightly different random tree construction heuristics with different properties are proposed.

The *Random Rooted* tree construction algorithm selects one arbitrary node as the tree's root node and iteratively adds randomly chosen, feasible edges each connecting a node from the growing tree fragment to a node not yet included. This algorithm is guaranteed to build spanning trees in sparse, connected graphs, but not each possible tree is constructed with the same probability. Nodes added early during construction are expected to have a higher degree as they are more often considered to be incident to edges connecting to nodes outside the growing tree fragment. This algorithm's complexity is $\mathcal{O}(n)$ in complete graphs given that finding an edge connecting a tree node with an outside tree costs constant time.

The *Random Prüfer* tree construction algorithm uses a random Prüfer sequence [158] to build trees. A Prüfer sequence for a labeled tree with $n$ nodes has length $n - 2$ (each element is in $\{1, \dots, n\}$) and, as a proof of CAYLEY's formula, it uniquely describes each of the $n^{n-2}$ possible spanning trees in a complete graph. Using a randomly generated Prüfer sequence, each possible tree is constructed with the same probability. In sparse graphs, however, it becomes unlikely that a random sequence corresponds to a valid edge set. The complexity to build trees from Prüfer sequences is $\mathcal{O}(n \log n)$.

Both random tree construction heuristics are expected to perform considerably worse than the more sophisticated approaches discussed below. The heuristics are included here for completeness only and will not be considered in later sections.

*Structured Trees*

Here, several structured trees are presented, where 'structured' refers to the fact that these trees are built by some rule following a given objective. In graph theory, a number of spanning tree types is known and each of them can be used as a construction heuristic for the OCST. A selection of three well-known trees is given here.

The *Minimum Spanning Tree* (MST) tree construction algorithm builds a minimum spanning tree on the graph. It has been argued by ROTHLAUF *et al.* [174] that good solutions for the OCST are biased towards the MST, which is supported by experiments as presented in [63]. The complexity of building minimum spanning trees is $\mathcal{O}(n^2)$ using PRIM's algorithm or $\mathcal{O}(m + n \log n)$ using KRUSKAL's algorithm and Fibonacci heaps.

*Star Trees* were proposed by PALMER and KERSHENBAUM [159] as initial solutions for the OCST, as star trees are optimal solutions for special cases [106]. This construction heuristic evaluates all $n$ star trees and uses the tree with minimal cost as its result. Evaluating all possible trees can be done in $\mathcal{O}(n^2)$ time, as described on p. 196.

For each graph node, the *Shortest Path Tree* tree construction algorithm builds a shortest path tree rooted at that node using DIJKSTRA's algorithm. For each tree, the sum over the distances from the tree's root to all other nodes is determined. The tree with the smallest sum is used as the heuristic's result. This is motivated by the fact that the SPT rooted at the median node of the network, i. e. the node that has the smallest sum in this regard, is already a 2-approximation to the MRT [205]. For Euclidean problems, the SPT is equivalent to a star, except for cases where three or more nodes are on a line. Finding the median in a graph with triangle inequality violations can be done in $\mathcal{O}(n^3)$ time using the algorithm of FLOYD and WARSHALL [69, 202].

*Problem-Specific Trees*

The most complex construction heuristic is from AHUJA and MURTY [3] (Fig. 47) and is related to the local search in the same paper. This construction heuristic was presented in detail in Sec. 5.1.2 (p. 193).

The most expensive part of this heuristic is determining the all-pairs shortest paths costing time $\mathcal{O}(n^3)$.

### 5.3.1    Results

The above construction heuristics were applied to the instances as shown in Tab. 42. Results for the following discussion are summarized in Tables 43–47. Experiments were repeated 20 times and both minimum and average values and their excess above the best known solutions were used for the discussion.

| Instance | RandomPrüfer | | RandomRooted | |
|---|---|---|---|---|
| | min | avg | min | avg |
| Palmer6 | $7.82 \cdot 10^5$ | $1.52 \cdot 10^6$ | $8.36 \cdot 10^5$ | $1.91 \cdot 10^6$ |
| | 12.87 | 119.73 | 20.63 | 175.09 |
| Palmer12 | $9.64 \cdot 10^6$ | $1.22 \cdot 10^7$ | $7.33 \cdot 10^6$ | $1.04 \cdot 10^7$ |
| | 181.29 | 257.01 | 113.67 | 204.49 |
| Berry6 | 1015 | 1380.9 | 883 | 1218.6 |
| | 90.07 | 158.60 | 65.36 | 128.20 |
| Berry35 | $2.44 \cdot 10^5$ | $3.82 \cdot 10^5$ | $2.12 \cdot 10^5$ | $3.22 \cdot 10^5$ |
| | 1340.81 | 2160.83 | 1152.95 | 1804.11 |
| Berry35u | 51063 | 72697.2 | 39887 | 55138.2 |
| | 215.85 | 349.66 | 146.72 | 241.05 |
| Raidl10 | $1.99 \cdot 10^5$ | $3.34 \cdot 10^5$ | $2.24 \cdot 10^5$ | $3.18 \cdot 10^5$ |
| | 271.11 | 522.48 | 317.78 | 492.78 |
| Raidl20 | $1.56 \cdot 10^6$ | $2.12 \cdot 10^6$ | $1.01 \cdot 10^6$ | $1.69 \cdot 10^6$ |
| | 887.55 | 1247.17 | 540.85 | 974.62 |
| Raidl35 | $7.27 \cdot 10^6$ | $9.09 \cdot 10^6$ | $4.49 \cdot 10^6$ | $6.76 \cdot 10^6$ |
| | 1663.31 | 2106.12 | 990.26 | 1539.23 |
| Raidl50 | $1.86 \cdot 10^7$ | $2.48 \cdot 10^7$ | $1.22 \cdot 10^7$ | $1.60 \cdot 10^7$ |
| | 2208.64 | 2975.81 | 1411.99 | 1881.16 |
| Raidl75 | $4.80 \cdot 10^7$ | $6.41 \cdot 10^7$ | $2.95 \cdot 10^7$ | $4.24 \cdot 10^7$ |
| | 2693.12 | 3630.39 | 1620.17 | 2369.10 |
| Raidl100 | $1.15 \cdot 10^8$ | $1.40 \cdot 10^8$ | $5.71 \cdot 10^7$ | $8.05 \cdot 10^7$ |
| | 4388.83 | 5382.84 | 2129.71 | 3042.15 |

Table 43: Results for random tree-based construction heuristics applied to standard benchmark instances. Large numbers denote the average final solution cost, smaller numbers below are the excess above the best-known value in percent.

For small benchmark instances, the best-known solution found by the algorithms presented in this thesis matches the values from other authors. Due to the size of the instances, it can be assumed that these values are optimal results. For larger instances, especially the ones that were created for this thesis, the best-known solutions found in any experiment have been used as upper bound. Lacking tight lower bound values, the excess is given as a percentage value, where 0.0 % represents a solution cost equal to the upper bound and positive values represent worse solutions.

As expected, both construction heuristics based on random trees perform worst among all construction heuristics (see Tables 43–44). Trees found by both heuristics have a considerable excess, which is > 100 % on average for each instance. Even in the best case, the excess

| Instance | RandomPrüfer | | RandomRooted | |
|---|---|---|---|---|
| | min | avg | min | avg |
| R100 | $9.27 \cdot 10^7$ | $1.42 \cdot 10^8$ | $6.77 \cdot 10^7$ | $8.45 \cdot 10^7$ |
| | 3718.44 | 5766.61 | 2687.48 | 3382.16 |
| R100-E | $1.27 \cdot 10^9$ | $1.51 \cdot 10^9$ | $6.98 \cdot 10^8$ | $8.61 \cdot 10^8$ |
| | 589.66 | 722.19 | 279.77 | 368.58 |
| R300 | $1.81 \cdot 10^9$ | $2.24 \cdot 10^9$ | $8.31 \cdot 10^8$ | $9.75 \cdot 10^8$ |
| | 11697.54 | 14528.39 | 5322.13 | 6260.24 |
| R300-E | $1.96 \cdot 10^{10}$ | $2.31 \cdot 10^{10}$ | $8.28 \cdot 10^9$ | $9.82 \cdot 10^9$ |
| | 1114.59 | 1332.80 | 414.34 | 509.40 |
| R500 | $6.87 \cdot 10^9$ | $8.39 \cdot 10^9$ | $2.52 \cdot 10^9$ | $3.04 \cdot 10^9$ |
| | 18098.58 | 22124.97 | 6585.89 | 7951.30 |
| R500-E | $6.78 \cdot 10^{10}$ | $8.30 \cdot 10^{10}$ | $2.65 \cdot 10^{10}$ | $3.16 \cdot 10^{10}$ |
| | 1413.77 | 1755.45 | 492.97 | 606.62 |
| R750 | $1.79 \cdot 10^{10}$ | $2.35 \cdot 10^{10}$ | $6.46 \cdot 10^9$ | $7.47 \cdot 10^9$ |
| | 22400.72 | 29331.81 | 8002.42 | 9276.92 |
| R750-E | $1.82 \cdot 10^{11}$ | $2.42 \cdot 10^{11}$ | $6.49 \cdot 10^{10}$ | $7.77 \cdot 10^{10}$ |
| | 1667.16 | 2250.09 | 529.51 | 654.54 |
| R1000 | $3.79 \cdot 10^{10}$ | $4.75 \cdot 10^{10}$ | $1.29 \cdot 10^{10}$ | $1.42 \cdot 10^{10}$ |
| | 27746.87 | 34800.64 | 9373.64 | 10298.30 |
| R1000-E | $3.98 \cdot 10^{11}$ | $4.83 \cdot 10^{11}$ | $1.20 \cdot 10^{11}$ | $1.40 \cdot 10^{11}$ |
| | 2124.27 | 2595.93 | 572.18 | 684.08 |
| R2000 | $2.26 \cdot 10^{11}$ | $2.87 \cdot 10^{11}$ | $5.16 \cdot 10^{10}$ | $6.24 \cdot 10^{10}$ |
| | 44338.16 | 56383.93 | 10046.57 | 12171.04 |
| R2000-E | $2.38 \cdot 10^{12}$ | $2.90 \cdot 10^{12}$ | $5.91 \cdot 10^{11}$ | $6.60 \cdot 10^{11}$ |
| | 3186.85 | 3895.90 | 715.49 | 810.93 |

Table 44: Results for random tree-based construction heuristics applied to randomly generated instances. Large numbers denote the average final solution cost, smaller numbers below are the excess above the best-known value in percent.

| Instance | Star | | | ShortestPath | | | MST | | | AM-C | | |
|---|---|---|---|---|---|---|---|---|---|---|---|---|
| | min | avg | t [s] | min | avg | t [s] | min | avg | t [s] | min | avg | t [s] |
| Palmer6 | $8.02 \cdot 10^5$ 15.69 | $8.02 \cdot 10^5$ 15.69 | 0.0 | $8.02 \cdot 10^5$ 15.69 | $9.95 \cdot 10^5$ 43.49 | 0.0 | $7.10 \cdot 10^5$ 2.39 | $7.10 \cdot 10^5$ 2.39 | 0.0 | $6.93 \cdot 10^5$ 0.00 | $6.99 \cdot 10^5$ 0.80 | 0.0 |
| Palmer12 | $5.96 \cdot 10^6$ 73.91 | $5.96 \cdot 10^6$ 73.91 | 0.0 | $5.96 \cdot 10^6$ 73.91 | $6.09 \cdot 10^6$ 77.76 | 0.0 | $3.88 \cdot 10^6$ 13.07 | $3.88 \cdot 10^6$ 13.07 | 0.0 | $3.43 \cdot 10^6$ 0.09 | $3.55 \cdot 10^6$ 3.52 | 0.0 |
| Raidl10 | $1.42 \cdot 10^5$ 165.00 | $1.42 \cdot 10^5$ 165.00 | 0.0 | 53674 0.00 | 56221.2 4.75 | 0.0 | 58352 8.72 | 58352.0 8.72 | 0.0 | 53674 0.00 | 53674.0 0.00 | 0.0 |
| Raidl20 | $6.87 \cdot 10^5$ 336.31 | $6.87 \cdot 10^5$ 336.31 | 0.0 | $1.61 \cdot 10^5$ 1.92 | $1.73 \cdot 10^5$ 9.70 | 0.0 | $1.66 \cdot 10^5$ 5.22 | $1.67 \cdot 10^5$ 5.78 | 0.0 | $1.58 \cdot 10^5$ 0.05 | $1.58 \cdot 10^5$ 0.14 | 0.0 |
| Raidl35 | $2.26 \cdot 10^6$ 448.23 | $2.26 \cdot 10^6$ 448.23 | 0.0 | $4.23 \cdot 10^5$ 2.62 | $4.58 \cdot 10^5$ 11.07 | 0.0 | $4.40 \cdot 10^5$ 6.72 | $4.48 \cdot 10^5$ 8.59 | 0.0 | $4.12 \cdot 10^5$ 0.00 | $4.17 \cdot 10^5$ 1.20 | 0.0 |
| Raidl50 | $4.37 \cdot 10^6$ 441.91 | $4.37 \cdot 10^6$ 441.91 | 0.0 | $8.12 \cdot 10^5$ 0.59 | $8.51 \cdot 10^5$ 5.52 | 0.0 | $8.90 \cdot 10^5$ 10.34 | $9.62 \cdot 10^5$ 19.17 | 0.0 | $8.07 \cdot 10^5$ 0.00 | $8.16 \cdot 10^5$ 1.08 | 0.1 |
| Raidl75 | $1.21 \cdot 10^7$ 607.28 | $1.21 \cdot 10^7$ 607.28 | 0.0 | $1.74 \cdot 10^6$ 1.22 | $1.89 \cdot 10^6$ 9.82 | 0.0 | $2.14 \cdot 10^6$ 24.88 | $2.27 \cdot 10^6$ 31.91 | 0.1 | $1.72 \cdot 10^6$ 0.08 | $1.79 \cdot 10^6$ 4.13 | 0.1 |
| Raidl100 | $2.07 \cdot 10^7$ 707.58 | $2.07 \cdot 10^7$ 707.58 | 0.0 | $2.59 \cdot 10^6$ 1.13 | $2.72 \cdot 10^6$ 6.38 | 0.0 | $3.10 \cdot 10^6$ 21.13 | $3.45 \cdot 10^6$ 34.88 | 0.1 | $2.57 \cdot 10^6$ 0.27 | $2.65 \cdot 10^6$ 3.39 | 0.2 |

Table 45: OCST construction heuristics' results for standard benchmark instances. Large numbers denote the average final solution cost, smaller numbers below are the excess above the best-known value in percent.

| Instance | Star | | | ShortestPath | | | MST | | | AM-C | | |
|---|---|---|---|---|---|---|---|---|---|---|---|---|
| | min | avg | t [s] | min | avg | t [s] | min | avg | t [s] | min | avg | t [s] |
| Berry6 | 734 | 734.0 | 0.0 | 606 | 631.6 | 0.0 | 534 | 534.0 | 0.0 | 534 | 534.0 | 0.0 |
| | 37.45 | 37.45 | | 13.48 | 18.28 | | 0.00 | 0.00 | | 0.00 | 0.00 | |
| Berry35 | 77799 | 77799.0 | 0.0 | 77799 | 91423.4 | 0.0 | 16915 | 16915.0 | 0.0 | 16915 | 16915.0 | 0.0 |
| | 359.94 | 359.94 | | 359.94 | 440.49 | | 0.00 | 0.00 | | 0.00 | 0.00 | |
| Berry35u | 21513 | 21513.0 | 0.0 | 21745 | 22516.3 | 0.0 | 21745 | 22516.3 | 0.0 | 17671 | 18365.7 | 0.0 |
| | 33.07 | 33.07 | | 34.50 | 39.27 | | 34.50 | 39.27 | | 9.30 | 13.60 | |
| R100 | $2.15 \cdot 10^7$ | $2.15 \cdot 10^7$ | 0.0 | $2.46 \cdot 10^6$ | $2.65 \cdot 10^6$ | 0.1 | $2.84 \cdot 10^6$ | $2.99 \cdot 10^6$ | 0.0 | $2.43 \cdot 10^6$ | $2.44 \cdot 10^6$ | 0.2 |
| | 786.11 | 786.11 | | 1.35 | 9.02 | | 16.95 | 23.28 | | 0.05 | 0.52 | |
| R100-E | $1.95 \cdot 10^8$ | $1.95 \cdot 10^8$ | 0.0 | $1.95 \cdot 10^8$ | $2.10 \cdot 10^8$ | 0.1 | $2.56 \cdot 10^8$ | $2.56 \cdot 10^8$ | 0.0 | $1.86 \cdot 10^8$ | $1.95 \cdot 10^8$ | 0.2 |
| | 6.17 | 6.17 | | 6.07 | 14.44 | | 39.47 | 39.50 | | 1.30 | 5.99 | |
| R300 | $2.03 \cdot 10^8$ | $2.03 \cdot 10^8$ | 0.0 | $1.58 \cdot 10^7$ | $1.64 \cdot 10^7$ | 0.3 | $2.10 \cdot 10^7$ | $2.46 \cdot 10^7$ | 0.1 | $1.53 \cdot 10^7$ | $1.58 \cdot 10^7$ | 3.7 |
| | 6.17 | 6.17 | | 3.27 | 6.68 | | 36.82 | 60.77 | | 0.10 | 3.14 | |
| R300-E | $1.70 \cdot 10^9$ | $1.70 \cdot 10^9$ | 0.0 | $1.70 \cdot 10^9$ | $1.75 \cdot 10^9$ | 0.3 | $2.70 \cdot 10^9$ | $2.71 \cdot 10^9$ | 0.1 | $1.64 \cdot 10^9$ | $1.68 \cdot 10^9$ | 3.7 |
| | 5.33 | 5.33 | | 5.25 | 8.56 | | 67.35 | 68.17 | | 1.75 | 4.48 | |

Table 46: OCST construction heuristics' results for standard benchmark and randomly generated instances with < 500 nodes. Large numbers denote the average final solution cost, smaller numbers below are the excess above the best-known value in percent.

| Instance | Star min | Star avg | Star $t$ [s] | ShortestPath min | ShortestPath avg | ShortestPath $t$ [s] | MST min | MST avg | MST $t$ [s] | AM-C min | AM-C avg | AM-C $t$ [s] |
|---|---|---|---|---|---|---|---|---|---|---|---|---|
| R500 | $5.83\cdot10^8$<br>1443.76 | $5.83\cdot10^8$<br>1443.76 | 0.1 | $3.84\cdot10^7$<br>1.81 | $4.06\cdot10^7$<br>7.53 | 0.9 | $5.84\cdot10^7$<br>54.84 | $6.59\cdot10^7$<br>74.57 | 0.2 | $3.78\cdot10^7$<br>0.27 | $3.90\cdot10^7$<br>3.39 | 18.3 |
| R500-E | $4.70\cdot10^9$<br>5.06 | $4.70\cdot10^9$<br>5.06 | 0.1 | $4.69\cdot10^9$<br>4.89 | $4.78\cdot10^9$<br>6.76 | 0.8 | $8.65\cdot10^9$<br>93.37 | $9.04\cdot10^9$<br>102.02 | 0.3 | $4.54\cdot10^9$<br>1.44 | $4.64\cdot10^9$<br>3.61 | 18.2 |
| R750 | $1.33\cdot10^9$<br>1566.06 | $1.33\cdot10^9$<br>1566.06 | 0.2 | $8.23\cdot10^7$<br>3.20 | $8.42\cdot10^7$<br>5.66 | 2.6 | $1.23\cdot10^8$<br>53.79 | $1.36\cdot10^8$<br>70.29 | 0.3 | $8.05\cdot10^7$<br>1.06 | $8.21\cdot10^7$<br>2.99 | 64.6 |
| R750-E | $1.08\cdot10^{10}$<br>5.24 | $1.08\cdot10^{10}$<br>5.24 | 0.2 | $1.08\cdot10^{10}$<br>5.08 | $1.11\cdot10^{10}$<br>7.30 | 1.9 | $2.59\cdot10^{10}$<br>151.27 | $2.61\cdot10^{10}$<br>153.77 | 1.1 | $1.05\cdot10^{10}$<br>2.15 | $1.09\cdot10^{10}$<br>5.40 | 63.5 |
| R1000 | $2.35\cdot10^9$<br>1621.49 | $2.35\cdot10^9$<br>1621.49 | 0.4 | $1.39\cdot10^8$<br>1.82 | $1.42\cdot10^8$<br>4.39 | 5.5 | $2.12\cdot10^8$<br>55.48 | $2.39\cdot10^8$<br>75.40 | 0.5 | $1.37\cdot10^8$<br>0.21 | $1.40\cdot10^8$<br>2.68 | 158.7 |
| R1000-E | $1.89\cdot10^{10}$<br>5.57 | $1.89\cdot10^{10}$<br>5.57 | 0.4 | $1.89\cdot10^{10}$<br>5.30 | $1.92\cdot10^{10}$<br>7.34 | 3.8 | $3.53\cdot10^{10}$<br>97.15 | $3.68\cdot10^{10}$<br>105.17 | 1.8 | $1.83\cdot10^{10}$<br>2.38 | $1.90\cdot10^{10}$<br>6.13 | 154.9 |
| R2000 | $9.62\cdot10^9$<br>1791.71 | $9.62\cdot10^9$<br>1791.71 | 1.7 | $5.22\cdot10^8$<br>2.52 | $5.31\cdot10^8$<br>4.43 | 35.4 | $8.03\cdot10^8$<br>57.94 | $9.25\cdot10^8$<br>81.92 | 2.3 | $5.17\cdot10^8$<br>1.65 | $5.22\cdot10^8$<br>2.65 | 1447.4 |
| R2000-E | $7.65\cdot10^{10}$<br>5.46 | $7.65\cdot10^{10}$<br>5.46 | 1.6 | $7.61\cdot10^{10}$<br>4.91 | $7.72\cdot10^{10}$<br>6.42 | 21.7 | $1.40\cdot10^{11}$<br>93.54 | $1.51\cdot10^{11}$<br>108.76 | 10.0 | $7.43\cdot10^{10}$<br>2.48 | $7.67\cdot10^{10}$<br>5.73 | 1394.9 |

Table 47: OCST construction heuristics' results for randomly generated instances with $\geq 500$ nodes. Large numbers denote the average final solution cost, smaller numbers below are the excess above the best-known value in percent.

of a random tree is 12.87 % (`Palmer6`, RandomPrüfer heuristic). It has to be noted that random rooted trees are generally better than Prüfer-based trees. As explained before, Prüfer sequences encode each tree with the same probability, but random rooted trees are biased towards star-like trees. Considering a star to be closer to an optimal solution than a purely random tree, the RandomRooted heuristic is able to find better solutions.

Comparing the excess between random instances with either Euclidean or non-Euclidean distances, the excess of non-Euclidean instances' solutions is generally larger than the excess for solutions to Euclidean instances of the same size. This due to the different distribution of edge lengths in both instance types: in Euclidean instances, shorter edges (compared to the maximum edge length) occur more often than longer edges, whereas for non-Euclidean instances, edge lengths are distributed equally. Shorter edges, again, lead to better solutions (more similar to MSTs), explaining the lower excess. In terms of computation times, the RandomPrüfer heuristic is slower than the Random Rooted heuristic. Whereas for instances with $\leq 500$ nodes computation times are negligible, the largest average computation times were recorded for problem instance `R2000-E`, where the RandomPrüfer heuristic required 9.5 s to construct a solution, whereas the Random Rooted required only 3.8 s (not shown in Tab. 44).

Among all construction heuristics, the construction heuristic from Ahuja and Murty (designated as 'AM-C') performs best for the classic benchmark instances by `Palmer`, `Berry`, and `Raidl`. For problem instances `Berry6` (534) and `Berry35` (16 915), the same solutions as in [30] are constructed. The best-constructed solution for `Raidl10` matches the previously best-known solution (53 674). The second best heuristic for both `Palmer` and `Berry` instances is the MST heuristic. For instances `Berry6` and `Berry35` the same solutions were found as before. For instances from the `Raidl` series, however, the minimum and average solution quality is inferior to the ShortestPath heuristic's results, except for the average values of `Raidl20` and `Raidl35`. Generally, the ShortestPath heuristic is, next to AM-C, the second best choice for `Raidl` instances. For example, for instance `Raidl10`, the best-known solution with cost 53 674 was constructed in 13 out of 20 runs. In contrast, for `Berry` and `Palmer` instances, this heuristic performs considerably worse and thus can not be recommended. For both series, the Star heuristic performs better, but its performance is not comparable to the top performers MST and AM-C, except for `Berry35u`. E. g. for `Berry35`, the average excess for the Star heuristic is 359.9 % and for the ShortestPathTree heuristic 440.5 %.

As there are only two types of graphs created by the random instance generator (either Euclidean or non-Euclidean), it is easier to draw conclusions. As before, the AM-C heuristic performs best, finding the best initial solutions for most problem instances. For some large Euclidean instances, however, the average solution cost is slightly higher than the Star heuristic. For example, for instance R2000-E, the Star heuristic finds the best solutions on average (excess 5.46 %); the AM-C heuristic find solutions with an excess of 5.73 %. Furthermore, with growing instance size, the computational costs to construct an initial solution are considerably larger than the other construction heuristics. Constructing an initial solution for an instance with 2000 nodes takes more than 20 CPU minutes in the used experimental environment.

Both the Star heuristic and the MST heuristic differ considerably in their performance, depending on whether they are applied to a Euclidean or a non-Euclidean instance. For Euclidean instances, the Star heuristic performs similarly to the ShortestPathTree heuristic, whereas the MST fails for this type of instance, resulting in the worst solutions of all structured heuristics. For example, for R1000-E, the excess for the Star, ShortestPathTree and MST heuristics are 5.57 %, 7.34 %, and 105.17 %, respectively. For non-Euclidean instances, the MST heuristic performs considerably better than the Star heuristic. Still, both heuristics perform worse than to the ShortestPathTree heuristic and the AM-C heuristic. For R1000, for example, the excess for the heuristics Star, MST, ShortestPathTree, and AM-C are 1621.49 %, 75.40 %, 4.39 %, and 2.68 %.

Among the construction heuristics, the Star heuristic is the fastest, requiring < 2 s even for the largest instances. Whereas, for this heuristic, the computation times for both Euclidean and non-Euclidean instances of the same size match, computation times differ for both the MST heuristic and ShortestPathTree. For the MST heuristic, constructing solutions takes up to 5 times longer for Euclidean instances than for non-Euclidean instances. This is due to the fact that paths in Euclidean instances are considerably longer (in terms of hop count) compared to non-Euclidean instances. For example, for R2000-E the average hop distance between two nodes is about 102.9, whereas it is only 9.4 for R2000. For the ShortestPathTree heuristic, constructing a non-Euclidean instance's solution takes up to 2 times longer than the construction for an Euclidean instance. Here, during construction of SPTs, twice as many decreaseKey operations [127] are performed on the Fibonacci heap in

Dijkstra's algorithm for non-Euclidean instances compared to Euclidean instances.

In summary, the AM-C heuristic is the best choice for small instances < 100 nodes as it results in the best solutions. For larger instances, large computation times prohibit its application, thus the ShortestPathTree heuristic becomes the best general choice: its solution quality is only slightly below the AM-C's average quality but computation times are much lower. For Euclidean problem instances, the Star heuristic can be used for even better results in a shorter time. Due to their high solution costs (large excess), random solutions should not be considered for any sophisticated solution-finding approach.

## 5.4  Local Search

One of the best-known local searches for the OCST is from Ahuja and Murty [3]. This local search (called 'tree improvement' by its authors and called 'AM-H' here) has been summarized in Sec. 5.1.2 (p. 194).

Although this local search is known for its good solutions, it requires a considerable amount of time to solve larger problem instances. The problem of high computation times is addressed here by the introduction of an improvement strategy that simplifies the computation of cost changes for possible 1-exchange moves by estimating only the change instead of computing the exact gain. Once an exchange move is actually performed, the correct cost is computed. As explained below, this guess on the cost change can be parametrized from being slow and precise (as the original algorithm) to fast and imprecise. Given a good choice of parameters, even a fast but imprecise setting can outperform the original algorithm, as more improving exchange steps can be performed in the same time.

Performance evaluations of the AM-H show that the computation of vector $h$ (Eq. (5.10)) is the most time-consuming part of the algorithm (see Fig. 46, p. 195). This is particularly noticeable for components $S$ and $\overline{S}$ with either $|S| \ll |\overline{S}|$ or $|S| \gg |\overline{S}|$. Therefore, a modification is proposed that examines a limited number of candidate nodes from both components $S$ and $\overline{S}$. The modified algorithm uses $S' \subseteq S$ and $\overline{S'} \subseteq \overline{S}$ to compute both $w$ and $h$. This approach reduces the computation time considerably, but renders $\alpha_{i,j}$ a heuristic value only instead of an exact measure to compute a 1-exchange's cost. Thus, using these $\alpha$-values may lead to exchange moves that actually degrade the current solution's quality. As the tree's new cost has to be computed when performing the exchange operation, the move can be made undone if necessary by restoring the previous solution.

The primary objective of the modified local search is to select subsets $S' \subseteq S$ and $\overline{S'} \subseteq \overline{S}$. There are two degrees of freedom in choosing nodes: the number of nodes determines the computation time for the subroutine ALPHA (Fig. 46, p. 195) and the quality of the resulting $\alpha$ values. Selecting nodes based on their location in the current tree or graph may influence the quality, too, as the selection strategy determines the neighborhood in this local search.

In previous publications [63, 66], the size of node sets $S'$ and $\overline{S'}$ was determined as a fraction $f \in (0.0, 1.0]$ resulting in $|S'| = f \cdot |S|$ and $|\overline{S'}| = f \cdot |\overline{S}|$. This fraction value was set to $0.1 \leq f \leq 0.3$ for most evaluated setups. Although this approach was successful, it introduced $f$ as a new experimental parameter. Therefore, a new approach is introduced, where the size of $S'$ and $\overline{S'}$ is limited by

$$|S'|, |\overline{S'}| \leq \lceil \sqrt{n} \rceil \tag{5.20}$$

Using the square root of $n$ allows us to reduce the complexity of computing $h$ from time $\mathcal{O}(n^2)$ down to $\mathcal{O}(n)$.

Once the number of nodes to be selected has been determined, the nodes to be included into $S'$ and $\overline{S'}$ have to be selected. For the following discussing, it is assumed that edge $e = (s, t)$ has been removed from the tree splitting it into two components. The following selection strategies were considered:

REQUIREMENT  Sorts nodes in each component by their requirement value to $s$ or $t$, respectively. Nodes are either sorted by increasing ('Req↑') or decreasing requirement ('Req↓').

DISTANCE  Sorts nodes by their distance value to $s$ or $t$, respectively. As a distance value, the edge between the node and $s$ or $t$, respectively, is used; if it is not available, the unique path's length in the component is used. Nodes are either sorted by increasing ('Dst↑') or decreasing distance ('Dst↓').

HOP COUNT  Sorts nodes by the hop count to node $s$ or $t$, respectively. This strategy is denoted as 'Hop'.

PATH LENGTH  Sorts nodes by the path length in the tree to node $s$ or $t$, respectively. This strategy is denoted as 'PLn'.

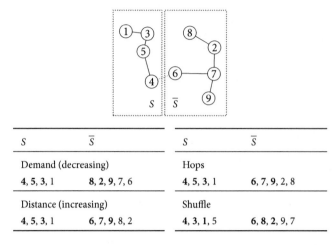

| $S$ | $\overline{S}$ | | $S$ | $\overline{S}$ |
|---|---|---|---|---|
| Demand (decreasing) | | | Hops | |
| **4, 5, 3**, 1 | **8, 2, 9**, 7, 6 | | **4, 5, 3**, 1 | **6, 7, 9**, 2, 8 |
| Distance (increasing) | | | Shuffle | |
| **4, 5, 3**, 1 | **6, 7, 9**, 8, 2 | | **4, 3, 1**, 5 | **6, 8, 2**, 9, 7 |

Figure 49: Examples of different node sorting strategies. Selected node ids are highlighted.

INDEX   Sorts nodes by their node index. This strategy is denoted as 'Idx'.

SHUFFLE   Performs no sorting, but choose nodes randomly instead. This strategy is denoted as 'Shf'.

In Fig. 49, an example of different selection strategies is shown. Here, a Euclidean problem instance with 9 nodes is given, where the edge $(s, t) = (4, 6)$ (gray edge) has been removed from the current solution. The tree is partitioned into two components denoted as $S = \{1, 3, 4, 5\}$ and $\overline{S} = \{2, 6, 7, 8, 9\}$. Furthermore, it is assumed $|S'| = |\overline{S'}| = \sqrt{n} = 3$. Note, it must hold that $s \in S$ and $t \in \overline{S}$ so that an $\alpha$ value is computed for the removed edge and thus the change in cost can be estimated. For the decreasing demand sorting, it holds that $r_{4,5} = 98 \geq r_{3,4} = 79 \geq r_{1,4} = 31$ in $S$ (similar for $\overline{S}$). For the other three example strategies in Fig. 49, the sorting is obvious. Once the nodes in both components are sorted, the first $\lceil \sqrt{n} \rceil$ nodes are used for $S'$ and $\overline{S'}$, respectively (highlighted as bold node ids).

### 5.4.1 Results

Experiments were conducted by applying both the original Ahuja-Murty local search algorithm and the improved algorithm on a set of benchmark instances as listed in Fig. 42. The solutions in Sec. 5.3 were used as initial solutions, with both random tree solution construction heuristics skipped due to their low quality. All the sorting strategies as described above were evaluated and compared to the Ahuja-Murty local search algorithm ('AM-H'). Experiments were repeated 20 times and average values were used for the following discussion. As a termination criterion, a time limit was imposed on the experimental setups, depending on the problem instance's size, with a minimum time limit of 1 s set. The time limit in CPU seconds for an instance with $n$ nodes was set to

$$t_{\max} = \max\left\{1, \left\lceil \frac{n}{100} \right\rceil^2\right\} \tag{5.21}$$

Detailed results on all the sorting strategies for the six selected problem instances are given in Tables 48–50. Results for all the problem instances, comparing only the best performing sorting strategy and the original Ahuja-Murty heuristic local search algorithm, are given in Tables 51–53.

### Sorting Strategies

For a detailed discussion, six problem instances were selected. Four small instances (Palmer12, Berry35, Raidl10, and Raidl35) were selected. For small instances, the number of alternatives when sorting and selecting nodes is rather limited, resulting in similar sets of $S'$ and $\overline{S'}$ for different strategies. Larger instances, such as R500 and R500-E, are expected to show a more predictable and stable performance.

For problem instance Palmer12, when starting from solutions constructed either by the Star or ShortestPathTree, the algorithm with Shuffle sorting is the best performing local search, with AM-H in second place. When starting from Star solutions, the Shuffle sorting strategy (excess 0.46 %) finds the best-known solution in 13 out of 20 runs; the AM-H setup (excess 1.22 %) finds this solution in 11 out of 20 runs. Starting from MST solutions, AM-H performs best (excess 1.28 %) and, furthermore, the Req↓ (1.34 %), Dst↑ (1.44 %), and PLn (1.44 %) sorting strategies outperform Shuffle (1.46 %). Starting from AM-C solutions, both AM-H (1.50 %) and Shuffle (0.81 %) are outperformed by Req↓,

| Instance | LS | Star | SPT | MST | AM-C |
|---|---|---|---|---|---|
| Palmer12 | AM-H | $3.47 \cdot 10^6$ | $3.50 \cdot 10^6$ | $3.47 \cdot 10^6$ | $3.48 \cdot 10^6$ |
| 1 s | | 1.22 | 2.06 | 1.28 | 1.50 |
| | Shf | $3.44 \cdot 10^6$ | $3.47 \cdot 10^6$ | $3.48 \cdot 10^6$ | $3.46 \cdot 10^6$ |
| | | 0.46 | 1.29 | 1.46 | 0.81 |
| | Idx | $4.20 \cdot 10^6$ | $4.91 \cdot 10^6$ | $3.51 \cdot 10^6$ | $3.51 \cdot 10^6$ |
| | | 22.45 | 43.09 | 2.44 | 2.30 |
| | Req↑ | $3.61 \cdot 10^6$ | $4.18 \cdot 10^6$ | $3.68 \cdot 10^6$ | $3.51 \cdot 10^6$ |
| | | 5.25 | 21.85 | 7.38 | 2.30 |
| | Req↓ | $5.93 \cdot 10^6$ | $5.78 \cdot 10^6$ | $3.47 \cdot 10^6$ | $3.44 \cdot 10^6$ |
| | | 73.05 | 68.55 | 1.34 | 0.33 |
| | Dst↑ | $5.93 \cdot 10^6$ | $5.78 \cdot 10^6$ | $3.48 \cdot 10^6$ | $3.44 \cdot 10^6$ |
| | | 73.05 | 68.55 | 1.44 | 0.33 |
| | Dst↓ | $3.66 \cdot 10^6$ | $4.32 \cdot 10^6$ | $3.69 \cdot 10^6$ | $3.51 \cdot 10^6$ |
| | | 6.67 | 26.07 | 7.56 | 2.30 |
| | PLn | $5.93 \cdot 10^6$ | $5.48 \cdot 10^6$ | $3.48 \cdot 10^6$ | $3.44 \cdot 10^6$ |
| | | 73.05 | 59.72 | 1.44 | 0.33 |
| | Hop | $4.27 \cdot 10^6$ | $4.63 \cdot 10^6$ | $3.53 \cdot 10^6$ | $3.51 \cdot 10^6$ |
| | | 24.56 | 35.09 | 2.91 | 2.30 |
| Berry35 | AM-H | 16915.0 | 16915.0 | 16915.0 | 16915.0 |
| 1 s | | 0.00 | 0.00 | 0.00 | 0.00 |
| | Shf | 16915.0 | 16915.0 | 16915.0 | 16915.0 |
| | | 0.00 | 0.00 | 0.00 | 0.00 |
| | Idx | 49201.0 | 59471.7 | 16915.0 | 16915.0 |
| | | 190.87 | 251.59 | 0.00 | 0.00 |
| | Req↑ | 19749.9 | 20074.1 | 16915.0 | 16915.0 |
| | | 16.76 | 18.68 | 0.00 | 0.00 |
| | Req↓ | 45574.2 | 24284.9 | 16915.0 | 16915.0 |
| | | 169.43 | 43.57 | 0.00 | 0.00 |
| | Dst↑ | 31001.7 | 58494.7 | 16915.0 | 16915.0 |
| | | 83.28 | 245.82 | 0.00 | 0.00 |
| | Dst↓ | 44115.2 | 53462.7 | 16915.0 | 16915.0 |
| | | 160.81 | 216.07 | 0.00 | 0.00 |
| | PLn | 68929.0 | 80795.6 | 16915.0 | 16915.0 |
| | | 307.50 | 377.66 | 0.00 | 0.00 |
| | Hop | 51157.1 | 58310.3 | 16915.0 | 16915.0 |
| | | 202.44 | 244.73 | 0.00 | 0.00 |

Table 48: Results for sorting strategies for instances Palmer12 and Berry35. Large numbers denote the average final solution cost, smaller numbers below are the excess above the best-known value in percent.

Dst↑, and PLn (all three 0.33%). This pattern of performance is specific for this problem instances and does not occur for other problem instances. All other sorting strategies perform worse than the strategies mentioned above. In some setups, such as PLn starting from Star solutions, there is basically no improvement in the initial solutions (excess 73.05 %); starting from AM solutions, however, this sorting strategy is a top performer.

For problem instance Berry35, both the MST and the AM-C construction heuristics find the best-known solution and are thus not considered in this analysis. For the other two construction heuristics, Shuffle is the best sorting strategy, producing the same results as AM-H. The second best sorting strategy is Req↑ with 16.76 % and 18.68 % excess starting from Star or ShortestPathTree solutions, respectively. All other sorting strategies perform considerably worse, up to cases where no improvements for the initial solutions were found.

For instance Raidl10, the AM-C construction heuristic finds the best-known solution (excluded from the following analysis). The same holds when starting from any other construction heuristic's solution and applying AM-H or the Shuffle sorting strategy. Furthermore, the best known solution is found in all runs when starting from Star solutions using Dem↑ or Dst↑ sorting strategies. The other sorting strategies' setups perform considerably worse; some do not even improve the initial solution (e. g. Dst↑ starting from MST solutions).

For Raidl35, using AM-H or the Shuffle sorting strategy results in the best-known solutions regardless of the initial solution. The only other setups that find solutions with an average excess of < 1% are those starting from AM-C solutions using any sorting strategies except for Dst↑, Dst↓, or Hop. Again, some setups (for example, starting from either AM-C or MST solutions using hop count sorting) do not improve the initial solution at all.

For the two largest instances in this detailed discussion (R500 and R500-E), a clear difference between both AM-H and the Shuffle sorting strategy compared to the other sorting strategies is visible. Whereas the Shuffle sorting strategy outperforms AM-H in terms of average solution quality for all four construction heuristics for R500-E and R500, none of the other sorting strategies is competitive. For example, for R500 starting from MST solutions, AM-H results in solutions with an average excess of 6.71 %, whereas Shuffle results in solutions with excess 6.34 %, but the best of the remaining sorting strategies (here, Dst↓) has an average excess of 44.43 %. Starting from AM-C results in best

| Instance | LS | Star | SPT | MST | AM-C |
|---|---|---|---|---|---|
| Raidl10 | AM-H | 53674.0 | 53674.0 | 53674.0 | 53674.0 |
| 1 s | | 0.00 | 0.00 | 0.00 | 0.00 |
| | Shf | 53674.0 | 53674.0 | 53674.0 | 53674.0 |
| | | 0.00 | 0.00 | 0.00 | 0.00 |
| | Idx | $1.01 \cdot 10^5$ | 56221.2 | 57910.4 | 53674.0 |
| | | 88.15 | 4.75 | 7.89 | 0.00 |
| | Req↑ | 53674.0 | 54958.5 | 55868.0 | 53674.0 |
| | | 0.00 | 2.39 | 4.09 | 0.00 |
| | Req↓ | 77101.0 | 55769.4 | 57354.0 | 53674.0 |
| | | 43.65 | 3.90 | 6.86 | 0.00 |
| | Dst↑ | 53674.0 | 55639.8 | 58352.0 | 53674.0 |
| | | 0.00 | 3.66 | 8.72 | 0.00 |
| | Dst↓ | 73283.0 | 55639.8 | 55309.1 | 53674.0 |
| | | 36.53 | 3.66 | 3.05 | 0.00 |
| | PLn | 60367.3 | 54481.3 | 57400.0 | 53674.0 |
| | | 12.47 | 1.50 | 6.94 | 0.00 |
| | Hop | 97967.0 | 54958.5 | 57957.0 | 53674.0 |
| | | 82.52 | 2.39 | 7.98 | 0.00 |
| Raidl35 | AM-H | $4.12 \cdot 10^5$ | $4.12 \cdot 10^5$ | $4.12 \cdot 10^5$ | $4.12 \cdot 10^5$ |
| 1 s | | 0.00 | 0.00 | 0.00 | 0.00 |
| | Shf | $4.12 \cdot 10^5$ | $4.12 \cdot 10^5$ | $4.12 \cdot 10^5$ | $4.12 \cdot 10^5$ |
| | | 0.00 | 0.00 | 0.00 | 0.00 |
| | Idx | $1.10 \cdot 10^6$ | $4.51 \cdot 10^5$ | $4.34 \cdot 10^5$ | $4.14 \cdot 10^5$ |
| | | 167.61 | 9.54 | 5.20 | 0.45 |
| | Req↑ | $1.02 \cdot 10^6$ | $4.50 \cdot 10^5$ | $4.39 \cdot 10^5$ | $4.14 \cdot 10^5$ |
| | | 147.56 | 9.20 | 6.55 | 0.49 |
| | Req↓ | $7.06 \cdot 10^5$ | $4.56 \cdot 10^5$ | $4.43 \cdot 10^5$ | $4.14 \cdot 10^5$ |
| | | 71.21 | 10.71 | 7.43 | 0.49 |
| | Dst↑ | $6.23 \cdot 10^5$ | $4.57 \cdot 10^5$ | $4.45 \cdot 10^5$ | $4.17 \cdot 10^5$ |
| | | 51.08 | 10.97 | 7.86 | 1.20 |
| | Dst↓ | $9.40 \cdot 10^5$ | $4.53 \cdot 10^5$ | $4.41 \cdot 10^5$ | $4.17 \cdot 10^5$ |
| | | 127.97 | 9.99 | 7.04 | 1.19 |
| | PLn | $6.75 \cdot 10^5$ | $4.50 \cdot 10^5$ | $4.47 \cdot 10^5$ | $4.14 \cdot 10^5$ |
| | | 63.67 | 9.14 | 8.45 | 0.46 |
| | Hop | $9.08 \cdot 10^5$ | $4.53 \cdot 10^5$ | $4.47 \cdot 10^5$ | $4.17 \cdot 10^5$ |
| | | 120.20 | 9.98 | 8.51 | 1.19 |

Table 49: Results for sorting strategies for two selected Raidl instances. Large numbers denote the average final solution cost, smaller numbers below are the excess above the best-known value in percent.

| Instance | LS | Star | SPT | MST | AM-C |
|---|---|---|---|---|---|
| R500 | AM-H | $4.19 \cdot 10^7$ | $3.94 \cdot 10^7$ | $4.03 \cdot 10^7$ | $3.89 \cdot 10^7$ |
| 25 s | | 11.07 | 4.30 | 6.71 | 3.04 |
| | Shf | $4.14 \cdot 10^7$ | $3.94 \cdot 10^7$ | $4.01 \cdot 10^7$ | $3.89 \cdot 10^7$ |
| | | 9.69 | 4.26 | 6.34 | 3.02 |
| | Idx | $1.15 \cdot 10^8$ | $4.06 \cdot 10^7$ | $5.81 \cdot 10^7$ | $3.90 \cdot 10^7$ |
| | | 203.38 | 7.44 | 54.00 | 3.38 |
| | Req↑ | $8.94 \cdot 10^7$ | $4.05 \cdot 10^7$ | $5.45 \cdot 10^7$ | $3.90 \cdot 10^7$ |
| | | 136.95 | 7.42 | 44.49 | 3.38 |
| | Req↓ | $9.07 \cdot 10^7$ | $4.05 \cdot 10^7$ | $5.49 \cdot 10^7$ | $3.90 \cdot 10^7$ |
| | | 140.33 | 7.42 | 45.45 | 3.37 |
| | Dst↑ | $6.87 \cdot 10^7$ | $4.05 \cdot 10^7$ | $5.83 \cdot 10^7$ | $3.90 \cdot 10^7$ |
| | | 82.13 | 7.43 | 54.44 | 3.39 |
| | Dst↓ | $8.92 \cdot 10^7$ | $4.05 \cdot 10^7$ | $5.45 \cdot 10^7$ | $3.90 \cdot 10^7$ |
| | | 136.45 | 7.40 | 44.43 | 3.38 |
| | PLn | $5.60 \cdot 10^7$ | $4.05 \cdot 10^7$ | $6.45 \cdot 10^7$ | $3.90 \cdot 10^7$ |
| | | 48.35 | 7.36 | 70.80 | 3.39 |
| | Hop | $2.00 \cdot 10^8$ | $4.06 \cdot 10^7$ | $6.57 \cdot 10^7$ | $3.90 \cdot 10^7$ |
| | | 431.05 | 7.51 | 73.99 | 3.39 |
| R500-E | AM-H | $4.51 \cdot 10^9$ | $4.53 \cdot 10^9$ | $4.55 \cdot 10^9$ | $4.55 \cdot 10^9$ |
| 25 s | | 0.78 | 1.29 | 1.67 | 1.74 |
| | Shf | $4.51 \cdot 10^9$ | $4.53 \cdot 10^9$ | $4.53 \cdot 10^9$ | $4.54 \cdot 10^9$ |
| | | 0.71 | 1.18 | 1.24 | 1.37 |
| | Idx | $4.61 \cdot 10^9$ | $4.65 \cdot 10^9$ | $4.70 \cdot 10^9$ | $4.61 \cdot 10^9$ |
| | | 3.00 | 3.89 | 5.11 | 3.10 |
| | Req↑ | $4.64 \cdot 10^9$ | $4.70 \cdot 10^9$ | $4.87 \cdot 10^9$ | $4.62 \cdot 10^9$ |
| | | 3.73 | 5.07 | 8.72 | 3.32 |
| | Req↓ | $4.62 \cdot 10^9$ | $4.69 \cdot 10^9$ | $4.90 \cdot 10^9$ | $4.63 \cdot 10^9$ |
| | | 3.23 | 4.73 | 9.43 | 3.43 |
| | Dst↑ | $4.58 \cdot 10^9$ | $4.61 \cdot 10^9$ | $6.23 \cdot 10^9$ | $4.60 \cdot 10^9$ |
| | | 2.23 | 3.10 | 39.31 | 2.87 |
| | Dst↓ | $4.70 \cdot 10^9$ | $4.78 \cdot 10^9$ | $8.66 \cdot 10^9$ | $4.64 \cdot 10^9$ |
| | | 5.06 | 6.75 | 93.46 | 3.61 |
| | PLn | $4.62 \cdot 10^9$ | $4.66 \cdot 10^9$ | $6.64 \cdot 10^9$ | $4.61 \cdot 10^9$ |
| | | 3.25 | 4.16 | 48.32 | 3.07 |
| | Hop | $4.70 \cdot 10^9$ | $4.77 \cdot 10^9$ | $8.51 \cdot 10^9$ | $4.64 \cdot 10^9$ |
| | | 4.92 | 6.66 | 90.17 | 3.60 |

Table 50: Results for sorting strategies for instances R500 and R500-E. Large numbers denote the average final solution cost, smaller numbers below are the excess above the best-known value in percent.

solutions for R500 (excess 3.04 % and 3.02 % for AM-H and Shuffle, respectively), followed by ShortestPathTree solutions (excess 4.30 % and 4.26 %, respectively). For R500-E, best solutions are found starting from Star solutions (excess 0.78 % and 0.71 %, respectively), again followed by ShortestPathTree solutions (excess 1.29 % and 1.18 %, respectively). As before, some sorting strategies do not enable the algorithm presented here to improve the initial solutions.

### 5.4.2 Random Shuffle

The good performance of the Shuffle strategy can be explained by the fact that this strategy is the only one where nodes from each component are selected with the same probability, whereas other strategies have a strong bias towards a small selection of nodes (for example, when sorting by node index). Comparing the average solution qualities when reaching the instance-specific time bound shows that, among all the sorting strategies, Shuffle is the only strategy that can compete with the Ahuja-Murty local search. Therefore, the following discussion for all other problem instances is restricted to AM-H and the sorting strategy 'Shuffle'. The algorithm presented here using the Shuffle sorting strategy is dubbed 'Random Shuffle Ahuja-Murty' (RS-AM).

Although the RS-AM was designed primarily for large problem instances, it performs comparably to the original AM-H for small instances. In about half of all setups (regarding problem instance and construction heuristic), the average solution quality using the Shuffle sorting strategy is better than the solution quality of the AM-H algorithm.

### Standard Benchmark Instances

For both Palmer instances, both algorithms find best solutions starting from Star solutions: for Palmer6 (Tab. 51) the best-known solution is always found; for Palmer12 (Tab. 48), AM-H has an average excess of 1.22 % and RS-AM has an excess of 0.46 %. For setups starting from one of the other three construction heuristics, RS-AM finds better average solutions, compared to AM-H, in four out of six cases (plus one 'draw').

Both Berry6 and Berry35 pose no challenge, as the best-known solution is found in each setup. Berry35u, however, is harder; even in the best setup (starting from AM-C solutions), the average excess is

| Instance | LS | Star | SPT | MST | AM-C |
|---|---|---|---|---|---|
| Palmer6 | AM-H | $6.93 \cdot 10^5$ | $6.98 \cdot 10^5$ | $7.01 \cdot 10^5$ | $6.97 \cdot 10^5$ |
| 1 s | | 0.00 | 0.65 | 1.08 | 0.54 |
| | RS-AM | $6.93 \cdot 10^5$ | $6.98 \cdot 10^5$ | $6.93 \cdot 10^5$ | $6.95 \cdot 10^5$ |
| | | 0.00 | 0.65 | 0.00 | 0.32 |
| Berry6 | AM-H | 534.0 | 534.0 | 534.0 | 534.0 |
| 1 s | | 0.00 | 0.00 | 0.00 | 0.00 |
| | RS-AM | 534.0 | 534.0 | 534.0 | 534.0 |
| | | 0.00 | 0.00 | 0.00 | 0.00 |
| Berry35u | AM-H | 17133.3 | 16986.2 | 16941.5 | 16198.9 |
| 1 s | | 5.98 | 5.07 | 4.79 | 0.20 |
| | RS-AM | 17194.0 | 16930.3 | 16932.7 | 16220.8 |
| | | 6.35 | 4.72 | 4.74 | 0.33 |
| Raidl20 | AM-H | $1.63 \cdot 10^5$ | $1.59 \cdot 10^5$ | $1.58 \cdot 10^5$ | $1.58 \cdot 10^5$ |
| 1 s | | 3.60 | 0.90 | 0.00 | 0.00 |
| | RS-AM | $1.62 \cdot 10^5$ | $1.59 \cdot 10^5$ | $1.58 \cdot 10^5$ | $1.58 \cdot 10^5$ |
| | | 2.70 | 1.12 | 0.00 | 0.00 |
| Raidl50 | AM-H | $8.07 \cdot 10^5$ | $8.07 \cdot 10^5$ | $8.08 \cdot 10^5$ | $8.07 \cdot 10^5$ |
| 1 s | | 0.01 | 0.05 | 0.10 | 0.07 |
| | RS-AM | $8.07 \cdot 10^5$ | $8.07 \cdot 10^5$ | $8.08 \cdot 10^5$ | $8.08 \cdot 10^5$ |
| | | 0.04 | 0.06 | 0.11 | 0.09 |
| Raidl75 | AM-H | $1.72 \cdot 10^6$ | $1.75 \cdot 10^6$ | $1.72 \cdot 10^6$ | $1.72 \cdot 10^6$ |
| 1 s | | 0.00 | 1.83 | 0.00 | 0.00 |
| | RS-AM | $1.73 \cdot 10^6$ | $1.75 \cdot 10^6$ | $1.72 \cdot 10^6$ | $1.76 \cdot 10^6$ |
| | | 0.51 | 1.91 | 0.01 | 2.32 |
| Raidl100 | AM-H | $2.64 \cdot 10^6$ | $2.65 \cdot 10^6$ | $2.56 \cdot 10^6$ | $2.64 \cdot 10^6$ |
| 1 s | | 2.98 | 3.42 | 0.11 | 2.88 |
| | RS-AM | $2.62 \cdot 10^6$ | $2.65 \cdot 10^6$ | $2.57 \cdot 10^6$ | $2.64 \cdot 10^6$ |
| | | 2.37 | 3.47 | 0.50 | 2.91 |

Table 51: Results of the Ahuja-Murty local search and RS-AM for known benchmark instances. Large numbers denote the average final solution cost, smaller numbers below are the excess above the best-known value in percent.

| Instance | LS | Star | SPT | MST | AM-C |
|---|---|---|---|---|---|
| R100 | AM-H | $2.43 \cdot 10^6$ | $2.43 \cdot 10^6$ | $2.43 \cdot 10^6$ | $2.43 \cdot 10^6$ |
| 1 s | | 0.00 | 0.10 | 0.00 | 0.00 |
| | RS-AM | $2.43 \cdot 10^6$ | $2.43 \cdot 10^6$ | $2.43 \cdot 10^6$ | $2.43 \cdot 10^6$ |
| | | 0.18 | 0.05 | 0.14 | 0.00 |
| R100-E | AM-H | $1.86 \cdot 10^8$ | $1.88 \cdot 10^8$ | $1.87 \cdot 10^8$ | $1.87 \cdot 10^8$ |
| 1 s | | 0.96 | 2.18 | 1.51 | 1.53 |
| | RS-AM | $1.86 \cdot 10^8$ | $1.87 \cdot 10^8$ | $1.88 \cdot 10^8$ | $1.86 \cdot 10^8$ |
| | | 1.17 | 1.99 | 2.05 | 1.33 |
| R300 | AM-H | $1.58 \cdot 10^7$ | $1.56 \cdot 10^7$ | $1.58 \cdot 10^7$ | $1.56 \cdot 10^7$ |
| 9 s | | 2.90 | 2.06 | 3.26 | 2.00 |
| | RS-AM | $1.59 \cdot 10^7$ | $1.57 \cdot 10^7$ | $1.60 \cdot 10^7$ | $1.56 \cdot 10^7$ |
| | | 3.91 | 2.17 | 4.06 | 2.06 |
| R300-E | AM-H | $1.62 \cdot 10^9$ | $1.63 \cdot 10^9$ | $1.63 \cdot 10^9$ | $1.62 \cdot 10^9$ |
| 9 s | | 0.60 | 1.27 | 1.32 | 0.88 |
| | RS-AM | $1.62 \cdot 10^9$ | $1.63 \cdot 10^9$ | $1.63 \cdot 10^9$ | $1.63 \cdot 10^9$ |
| | | 0.66 | 1.12 | 1.37 | 0.98 |
| R500 | AM-H | $4.19 \cdot 10^7$ | $3.94 \cdot 10^7$ | $4.03 \cdot 10^7$ | $3.89 \cdot 10^7$ |
| 25 s | | 11.07 | 4.30 | 6.71 | 3.04 |
| | RS-AM | $4.14 \cdot 10^7$ | $3.94 \cdot 10^7$ | $4.01 \cdot 10^7$ | $3.89 \cdot 10^7$ |
| | | 9.69 | 4.26 | 6.34 | 3.02 |
| R500-E | AM-H | $4.51 \cdot 10^9$ | $4.53 \cdot 10^9$ | $4.55 \cdot 10^9$ | $4.55 \cdot 10^9$ |
| 25 s | | 0.78 | 1.29 | 1.67 | 1.74 |
| | RS-AM | $4.51 \cdot 10^9$ | $4.53 \cdot 10^9$ | $4.53 \cdot 10^9$ | $4.54 \cdot 10^9$ |
| | | 0.71 | 1.18 | 1.24 | 1.37 |
| R750 | AM-H | $9.02 \cdot 10^7$ | $8.21 \cdot 10^7$ | $8.46 \cdot 10^7$ | – |
| 57 s | | 13.23 | 2.99 | 6.12 | |
| | RS-AM | $8.61 \cdot 10^7$ | $8.21 \cdot 10^7$ | $8.45 \cdot 10^7$ | – |
| | | 7.99 | 2.96 | 5.96 | |
| R750-E | AM-H | $1.04 \cdot 10^{10}$ | $1.05 \cdot 10^{10}$ | $1.08 \cdot 10^{10}$ | – |
| 57 s | | 0.78 | 1.48 | 5.15 | |
| | RS-AM | $1.04 \cdot 10^{10}$ | $1.04 \cdot 10^{10}$ | $1.06 \cdot 10^{10}$ | – |
| | | 0.46 | 0.90 | 2.62 | |

Table 52: Results of the Ahuja-Murty local search and RS-AM for random instances with < 1000 nodes. Large numbers denote the average final solution cost, smaller numbers below are the excess above the best-known value in percent.

| Instance | LS | Star | SPT | MST | AM-C |
|----------|-----|------|-----|-----|------|
| R1000 | AM-H | $1.44 \cdot 10^8$ | $1.39 \cdot 10^8$ | $1.46 \cdot 10^8$ | – |
| 100 s | | 5.63 | 2.38 | 7.34 | |
| | RS-AM | $1.43 \cdot 10^8$ | $1.39 \cdot 10^8$ | $1.45 \cdot 10^8$ | – |
| | | 4.93 | 2.36 | 6.42 | |
| R1000-E | AM-H | $1.81 \cdot 10^{10}$ | $1.83 \cdot 10^{10}$ | $1.82 \cdot 10^{10}$ | – |
| 100 s | | 1.15 | 1.96 | 1.60 | |
| | RS-AM | $1.80 \cdot 10^{10}$ | $1.81 \cdot 10^{10}$ | $1.81 \cdot 10^{10}$ | – |
| | | 0.38 | 1.01 | 1.22 | |
| R2000 | AM-H | $1.89 \cdot 10^9$ | $5.24 \cdot 10^8$ | $5.68 \cdot 10^8$ | – |
| 400 s | | 271.25 | 2.91 | 11.58 | |
| | RS-AM | $5.35 \cdot 10^8$ | $5.19 \cdot 10^8$ | $5.34 \cdot 10^8$ | – |
| | | 5.15 | 1.98 | 4.95 | |
| R2000-E | AM-H | $7.55 \cdot 10^{10}$ | $7.54 \cdot 10^{10}$ | $7.50 \cdot 10^{10}$ | – |
| 400 s | | 4.15 | 4.05 | 3.43 | |
| | RS-AM | $7.29 \cdot 10^{10}$ | $7.31 \cdot 10^{10}$ | $7.33 \cdot 10^{10}$ | – |
| | | 0.53 | 0.88 | 1.15 | |

Table 53: Results of the Ahuja-Murty local search and RS-AM for random instances with $\geq$ 1000 nodes. Large numbers denote the average final solution cost, smaller numbers below are the excess above the best-known value in percent.

0.20 % and 0.33 % for AM-H and RS-AM, respectively. Here, the best known solution is only found twice by AM-H.

From the Raidl series, problem instance Raidl10 poses no challenge to both algorithms, as the best-known solution is found in each setup. For Raidl20 both algorithms always find the best known solution when starting from either the MST or AM-C solutions, given that both construction heuristics already provide the best initial solutions on average. Starting from Star solutions, AM-H results in the highest average excess (3.60 %) observed for any setup on Raidl instances, whereas the RS-AM has an average excess of only 2.70 %. For Raidl50, all setups (regardless of construction heuristic or local search) find solutions with an excess ranging from 0.01 % to 0.11 %. Here, most setups find the best-known solution with cost 806 864 in at least one of 20 runs. For example, starting from Star solutions, AM-H finds this solution in 15 out of 20 runs; RS-AM finds it in 16 runs. With instance Raidl75, AM-H performs better than RS-AM for each of the four construction heuristics. For example, the average initial solution with AM-C had an excess of 4.13 % and AM-H finds solutions with an excess of 0.0 % (cost 1 717 491) and 2.32 % (RS-AM), but starting with Star solutions (excess 607.3 %) the local searches' average excess is 0.0 % and 0.51 % (finding the best known solution 19 out of 20 times). Finally, for `Raidl100`, the best results are found starting from MST solutions using AM-H (excess 0.11 %), where the best solution (cost 2 561 543) is found 6 times; RS-AM finds this solution 16 times with an average excess of 0.50 %. Although the ShortestPathTree construction heuristic provided the second best initial solutions for this problem instance, after applying a local search to these solutions the quality falls behind solutions found when starting from other construction heuristics' solutions. Here, the ShortestPathTree heuristic average solution has an excess of 6.38 % and, after applying AM-H or RS-AM, the excess becomes 3.42 % or 3.47 %, respectively. Stars solutions have an initial excess of 707.6 % but, using either AM-H or RS-AM, solutions with an average excess of 2.98 % or 2.37 %, respectively, can be found.

*Randomly Generated Instances*

In terms of the random instances generated, results show that the smallest non-Euclidean instance (`R100`) is easy to solve for all setups. A non-optimal solution was only found in a few cases after applying a local search resulting in average excesses of < 0.2 %. This is interesting, given the fact that the average quality of initial solutions ranges from 0.5 % (AM-C) to more than 700 % (Star). For the Euclidean variant, the best results are found when starting from Star solutions. This observation holds for all other random Euclidean instances, too. For example, the average excess for RS-AM is 0.96 % starting from a Star solution, but 1.17 % when starting from AM-C solutions. For both instances with 100 nodes, no clear preference for either AM-H or RS-AM can be determined.

For both instances with 300 nodes, it holds that starting from AM-C solutions results in the best solutions for both local search algorithms for the non-Euclidean instance; for the Euclidean instance, the Star heuristic allows the best solutions to be found. Still, the average results are very homogeneous considering that initial solutions from different construction heuristics have a considerable excess (for example, Star solutions for non-Euclidean instances and MST instances for Euclidean instances). For `R300`, AM-H finds best solutions for all four setups (in terms of initial solutions); for `R300-E`, all setups except for ShortestPathTree outperform RS-AM.

For instances with a size of 500 nodes and more, however, the advantage of the RS-AM compared to the original AM-H algorithm is clearly visible. Here, the RS-AM approach finds the best average solutions (excess 0.71 %) for R500-E using the Star construction heuristic and for R500 starting from AM-C solutions (3.02 %, Tab. 50).

Starting from instance sizes of 750 nodes, AM-C has been removed from the set of construction heuristics as the computation times to construct an initial solution exceeded the time bound for these large instances. Therefore, for large non-Euclidean instances, the Shortest-PathTree heuristic not only provides the best initial solutions, it also allows both local search algorithms to find the best solutions for this type of problem instance. For instance R750, the average excess for both local search algorithms is 2.99 % (AM-H) and 2.96 % (RS-AM). But starting from MST solutions, for example, the excess is 6.12 % (AM-H) and 5.96 % (RS-AM). For Euclidean problem instances, the Star construction heuristic provides the best initial solutions and enables both local search algorithms to find the best solutions. For R750-E, the average excess with this construction heuristic is 0.78 % (AM-H) and 0.46 % (RS-AM), which is better than starting with MST, for example, which results in an excess of 5.15 % and 2.62 %, respectively.

For the largest instances with 1000 and 2000 nodes, the pattern of behavior is the same (see also Tab. 53). Again, best results for non-Euclidean instances are found with the Shuffle sorting strategy starting from SPT solutions and best results for Euclidean instances are found with the Shuffle sorting strategy starting from Star solutions. For example, for instance R2000-E, the average excess starting from Star solutions is 4.15 % (AM-H) and 0.53 % (RS-AM, best average excess for this instance). For R2000, the excess using the Shuffle sorting strategy is only 1.98 % starting from shortest path trees, but it is 5.15 % and 4.95 % starting from Star trees or MST solutions, respectively. Still, this excess is below the results from the AM-H algorithm, which results in an excess of 2.91 %, 271.25 %, and 11.58 %, respectively, for the above setups.

*Summary*

Experimental data as presented above shows the advantages of the Random Shuffle Ahuja-Murty algorithm (RS-AM) compared to the original AM-H. The RS-AM approach is considerably faster and can thus find better solutions given only a limited amount of time. This becomes

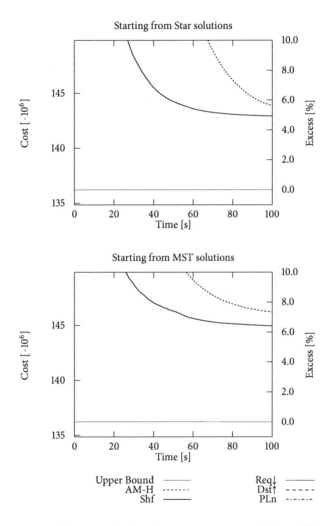

Figure 50: Performance of selected sorting strategies applied to problem instance R1000.

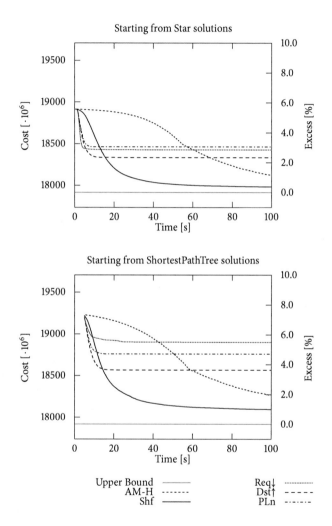

Figure 51: Performance of selected sorting strategies applied to problem instance R1000-E.

more and more apparent with larger problem instance sizes and can be best observed for problem instances with Euclidean distances.

To achieve best results, for problem instances with non-Euclidean distances the ShortestPathTree construction heuristic should be combined with RS-AM; for Euclidean distance-based instances, the Star construction heuristic should be preferred. If the problem instance at hand is small enough, the AM-C construction heuristic is also a good choice.

## 5.5    Memetic Algorithm

The RS-AM approach represents an improvement on the previously best-known algorithms for the OCST, especially for large instances ($\geq$ 500 nodes). To improve these results further, a memetic algorithm was developed. Some components of the memetic algorithm, such as solution construction and local search, have been presented before. The remaining components will be presented in this section, the most important of which are several recombination operators.

The general framework of the memetic algorithm is shown in Fig. 52, which is a variant of the generic form shown in Fig. 5. One of the construction heuristics can be used to initialize an individual, as presented in Sec. 5.3. For recombination, one of the operators introduced in the following section is available. The local search operator employed here is the RS-AM (Sec. 5.4), although some experiments have been conducted with the original AM-H for comparison. To select individuals of the next generation, a tournament selection is performed by drawing two individuals from the combined set of the current population and offspring as often as required, keeping the better one for the next generation. The best individual is always kept (elitism).

Whereas the local search in the previous section was limited by a time limit depending on the instance size (see Sec. 5.4.1), for experiments with the memetic algorithm, the local search was limited by the number of rounds (number of outer loops in Fig. 48). Using the original AM-H local search, finding a local optimum can take a considerable amount of computation time, effectively starving the other MA operators. Therefore, the number of rounds was limited to 1 for AM-H. As RS-AM would restrict its internal cost computations due to the component sizes of $\mathcal{O}(\sqrt{n})$ (cf Eq. (5.20)), the number of rounds was set to $\lceil \sqrt{n} \rceil$ here, with $n$ as the problem size.

A dedicated mutation operator was not integrated into the memetic algorithm for several reasons. Firstly, minor changes in the tree for the OCST (for example, random 1-exchange) may have a major impact on the solution cost. Thus, whereas a too-simple mutation will be undone by the local search at best, a too-strong mutation will degenerate the current solution considerably. Secondly, stochastic elements both in the local search (especially RS-AM) and in the recombination operators introduce new features to the population. As the local search is limited, premature convergence is not expected.

### 5.5.1 Recombination

Recombination (see Sec. 2.1.4) is a technique in evolutionary and memetic algorithms that combines existing solutions to create new solutions. These offspring solutions contain features from all parent solutions and are supposed to be closer to an optimal solution, as the recombination acts as a weak intensification operator (depending on the actual implementation). In [66], several recombination operators for the OCST were introduced and will be discussed here.

*Exhaustive Recombination*

The *exhaustive recombination algorithm* (Fig. 53) is inspired by the exact algorithm in [3] (see also Sec. 5.1.1, p. 189). This recombinator evaluates all possible trees built from a combined set of edges from both parents and returns the tree with minimal cost. The major differences from the exact algorithm are that only edges from parent trees $T_a$ and $T_b$ are considered in the search and that no lower bound is used. Following the categorization from RADCLIFFE and SURRY [164, 165] (Sec. 2.1.4, p. 16), this recombination operator is respectful and transmitting. The algorithm begins with two initialization steps before performing the main loop. In the first initialization step (lines 2–7), several variables are initialized, such as the initial partial solution $T'$, containing only edges common to both parent trees, and edge sets $E^*$ and $E'$ containing edges occurring only in the better or worse parent, respectively. The second initialization step (lines 8–13) builds a stack of partial solutions and candidate edge sets starting from the partial solution $T'$ containing only common edges. Iteratively, edges from $E^*$ are added to the tree, which is pushed on the stack together with the edge set $E'$. This strategy fills the branch and bound-like algorithm's stack as if the algorithm had always branched by selecting edges from the better parent solution. Thus the main loop (lines 14–32) starts with partial solutions close to the better solution parent solution $T_a$, but departs from it when exploring the search space further. At the beginning of each loop iteration, a position in the search space, consisting of a partial solution $T'$ and a set of candidate edges $E'$, is fetched from the stack. If the partial solution $T'$ is actually a valid solution, it may be stored as a candidate final solution and the upper bound is lowered. Otherwise, an edge $e$ is selected. The algorithm branches in two possible search space regions containing trees with or without $e$, respectively. To increase the efficiency of the search, the partial solution and the candidate edge set are checked to see if both edge sets combined hold enough edges for future valid solutions (line 24) and whether the partial solution including $e$ contains a cycle and is below the upper bound (line 28). For each passed check, the modified partial solution and candidate edge sets are pushed on the stack. The main loop terminates when the stack is empty, but may terminate earlier, once a given time bound or iteration count is reached. This algorithm can be adapted easily to a multi-parent recombination by modifying the first initialization step, especially $T'$, $E^*$, and $E'$.

Preliminary experiments suggested that this recombination operator could not be used in practical approaches due to its excessive computation requirements. It is discussed here for the completeness of the recombination approaches developed for the OCST.

### Tree Building Recombination

The *tree building recombination algorithm* ('TBd' or 'TreeBuilding', Fig. 54) reuses concepts from the tree building algorithm by [3] (see also Sec. 5.1.2, p. 193) and performs a respectful but not transmitting recombination. This recombination operator first determines the set of common tree fragments $\mathcal{T}$ from both parents $T_a$ and $T_b$. A fragment is defined as a connected set of node and edges that are contained in both parents. Single nodes may be fragments, too, if they have different edges in both parents. A path length matrix $c(p_{i,j}^{\mathcal{T}})$ is initialized with the all-pairs shortest paths' length in $G$ and updated with the unique paths' lengths from the fragments. The offspring solution is initialized by the fragment that contains a randomly selected node $s$ (line 5). As long as not all fragments are connected in the offspring, the edge $(p, q) \in S \times \bar{S}$ that increases the offspring cost the least is selected for insertion, evaluating the set of fragments in ALPHA (see Sec. 46). Once $q$ has been determined, its fragment is inserted into the partial tree and the path length matrix is updated with the new edges in the partial solution.

### Path Merging Recombination

The *path merging recombination algorithm* ('Pth' or 'PathMerger', Fig. 55) is the only operator that does not use the OCST cost function during recombination, but is still respectful and transmitting. For this operator, the set of nodes is divided into two complementary node sets $S$ and $\overline{S}$, where one set $S$ is initialized by a randomly selected node (lines 3–4). During the recombination operation, $S$ represents the nodes contained in the partial solution. Starting with a random seeding node in $S$ and $\overline{S} = V \setminus S$, a node $s \in \overline{S}$ and one parent $T \in \{T_a, T_b\}$ are selected iteratively (lines 7 and 8) until all nodes are connected by the partial solution. Here, the recombination operator alternates between both parents. Using DIJKSTRA's shortest path algorithm, the shortest path in $T$ from $s$ to the closest node in $S$ is determined. All edges from this path are added to the partial tree (line 10); nodes from the path are added to $S$. No cycles can occur. This algorithm can be transferred easily into a multi-parent algorithm by using a larger pool of parent trees to find paths inside. The implementation used here employs a round-robin strategy to select parents.

### Replace Recombination

For comparison, a simple replace recombination ('Rpl' or 'Replace', Fig. 56) was used, which returns the better of two parents as the offspring solution. This recombination operator is depicted in Fig. 56. Again, this algorithm can be easily enhanced for multi-parent setups.

### 5.5.2 Distribution

The non-distributed memetic algorithm (MA) as shown in Fig. 52 has been enhanced to an distributed memetic algorithm (DMA, Fig. 57) by applying the following changes:

- Instead of maintaining a population of individuals, each algorithm instance of the DMA represents an evolutionary algorithm island maintaining a subpopulation of a single individual each. In comparative experiments, the number of algorithm instances in DMA setups was set equal to the population size in non-distributed MAs.

- An asynchronous thread receives individuals coming from other islands. Received individuals are stored in a queue $Q$, holding 16 messages at most.

- The DMA will only recombine if the queue $Q$ is not empty. In this case, the head individual is removed from the queue and a recombination between the island's current solution and the solution from the queue is performed. If the queue is empty, the following operators are performed on the island's current solution instead of the recombination's offspring.

- The selection of the next generation's individual is basically the same TOURNAMENTSELECTION as used for the MA, but it is simplified, as only one individual from the current population and the result of the local search are available.

- The next generation's individual is sent to a randomly selected island, but only if it represents an improvement compared to the previous generation's individual.

For the distributed algorithm's experiments, a simple epidemic algorithm (see Sec. 2.2.1) is used to supply each node with a list of neighbors (membership protocol). This list is used to exchange individuals between the islands participating in the computation. In the controlled environment used here, the epidemic algorithm was configured to build a complete list of all participating nodes for each node. As building the neighbor list was performed in parallel to the initialization of the OCST, a stable neighbor list was provided for each setup.

## 5.6    EXPERIMENTAL SETUP & RESULTS

For the evaluation of the memetic algorithm, experiments with different recombination operators and population sizes were conducted. In the following result discussion, results of both AM-H or RS-AM as local search (also given four times as long as in Sec. 5.4) were compared to both distributed and non-distributed setups. As recombination operators, either PathMerger (Pth), TreeBuilding (TBd), or Replace (Rpl) were used. Each setup was repeated 20 times and average values were used for discussion.

The population size or number of islands in the DMA, respectively, was set to either 2, 4, or 8. As both sophisticated local search and recombination operators were used, small population sizes were considered to be sufficient. In the non-distributed case, a single program instance maintained a set of individuals. In the distributed case, as many algorithm instances as the population size in corresponding non-distributed setups were started, where each program instance maintained only one individual.

As termination criterion, time limits depend on the problem instance's size, similar to the local search algorithm (see Sec. 5.4.1), but all limits were multiplied by 4 to take the additional efforts for population-based setups into account. To compare the results from non-distributed and distributed setups at any given point in time, the following technique was used: for non-distributed setups, the best known individual of the population was used; for distributed setups, again the best known solution over all islands was used, but the computation time was multiplied by the number of islands, as each island counts its CPU time independently. It can be assumed that all islands started at the same time and consumed CPU resources at the same rate. Thus, for both types of setups the total CPU time spent was considered.

For the experiments conducted here, the primary focus was on large problem instances ($\geq$ 500 nodes). The limited effort required to reach (near-)optimal results for smaller instances does not justify the application of (distributed) memetic algorithms. For comparison, however, three smaller instances with 100 nodes (Raidl100, R100, and R100-E) were included.

*Results*

With a medium-size problem instance such as Raidl100 (Tab. 54), small effects of different recombination operators and population sizes can be observed. Using the ShortestPathTree construction heuristic, the average solution quality of non-distributed population-based setups improves with growing population size for all recombination operators, suggesting that the larger population size allows the MA to concentrate on better solutions, with little influence from the recombination operator actually used. For distributed setups, the same pattern of behavior can be observed, with the exception of setups with population size 8. Except for these three distributed setups, all population-based setups find better solutions on average compared to the single-individual setups

AM-H and RS-AM. Using the MST solution factory which was used in the local search experiments to find the best solutions for this problem instance, there is no tendency of larger population sizes resulting in better solutions. Again, compared to the other setups, distributed setups with 8 individuals converge to worse solutions. The reason for this disappointing performance is that each node has only $1/8$ of the total time of 100 s which is not sufficient to reach competitive results.

Problem instances R100 and R100-E (Tab. 55) are the smallest random instances created for this thesis. For R100, initial solutions were created using the ShortestPathTree heuristic; for R100-E the Star heuristic was used. Both construction heuristics perform best for non-Euclidean and Euclidean instances, respectively, and will be used in the remainder of this discussion. Except for distributed setups with 8 individuals, all setups find good solutions resulting in an average excess of < 0.05 %. Setups with a low excess basically differ only in the number of runs that find the best-known solution (cost 2 427 890). For example, for the non-distributed setup with 2 individuals using the Replace recombinator, only two runs result in non-optimal solutions (excess 0.17 %). For R100-E, non-distributed recombination steps perform better with increasing population size. Interestingly, the Replace recombination has the worst performance among all three recombinators. Best average results are achieved using the TreeBuilding recombination and 8 individuals (excess 0.26 %) followed by a similar setup using the PathMerger recombination (excess 0.30 %). Both perform better than the corresponding Replace recombinator (excess 0.56 %) and the single-individual setups AM-H and RS-AM sorting (excess 0.96 % and 1.16 %, respectively). For setups with 4 individuals, distributed setups outperform non-distributed setups but degrade with larger population sizes. For a setup using the Replace recombinator, for example, the non-distributed setup's average excess is 0.88 %, whereas it is 0.78 % for the distributed setup.

For problem instance R500 (Tab. 56) the TreeBuilding recombinator in non-distributed setups performs best. With growing population size, the average decreases down to 0.33 % (population size 8), whereas all other setups have an average excess of > 1.0 %. In terms of the population size, it holds that that larger population setups perform better than small population setups for most setups. For the Replace recombinator, for example, the distributed setup's excess decreases from 3.12 % (population size 2) down to 1.58 % (population size 8). The exception here is the distributed setup using the TreeBuilding recombinator, where the

| Instance | Setup | Population Size | | |
|---|---|---|---|---|
| | | $1/2^{\dagger}$ | 4 | 8 |
| Raidl100 4 s | AM-H | $2.65{\cdot}10^6$ 3.42 | | |
| | RS-AM | $2.65{\cdot}10^6$ 3.43 | | |
| | Pth | $2.59{\cdot}10^6$ 56.2 1.07 | $2.56{\cdot}10^6$ 60.0 0.04 | $2.56{\cdot}10^6$ 60.0 0.03 |
| | Pth-dist | $2.59{\cdot}10^6$ 7.9 1.08 | $2.56{\cdot}10^6$ 13.1 0.09 | $2.57{\cdot}10^6$ 6.8 0.30 |
| | TBd | $2.59{\cdot}10^6$ 54.6 1.09 | $2.56{\cdot}10^6$ 57.4 0.04 | $2.56{\cdot}10^6$ 56.5 0.01 |
| | TBd-dist | $2.58{\cdot}10^6$ 7.3 0.77 | $2.56{\cdot}10^6$ 12.4 0.03 | $2.57{\cdot}10^6$ 4.9 0.30 |
| | Rpl | $2.59{\cdot}10^6$ 57.8 1.09 | $2.56{\cdot}10^6$ 61.1 0.05 | $2.56{\cdot}10^6$ 62.8 0.02 |
| | Rpl-dist | $2.60{\cdot}10^6$ 9.6 1.44 | $2.56{\cdot}10^6$ 15.5 0.05 | $2.57{\cdot}10^6$ 8.2 0.16 |
| Raidl100 4 s | AM-H | $2.56{\cdot}10^6$ 0.11 | | |
| | RS-AM | $2.57{\cdot}10^6$ 0.43 | | |
| | Pth | $2.56{\cdot}10^6$ 55.5 0.02 | $2.56{\cdot}10^6$ 59.0 0.04 | $2.56{\cdot}10^6$ 59.4 0.00 |
| | Pth-dist | $2.56{\cdot}10^6$ 7.8 0.03 | $2.56{\cdot}10^6$ 15.0 0.04 | $2.58{\cdot}10^6$ 9.9 0.58 |
| | TBd | $2.56{\cdot}10^6$ 53.5 0.00 | $2.56{\cdot}10^6$ 56.2 0.02 | $2.56{\cdot}10^6$ 56.4 0.02 |
| | TBd-dist | $2.56{\cdot}10^6$ 5.5 0.01 | $2.56{\cdot}10^6$ 11.9 0.00 | $2.57{\cdot}10^6$ 8.0 0.27 |
| | Rpl | $2.56{\cdot}10^6$ 57.6 0.02 | $2.56{\cdot}10^6$ 61.0 0.03 | $2.56{\cdot}10^6$ 61.4 0.04 |
| | Rpl-dist | $2.56{\cdot}10^6$ 7.2 0.02 | $2.56{\cdot}10^6$ 15.1 0.04 | $2.57{\cdot}10^6$ 11.8 0.24 |

$^{\dagger}$ For 'AM-H' and 'RS-AM' population size is 1, otherwise it is 2.

Table 54: Results from the recombination experiments for instance Raidl100. The table's upper half uses ShortestPathTree solutions (worst performance in iterated setups) as initial solutions; the lower half uses MST solutions (best performance in iterated setup). Large numbers denote the average final solution cost, smaller numbers below are average number of recombinations (left) and the excess above the best-known value in percent (right).

| Instance | Setup | Population Size | | |
|---|---|---|---|---|
| | | $1/2^{\dagger}$ | 4 | 8 |
| R100 | AM-H | $2.43{\cdot}10^6$ | | |
| 4 s | | 0.00 | | |
| | RS-AM | $2.43{\cdot}10^6$ | | |
| | | 0.04 | | |
| | Pth | $2.43{\cdot}10^6$ | $2.43{\cdot}10^6$ | $2.43{\cdot}10^6$ |
| | | 57.2  0.01 | 60.4  0.00 | 59.0  0.01 |
| | Pth-dist | $2.43{\cdot}10^6$ | $2.43{\cdot}10^6$ | $2.43{\cdot}10^6$ |
| | | 6.2  0.03 | 13.2  0.02 | 7.3  0.26 |
| | TBd | $2.43{\cdot}10^6$ | $2.43{\cdot}10^6$ | $2.43{\cdot}10^6$ |
| | | 54.4  0.01 | 58.4  0.01 | 57.4  0.00 |
| | TBd-dist | $2.43{\cdot}10^6$ | $2.43{\cdot}10^6$ | $2.43{\cdot}10^6$ |
| | | 5.5  0.00 | 9.8  0.00 | 5.1  0.21 |
| | Rpl | $2.43{\cdot}10^6$ | $2.43{\cdot}10^6$ | $2.43{\cdot}10^6$ |
| | | 58.4  0.02 | 61.2  0.00 | 62.8  0.00 |
| | Rpl-dist | $2.43{\cdot}10^6$ | $2.43{\cdot}10^6$ | $2.43{\cdot}10^6$ |
| | | 6.5  0.01 | 13.2  0.00 | 8.1  0.11 |
| R100-E | AM-H | $1.86{\cdot}10^8$ | | |
| 4 s | | 0.96 | | |
| | RS-AM | $1.86{\cdot}10^8$ | | |
| | | 1.16 | | |
| | Pth | $1.85{\cdot}10^8$ | $1.85{\cdot}10^8$ | $1.84{\cdot}10^8$ |
| | | 53.4  0.74 | 56.1  0.60 | 58.4  0.30 |
| | Pth-dist | $1.85{\cdot}10^8$ | $1.85{\cdot}10^8$ | $1.86{\cdot}10^8$ |
| | | 12.7  0.83 | 18.9  0.41 | 11.7  1.19 |
| | TBd | $1.86{\cdot}10^8$ | $1.85{\cdot}10^8$ | $1.84{\cdot}10^8$ |
| | | 51.8  0.95 | 52.0  0.67 | 49.8  0.26 |
| | TBd-dist | $1.85{\cdot}10^8$ | $1.84{\cdot}10^8$ | $1.86{\cdot}10^8$ |
| | | 11.7  0.89 | 16.1  0.33 | 8.2  0.91 |
| | Rpl | $1.86{\cdot}10^8$ | $1.85{\cdot}10^8$ | $1.85{\cdot}10^8$ |
| | | 55.3  0.99 | 58.2  0.88 | 59.4  0.56 |
| | Rpl-dist | $1.86{\cdot}10^8$ | $1.86{\cdot}10^8$ | $1.86{\cdot}10^8$ |
| | | 10.7  1.30 | 18.6  1.01 | 13.0  1.07 |

$^{\dagger}$ For 'AM-H' and 'RS-AM' population size is 1, otherwise it is 2.

Table 55: Results from the recombination experiments for instances R100 and R100-E. The table's upper half uses ShortestPathTree solutions (best performance for R100) as initial solutions; the lower half uses Star solutions (best performance for R100-E). Large numbers denote the average final solution cost, smaller numbers below are average number of recombinations (left) and the excess above the best-known value in percent (right).

non-distributed setups result in an average excess of 0.33 %, but the distributed setups result in an excess of 2.11 %. For problem instance R500-E, the TreeBuilding recombinator falls behind the other two recombination operators for solution quality, which holds for both non-distributed and distributed setups. Whereas the solutions qualities of all six setups with population size 2 are comparable (excess ranging from 0.51 % to 0.62 %), both TreeBuilding setups perform worse than the other setups for both larger population sizes. For example, the TreeBuilding setups with population size 4 have an excess of 0.81 % (non-distributed) and 0.75 %; the corresponding setups using the PathMerger setup result in excesses of 0.40 % and 0.44 %, respectively.

For problem instance R750 (Tab. 57), the TreeBuilding recombinator is the best recombination operator for non-distributed setups, outperforming both other recombinators in each case. For population size 2, for example, the TreeBuilding recombinator finds solutions with an excess of 2.12 % (non-distributed) and 2.14 % (distributed), whereas the PathMerger recombination results in an excess of 2.29 % and 2.29 %, respectively, and the Replace recombinator in 2.28 % and 2.30 %. For distributed setups (except for population size 2), the Replace recombinator performs best, followed by the PathMerger recombinator. For problem instance R750-E, the TreeBuilding recombinator performs worst, failing to reach the solution quality levels of both AM-H and RS-AM sorting. Best results are achieved with population size 4 and either the Path-Merger recombinator or Replace recombinator. For these four setups (distributed and non-distributed) the average excess is between 0.30 % and 0.32 % and thus well below both single individual setups (excess ≥ 0.37 %). Whereas the best solution for this problem instance was found by an AM-H setup, among the 10 best solutions (max. excess 0.075 %), 6 where found by PathMerger setups, 1 by a TreeBuilding setup and 2 by Replacemet setups.

With problem instance R1000 (Tab. 58), all population-based setups perform better than single-individual setups. Furthermore, the average solution quality becomes better with increased population size. For population size 2, the TreeBuilding recombinator performs best: the excess for non-distributed setups is 1.52 %, while all other setups show an excess of > 1.6 %. However, the overall smallest excess is found by the distributed Replace setup using a population size of 8. For problem instance R1000-E, the TreeBuilding recombination operator fails to achieve solution quality levels that match the results from single-individual setups. The best average excess for any TreeBuilding setup is 0.45 % (4 individ-

| | | Population Size | | |
|---|---|---|---|---|
| Instance | Setup | $1/2^\dagger$ | 4 | 8 |
| R500 | AM-H | $3.93{\cdot}10^7$ | | |
| 100 s | | 4.24 | | |
| | RS-AM | $3.93{\cdot}10^7$ | | |
| | | 4.19 | | |
| | Pth | $3.88{\cdot}10^7$ | $3.85{\cdot}10^7$ | $3.83{\cdot}10^7$ |
| | | 28.5  2.91 | 27.4  1.90 | 24.8  1.60 |
| | Pth-dist | $3.89{\cdot}10^7$ | $3.88{\cdot}10^7$ | $3.84{\cdot}10^7$ |
| | | 20.6  3.07 | 22.0  2.85 | 19.5  1.77 |
| | TBd | $3.88{\cdot}10^7$ | $3.82{\cdot}10^7$ | $3.79{\cdot}10^7$ |
| | | 24.8  2.71 | 20.6  1.19 | 13.6  0.33 |
| | TBd-dist | $3.83{\cdot}10^7$ | $3.83{\cdot}10^7$ | $3.85{\cdot}10^7$ |
| | | 18.2  1.55 | 8.9  1.46 | 6.8  2.11 |
| | Rpl | $3.89{\cdot}10^7$ | $3.86{\cdot}10^7$ | $3.83{\cdot}10^7$ |
| | | 28.8  3.12 | 28.6  2.24 | 27.9  1.49 |
| | Rpl-dist | $3.89{\cdot}10^7$ | $3.87{\cdot}10^7$ | $3.83{\cdot}10^7$ |
| | | 26.7  3.12 | 34.6  2.61 | 29.1  1.51 |
| R500-E | AM-H | $4.51{\cdot}10^9$ | | |
| 100 s | | 0.68 | | |
| | RS-AM | $4.51{\cdot}10^9$ | | |
| | | 0.68 | | |
| | Pth | $4.50{\cdot}10^9$ | $4.49{\cdot}10^9$ | $4.50{\cdot}10^9$ |
| | | 26.3  0.62 | 25.6  0.40 | 23.6  0.54 |
| | Pth-dist | $4.50{\cdot}10^9$ | $4.50{\cdot}10^9$ | $4.51{\cdot}10^9$ |
| | | 28.1  0.53 | 23.3  0.44 | 20.9  0.67 |
| | TBd | $4.50{\cdot}10^9$ | $4.51{\cdot}10^9$ | $4.53{\cdot}10^9$ |
| | | 20.4  0.51 | 14.2  0.81 | 15.6  1.32 |
| | TBd-dist | $4.50{\cdot}10^9$ | $4.51{\cdot}10^9$ | $4.51{\cdot}10^9$ |
| | | 8.7  0.62 | 6.4  0.75 | 6.7  0.76 |
| | Rpl | $4.50{\cdot}10^9$ | $4.50{\cdot}10^9$ | $4.50{\cdot}10^9$ |
| | | 26.3  0.58 | 25.8  0.54 | 27.1  0.49 |
| | Rpl-dist | $4.50{\cdot}10^9$ | $4.50{\cdot}10^9$ | $4.50{\cdot}10^9$ |
| | | 37.1  0.58 | 31.1  0.47 | 21.9  0.56 |

$^\dagger$ For 'AM-H' and 'RS-AM' population size is 1, otherwise it is 2.

Table 56: Results from the recombination experiments for instances R500 and R500-E. The table's upper half uses ShortestPathTree solutions (best performance for R500) as initial solutions; the lower half uses Star solutions (best performance for R500-E). Large numbers denote the average final solution cost, smaller numbers below are average number of recombinations (left) and the excess above the best-known value in percent (right).

| Instance | Setup | Population Size $1/2^{\dagger}$ | 4 | 8 |
|---|---|---|---|---|
| R750 228 s | AM-H | $8.21{\cdot}10^7$ 2.96 | | |
| | RS-AM | $8.20{\cdot}10^7$ 2.93 | | |
| | Pth | $8.15{\cdot}10^7$ 22.9 2.29 | $8.11{\cdot}10^7$ 22.4 1.78 | – |
| | Pth-dist | $8.15{\cdot}10^7$ 17.8 2.29 | $8.14{\cdot}10^7$ 16.6 2.13 | $8.12{\cdot}10^7$ 13.3 1.93 |
| | TBd | $8.14{\cdot}10^7$ 18.8 2.12 | $8.10{\cdot}10^7$ 12.8 1.62 | – |
| | TBd-dist | $8.14{\cdot}10^7$ 8.7 2.14 | $8.17{\cdot}10^7$ 4.2 2.50 | $8.13{\cdot}10^7$ 6.8 1.95 |
| | Rpl | $8.15{\cdot}10^7$ 23.6 2.28 | $8.11{\cdot}10^7$ 22.8 1.71 | – |
| | Rpl-dist | $8.15{\cdot}10^7$ 31.8 2.30 | $8.13{\cdot}10^7$ 27.2 1.94 | $8.10{\cdot}10^7$ 21.5 1.58 |
| R750-E 228 s | AM-H | $1.03{\cdot}10^{10}$ 0.37 | | |
| | RS-AM | $1.03{\cdot}10^{10}$ 0.38 | | |
| | Pth | $1.03{\cdot}10^{10}$ 21.4 0.33 | $1.03{\cdot}10^{10}$ 19.9 0.30 | – |
| | Pth-dist | $1.03{\cdot}10^{10}$ 22.3 0.26 | $1.03{\cdot}10^{10}$ 17.7 0.32 | $1.04{\cdot}10^{10}$ 15.2 0.50 |
| | TBd | $1.04{\cdot}10^{10}$ 12.8 0.53 | $1.04{\cdot}10^{10}$ 10.3 0.87 | – |
| | TBd-dist | $1.04{\cdot}10^{10}$ 5.3 0.50 | $1.04{\cdot}10^{10}$ 3.3 0.52 | $1.04{\cdot}10^{10}$ 6.7 0.57 |
| | Rpl | $1.03{\cdot}10^{10}$ 21.4 0.37 | $1.03{\cdot}10^{10}$ 21.4 0.32 | – |
| | Rpl-dist | $1.03{\cdot}10^{10}$ 30.6 0.36 | $1.03{\cdot}10^{10}$ 23.6 0.31 | $1.03{\cdot}10^{10}$ 15.1 0.38 |

$^{\dagger}$ For 'AM-H' and 'RS-AM' population size is 1, otherwise it is 2.

Table 57: Results from the recombination experiments for instances R750 and R750-E. The table's upper half uses ShortestPathTree solutions (best performance for R750) as initial solutions; the lower half uses Star solutions (best performance for R750-E). Large numbers denote the average final solution cost, smaller numbers below are average number of recombinations (left) and the excess above the best-known value in percent (right).

uals, distributed), which is still worse than AM-H and RS-AM sorting (0.35 % and 0.33 %, respectively). For small population sizes, both Path-Merger recombination and Replace recombination perform similarly, but the latter recombination performs better with growing population size. With population size 4, all distributed setups perform better than their corresponding non-distributed setups, resulting in the best overall excess of 0.24 % using the Replace recombinator.

For both problem instances with 2000 individuals (Tab. 59), the Tree-Building recombinator performs worst, due to its excessive computation demand resulting in fewer iterations within the given time bounds. For problem instance R2000 and 2 individuals in non-distributed setups, for example, setups using the Replace recombinator performed 11.8 iterations on average, but only 3.4 iterations using the TreeBuilding recombinator. For problem instance R2000-E, the values for the corresponding setups are similar, with 9.8 and 2.5 iterations, respectively. For this problem instance, as for smaller Euclidean instances, the TreeBuilding recombinator fails to find acceptable solutions; it is the only recombination setup that fails to achieve the same level of single-individual setups. Best results are achieved using either PathMerger or Replace recombination and 2 individuals, as the average excess is $\leq 0.40$ % for these setups compared to the single individual setup with a minimum excess of 0.46 %.

*Summary*

For the OCST, a number of recombination operators have been presented here that differ in their strategies and complexity, ranging from simple replace operators to a recombination operator inspired by an exact algorithm. It has to be noted, that designing recombination operators for the OCST is not trivial. The application of the sophisticated recombination operators does not result in significant improvements compared to a simple Replace recombination. The recombination operators' two main drawbacks are their time consumption and the sensitivity of the OCST to minor tree changes, leading to recombination offspring that can be considerably worse than their parents. The local search applied on a offspring has to compensate for this decrease in quality but may not be sufficiently strong to improve the offspring to a quality level similar to that of the parents. Still, in some cases, the recombination operators are able to extract the essential features, allowing the memetic

| Instance | Setup | Population Size | | |
|---|---|---|---|---|
| | | $1/2^{\dagger}$ | 4 | 8 |
| R1000<br>400 s | AM-H | $1.39{\cdot}10^8$<br>2.33 | | |
| | RS-AM | $1.39{\cdot}10^8$<br>2.31 | | |
| | Pth | $1.38{\cdot}10^8$<br>20.3  1.61 | $1.38{\cdot}10^8$<br>18.9  1.10 | – |
| | Pth-dist | $1.39{\cdot}10^8$<br>15.2  1.68 | $1.38{\cdot}10^8$<br>13.9  1.47 | $1.38{\cdot}10^8$<br>13.1  1.16 |
| | TBd | $1.38{\cdot}10^8$<br>14.6  1.52 | $1.38{\cdot}10^8$<br>8.8  1.31 | – |
| | TBd-dist | $1.39{\cdot}10^8$<br>4.4  1.91 | $1.39{\cdot}10^8$<br>3.5  1.75 | $1.38{\cdot}10^8$<br>6.5  1.27 |
| | Rpl | $1.38{\cdot}10^8$<br>20.6  1.61 | $1.38{\cdot}10^8$<br>20.4  1.02 | – |
| | Rpl-dist | $1.38{\cdot}10^8$<br>28.4  1.61 | $1.38{\cdot}10^8$<br>20.7  1.27 | $1.37{\cdot}10^8$<br>15.3  0.89 |
| R1000-E<br>400 s | AM-H | $1.80{\cdot}10^{10}$<br>0.35 | | |
| | RS-AM | $1.80{\cdot}10^{10}$<br>0.33 | | |
| | Pth | $1.80{\cdot}10^{10}$<br>18.3  0.27 | $1.80{\cdot}10^{10}$<br>16.8  0.34 | – |
| | Pth-dist | $1.80{\cdot}10^{10}$<br>18.4  0.28 | $1.80{\cdot}10^{10}$<br>15.6  0.31 | $1.80{\cdot}10^{10}$<br>10.9  0.45 |
| | TBd | $1.80{\cdot}10^{10}$<br>10.4  0.71 | $1.81{\cdot}10^{10}$<br>8.3  0.90 | – |
| | TBd-dist | $1.80{\cdot}10^{10}$<br>3.6  0.72 | $1.80{\cdot}10^{10}$<br>3.5  0.45 | $1.80{\cdot}10^{10}$<br>6.4  0.48 |
| | Rpl | $1.80{\cdot}10^{10}$<br>18.4  0.33 | $1.80{\cdot}10^{10}$<br>16.9  0.31 | – |
| | Rpl-dist | $1.80{\cdot}10^{10}$<br>24.7  0.26 | $1.80{\cdot}10^{10}$<br>17.2  0.24 | $1.80{\cdot}10^{10}$<br>15.5  0.36 |

$^{\dagger}$ For 'AM-H' and 'RS-AM' population size is 1, otherwise it is 2.

Table 58: Results from the recombination experiments for instances R1000 and R1000-E. The table's upper half uses ShortestPathTree solutions (best performance for R1000) as initial solutions; the lower half uses Star solutions (best performance for R1000-E).

| | | Population Size | | |
|---|---|---|---|---|
| Instance | Setup | $1/2^{\dagger}$ | 4 | 8 |
| R2000 | AM-H | $5.18{\cdot}10^{8}$ | | |
| 1600 s | | 1.92 | | |
| | RS-AM | $5.18{\cdot}10^{8}$ | | |
| | | 1.82 | | |
| | Pth | $5.16{\cdot}10^{8}$ | – | – |
| | | 14.8  1.45 | | |
| | Pth-dist | $5.16{\cdot}10^{8}$ | $5.17{\cdot}10^{8}$ | $5.16{\cdot}10^{8}$ |
| | | 9.0  1.52 | 8.2  1.63 | 8.7  1.45 |
| | TBd | $5.21{\cdot}10^{8}$ | – | – |
| | | 7.0  2.48 | | |
| | TBd-dist | $5.21{\cdot}10^{8}$ | $5.18{\cdot}10^{8}$ | $5.17{\cdot}10^{8}$ |
| | | 2.0  2.37 | 3.2  1.83 | 5.9  1.57 |
| | Rpl | $5.16{\cdot}10^{8}$ | – | – |
| | | 15.4  1.40 | | |
| | Rpl-dist | $5.16{\cdot}10^{8}$ | $5.15{\cdot}10^{8}$ | $5.15{\cdot}10^{8}$ |
| | | 18.4  1.40 | 12.8  1.26 | 8.3  1.19 |
| R2000-E | AM-H | $7.28{\cdot}10^{10}$ | | |
| 1600 s | | 0.46 | | |
| | RS-AM | $7.29{\cdot}10^{10}$ | | |
| | | 0.53 | | |
| | Pth | $7.28{\cdot}10^{10}$ | – | – |
| | | 13.6  0.39 | | |
| | Pth-dist | $7.28{\cdot}10^{10}$ | $7.29{\cdot}10^{10}$ | $7.30{\cdot}10^{10}$ |
| | | 11.7  0.40 | 9.1  0.49 | 3.8  0.64 |
| | TBd | $7.33{\cdot}10^{10}$ | – | – |
| | | 7.0  1.03 | | |
| | TBd-dist | $7.31{\cdot}10^{10}$ | $7.29{\cdot}10^{10}$ | $7.30{\cdot}10^{10}$ |
| | | 2.0  0.86 | 3.4  0.58 | 4.0  0.64 |
| | Rpl | $7.28{\cdot}10^{10}$ | – | – |
| | | 14.2  0.37 | | |
| | Rpl-dist | $7.28{\cdot}10^{10}$ | $7.28{\cdot}10^{10}$ | $7.29{\cdot}10^{10}$ |
| | | 14.8  0.39 | 11.0  0.41 | 3.9  0.60 |

$^{\dagger}$ For 'AM-H' and 'RS-AM' population size is 1, otherwise it is 2.

Table 59: Results from the recombination experiments for instances R2000 and R2000-E. The table's upper half uses ShortestPathTree solutions (best performance for R2000) as initial solutions; the lower half uses Star solutions (best performance for R2000-E).

algorithm to find solutions that are better than those from the local search alone, given the same amount of CPU time.

Considering the overall performance, the Replace recombination operator is the best choice with growing instance size, as it is computationally cheap and the generated offspring have the same level of quality as the parent individuals. Its main drawback is that this strategy may lead to low diversity in the population. Using a population-based approach (both distributed and non-distributed) results in better solutions compared to single-individual setups (AM-H and RS-AM) given the same computation time.

Using a distributed, population-based setup reduces the absolute time spent to reach a given solution quality level, compared to both single and non-distributed population-based setups. Although the structure of both the distributed and the non-distributed algorithms were designed to match in several aspects, different concepts led to different results. The major difference is that distributed setups exchange individuals less often than non-distributed setups. In distributed setups, recombining individuals is only performed if a solution was received from another computing node; in non-distributed setups, recombination could be performed regularly due to the availability of recombination partners.

For large problem instances, solutions including their auxiliary data structures require a considerable amount of system resources. It is an advantage of distributed setups that only one active solution is maintained per island, whereas non-distributed setups are limited in their population size, reaching memory limits. The disadvantage of distributed setups, however, is the effort of redundant computations and synchronization between participating nodes.

## 5.7    Solution Analysis

The problems arising when solving OCST problem instances, and the performance of the algorithms in particular, motivate a deeper analysis. Here, two problem instances with either Euclidean (R500-E) or non-Euclidean (R500) inter-node distances are used. For a broader pool of data, additional solutions were created using the algorithms discussed in previous sections. For problem instance R500, a total of 200 solutions were created using the ShortestPathTree construction heuristic. For problem instance R500-E, the same number of solutions were created using the Star construction heuristic. Both sets of solutions were solved using (a) the original Ahuja-Murty local search algorithm (AM-H) (b) the improved local search using the Shuffle sorting strategy (RS-AM) (c) a non-distributed memetic algorithm using the TreeBuilding recombinator with 4 individuals (d) a distributed memetic algorithm using the TreeBuilding recombinator with 4 individuals. The time constraint used in previous section was not strictly applied[2] leading to more varied running times and solutions not comparable to the previous sections' results.

In this analysis, interest focused on the distribution of solutions in the search space in relation to the best-known solutions. Here, the number of best-known solutions, the minimum distance between a given solution to its closest best-known solution (min $d_{best}$), the average distance between the solutions and their closest best-known solution ($\overline{d}_{best}$), the average distance between solutions ($\overline{d}_{sol}$), and the number of distinct solutions ($N$) out of 200 were determined. The fitness of a solution is its excess above the best-known solution's quality; the distance is the number of edges differing between two solutions. Additionally, the fitness distance correlation (FDC) coefficient $\rho$ [116] was determined, describing the difficulty of the search space for heuristic algorithms. As the RWA is defined as a minimization problem here, a correlation value $\rho \to 1$ indicates that there is a relation between decreasing distance and decreasing excess. Given a set of solutions $S$, for each solution $s \in S$ the fitness $f_s$ and distance $d_s$ is determined. Furthermore, both average values $\overline{d}$ and $\overline{f}$ and standard deviations $\sigma_d$ and $\sigma_f$ are determined for all $\{d_s : s \in S\}$ and $\{f_s : s \in S\}$, respectively. The covariance on fitness and distance and the correlation coefficient $\rho$ are determined as follows:

$$C_{FD} = \frac{1}{n} \sum_{s \in S} \left( f_s - \overline{f} \right) \cdot \left( d_s - \overline{d} \right) \qquad \rho = \frac{C_{FD}}{\sigma_f \cdot \sigma_d} \qquad (5.22)$$

As the OCST is a minimization problem, $\rho \to 1$ is preferred, as this implies that solutions that have better objective values also have more paths in common with optimal solutions. If $\rho \to -1$, solutions have better objective values with less common paths and for $\rho \approx 0$, no correlation between fitness and distance is observed.

For problem instance R500, one unique solution is known to be the best-known solution with cost 37 744 037. For instance R500-E, one unique solution with cost 4 473 402 563 is known.

In Tab. 60, the results of the analysis are summarized for both problem instances. The minimum distances between the found solutions

---

2 For example, local search operations were allowed to converge instead of being canceled when they reached the time limit.

|        | Solver  | min $d_{\text{best}}$ | $\overline{d}_{\text{best}}$ | $\overline{d}_{\text{sol}}$ | $N$ | $\rho$ |
|--------|---------|----------|----------|----------|-----|--------|
| R500   | Constr  | 158 | 350.95 | 375.5596 | 58  | 0.587 |
|        | AM-LS   | 0   | 298.74 | 324.4158 | 106 | 0.621 |
|        | Shuffle | 0   | 299.21 | 324.0010 | 166 | 0.619 |
|        | MA      | 4   | 204.72 | 256.4864 | 200 | 0.758 |
|        | DMA     | 9   | 196.50 | 250.5436 | 200 | 0.720 |
| R500-E | Constr  | 492 | 492.00 | $-^{\dagger}$ | 1   | $-^{\dagger}$ |
|        | AM-LS   | 254 | 319.95 | 261.4488 | 200 | 0.394 |
|        | Shuffle | 230 | 284.10 | 277.6340 | 200 | 0.429 |
|        | MA      | 197 | 272.54 | 272.0870 | 200 | 0.578 |
|        | DMA     | 200 | 269.49 | 276.4070 | 200 | 0.640 |

$^{\dagger}$ Only one solution available

Table 60: Results from solution analysis and fitness distance correlation analysis for problem instances R500 and R500-E applied to different types of solutions.

and the best-known solution imply that it is easier for problem instance R500 to find solutions close to the best-known solution starting from ShortestPathTree solutions, compared to the Euclidean counterpart R500-E starting from Star solutions. For the former instance, the closest solution constructed by the ShortestPathTree heuristic has about 68 % of all edges in common with the best-known solution (min $d_{\text{best}}$); on average, initial solutions share about 30 % of their edges with the best-known solution ($\overline{d}_{\text{best}}$). For the latter instance, the unique Star used as the initial solution shares only 8 edges with the best-known solution. All approaches using some kind of local search are able to find solutions identical or very close to the best-known solution for R500 (min $d_{\text{best}} \leq 9$). Whereas both memetic algorithm setups fail to find the best known solution, solutions found by both the MA and DMA setup are, on average, closer to the best-known solution ($\overline{d}_{\text{best}} < 257$) compared to the construction heuristic and both local search approaches ($\overline{d}_{\text{best}} > 324$). For problem instance R500-E, solutions found by the setups under consideration are much further away from the best-known solution. Even the closest solutions found by either AM-H or RS-AM share only about half of all edges with the best-known solution (254 and 230 edge distance, respectively), on average only 36.0 % and 43.2 %

of all edges are shared between the best-known solution and these local optima. Both memetic algorithms perform better here, having a minimum distance of about 200 edges and average distances of 272.5 edges (MA) and 269.5 edges (DMA).

For the average distance between local optima ($\overline{d}_{sol}$), this distance decreases with 'better' algorithms for instance R500, but stays approximately constant for R500-E, regardless of the solver. For R500, $\overline{d}_{sol}$ is 375.6 for initial solutions, about 324 for both local search algorithms, and about 255 for both memetic algorithms. These distances are always larger than the corresponding $\overline{d}_{best}$: for the initial solutions and the local optima from AM-H and RS-AM, it holds that $\overline{d}_{sol} \approx \overline{d}_{best} + 25$, whereas for both memetic algorithms it holds that $\overline{d}_{sol} \approx \overline{d}_{best} + 50$. Thus, local optima are closer to the best-known solution than to other local optima. For R500-E, $\overline{d}_{sol}$ is 261.4 for the Ahuja-Murty local search and between 272 and 278 for the other three approaches. Especially for 'better' solvers, $\overline{d}_{best} \approx \overline{d}_{sol}$ suggests that local optima and the best-known solution are evenly distributed in the search space.

The ShortestPathTree construction heuristic used for R500 finds $N = 58$ distinct solutions within the set of 200 solutions created for this analysis. Starting from these solutions, the local search algorithms result in 106 (AM-H) and 166 (RS-AM) distinct solutions. For both memetic algorithms, it holds that no two solutions are identical. Whereas a single star is used as the initial solution for R500-E, all four solvers find different solutions in each of their 200 runs. This observation and the values of $\overline{d}_{sol}$ suggest that the choice of this unique initial solution does not limit the search to a small part of the search space.

*Fitness Distance Correlation*

The *fitness distance correlation* coefficient ($\rho$) for instance R500 ranges from 0.587 for initial solutions to 0.758 (depending on the solver applied to the initial solutions) for local optima found by the non-distributed memetic algorithm. These values support the observation of low values for min $d_{best}$, as local optima are close to the best-known solution, in terms of both fitness and distance. For R500-E, however, the correlation coefficients are below 0.5 for both local search approaches, reaching higher values only for both memetic approaches (0.578 and 0.640, respectively). For the setups discussed above, fitness distance plots were generated for an additional analysis. The five rows in Fig. 60 correspond to the setups shown in Tab. 60.

For problem instance R500 (left column), the five plots can be seen as pages of a 'flip-book', where the distribution of the 200 solutions in each plot changes with increasingly better solvers from top to bottom. For the construction heuristic, most solutions have an excess of 6–12 % and a distance of 300–400 edges to the best-known solution. With both AM-H and RS-AM, the main field of solutions moves to the left (lower excess of about 3–9 %), but it also divides into two branches. Although both branches contain solutions with an excess of < 3 %, one branch contains only solutions with $d_{best} > 300$, regardless of solution quality ($\approx$ 150 solutions), whereas the second branch contains solutions where both excess and distance to the best-known solution decrease, thus aligning the solutions along the diagonal in the plot. This effect is strongest for both memetic algorithms, as there are only a few solutions with an excess of > 6 % left and each solution is located in either branch. Here, about 70 solutions have a distance of more than 300 edges to the best-known solution.

For problem instance R500-E (right column), the initial solution is not shown in the first plot due to its too high excess (5.06 %). For the other four plots, the solutions are distributed in a dense cloud. For both local search algorithms, the cloud's center is located at an excess of 0.5–1.0 % and a distance of about 300–350; the distribution of solutions has a nearly horizontal stretch with a minor tendency towards the diagonal. For the memetic setups, the cloud approaches the diagonal; the center's excess is now at about 0.5 % and most solutions have a distance of < 300 edges.

Whereas it is possible to find very good solutions for instance R500 that are close to the best-known solution in terms of both distance and fitness (given that the solutions are located on the diagonal branch), the setups under consideration for R500-E fail to find a solution close to the best-known solution for distance, although the achieved excess is lower than the one for the non-Euclidean instance of the same size on average.

*Summary*

Both problem instances show that finding good or even optimal solutions for the OCST using local search is not trivial. In the search space of instance R500, a large number of local optima with low excess but large distance to the best-known solution were found. It is possible that the global optimal solution is closer to these solutions than the best-known solution found for this instance. The distribution of solutions in the plots for R500-E suggest that it is relatively easy to find sufficiently good local optima, but a 'gap' of 200 edges must be bridged for best (or even optimal) solutions.

## 5.8   Summary

The Optimum Communication Spanning Tree Problem is important for the planning of communication networks where the communication volume between participating nodes is considered in the topology design. The results of this chapter can be summarized as follows:

- Existing algorithms for the OCST were presented, with the focus on the algorithms by Ahuja and Murty. Furthermore, several EAs and GAs were presented.

- The selection of problem instances was addressed. As available benchmark instances are small by today's standards, random instances were generated following a 'recipe' documented in related literature.

- Several solution construction heuristics were discussed and compared. Two random tree generation algorithms were included for comparison, but results showed that their quality is not competitive with more sophisticated approaches. Although any structured[3] tree generation algorithm can produce feasible solutions, three structured construction heuristics (star, MST, shortest path tree) were selected and their viablity for the OCST was examined. The results suggest that stars are best suited for Euclidean instances, whereas shortest path trees are best suited for non-Euclidean instances. The construction heuristic from Ahuja and Murty performs best in most cases, but has a prohibitive runtime behavior.

- Based on the local search by Ahuja and Murty ('AH-H'), a faster local search algorithm was developed. The key issue with AM-H is its extensive cost when determining the objective value's change for a potential 1-exchange move. In contrast to the original algorithm, the improved algorithm presented here used only

---

3  Here, 'structured' refers to building a tree with a bias towards some objective.

a subset of all node pairs for cost evaluation and thus was considerably faster. Different techniques to sample nodes for the subset were evaluated; the strategy to select nodes at random performed best.

- Several recombination operators for the OCST were proposed to enable the development of a memetic algorithm (MA). The design of recombination operators, however, turned out to be difficult, as the OCST is very sensitive to small changes in the tree structure result in large changes in the objective value. Three recombination algorithms were proposed; the recombination operator based on the exact algorithm by AHUJA and MURTY was not used in the experimental analysis due to its prohibitive computation times. Recombination heuristics based on the concept of merging tree fragments common to both parents and the concept of reusing path from either parents were proposed, too, and used in the experimental analysis. Both recombination operators, however, did not perform significantly better than a replace operator, due to its advantage in speed and non-destructiveness.

- Analgous to the memetic algorithm, a distributed memetic algorithm (DMA) was developed using the concept of an island model. For corresponding setups of the distributed and non-distributed algorithms, the same total CPU time was used as the limit (termination criterion). Results for the distributed algorithm showed that it is competitive to the original algorithm, finding results in less absolute time due to the parallelization of the solution finding process. Given that the resources per computing node are limited, the distributed algorithm can handle larger problem instances, as only one individual per island is maintained. The original memetic algorithm, in contrast, has to maintain the complete population on a single system.

- A search space analysis for two selected problem instances was conducted, considering indicators such as average distance between solutions. Results suggest that although it is possible to find good solutions for both problem instances using local search or memetic algorithms, these results may have a considerable distance (in number of different edges) to global optima[4]. In one of the two examples discussed in this analysis, the set of

---

4  Here, the best known solution was used as the point of reference.

local optima was split between solutions with a large distance to the best-known solution regardless of quality, and solutions that became increasingly similar to the best-known solution with better fitness. For the other example, only a weak relation between better solution quality and distance to the best-known solution was observed and even solutions with minimal excess only had about half of all edges in common with the best-known solution.

For small problem instances, the algorithms by AHUJA and MURTY are sufficient, as here a more complete search is performed and the runtime complexity does not yet seriously affect its applicability. With increasing problem size, the random sample algorithm (RS-AM) is the better choice as it finds competitive results in a fraction of the time required by the original local search. Solution quality can be improved by the choice of construction heuristics, as discussed previously. For very large problem instances, the distributed memetic algorithm can be used to reduce the absolute time to find good solutions for the problem instance at hand. Here, the replace recombination is the best choice in most cases.

```
1: function INITIALIZEPOPULATION(Graph G, Requests R)
2:     S ← ∅
3:     for i ← 1, . . . , n do
4:         s ← INITIALIZEINDIVIDUAL(G)
5:         S ← S ∪ {s}
6:     end for
7:     return S
8: end function
```

```
1: function TOURNAMENTSELECTION(Population S, S′)
2:     S* ← BEST(S ∪ S′)
3:     for i ∈ {2, . . . , n} do
4:         s₁ ← CHOOSEINDIVIDUAL(S ∪ S′)
5:         s₂ ← CHOOSEINDIVIDUAL(S ∪ S′, s₁)
6:         if s₁ < s₂ then
7:             S* ← S* ∪ {s₁}
8:         else
9:             S* ← S* ∪ {s₂}
10:        end if
11:    end for
12:    return S*
13: end function
```

```
1: function MEMETICALGORITHM(Graph G = (V, E, d, r))
2:     S ← INITIALIZEPOPULATION(G)
3:     while ¬ time limit reached do
4:         S′ ← ∅
5:         for all s ∈ S do
6:             s̄ ← CHOOSEINDIVIDUAL(S, s)
7:             s′ ← RECOMBINE(G, s, s̄)
8:             s″ ← LOCALSEARCH(G, s′)
9:             S′ ← S′ ∪ {s″}
10:        end for
11:        S ← TOURNAMENTSELECTION(S, S′)
12:    end while
13:    return S
14: end function
```

Figure 52: Memetic algorithm for the OCST.

```
 1: function ExhaustiveRecombination(T_a, T_b)
 2:     S ← ∅                                    ▷ Start with empty stack
 3:     T* ← T_a                                 ▷ Initial best solution
 4:     z* ← c(T_a)                              ▷ Set upper bound
 5:     T' ← E_{T_a} ∩ E_{T_b}                   ▷ Initial partial solution
 6:     E* ← E_{T_a} \ E_{T_b}                   ▷ Edges only in better parent
 7:     E' ← E_{T_b} \ E_{T_a}                   ▷ Edges only in worse parent

 8:     while |E*| > 0 do                        ▷ Prepare stack
 9:         Push(S, (T', E'))                    ▷ Put current state on stack
10:         e ← arg min_{e∈E*} d(e)              ▷ Fetch shortest edge from E*
11:         T' ← T' ∪ {e}                        ▷ Add e to growing partial solution
12:         E* ← E* \ {e}
13:     end while

14:     while |S| > 0 do
15:         (T', E') ← Pop(S)                    ▷ Fetch current state from stack
16:         if IsTree(T') then                   ▷ Valid solution found
17:             if c(T') < c(T*) then            ▷ New best tree found
18:                 T* ← T'                      ▷ Store new best tree
19:                 z* ← c(T*)                   ▷ Update upper bound
20:             end if
21:         else if |E'| > 0 then                ▷ Branch search
22:             e ← arg min_{e∈E'} d(e)          ▷ Fetch shortest edge
23:             E' ← E' \ {e}
24:             if |E'| + |E_{T'}| ≥ |V| - 1 then  ▷ Enough edges left?
25:                 Push(S, (T', E'))            ▷ Branch without e
26:             end if
27:             T' ← T' ∪ {e}
28:             if IsValid(T') ∧ c'(T') < z* then    ▷ Below LB?
29:                 Push(S, (T', E'))            ▷ Branch with edge e
30:             end if
31:         end if
32:     end while
33:     return T*                                ▷ Return best solution
34: end function
```

Figure 53: Recombination of parent trees $T_a$ and $T_b$ to an offspring tree $T^*$ using the Exhaustive algorithm. W. l. o g. $c(T_a) \leq c(T_b)$

1: **function** TREEBUILDINGRECOMBINATION($T_a$, $T_b$)
2:   $\mathcal{T} \leftarrow \{T_1, \ldots, T_k\}$       ▷ Determine fragments
3:   $p^{\mathcal{T}} \leftarrow$ ALLPAIRSSHORTESTPATH($G$)
4:   $s \leftarrow$ SEED($G$)        ▷ Select seeding node
5:   $T^* \leftarrow \arg_{s \in T} T \in \mathcal{T}$     ▷ Initialize partial solution
6:   $\mathcal{T} \leftarrow \mathcal{T} \setminus \{T^*\}$      ▷ Update fragment set
7:   $S \leftarrow V_{T^*}$        ▷ Update components
8:   $\overline{S} \leftarrow V \setminus S$

9:   **while** $|S| < |V|$ **do**
10:    $\alpha \leftarrow$ ALPHA($S, \overline{S}, p_{i,j}^{\mathcal{T}}, p_{i,j}^{\mathcal{T}}$)     ▷ Determine $\alpha$
11:    $(p, q) \leftarrow \arg\min_{(p,q) \in (S \times \overline{S})} \{\alpha_{p,q}\}$   ▷ Select edge
12:    $T' \leftarrow \arg_{q \in T} T \in \mathcal{T}$     ▷ Determine $q$'s fragment
13:    $\mathcal{T} \leftarrow \mathcal{T} \setminus \{T'\}$      ▷ Update fragment set
14:    $T^* \leftarrow T^* \cup T'$   ▷ Add $q$'s fragment to partial solution
15:    **for** each $(i, j) \in (S \times V_{T'})$ **do**
16:     $c(p_{i,j}^{\mathcal{T}}) \leftarrow c(p_{i,p}^{\mathcal{T}}) + d(p, q) + c(p_{q,j}^{\mathcal{T}})$
17:    **end for**
18:    $S \leftarrow S \cup V_{T'}$       ▷ Update components
19:    $\overline{S} \leftarrow V \setminus S$
20:   **end while**
21:   **return** $T^*$        ▷ Return solution
22: **end function**

Figure 54: Recombination of two parent trees $T_a$ and $T_b$ to an offspring tree $T^*$ using the TreeBuilding recombination algorithm.

```
 1: function PATHMERGERRECOMBINATION(T_a, T_b)
 2:     T* ← ∅
 3:     s ← SEED(G)                           ▷ Select seeding node
 4:     S ← {s}                               ▷ Initialize components
 5:     S̄ ← V ∖ S
 6:     while |S| < |V| do
 7:         s ← SEED(S̄)                       ▷ Select node not in S
 8:         T ← SELECT(T_a, T_b)              ▷ Alternating btw. T_a and T_b
 9:         p ← arg min_{p^T_{s,s'} with s'∈S} |p^T_{s,s'}|   ▷ Find path to node in S
10:         T* ← T* ∪ p                       ▷ Add path to partial solution
11:         S ← S ∪ V_p                       ▷ Update components
12:         S̄ ← S̄ ∖ V_p
13:     end while
14:     return T*                             ▷ Return solution
15: end function
```

Figure 55: Recombination of two parent trees $T_a$ and $T_b$ to an offspring tree $T^*$ using the Path recombination algorithm.

```
 1: function REPLACERECOMBINATION(T_a, T_b)
 2:     if c(T_a) < c(T_b) then
 3:         return T_a
 4:     else
 5:         return T_b
 6:     end if
 7: end function
```

Figure 56: Recombination of two parent trees $T_a$ and $T_b$ to an offspring tree $T^*$ using the Replace recombination algorithm.

```
 1: function DISTRIBUTEDMA(Graph G = (V, E, d, r))
 2:     s ← INITIALIZEINDIVIDUAL(G)
 3:     while ¬TERMINATIONDETECTED do
 4:         if {q₁, . . . , qₖ} = Q ≠ ∅ then
 5:             s̄ = q₁, Q ← {q₂, . . . , qₖ}
 6:             s' ← RECOMBINE(G, s, s̄)
 7:         else
 8:             s' ← s
 9:             s'' ← LOCALSEARCH(G, s')
10:         end if
11:         if s'' < s then
12:             s ← s''
13:             SENDTORANDOMNEIGHBOR(s)
14:         end if
15:     end while
16:     return s
17: end function
```

Figure 57: Distributed memetic algorithm for the OCST.

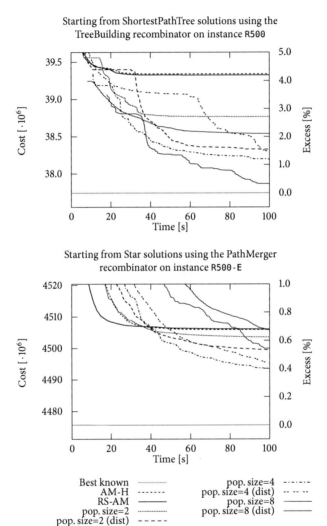

Figure 58: Different recombination operators applied on problem instances with 500 nodes.

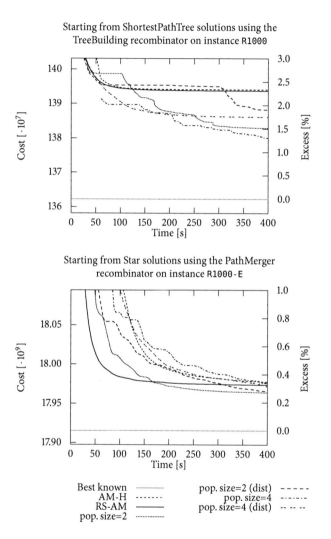

Figure 59: Different recombination operators applied on problem instances with 1000 nodes.

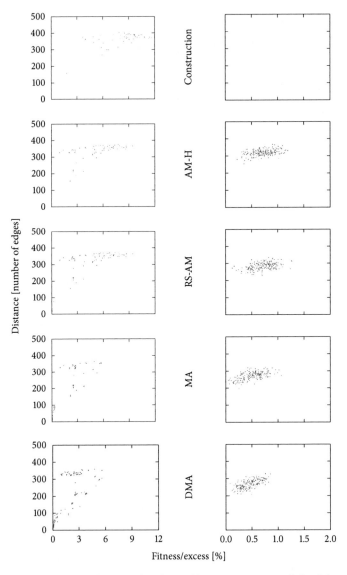

Figure 60: Fitness-distance plots for problem instances R500 (left side) and R500-E (right side). The five rows correspond to the setups shown in Tab. 60.

# 6

## CONCLUSIONS

In the preceding chapters, heuristic algorithms for the three selected NP-complete combinatorial optimization problems were presented. For each of the problems, distributed and memetic algorithms were discussed and evaluated by experimental research. Details on the findings are given in the summary sections of the chapters for each problem.

### Distributed Algorithms

Using either a hypercube topology or an epidemic algorithm as a 'middleware' allows the distribution of evolutionary or memetic algorithms. Whereas a hypercube topology is a structured approach with predictable features best suited for static[1] network environments, epidemic algorithms are more robust and thus applicable in both static and dynamic environments.

A contribution of this thesis is the evaluation of the concept for distributed memetic algorithms for three selected combinatorial optimization problems. It can be argued that if a memetic algorithm including a recombination operator is available for an optimization problem, the algorithm can be distributed with little effort, using the distribution approach as described in this thesis.

### Problem-Specific Algorithms

Distributing the computation is not the only feasible approach for addressing large problem instances. Restricting the search space is a viable concept as shown, for example, by don't-look-bits or restricted candidate lists for various problems.

Each simplification technique presented in this thesis was designed for a specific problem. The techniques include heuristics to detect components of optimal solutions in suboptimal solutions and fixing those components for subsequent local search (TSP), simplification of the

---

1 In static networks, it is assumed that nodes and network connections do not change (leave or fail) during the computation, whereas in dynamic networks nodes may fail, unannounced, at any time and new nodes may join the network.

cost function (OCST), and homogeneous reduction of the complexity of a problem instance (RWA). However, each of these techniques can be generalized and transferred to other NP-complete problems.

Fixing edges or components in general is a simple idea. The challenging part is the selection of components. The approach of selecting components to be fixed can be used for NP-complete problems where similar but less complex problems exist. For the TSP, both the MST and finding nearest neighbors are related problems, but can be solved in polynomial time (problem class P). In addition to the TSP, the MST and nearest neighbor list can be used in general for graph problems that prefer short edges while maintaining some connectivity properties. The vehicle routing problem, where customers have to be served by a fleet of vehicles each making round trips from a central depot, is an example of such a problem.

Simplifying the cost function that is also a search space simplification is an approach that can be used in flow problems with many different commodities. In this approach, some commodities are excluded from the cost function evaluation, but the choice of which commodities to exclude may be a sensitive issue. An example of where the approach of excluding commodities is feasible is the supply chain management problem[2] (certain factories and customers are excluded).

Homogeneous reductions can be applied on problems where many similar elements have to be arranged or categorized. Assuming that different types of items are given and a large number of items for each type is available, the same search space reduction technique can be used as for the RWA. From the $n_i$ items of the same type $i$, only $\left\lceil \frac{n_i}{k} \right\rceil$ items are kept in a multilevel reduction step. A solution can be found more easily in the reduced instance, . In the expansion step, all the features of the reduced instance's solution are copied $k$ times to get a solution for the original problem instance. Motivated by the RWA construction heuristics presented here, the bin packing problem is an example of where this concept can be used.

*Contributions*

In the introduction, it was stated that this thesis strives to solve large problem instances of the three problems TSP, OCST, and RWA. With

---

2  In the supply chain management problem, a subset has to be selected from a set of factories and distribution centers and activated, minimizing the total costs while supplying the customers with the required goods.

a focus on the development on problem-size reduction and speed-up techniques, this objective has been clearly reached. For the OCST and the RWA problems, new and larger problem instances had to be created to benchmark the presented algorithms, as known benchmark instances had to be considered as trivial. For the RWA, tight lower bounds are available, proving the quality of the algorithms from this thesis. For the OCST, direct comparisons between the best algorithm from literature and the random shuffle algorithm (RS-AM) have shown that this RS-AM algorithm is able to find good solutions faster for all relevant problem instances. For the TSP, the edge fixing heuristic can be used as a building block of a larger algorithm.

*Areas of Future Research*

Future research based on the findings of this thesis can be divided into short-term objectives and long-term directions. Short-term objectives are a direct continuation of the research for each of the three problems considered here. Long-term directions are derived from the more abstract techniques and contributions from this work.

SHORT-TERM OBJECTIVES    Since the original research for the TSP part of this section was carried out in 2005, new and improved algorithms for the TSP have emerged. Most notably, HELSGAUN has published a new version of his LK-H algorithm, which includes some interesting features, such as a new recombination operator. The next logical step, therefore, is to integrate the new LK-H into a distributed algorithm, similar to the process with CLK in this thesis. From the LK-H, both the local search and the recombination parts can be used in the DMA, where the local search operator is enriched with an edge fixing component.

The research performed for this thesis on the RWA focused on the static variant. The current algorithm can be expanded to several other optimization objectives, such as selecting requests if the number of wavelengths is limited and each request is associated with a gain. In addition, the concepts of the discussed algorithms can be adapted for dynamic or online RWA variants. Other constraints to be considered are the availability of wavelength converters (only at some nodes, adding cost) and different sets of wavelengths available at each link or even multiple fibers per link.

For the OCST, new concepts of recombination are required to handle large problem instances, as 'conventional' operators have drawbacks, as described. Instead of performing a dedicated recombination, the structure of a solution received in the DMA can be analyzed. For example, edges from received solutions can be considered with a higher priority in a local search exchange step. For inclusion, a feasible edge is selected from the collection of received solutions instead of testing all $\mathcal{O}(n^2)$ candidate edges. For more realistic experiments, random instances modeling metropolitan area networks (clusters of nodes with high inter-node communication volume) and instances based on real-world communication traffic patterns have to be generated.

LONG-TERM DIRECTIONS    Practical approaches on distributed computation outside controlled environments fail because of different reasons. The PlanetLab system, an international project where researchers contribute computation resources and in return may use other systems, allows the execution of distributed computations in theory. However, only a small fraction of nodes that are listed as 'participating' are actually reachable due to software and hardware problems. This makes the PlanetLab system more interesting for research on fault-tolerant algorithms than for distributed computations. 'Cloud computing', which can be seen as a successor to grid computing, may become a future alternative. In cloud computing, computational resources are provided as a service and billed by pay-per-use. Whereas grid computing was perceived as a niche application for research-oriented users, large Internet companies such as Google and Amazon already offer services for cloud computing to end users. As a business model, solving large problem instances can be advertised as a service, where the service provider rents computational resources and runs a distributed algorithm on the cloud's resources.

Desktop computing systems struggle with practical problems, too. Given the lack of free IPv4 network addresses, desktop PCs are often located in subnets that cannot be reached due to NAT at intermediate routers. In addition, nodes are no longer reachable at the address they used for joining the network after some time. This is due to regular changes in the online status, dynamic host configuration, and changing network parameters that are location-dependent (for mobile equipment). The above problems can be solved by using IPv6 addresses that allow unique addresses to be assigned each node.

In the foreseeable future, the computational resources available for both workstation PCs and cluster computers will grow. This allows larger problem instances than before to be addressed, which will put additional demands on heuristic algorithms. Components of algorithms with a small constant factor but high polynomial degree in their run-time complexity will have a larger influence on the performance of the algorithm. Using the problem reduction techniques presented here (using the random sample approach as an example), these high complexity components can be simplified effectively. Still, the consequences of these simplifications have to be considered in the algorithm design, as assumptions that hold in the original variant may no longer be valid.

In classical, non-distributed evolutionary and memetic algorithms, there are distinct phases for each operator: recombination, mutation, local search, and selection of the next generation's individuals. In distributed memetic algorithms with only one individual per island, these phases are less strict as computing nodes operate asynchronously. If no individual is stored in the message queue, no recombination is performed. If too many individuals are stored in the queue, recombination is performed more often than expected from the experiment setup's parameter set. This issue can be addressed by 'merging' local search and recombination. Local search algorithms usually use data structures with candidate components in exchange moves, queues that determine the order in which elements are considered for improvement steps, or some memory on the history of the local search process. Here, the idea is to integrate components from received individuals into these data structures *while the local search is still running*. As an example for the TSP, don't look bits are cleared for nodes that have different edges in both the current and the received solution. Considering only minor changes on the data structures, the influence can be expected to be weaker than using a 'real' recombination operator. Still, positive effects may be achieved in the long run and a dedicated recombination operator can be used in addition, if necessary.

# APPENDIX

In this appendix, additional material is provided on each of the three combinatorial optimization problems. Descriptions of lower bound and polylog algorithms and proofs of NP-completeness are from the authors referred to in the literature references and not the author of this thesis. The materials are included for the sake of completeness.

## A.1 TRAVELLING SALESMAN PROBLEM

### A.1.1 *Lower Bounds for the TSP*

An introduction to lower bounds for the TSP was given in Sec. 3.1.2. Here, more details on the lower bound algorithm by HELD and KARP [97, 98] are provided.

VALENZUELA *et al.* [195] discuss variants and extensions of the Held-Karp lower bound ($LB_{HK}$), which is determined as follows: Given is a graph $G = (V, E, d)$. Define an arbitrary weight $p_i$ for each node $i \in V$. This weight will be modified during the *subgradient optimization* later. Modify the edge weight for each edge $e$ as defined in Eq. (A.1) where $(i, j) = e \in E$. Let $\mathcal{U}$ be the set of all 1-trees in $G$ and $\mathcal{T}$ the set of all tours in $G$. As every tour is a 1-tree, it holds that $\mathcal{T} \subseteq \mathcal{U}$ and thus Eq. (A.2) holds, where $c'(U)$ is the sum of all modified weights for edges in $U$. Due to Eq. (A.1), Eq. (A.3) holds for each 1-tree (and thus each tour) $U$ with node degree $\delta_i^U$ for each node $i$ in $U$. If $U$ is a tour, it holds that $\delta \equiv 2$. Combining equations (A.2) and (A.3) using $T^\star = \arg\min_{T \in \mathcal{T}} c(T)$ as best tour in $G$, Eq. (A.4) can be derived and subsequently Eq. (A.5) using $c$ instead of $c'$ as weight function. Finally, Eq. (A.6) holds for an inequality for the cost of the best tour $T^\star$.

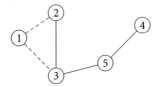

Figure 61: Example of an 1-tree. Dashed edges are the two edges incident to node 1; solid edges (together with the dotted edges) correspond to the minimum 1-tree for this graph.

$$d'_{i,j} = d_{i,j} + p_i + p_j \tag{A.1}$$

$$\min_{U \in \mathcal{U}} c'(U) \le \min_{T \in \mathcal{T}} c'(T) \tag{A.2}$$

$$c'(U) = c(U) + \sum_{i \in V} p_i \delta_i^U \tag{A.3}$$

$$\min_{U \in \mathcal{U}} c'(U) \le c(T^\star) + 2 \sum_{i \in V} p_i \tag{A.4}$$

$$\min_{U \in \mathcal{U}} \left\{ c(U) + \sum_{i \in V} p_i \delta_i^U \right\} \le c(T^\star) + 2 \sum_{i \in V} p_i \tag{A.5}$$

$$\min_{U \in \mathcal{U}} \left\{ c(U) + \sum_{i \in V} p_i \left( \delta_i^U - 2 \right) \right\} \le c(T^\star) \tag{A.6}$$

The Held-Karp lower bound $\text{LB}_{\text{HK}}$ is thus defined as

$$\text{LB}_{\text{HK}} = \max_p \left[ \min_{U \in \mathcal{U}} \left\{ c(U) + \sum_{i \in V} p_i \left( \delta_i^U - 2 \right) \right\} \right] \tag{A.7}$$

To determine an approximation of the lower bound, $p$ is iteratively modified using a Lagrangian relaxation scheme. Due to the minimization component in the HK bound, the relaxation results in a series of $p$ vectors used in the modified edge weight function Eq. (A.1) to create 1-trees more and more similar to a tour (node degree 2). Vector $p$ is updated in each iteration $m + 1$ as shown in Eq. (A.9), where $\delta_i^m$ is the node degree of node $i$ in the minimum 1-tree defined by the modified edge weight function using $p^m$.

$$p_i^0 = 0 \qquad\qquad \text{for each } i \in V \tag{A.8}$$

$$p_i^{m+1} = p_i^m + t^m \left( \delta_i^m - 2 \right) \qquad\qquad \text{for each } i \in V \tag{A.9}$$

Every node $i$ having a degree $\delta_i > 2$ will have a larger $p_i$ value in the next iteration and thus the incident edges have a lower probability of being included in the next iteration's 1-tree due to higher edge costs. Conversely, a node $i$ having a degree $\delta_i < 2$ will have a smaller $p_i$ value and thus is expected to have more incident edges in the next 1-tree by equivalent argumentation. Variable $t^m$ acts as a scaling factor, which has to comply to the following two conditions in order let the algorithm to converge to $\text{LB}_{\text{HK}}$:

$$\lim_{m \to \infty} t^m = 0 \qquad\qquad \sum_{m=1}^{\infty} t^m = \infty \qquad (A.10)$$

Different strategies exist on how to modify $t^m$ and optionally $p_i^m$. An early strategy by HELD [99] updates $t^m$ as follows:

$$t^m = \frac{\lambda (U - L)}{\sum_{i \in V} \left( \delta_i^m - 2 \right)^2} \qquad (A.11)$$

where $U$ and $L$ are upper and lower bounds, respectively, and $\lambda$ is a positive scalar $< 2$.

An alternative strategy was proposed by VOLGENANT and JONKER [198], which uses the following update rules:

$$p_i^{m+1} = p_i^m + 0.6t^m \left( \delta_i^m - 2 \right)$$
$$+ 0.4t^m \left( \delta_i^{m-1} - 2 \right) \qquad \text{for each } i \in V \quad (A.12)$$

where

$$\delta_i^0 = \delta_i^1 \qquad (A.13)$$

$$t^{m+1} - 2t^m + t^{m-1} = \text{constant} \qquad (A.14)$$

$$t^1 = \frac{l^*}{100} \qquad (A.15)$$

$$t^1 - t^2 = 3 \left( t^{M-1} - t^M \right) \qquad \text{with } t^M = 0 \qquad (A.16)$$

where $l^*$ is the best known minimal 1-tree (new trees automatically update $t^1$) and $M$ is the number of iterations. The advantage of this approach compared to the original approach is that lower and upper bounds now have to be known.

The Held-Karp lower bound is known to be at most $1/3$ below the optimum, given that the triangle inequality holds. For common problems, however, it has been reported that the lower bound is less than 1 % below the optimum in most cases. The runtime complexity is dominated by the computations of 1-trees ($\mathcal{O}(|E|\log|E|)$ per tree) given a constant number of iterations.

## A.2    Optimum Communication Spanning Trees

### A.2.1    Proof of NP-Completeness of the OCST

The OCST is known to be NP-complete as shown by Johnson, Lenstra, and Rinnooy Kan in [114]. The proof shows that the problem of *Exact 3-Cover* can be reduced to a special case of the decision variant of the OCST. The OCST's decision variant is defined as follows according to [82, ND7]: Given a complete graph $G = (V, E, d, r)$ with a distance function $d : E \to \mathbb{Z}_0^+$, a requirement (or demand) function $r : V \times V \to \mathbb{Z}_0^+$, and a bound $B \in \mathbb{Z}_0^+$, does a spanning tree $T \subseteq G$ exist with

$$c(T) = \sum_{i,j\in V} r_{i,j} \cdot c(p_{i,j}^T) \leq B \;? \tag{A.17}$$

A special case of the OCST called *simple network design problem* (SNDP) is used to show the NP-completeness. The SNDP sets $r_{i,j} = 1$ for all $i, j \in V$ and $d(e) = 1$ for all $e \in E$. Note that the SNDP is not a special case of optimum requirement spanning tree problem (ORST, [106]), which can be solved in polynomial time. The SNDP does not require the graph to be fully-connected (only connectivity is required), which is a prerequisite for the ORST. The *Exact 3-Cover* problem is defined as follows (according to [114]): Given a family $S = \{\sigma_1, \ldots, \sigma_s\}$ of 3-element subsets of a set $P = \{\pi_1, \ldots, \pi_{3t}\}$ (it holds that $|\sigma_i| = 3$ and $\sigma_i \subset P$ for $i = 1, \ldots, s$), is there a subfamily $S' \subset S$ of pairwise disjoint sets, such that $\bigcup_{\sigma\in S'} \sigma = P$?

The proof in [114] as reproduced below shows that, for any given problem instance for the Exact 3-Cover problem, a problem instance for the SNDP can be constructed. Any valid solution found in the SNDP instance corresponds to a valid solution for the original Exact 3-Cover problem instance. The proof performs the following steps: Firstly, a graph $G = (V, E)$ and a bound $B$ is derived for the SNDP instance. Then, it is shown that only trees $T = (V, E')$ for which $c(T) \leq B$ holds contain a solution for the cover problem (by evaluating which edges of $E$ are actually included in $E'$).

This SNDP instance with graph $G = (V, E)$ is constructed as follows: Nodes $V$ consist of three sets $R$, $S$, and $P$ holding $V = R \cup S \cup P$. Node set $S$ contains one node for each $\sigma$ in the Exact 3-Cover problem instance, set $P$ contains one node per $\pi$ in the Exact 3-Cover problem instance. Node set $R$ contains $r + 1$ nodes denoted as $\rho_0$ to $\rho_r$, where the choice on $r$ is defined below. Furthermore, a set of constants associated with these three node sets is defined as follows:

$$s = |S|$$
$$p = |P|$$
$$b_{S,S} = s^2 - s$$
$$b_{S,P} = 9sp - 6p$$
$$b_{P,P} = 18p^2 - 12p$$
$$r = b_{S,S} + b_{S,P} + b_{P,P}$$
$$b_{R,R} = r^2$$
$$b_{R,S} = 2rs + s$$
$$b_{R,P} = 9rp + 6p$$
$$B = b_{R,R} + b_{R,S} + b_{R,P} + b_{S,S} + b_{S,P} + b_{P,P}$$

The edge set $E$ contains the following edges: (i) nodes $\rho_1$ to $\rho_r$ are connected only to $\rho_0$, (ii) node $\rho_0$ is connected to each node $\sigma \in S$, and (iii) each node $\sigma \in S$ is connected to exactly three nodes $\pi \in P$, where in the corresponding Exact 3-Cover problem instance $\pi \in \sigma$. An example of such a graph $G = (V, E)$ is shown in Fig. 62.

Now the objective is to find a spanning tree $T$ in $G$ which fulfills the constraints as stated above. For brevity, let $c_{X,Y} = \sum_{i \in X, j \in Y} c(p_{i,j}^T)$. The cost for this tree is

$$c(T) = \sum_{i,j \in V} c(p_{i,j}^T) \tag{A.18}$$

$$= c_{R,R} + c_{R,S} + c_{R,P} + c_{S,S} + c_{S,P} + c_{P,P} \tag{A.19}$$

Every edge $(\rho_0, \rho_i)$ with $i = 1, \ldots, r$ will be included in $T$, as each $\rho_i$ is a leaf in $G$. Thus, $c_{R,R} = r^2 = b_{R,R}$. Furthermore, each edge $(\rho_0, \sigma)$ for all $\sigma \in S$ is included in $T$. The proof assumes that there is an edge $(\rho_0, \sigma) \notin E'$ for some $\sigma \in S$. In this case, each path from any $\rho \in R$ to $\sigma$ has to be routed over some $\pi \in P$ and thus would be longer by 2 units

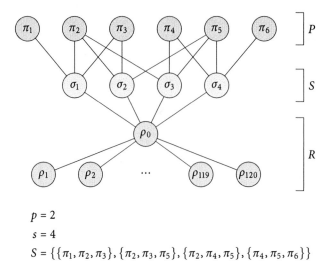

$p = 2$

$s = 4$

$S = \{\{\pi_1, \pi_2, \pi_3\}, \{\pi_2, \pi_3, \pi_5\}, \{\pi_2, \pi_4, \pi_5\}, \{\pi_4, \pi_5, \pi_6\}\}$

Figure 62: SNDP graph constructed for an exact 3-cover problem instance.

compared to the case where $(\rho_0, \sigma) \in E'$. This increase in cost can be used for a contradiction:

$$
\begin{aligned}
c(T) &> c_{R,R} + c_{R,S} + c_{R,P} \\
&\geq b_{R,R} + (b_{R,S} + 2|R|) + b_{R,P} \quad \text{(A.20)} \\
&> B \quad \text{(A.21)}
\end{aligned}
$$

As every edge between $(\rho_0, \sigma)$ with $\sigma \in S$ must be included in $T$, any node $\pi \in P$ may only be connected to one $\sigma \in S$, i. e. any node $\pi \in P$ is a leaf in $T$, as otherwise a cycle is introduced in $T$.

So far, it can be concluded that $c_{X,Y} = b_{X,Y}$ for all of the six node set pairs except for $\{X, Y\} = \{P, P\}$. The routing cost $c_{P,P}$ within $P$ can be determined as follows:

$$
\begin{aligned}
c_{P,P} &= 4 \cdot \frac{3t(3t-1)}{2} - (2s_2 + 6s_3) \\
&= b_{P,P} + 6(t - s_3) - 2s_2 \quad \text{(A.22)}
\end{aligned}
$$

Here, $s_h$ denotes the number of nodes in $S$ that are connected to exactly $h$ nodes in $P$. In the above equation, $2s_2$ and $6s_3$ are subtracted, as path lengths between nodes in $T$ become shorter if both nodes are attached to the same node in $S$. To ensure that $c(T) \leq B$, it must hold $6(t - s_3) - 2s_2 = 0$ (cmp Eq. (A.18)), which is given for $s_3 = t$, $s_2 = 0$, $s_1 = 0$, and $s_0 = s - t$, i. e. nodes in $S$ are connected either to three nodes in $P$ or no node in $P$. The solution for the exact 3-cover problem instance can now be derived by setting $S'$ to those nodes in $S$ that have degree 4.

### A.2.2    Lower Bounds for the OCST

Several authors, such as HOANG [103], GALLO [81], and AHUJA and MURTY [4], proposed lower bounds for the *Network Design Problem* (NDP). With some minor modifications, lower bounds for the OCST can be derived from lower planes as proposed in these publications. Common to all three publications is the general approach: starting from some connected graph with known cost, iteratively edges are removed and the increase in cost is determined. The lower bound algorithms differ in their strategy on how to choose edges to be removed.

A naive lower bound for the OCST is to use a connected graph $\tilde{G} = (V, \tilde{E})$ and determine the shortest path length $c(p^{\tilde{G}}(i, j))$ between each node pair $(i, j) \in Q$. The cost $\mu_0$ of such a lower bound is

$$\mu_0 = \sum_{(i,j) \in Q} r_{i,j} \cdot c(p^{\tilde{G}}(i, j)) \tag{A.23}$$

As $\tilde{E}$ is defined to contain all feasible solutions' edges, each node pair's shortest path in $\tilde{G}$ is at most as long as the shortest path in any solution between the node pair.

In a preparatory step, a function $L$ is defined that determines the cost of a partial solution restricted to node pairs $\tilde{Q} \subseteq Q$ and routing only on edges in set $\tilde{E} \subseteq E$:

$$L(\tilde{E}, \tilde{Q}) = \sum_{(i,j) \in \tilde{Q}} r_{i,j} \cdot c(p^{\tilde{G}}(i, j)) \quad \text{with } \tilde{G} = (V, \tilde{E}) \tag{A.24}$$

The objective of the OCST can thus be rewritten as to minimize $L(E \setminus X, Q)$ where $X \subset E$ holds and $E \setminus X$ are the edges of a graph spanning all nodes. Let $x$ be the *characteristic vector* of $X$, i. e. $x$ is a vector of length $|E|$ where each element $x_i$ maps to an edge $e_i \in E$ and $x_i = 1$ if $e_i \in X$, otherwise $x_i = 0$. Let $S$ be the set of all characteristic vectors representing valid solutions. A function $h(x)$ is a lower plane for the OCST if it holds for all $x \in S$ that $h(x) \leq L(E \smallsetminus X, Q)$.

To determine lower bounds, a *penalty function* is defined based on the increase of cost if a given set of edges is not available for routing paths in the graph. The penalty $\Pi(X, Y)$ for a set edges $X \subset E$ and set of node pairs $Y \subseteq Q$ is defined as

$$\Pi(X, Y) = L(E \smallsetminus X, Y) - L(E, Y) \tag{A.25}$$

Now, let a set $Y = Y_1 \cup \ldots \cup Y_m \subseteq Q$ be an $m$-partition ($m = |E|$, for all $i \neq j$ it holds that $Y_i \cap Y_j = \varnothing$) of $Q$. Let $\mu$ denote a $m$-vector where each component is defined as $\mu_k = \Pi(\{e_k\}, Y_k)$. A lower plane can be derived as $h(x) = L(E, Q) + \mu \cdot x$.

The proof that $h(x)$ is actually a lower plane is described in detail in [81]. The idea is that the actual increase in cost by removing edges $X$ from a solution (denoted as $\Pi(X, Q)$) is always at least as high as $\mu \cdot x = \sum_{j=1}^{m}(\{e_j\}, Y_j) \cdot x_j$ for any $m$-partition $Y \subseteq Q$. Different lower planes, as discussed below, basically differ only in the choice of the partition.

The most simple lower plane following the pattern above is by HOANG [103], with a definition for each edge $e_k$ with $1 \leq k \leq m$

$$\mu_k^{\text{HOANG}} = \Pi(\{e_k\}, \{(i_k, j_k)\}) \quad \text{where } e_k = (i_k, j_k) \tag{A.26}$$

Here, only the additional cost between the nodes incident to the removed edge are considered.

This lower plane has been refined by GALLO [81], which implies some sorting order on the edges and defines node pair sets for each edge $e_k$:

$$Q_k = \{(i, j) \in Q : \Pi(\{e_k\}, \{(i, j)\}) > 0$$
$$\wedge (i, j) \notin Q_p \quad \text{where } 1 \leq p < k\} \tag{A.27}$$

and the cost approximation becomes

$$\mu_k^{\text{GALLO}} = \sum_{(i,j) \in Q_k} \Pi(\{e_k\}, \{(i, j)\}) \quad \text{for each } e_k \in E \tag{A.28}$$

Note that $\Pi(\{e_k\}, \{(i, j)\}) > 0$ equals that edge $e_k$ on the shortest path between nodes $i$ and $j$.

Finally, AHUJA and MURTY define a lower bound based $\mu^3$ as follows:

$$\beta^k_{(i,j)} = \begin{cases} 0 & k = 0 \\ \max_{1 \le p \le k} \left\{ \Pi\left(\{e_p\}, \{(i,j)\}\right) \right\} & 1 \le k \le m \end{cases} \tag{A.29}$$

$$\mu^3_k = \sum_{(i,j) \in Q} \max\{0, \Pi\left(\{e_k\}, \{(i,j)\}\right) - \beta^{k-1}_{(i,j)}\} \tag{A.30}$$

Next, it is the consideration that GALLO's lower plane dominates HOANG's lower plane, but is itself dominated by AHUJA and MURTY's lower plane. Then, lower bounds will be derived from the lower planes and examples for each lower bound given in an example graph. Finally, some pseudo code will be shown to determine a lower bound.

GALLO's lower plane dominates HOANG's lower plane as it holds that

$$\Pi\left(\{e_k\}, \{(i_k, j_k)\}\right) \le \sum_{(i,j) \in Q_k} \Pi\left(\{e_k\}, \{(i,j)\}\right) \tag{A.31}$$

for $1 \le k \le m$, $e_k = (i_k, j_k)$, and $Q_k$ as defined above. To prove this, three cases have to be considered: (i) if $e_k$ is not on the shortest path between $i$ and $j$ it holds that

$$\Pi\left(\{e_k\}, \{(i_k, j_k)\}\right) = \sum_{(i,j) \in Q_k} \Pi\left(\{e_k\}, \{(i,j)\}\right) = 0 \tag{A.32}$$

(ii) if $e_k$ is on the unique shortest path between $i$ and $j$ then $e_k$ is the only edge $e$ with $\Pi(\{e\}, \{(i,j)\}) > 0$ and thus $e_k \in Q_k$; as $Q_k$ may contain more node pairs the inequality

$$\Pi\left(\{e_k\}, \{(i,j)\}\right) \le \sum_{(i,j) \in Q_k} \Pi\left(\{e_k\}, \{(i,j)\}\right) \tag{A.33}$$

holds. (iii) if $e_k$ is one of several shortest paths between $i$ and $j$ then

$$\Pi\left(\{e_k\}, \{(i_k, j_k)\}\right) = \sum_{(i,j) \in Q_k} \Pi\left(\{e_k\}, \{(i,j)\}\right) = 0 \tag{A.34}$$

as removing $e_k$ does not increase the length of the shortest paths between $i$ and $j$.

AHUJA and MURTY's lower plane dominates GALLO's lower plane as it holds that

$$\sum_{(i,j) \in Q_k} \Pi\left(\{e_k\}, \{(i,j)\}\right)$$
$$\le \sum_{(i,j) \in Q} \max\left\{0, \Pi\left(\{e_k\}, \{(i,j)\}\right) - \beta^{k-1}_{(i,j)}\right\} \tag{A.35}$$

for $1 \leq k \leq m$, and $Q_k$ as defined above. From the definition of $Q_k$, it follows for each edge $(i, j) \in Q_k$ that $\beta_{(i,j)}^{k-1} = 0$ and thus

$$\max\{0, \Pi(\{e_k\}, \{(i,j)\}) - \beta_{(i,j)}^{k-1}\} = \Pi(\{e_k\}, \{(i,j)\}).$$

$$(A.36)$$

For edges $(i, j) \in Q \setminus Q_k$ it can be assumed that there is a node pair $(i, j)$ with $\beta_{(i,j)}^{k-1} > 0$ and $\Pi(\{e_k\}, \{(i,j)\}) > \beta_{(i,j)}^{k-1}$. Both cases combined establish the above domination.

To compute a lower bound based on the lower planes as defined above, the function $h(x) = L(E, Q) + \sum_{k=1}^{m} \mu_k \cdot x_k$ has to be minimized. Thereto, $X' = E \setminus X$ is defined as the edges of a spanning graph and $x'$ as its characteristic vector. Applying this change on the objective function results in $L(E, Q) + \sum_{k=1}^{m} \mu_k - \sum_{k=1}^{m} \mu_k \cdot x_k'$. To minimize this function, $X'$ must be chosen to be a spanning tree $T^*$ of maximum weight[1], where the edge weight of an edge $e_k$ corresponds to $\mu_k$. Thus, the lower bound for an OCST problem instance defined on a graph $G = (V, E)$ is

$$\text{LB}_{\text{OCST}} = L(E, Q) + \sum_{k=1}^{m} \mu_k - \sum_{e_k \in T^*} \mu_k \qquad (A.37)$$

$$= \mu_0 + \sum_{e_k \in E} \begin{cases} 0 & e_k \in T^* \\ \mu_k & \text{else} \end{cases} \qquad (A.38)$$

In Fig. 63 an example graph with 5 nodes is given, for which all of the above lower bounds algorithms are applied. In this example graph, node distances are printed next to the edge, whereas the requirement matrix is defined as on the right side as matrix $R$. Table 61 shows the results for each of above lower plane algorithms. The row denoted with '$\mu^1$' contains the coefficient as derived by HOANG's algorithm. Rows '$Q$' and '$\mu^2$' contain the set of node pairs affected by edge removals in GALLO's algorithm and the resulting coefficient, respectively. Rows '$S$' and '$\mu^3$' contain the set of node pairs affected by edge removals in AHUJA and MURTY's algorithm and the resulting coefficient, respectively. As can be seen, it holds that $\mu_k^1 \leq \mu_k^2 \leq \mu_k^3$ for each $1 \leq k \leq 7$ (for each edge). The resulting maximum spanning tree using HOANG's coefficient contains the edges $\{(1, 2), (1, 4), (2, 3), (4, 5)\}$, whereas both

---

1 This can be done by negating all edge weights and constructing a minimum spanning tree.

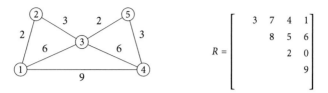

Figure 63: Example graph for lower bound computation.

GALLO and AHUJA and MURTY's algorithms result in a tree with edges $\{(1,2),(2,3),(3,5),(4,5)\}$. As $L(E,Q) = 215$, the resulting lower bounds are $LB_1 = 215$ for HOANG's algorithm; $LB_2 = LB_3 = 215 + 4 = 219$ for the other two lower bound algorithms. An optimal solution for the example in Fig. 63 can be easily found by memetic algorithm, where the optimal solution equals the maximum spanning tree found by the latter two lower bound algorithms.

In Fig. 64 the pseudo code to determine the lower plane coefficients from AHUJA and MURTY's algorithm is given. As a new data structure, $S$ contains those node pairs that are affected in their shortest connecting paths by the removal of the edge $e_k$ in each outer loop. Furthermore, $u_{i,j}$ denotes the shortest path length between nodes $i$ and $j$ in $G$, whereas $v_{i,j}$ denotes the shortest path lengths in $G'$ which equals the original graph without edge $e_k$.

### A.2.3   Polylog Approximation

Some details on the algorithm by PELEG and RESHEF [161, 162] as introduced in Sec. 5.1.1 (p. 190) will be discussed here.

A partition of a graph $G = (V,E)$ is a set $S = \{S^1,\ldots,S^k\}$ (set of node cluster) holding $S^i \cap S^j = \varnothing$ for any $i \neq j$ and $\bigcup_i S^i = V$. The set of edges connecting nodes in different clusters is designated as $C(S)$. The set of $\gamma$-heavy edges is defined as $H^\gamma(G) = \{(i,j) \in E : d(i,j) \geq \frac{D}{\gamma \cdot |V|^3}\}$ where $D = \max_{(i,j) \in Q} c(p^G(i,j))$. For each edge set $F \subseteq E$, it is defined

$$\mathcal{M}(F) = \sum_{e \in F} m(e) \tag{A.39}$$

$$\psi(F) = \sum_{e \in F} \frac{m(e)}{d(e)} \tag{A.40}$$

| k | 1 | 2 | 3 | 4 | 5 | 6 | 7 |
|---|---|---|---|---|---|---|---|
| Edge ▶ | (3,4) | (3,5) | (2,3) | (4,5) | (1,2) | (1,4) | (1,3) |
| **Method** | | | | HOANG | | | |
| $\mu^1$ | 0 | 0 | $(8-3) \cdot 8 = 40$ | $(8-3) \cdot 9 = 45$ | $(9-2) \cdot 3 = 21$ | $(10-9) \cdot 4 = 4$ | 0 |
| **Method** | | | | GALLO | | | |
| Q | ∅ | $\{\{1,5\}, \{2,5\}, \{3,4\}, \{3,5\}\}$ | $\{\{1,3\}, \{2,3\}, \{2,4\}\}$ | $\{\{4,5\}\}$ | $\{\{1,2\}\}$ | $\{\{1,4\}\}$ | ∅ |
| $\mu^2$ | 0 | $5 \cdot 1 + 7 \cdot 6 + 1 \cdot 2 + 7 \cdot 0 = 51$ | $1 \cdot 7 + 5 \cdot 8 + 2 \cdot 5 = 57$ | $1 \cdot 2 + 5 \cdot 9 = 47$ | $7 \cdot 3 = 21$ | $1 \cdot 4 = 4$ | 0 |
| **Method** | | | | AHUJA and MURTY | | | |
| S | ∅ | $\{\{1,5\}, (2,4), (2,5), (3,4), (3,5)\}$ | $\{\{1,3\}, (1,5), (2,3), (2,4), (2,5)\}$ | $\{\{4,2), (4,3), (4,5)\}$ | $\{\{1,2), (1,3), (1,5)\}$ | $\{\{1,4)\}$ | ∅ |
| $\mu^3$ | 0 | 54 | 57 | 45 | 21 | 4 | 0 |

Table 61: Intermediate and final results for different lower bound algorithms (HOANG, GALLO, and AHUJA and MURTY) applied to the example in Fig. 63.

**function** AHUJAMURTYLOWERBOUND(Graph $G = (V, E, d, r)$)
    $Q \leftarrow$ UNIQUENODEPAIRS($V$)
    $u \leftarrow$ ALLPAIRSSHORTESTPATH($G$)
    $\beta \leftarrow 0, \mu^3 \leftarrow 0$
    $\mu_0 \leftarrow \sum_{\{i,j\} \in Q} r_{i,j} \cdot u_{i,j}$
    **for all** $e_k \in E$ **do**
        $G' \leftarrow (V, E \setminus \{e_k\}, d)$
        $(p, q) \leftarrow e_k$
        $S \leftarrow \{(i, j) : (i, j) \in Q \wedge u_{i,j} = u_{i,p} + d(p, q) + u_{q,j}\}$
        **for all** $(i, j) \in S$ **do**
            $v_{i,j} \leftarrow c(p^{G'}(i, j))$
            **if** $v_{i,j} - u_{i,j} > \beta_{i,j}$ **then**
                $\mu_k^3 \leftarrow \mu_k^3 + r_{i,j} \cdot (v_{i,j} - u_{i,j} - \beta_{i,j})$
                $\beta_{i,j} = v_{i,j} - u_{i,j}$
            **end if**
        **end for**
    **end for**
    **return** $\mu^3$
**end function**

Figure 64: Lower bound as defined by AHUJA and MURTY in [4].

An $(\alpha, \beta, \gamma)$-separated partition $S$ must hold the following constraints:

$$\max_{(i,j) \in S^l \times S^l} c(p^G(i, j)) \le \beta \cdot D \quad \text{for } 1 \le l \le k \tag{A.41}$$

$$\psi(C(S)) \le \frac{\alpha \cdot \mathcal{M}(H^\gamma)}{D} \tag{A.42}$$

$$C(S) \subseteq H^\gamma \tag{A.43}$$

where $a > 0, 0 \le \beta < 1$ and $\gamma = \mathcal{O}(1)$. A construction algorithm recursively $(\alpha, \beta, \gamma)$-partitions the graph in each step into $k$ subgraphs until each subgraph contains only a single node. The tree at this level equals the single node. At higher levels, each subgraph $G_l$ with $1 \le l \le k$ provides a spanning tree $T_l$. Choosing a non-empty $S^1$ with $w_1 \in S^1$ w. l. o. g., find in each $S^l$ with $2 \le l \le k$ the node $w_l$ closest to $w_1$; ignore empty $S^l$. Create a tree $T$ for the current recursion level by connecting the subgraphs' trees by adding the edges $(w_1, w_l)$ for $2 \le l \le k$. The average stretch $\overline{S}(T)$ for such a tree $T$ can be derived by arguing over the properties of each subgraph and the constraints of the $(\alpha, \beta, \gamma)$-

separated partitions. The detailed proof is omitted here but available in [161, 162].

Now, it can be shown that for a 2-dimensional complete Euclidean multigraph $G = (V, E, d, m)$ there is an $(\alpha, \beta, \gamma)$-separated partition $S$ with

$$k = 4 \tag{A.44}$$

$$\alpha = \gamma = 6\left(1 + \sqrt{2}\right) \tag{A.45}$$

$$\beta = \sqrt{\frac{8}{9}} \tag{A.46}$$

It is assumed w. l. o. g. that the coordinates of each node are within $[0, D] \times [0, D]$. Let $k$ be an integer with $0 \leq k \leq \frac{2D}{3} = 2\mathcal{K}$ having a corresponding $q_k = \mathcal{K} + \frac{k}{2}$ resulting in $\mathcal{K} \leq q_k \leq 2\mathcal{K}$. For every $k$, a partition $S_k = \{S_k^1, \ldots S_k^4\}$ is defined, where each partition is constructed by cutting along $x = q_k$ and $y = q_k$. The first property (Eq. (A.41)) holds for $\beta = \sqrt{\frac{8}{9}}$ as the longest distance between any node in any region is at most $\sqrt{2\left(\frac{2D}{3}\right)^2}$. If $\gamma = 6\left(1 + \sqrt{2}\right)$ holds, it can be shown that by counting the partitions that intersect 'light' edges (as opposed to 'heavy' edges) that at least half of all partitions fulfill the property from Eq. (A.42). The third property (Eq. (A.43)) holds for at least one partition fulfilling the first two properties if $\alpha = 6\left(1 + \sqrt{2}\right)$ by arguing on the average of $\psi$ for different partitions.

In a case where different partitions result in the same segmentation of nodes, only one partition has to be considered. Thus, at most $\mathcal{O}(n)$ different partitions have to be considered in total.

## A.3    ROUTING AND WAVELENGTH ASSIGNMENT PROBLEM

### A.3.1    Benchmark Instances

Converting a network model from the SND benchmark library [156] to a problem instance for the RWA as used in this thesis is shown here. The SND library offers two files per problem instance: firstly, a network file describing the topology, demands, and special constraints; secondly, a model file describing, for example, the direction of edges (directional, bidirectional, undirected), survivability model, and hop limits. The network file may be shared among several related problem instances. For the conversion to an RWA problem instance, only the network file is of relevance; its format is explained in [156]. The file consists of four sections: NODES (number of nodes, position in the plane), LINKS (incident nodes, capacity, and more), DEMANDS (communication demand between node pairs), and ADMISSIBLE_PATHS (list of paths to be used between node pairs). The last section's default paths are of no relevance to the RWA. Both the link and the demand section can be interpreted directed or undirected, depending on the RWA definition under consideration. For the experiments conducted in this thesis, it is assumed that every link is undirected (the link can be used from any direction, but only once). Demand between any unordered pair of nodes was determined by summing up the values[2] from column 'value'.

For the smallest problem instance pdh (in number of nodes), the resulting demand matrix and the adjacency matrix are given in Fig. 65. In the adjacency matrix, a positive value corresponds to an existing link between two nodes in the RWA problem instance.

The original network file is available at the SND library homepage[3].

---

2 There may be multiple entries per node pair, not only due to direction, but also due to different routing units used in the SND problem instance.

3 http://sndlib.zib.de/coredata.download.action?objectName=
pdh&objectType=network&format=native

$$
\begin{matrix}
0 & 0 & 0 & 0 & 0 & 0 & 138 & 0 & 258 & 115 & 0 \\
 & 0 & 278 & 237 & 144 & 237 & 0 & 160 & 384 & 0 & 266 \\
 & & 0 & 215 & 124 & 0 & 0 & 0 & 0 & 197 & 99 \\
 & & & 0 & 105 & 0 & 0 & 0 & 0 & 0 & 0 \\
 & & & & 0 & 95 & 0 & 108 & 0 & 0 & 0 \\
 & & & & & 0 & 0 & 115 & 0 & 0 & 0 \\
 & & & & & & 0 & 212 & 247 & 0 & 0 \\
 & & & & & & & 0 & 100 & 0 & 0 \\
 & & & & & & & & 0 & 263 & 160 \\
 & & & & & & & & & 0 & 364 \\
 & & & & & & & & & & 0
\end{matrix}
$$

(a) Demand matrix.

$$
\begin{matrix}
0 & 0 & 0 & 0 & 0 & 0 & 1 & 1 & 1 & 1 & 0 \\
 & 0 & 1 & 1 & 1 & 1 & 0 & 1 & 1 & 1 & 1 \\
 & & 0 & 1 & 1 & 1 & 0 & 0 & 0 & 1 & 1 \\
 & & & 0 & 1 & 1 & 0 & 0 & 0 & 0 & 0 \\
 & & & & 0 & 1 & 1 & 1 & 0 & 0 & 0 \\
 & & & & & 0 & 0 & 1 & 1 & 0 & 0 \\
 & & & & & & 0 & 1 & 1 & 1 & 1 \\
 & & & & & & & 0 & 1 & 1 & 1 \\
 & & & & & & & & 0 & 1 & 1 \\
 & & & & & & & & & 0 & 1 \\
 & & & & & & & & & & 0
\end{matrix}
$$

(b) Adjacency matrix.

Figure 65: Demand and adjacency matrix for pdh.

[1] RAND Corporation. http://www.rand.org/, August 2008.

[2] AGRAWAL, G. P. *Fiber-Optic Communication Systems*. John Wiley & Sons, Inc., New York, 3rd edition, June 2002.

[3] AHUJA, R. K. and MURTY, V. V. S. Exact and Heuristic Algorithms for the Optimum Communication Spanning Tree Problem. *Transportation Science*, 21(3):163–170, August 1987.

[4] AHUJA, R. K. and MURTY, V. V. S. New Lower Planes for the Network Design Problem. *Networks*, 17(2):113–127, 1987.

[5] ALKAN, A. and ÖZCAN, E. Memetic Algorithms for Timetabling. *Congress on Evolutionary Computation (CEC'03)*, 2003.

[6] ANDERSON, D. P. BOINC: A System for Public-Resource Computing and Storage. *5th IEEE/ACM International Workshop on Grid Computing*, August 2004.

[7] ANDERSON, D. P., COBB, J., KORPELA, E., LEBOFSKY, M., and WERTHIMER, D. SETI@home: An Experiment in Public-Resource Computing. *Communications of the ACM*, 45(11):56–61, November 2002.

[8] APPLEGATE, D. USA13509 Computation Status. http://www.tsp.gatech.edu/usa13509/usa13509.html, June 2001.

[9] APPLEGATE, D., BIXBY, R. E., CHVÁTAL, V., COOK, W. J., ESPINOZA, D., GOYCOOLEA, M., and HELSGAUN, K. Optimal 85,900-City Tour. http://www.tsp.gatech.edu/pla85900/, March 2008.

[10] APPLEGATE, D. L., BIXBY, R. E., CHVÁTAL, V., and COOK, W. J. Finding Cuts in the TSP (a Preliminary Report). Technical Report 95-05, Rutgers University, Piscataway, NJ, USA, March 1995.

[11] APPLEGATE, D. L., BIXBY, R. E., CHVÁTAL, V., and COOK, W. J. Finding Tours in the TSP. Technical Report 99885, Research Institute for Discrete Mathematics, University of Bonn, 1999.

[12] APPLEGATE, D. L., BIXBY, R. E., CHVÁTAL, V., and COOK, W. J. Implementing the Dantzig-Fulkerson-Johnson Algorithm for large Traveling Salesman Problems. *Mathematical Programming*, 97:91–153, 2003.

[13] APPLEGATE, D. L., COOK, W. J., and ROHE, A. Chained Lin-Kernighan for Large Traveling Salesman Problems. *INFORMS Journal on Computing*, 15(1):82–92, January 2003.

[14] APPLEGATE, D. L., BIXBY, R. E., CHVÁTAL, V., and COOK, W. J. Concorde TSP Solver. http://www.tsp.gatech.edu/concorde/, October 2005.

[15] APPLEGATE, D. L., BIXBY, R. E., CHVÁTAL, V., and COOK, W. J. *The Traveling Salesman Problem: A Computational Study*. Princeton Series in Applied Mathematics. Princeton University Press, 2006.

[16] APPLEGATE, D. L., BIXBY, R. E., CHVÁTAL, V., COOK, W. J., ESPINOZA, D. G., GOYCOOLEA, M., and HELSGAUN, K. Certification of an optimal TSP tour through 85,900 cities. *Operations Research Letters*, September 2008. to appear.

[17] ARENAS, M. G., COLLET, P., EIBEN, A. E., JELASITY, M., MERELO, J. J., BAECHTER, B., PREUSS, M., and SCHOENAUER, M. A Framework for Distributed Evolutionary Algorithms. In *Proceedings of PPSN VII*, volume 2439, pages 665–675, Granada, September 2002.

[18] ATAMTÜRK, A. and RAJAN, D. Partition inequalities for capacitated survivable network design based on directed p-cycles. *Discrete Optimization*, 5(2):415–433, May 2008. Instances available at http://ieor.berkeley.edu/~atamturk/data/.

[19] ATTIYA, H. and WELCH, J. *Distributed Computing – Fundamentals, Simulations and Advanced Topics*. McGraw-Hill, 1998.

[20] BÄCK, T., HAMMEL, U., and SCHWEFEL, H.-P. Evolutionary Computation: Comments on the History and Current State. *IEEE Transactions on Evolutionary Computation*, 1(1):3–17, May 1997.

[21] BALAS, E. and TOTH, P. *Branch and bound*, pages 361–401. In , Lawler et al. [124], 1985.

[22] BANERJEE, D. and MUKHERJEE, B. A Practical Approach for Routing and Wavelength Assignment in Large Wavelength-Routed Optical Networks. *IEEE Journal on Selected Areas in Communications*, 14(5):903–908, 1996.

[23] BANERJEE, N. and SHARAN, S. A Evolutionary Algorithm for Solving the Single Objective Static Routing and Wavelength Assignment Problem in WDM Networks. In *Proceedings of International Conference on Intelligent Sensing and Information Processing (ICISIP 2004)*, pages 13–18, 2004.

[24] BANERJEE, N., MEHTA, V., and PANDEY, S. A Genetic Algorithm Approach for Solving the Routing and Wavelength Assignment Problem in WDM Networks. In *Proc. of the International Conference on Networks (ICN'04)*, 2004.

[25] BANERJEE, S. and CHEN, C. Design of Wavelength-Routed Optical Networks for Circuit Switched Traffic. In *Global Telecommunications Conference, GLOBECOM '96*, volume 1, pages 306–310, November 1996.

[26] BARONI, S. and BAYVEL, P. Wavelength Requirements in Arbitrarily Connected Wavelength-Routed Optical Networks. *Journal of Lightwave Technology*, 15(2):242–251, 1997.

[27] BAUER, K., FISCHER, T., KRUMKE, S. O., GERHARDT, K., WESTPHAL, S., and MERZ, P. Improved Construction Heuristics and Iterated Local Search for the Routing and Wavelength Assignment Problem. In VAN HEMERT, J. and COTTA, C., editors, *EvoCOP 2008 – Eighth European Conference on Evolutionary Computation in Combinatorial Optimization*, volume 4972 of *Lecture Notes in Computer Science*, pages 158–169. Springer, March 2008. (Cited on pages 116 and 119.)

[28] BEARDWOOD, J. E., HALTON, J. H., and HAMMERSLEY, J. M. The Shortest Path Through Many Points. In *Proc. Cambridge Philosophical Society*, volume 55, pages 299–327, 1959.

[29] BENTLEY, J. L. Experiments on Traveling Salesman Heuristics. In *Proceedings of the First Annual ACM-SIAM Symposium on Discrete Algorithms*, pages 91–99, January 1990.

[30] BERRY, L. T. M., MURTAGH, B. A., and McMAHON, G. Applications of a genetic-based algorithm for optimal design of tree-structured communication networks. In *Proceedings of the Regional Teletraffic Engineering Conference of the International Teletraffic Congress*, pages 361–370, 1995.

[31] BLUM, C. and ROLI, A. Metaheuristics in Combinatorial Optimization: Overview and Conceptual Comparison. *ACM Computing Surveys (CSUR)*, 35(3):268–308, September 2003.

[32] BOLLOBÁS, B. *Random Graphs*. Cambridge Studies in Advanced Mathematics. Cambridge University Press, 2001.

[33] BORŮVKA, O. On a minimal problem. *Práce Moravské Přídovědecké Společnosti v Brně (Acta Societas Scientiarum Naturalium Moravicae)*, III:37–58, 1926. (in Czech).

[34] BOUHMALA, N., NATVIG, T., and JAKOBSEN, M. A Multilevel Construction Algorithm for the Traveling Salesman Problem. In *Proceedings of the 5th Metaheuristics International Conference*, Kyoto, Japan, August 2003.

[35] CAMERINI, P. M., FRATTA, L., and MAFFIOLI, F. Some Results on the Design of Tree-Structured Communication Networks. In *Proceedings of the 9th International Teletraffic Congress*, pages 1–4, 1979.

[36] CHIAPUSIO, C., YARNELL, C., AVERY, D., McNETT, D., LAWSON, J., NASBY, J., DeNITTO, P. A., and GILDEA, P. distributed.net, June 2008.

[37] CHLAMTAC, I., GANZ, A., and KARMI, G. Lightpath Communications: An Approach to High Bandwidth Optical WANs. *IEEE Transactions on Communications*, 40(7):1171–1182, July 1992.

[38] CHLAMTAC, I., FARAGÓ, A., and ZHANG, T. Lightpath (Wavelength) Routing in Large WDM Networks. *IEEE Journal on Selected Areas in Communications*, 14(5), June 1996.

[39] CHRISTOFIDES, N. Worst-Case Analysis of a New Heuristic for the Traveling Salesman Problem. In TRAUB, J. F., editor, *Symposium on New Directions and Recent Results in Algorithms and Complexity*, page 441, 1976.

[40] CHRISTOFIDES, N. and EILON, S. Algorithms for Large-Scale Travelling Salesman Problems. *Operational Research Quarterly*, 23(4):511–518, December 1972.

[41] COLLETTE, Y. and SIARRY, P. *Multiobjective Optimization: Principles and Case Studies.* Springer, Berlin, 2004.

[42] COOK, S. A. The Complexity of Theorem-Proving Procedures. In *Proceedings of the 3rd Annual ACM Symposium on Theory of Computing*, pages 151–158. ACM Press, 1971.

[43] COOK, W. J. VLSI Data Sets. http://www.tsp.gatech.edu/vlsi/, March 2003.

[44] COOK, W. J. Log of SW24978 Computation. http://www.tsp.gatech.edu/sweden/, June 2004.

[45] COOK, W. J. National Traveling Salesman Problems. http://www.tsp.gatech.edu/world/countries.html, May 2005.

[46] COOK, W. J. World Traveling Salesman Problem. http://www.tsp.gatech.edu/world/, July 2008.

[47] COOK, W. J. FI10639 – Finland Computation Log. http://www.tsp.gatech.edu/world/filog.html, August 2001.

[48] COOK, W. J. and SEYMOUR, P. Tour Merging via Branch-Decomposition. *INFORMS Journal on Computing*, 15(3):233–248, 2003.

[49] COOK, W. J. et al. Concorde TSP Solver. http://www.tsp.gatech.edu/concorde.html, January 2005.

[50] COULOURIS, G. F. and DOLLIMORE, J. *Distributed Systems – Concepts and Design.* International Computer Science Series. Addison-Wesley, 1988.

[51] CROES, G. A. A Method for Solving Traveling Salesman Problems. *Operations Research*, 5:791–812, 1958.

[52] DANTZIG, G. B., FULKERSON, R., and JOHNSON, S. Solution of a Large-Scale Traveling-Salesman Problem. *Journal of the Operations Research Society of America*, 2:393–410, 1954.

[53] DAWKINS, R. *The Selfish Gene*. Clarendon Press, Oxford, 2nd edition, 1989.

[54] DE NORONHA, T. F. and RIBEIRO, C. C. Routing and wavelength assignment by partition colouring. *European Journal of Operational Research*, 171(3):797–810, 2006.

[55] DE NORONHA, T. F., RESENDE, M. G. C., and RIBEIRO, C. C. A Random-Keys Genetic Algorithm for Routing and Wavelength Assignment. In *Proceedings of the Seventh Metaheuristics International Conference (MIC 2007)*, June 2007.

[56] DELAUNAY, B. Sur la sphère vide. *Otdelenie Matematicheskikh i Estestvennykh Nauk*, 8:793–800, 1934.

[57] DEMERS, A., GREENE, D., HAUSER, C., IRISH, W., LARSON, J., SHENKER, S., STURGIS, H., SWINEHART, D., and TERRY, D. Epidemic Algorithms for Replicated Database Maintenance. In SCHNEIDER, F. B., editor, *Proceedings of the 6th Annual ACM Symposium on Principles of Distributed Computing*, pages 1–12. ACM Press, August 1987.

[58] DIJKSTRA, E. W. A Note on Two Problems in Connection with Graphs. *Numerische Mathematik*, 1(269-270):269–271, 1959.

[59] DORIGO, M. and STÜTZLE, T. *Ant Colony Optimization*. MIT Press, July 2004.

[60] ERDŐS, P. and RÉNYI, A. On Random Graphs I. *Publ. Math. Debrecen*, 6:290–297, 1959.

[61] EUGSTER, P. T. and GUERRAOUI, R. Probabilistic Multicast. In *Proceedings of the 3rd IEEE International Conference on Dependable Systems and Networks (DSN 2002)*, pages 313–322, June 2002.

[62] EUGSTER, P. T., GUERRAOUI, R., KERMARREC, A.-M., and MASSOULIÉ, L. From Epidemics to Distributed Computing. *IEEE Computer*, 2004.

[63] FISCHER, T. Improved Local Search for Large Optimum Communication Spanning Tree Problems. In *MIC'2007 – 7th Metaheuristics International Conference*, June 2007. (Cited on pages 208 and 217.)

[64] FISCHER, T. and MERZ, P. Embedding a Chained Lin-Kernighan Algorithm into a Distributed Algorithm. Interner Bericht 331/04, University of Kaiserslautern, Kaiserslautern, Germany, August 2004.

[65] FISCHER, T. and MERZ, P. Embedding a Chained Lin-Kernighan Algorithm into a Distributed Algorithm. In DOERNER, K. F., GENDREAU, M., GREISTORFER, P., GUTJAHR, W. J., HARTL, R. F., and REIMANN, M., editors, *MIC'2005 - 6th Metaheuristics International Conference*, Vienna, Austria, August 2005. (Cited on page 49.)

[66] FISCHER, T. and MERZ, P. A Memetic Algorithm for the Optimal Communication Spanning Tree Problem. In BARTZ-BEIELSTEIN, T., AGUILERA, M. J. B., BLUM, C., NAUJOKS, B., ROLI, A., RUDOLPH, G., and SAMPELS, M., editors, *Hybrid Metaheuristics, 4th International Workshop, HM 2007, Dortmund, Germany, October 8-9, 2007, Proceedings*, volume 4771 of *Lecture Notes in Computer Science*, pages 170–184. Springer, October 2007. (Cited on pages 217 and 233.)

[67] FISCHER, T., BAUER, K., and MERZ, P. A Distributed Memetic Algorithm for the Routing and Wavelength Assignment Problem. In RUDOLPH, G., JANSEN, T., LUCAS, S., POLONI, C., and BEUME, N., editors, *Parallel Problem Solving from Nature - PPSN X - 10th International Conference*, volume 5199/2008 of *Lecture Notes in Computer Science*, pages 879–888. Springer, September 2008. (Cited on pages 119 and 141.)

[68] FISCHER, T., BAUER, K., and MERZ, P. A Multilevel Approach for the Routing and Wavelength Assignment Problem. In KÖPPEN, M. and RAIDL, G., editors, *Workshop on Heuristic Methods for the Design, Deployment, and Reliability of Networks and Network Applications (HEUNET 2008) at the International Symposium on Applications and the Internet (SAINT 2008)*, pages 225–228, Turku, Finland, July 2008. IEEE Computer Society. (Cited on pages 52 and 119.)

[69] FLOYD, R. W. Algorithm 97: Shortest path. *Communications of the ACM*, 5(6):345, 1962.

[70] FOGEL, D. B. *Evolutionary Computation: The Fossil Record*. Wiley-IEEE Press, 1998.

[71] FOGEL, L. J. Autonomous Automata. *Industrial Research*, 4(2): 14–19, 1962.

[72] FOSTER, I. The Grid: A New Infrastructure for 21st Century Science. *Physics Today*, 55(2):42–47, February 2002.

[73] FOSTER, I. Globus Toolkit Version 4: Software for Service-Oriented Systems. *Journal of Computer Science and Technology*, 21(4):513–520, July 2006.

[74] FOSTER, I. and KESSELMAN, C. Globus: A Metacomputing Infrastructure Toolkit. *Intl J. Supercomputer Applications*, 11(2): 115–128, 1997.

[75] FOSTER, I. and KESSELMANN, C. *The Grid: Blueprint for a New Computing Infrastructure*, chapter Computational Grids. Morgan-Kaufman, 1999.

[76] FREDMAN, M. L., JOHNSON, D. S., MCGEOCH, L. A., and OSTHEIMER, G. Data Structures for Traveling Salesmen. *Journal of Algorithms*, 18(3):432–479, 1995.

[77] FREISLEBEN, B. and MERZ, P. A Genetic Local Search Algorithm for Solving Symmetric and Asymmetric Traveling Salesman Problems. In BÄCK, T., KITANO, H., and MICHALEWICZ, Z., editors, *IEEE International Conference on Evolutionary Computation*, pages 616–621, Piscataway, NJ, USA, 1996. IEEE Press.

[78] FREISLEBEN, B. and MERZ, P. New Genetic Local Search Operators for the Traveling Salesman Problem. In VOIGT, H.-M., EBELING, W., RECHENBERG, I., and SCHWEFEL, H.-P., editors, *Parallel Problem Solving from Nature IV*, volume 1141 of *Lecture Notes in Computer Science*, pages 890–900. Springer, 1996.

[79] FRIEDMAN, J. H., BASKETT, F., and SHUSTEK, L. H. An Algorithm for Finding Nearest Neighbors. *IEEE Transactions on Computers (TOC)*, C-24:1000–1006, October 1975.

[80] GABRIEL, K. and SOKAL, R. A new statistical approach to geographic variation analysis. *Systematic Zoology*, 18(3):259–278, 1969.

[81] GALLO, G. Lower planes for the network design problem. *Networks*, 13(3):411–425, February 1983.

[82]  GAREY, M. R. and JOHNSON, D. S. *Computers and Intractability: A Guide to the Theory of NP-Completeness.* W. H. Freeman, New York, June 1979.

[83]  GENDREAU, M. and POTVIN, J.-Y. Metaheuristics in Combinatorial Optimization. *Annals of Operations Research*, 140(1):189–213, November 2005.

[84]  GLOVER, F. Future paths for integer programming and links to artificial intelligence. *Computers and Operations Research*, 13(5): 533–549, May 1986.

[85]  GLOVER, F. Tabu Search – Part I. *ORSA Journal on Computing*, 1 (3):190–206, 1989.

[86]  GLOVER, F. Tabu Search – Part II. *ORSA Journal on Computing*, 2(1):4–32, 1990.

[87]  GLOVER, F. W. and KOCHENBERGER, G. A., editors. *Handbook of Metaheuristics*, volume 57 of *International Series in Operations Research & Management Science*. Kluwer Academic Publishers, Boston, MA, USA, January 2003.

[88]  GOLDBERG, D. E. and LINGE, R. Alleles, Loci and TSP. In GREFENSTETTE, J. J., editor, *Proceedings of the First International Conference on Genetic Algorithms*, pages 154–159. Hillsdale, NJ, Lawrence Erlbaum Associates, 1985.

[89]  GOMORY, R. E. Outline of an algorithm for integer solutions to linear programs. *Bulletin of the American Mathematical Society*, 64(5):275–278, 1958.

[90]  GORGES-SCHLEUTER, M. *Genetic Algorithms and Population Structures: A Massively Parallel Algorithm.* PhD thesis, University of Dortmund, Dortmund, Germany, 1991.

[91]  GORGES-SCHLEUTER, M. Asparagos96 and the Traveling Salesman Problem. In BÄCK, T., MICHALEWICZ, Z., and YAO, X., editors, *Proceedings of the 1997 IEEE International Conference on Evolutionary Computation, Indianapolis, USA*, pages 171–174. IEEE Press, April 1997.

[92] GROPP, W., LUSK, E., and SKJELLUM, A. *Using MPI – Portable Parallel Programming with the Message Passing Interface*. MIT Press, 2nd edition, November 1999.

[93] GROTE, N. and VENGHAUS, H. *Fibre Optic Communication Devices*. Springer, Berlin, 2001.

[94] GRUBER, G. Ein Genetischer Algorithmus für das Optimum Communication Spanning Tree Problem. Master's thesis, Institut für Computergraphik und Algorithmen, Technische Universität Wien, Vienna, Austria, 2004.

[95] HANSEN, P. and MLADENOVIĆ, N. First vs. best improvement: An empirical study. *Discrete Applied Mathematics*, 154:802–817, 2006.

[96] HART, W. E., KRASNOGOR, N., and SMITH, J. E. Memetic evolutionary algorithms. In HART, W. E., KRASNOGOR, N., and SMITH, J. E., editors, *Recent Advances in Memetic Algorithms*, volume 166 of *Studies in Fuzziness and Soft Computing*, pages 3–27. Springer, 2005.

[97] HELD, M. and KARP, R. The Travelling Salesman Problem and Minimum Spanning Trees. *Operations Research*, 18:1138–1162, 1970.

[98] HELD, M. and KARP, R. The Travelling Salesman Problem and Minimum Spanning Trees: Part II. *Mathematical Programming*, 1(1):6–25, 1971.

[99] HELD, M., WOLFE, P., and CROWDER, H. P. Validation of subgradient algorithm. *Mathematical Programming*, 6(1):62–88, 1974.

[100] HELSGAUN, K. An Effective Implementation of the Lin-Kernighan Traveling Salesman Heuristic. DATALOGISKE SKRIFTER (Writings on Computer Science) 81, Roskilde University, 1998.

[101] HELSGAUN, K. An Effective Implementation of the Lin-Kernighan Traveling Salesman Heuristic. *European Journal of Operational Research*, 126(1):106–130, 2000.

[102] HELSGAUN, K. An Effective Implementation of $k$-opt Moves for the Lin-Kernighan TSP Heuristic. Technical Report 109, Roskilde University, 2006. Revised November 2007.

[103]  Hoc, H. H. A Computational Approach to the Selection of an
       Optimal Network. *Management Science*, 19(5):488–498, January
       1973.

[104]  HOLLAND, J. H. Outline for a Logical Theory of Adaptive Systems.
       *J. ACM*, 9(3):297–314, 1962.

[105]  Hoos, H. H. and STÜTZLE, T. *Stochastic Local Search: Foundations
       and Applications.* The Morgan Kaufmann Series in Artificial
       Intelligence. Morgan Kaufmann, September 2004.

[106]  Hu, T. C. Optimum Communication Spanning Trees. *SIAM
       Journal of Computing*, 3(3):188–195, September 1974.

[107]  HYYTIÄ, E. and VIRTAMO, J. Wavelength Assignment and Rout-
       ing in WDM Networks. In *Fourteenth Nordic Teletraffic Seminar,
       NTS-14*, pages 31–40, Lyngby, Denmark, August 1998.

[108]  JARNÍK, V. O jistém problému minimálním (About a Certain
       Minimal Problem). *Práce Moravské Přídovědecké Společnosti
       v Brně (Acta Societas Scientiarum Naturalium Moravicae)*, VI:
       57–63, 1930. (in Czech).

[109]  JELASITY, M., VOULGARIS, S., GUERRAOUI, R., KERMARREC, A.-
       M., and van STEEN, M. Gossip-based peer sampling. *ACM
       Transactions on Computer Systems*, 25(3), 2007.

[110]  JOHNSON, D., McGEOCH, L., GLOVER, F., and REGO, C. 8th
       DIMACS Implementation Challenge: The Traveling Salesman
       Problem. http://www.research.att.com/~dsj/chtsp/, Au-
       gust 2006.

[111]  JOHNSON, D. S. Local Optimization and the Traveling Salesman
       Problem. In *Proceedings of the 17th International Colloquium on
       Automata, Languages and Programming*, number 443 in Lecture
       Notes in Computer Science, pages 446–461. Springer-Verlag, July
       1990.

[112]  JOHNSON, D. S. and McGEOCH, L. A. The Traveling Salesman
       Problem: A Case Study in Local Optimization. In AARTS, E.
       H. L. and LENSTRA, J. K., editors, *Local Search in Combinatorial
       Optimization*, pages 215–310. John Wiley & Sons, London, 1997.

[113] JOHNSON, D. S. and McGEOCH, L. A. Experimental Analysis of Heuristics for the STSP. In *The Traveling Salesman Problem and Its Variations*, pages 369–443. Kluwer Academic Publishers, 2002.

[114] JOHNSON, D. S., LENSTRA, J. K., and RINNOOY KAN, A. H. G. The Complexity of the Network Design Problem. *Networks*, 8(4): 279–285, 1978.

[115] JOHNSON, D. S., McGEOCH, L. A., and ROTHBERG, E. E. Asymptotic Experimental Analysis for the Held-Karp Traveling Salesman Bound. In *Proceedings of the 7th Annual ACM-SIAM Symposium on Discrete Algorithms*, pages 341–350. Society for Industrial and Applied Mathematics, 1996.

[116] JONES, T. and FORREST, S. Fitness Distance Correlation as a Measure of Problem Difficulty for Genetic Algorithms. In ESHELMAN, L. J., editor, *Proceedings of the 6th International Conference on Genetic Algorithms*, pages 184–192. Morgan Kaufmann, 1995.

[117] KATAYAMA, K. and NARIHISA, H. Iterated Local Search Approach using Genetic Transformation to the Traveling Salesman Problem. In BANZHAF, W., DAIDA, J., EIBEN, A. E., GARZON, M. H., HONAVAR, V., JAKIELA, M., and SMITH, R. E., editors, *Proceedings of the Genetic and Evolutionary Computation Conference*, volume 1, pages 321–328, Orlando, Florida, USA, July 1999. Morgan Kaufmann.

[118] KIRKPATRICK, S., GELATT, C. D., and VECCHI, M. P. Optimization by Simulated Annealing. *Science, New Series*, 220(4598):671–680, May 1983.

[119] KLEINBERG, J. *Approximation Algorithms for Disjoint Paths Problems*. PhD thesis, Dept. of EECS, MIT, Cambridge, May 1996.

[120] KOZA, J. R. *Genetic Programming: On the Programming of Computers by Means of Natural Selection*. MIT Press, Cambridge, MA, USA, 1992.

[121] KRUSKAL, J. B. On the Shortest Spanning Subtree of a Graph and the Traveling Salesman Problem. *Proceedings of the American Mathematical Society*, 7:48–50, February 1956.

[122] LAMPORT, L., SHOSTAK, R. E., and PEASE, M. C. The Byzantine Generals Problem. *ACM Transactions on Programming Languages and Systems (TOPLAS)*, 4(3):382–401, 1982.

[123] LAND, A. and DOIG, A. An automatic method for solving discrete programming problems. *Econometrica*, 28(3):497–520, 1960.

[124] LAWLER, E. L., LENSTRA, J. K., RINOOY KAN, A. H. G., and SHMOYS, D. B. *The Traveling Salesman Problem: A Guided Tour of Combinatorial Optimization*. John Wiley & Sons, New York, 1985.

[125] LI, G. and SIMHA, R. The Partition Coloring Problem and its Application to Wavelength Routing and Assignment. In *Prof. of Optical Networks Workshop*, February 2000.

[126] LI, Y. and BOUCHEBABA, Y. A New Genetic Algorithm for the Optimal Communication Spanning Tree Problem. In *Artificial Evolution*, pages 162–173, London, UK, 1999. Springer-Verlag.

[127] LIAO, A. Three priority queue applications revisited. *Algorithmica*, 7(1):415–427, 1992.

[128] LIN, S. Computer Solutions of the Traveling Salesman Problem. *The Bell System Technical Journal*, 44:2245–2269, December 1965.

[129] LIN, S. and KERNIGHAN, B. W. An Effective Heuristic Algorithm for the Traveling Salesman Problem. *Operations Research*, 21(2): 498–516, March 1973.

[130] LINIAL, N., LONDON, E., and RABINOVICH, Y. The Geometry of Graphs and Some of its Algorithmic Applications. *Combinatorica*, 15(2):215–245, 1995.

[131] LOURENCO, H. R., MARTIN, O., and STÜTZLE, T. A Beginners Introduction to Iterated Local Search. In *Proceedings of the Metaheuristics International Conference 2001 (MIC 2001)*, Porto, Portugal, 2001.

[132] MANOHAR, P., MANJUNATH, D., and SHEVGAONKAR, R. K. Routing and Wavelength Assignment in Optical Networks From Edge Disjoint Path Algorithms. *IEEE Communications Letters*, 6(5): 211–213, May 2002.

[133] MARGARA, L. and SIMON, J. Wavelength Assignment Problem on All-Optical Networks with k Fibres per Link. In *Automata, Languages and Programming*, pages 768–779, 2000.

[134] MARTIN, O., OTTO, S. W., and FELTEN, E. W. Large-Step Markov Chains for the Traveling Salesman Problem. *Complex Systems*, 5: 299–326, 1991.

[135] MARTIN, O., OTTO, S. W., and FELTEN, E. W. Large-Step Markov Chains for the TSP Incorporating Local Search Heuristics. *Operation Research Letters*, 11(4):219–224, 1992.

[136] MARTIN, W. N., LIENING, J., and COHOON, J. P. Island (migration) models: evolutionary algorithms based on punctuated equilibria. In BÄCK, T., FOGEL, D. B., and MICHALEWICZ, Z., editors, *Handbook of Evolutionary Computation*, pages 1–6, sect. C6.3. Oxford University Press, 1997.

[137] MATTERN, F. Algorithms for Distributed Termination Detection. *Distributed Computing*, 2(3):161–175, 1987.

[138] MENGER, K. Ein Theorem über die Bogenlänge. *Anzeiger*, 65: 264–266, 1928.

[139] MERRIAM-WEBSTER, INCORPORATED. Dictionary and Thesaurus – Merriam-Webster Online. http://www.merriam-webster. com/, May 2008. Last visited May 2008.

[140] MERZ, P. *Memetic Algorithms for Combinatorial Optimization Problems: Fitness Landscapes and Effective Search Strategies*. PhD thesis, University of Siegen, Germany, Siegen, Germany, December 2000.

[141] MERZ, P. A Comparison Of Memetic Recombination Operators For The Traveling Salesman Problem. In LANGDON, W. B., CANTÚ-PAZ, E., MATHIAS, K., ROY, R., DAVIS, D., POLI, R., BALAKRISHNAN, K., HONAVAR, V., RUDOLPH, G., WEGENER, J., BULL, L., POTTER, M. A., SCHULTZ, A. C., MILLER, J. F., BURKE, E., and JONOSKA, N., editors, *GECCO 2002: Proceedings of the Genetic and Evolutionary Computation Conference*, pages 472–479, New York, July 2002. Morgan Kaufmann Publishers.

[142]  MERZ, P. and FISCHER, T. A Memetic Algorithm for Large Traveling Salesman Problem Instances. In *MIC'2007 – 7th Metaheuristics International Conference*, June 2007.

[143]  MERZ, P. and FREISLEBEN, B. Memetic Algorithms for the Traveling Salesman Problem. *Complex Systems*, 13(4):297–345, 2001.

[144]  MICHALEWICZ, Z. *Genetic Algorithms + Data Structures = Evolution Programs*. Springer-Verlag, Berlin, Germany, 1996.

[145]  MICHALEWICZ, Z. and FOGEL, D. B. *How to Solve It: Modern Heuristics*. Springer-Verlag, 2000.

[146]  MLADENOVIĆ, N. and HANSEN, P. Variable neighborhood search. *Computers and Operations Research*, 24(11):1097–1100, November 1997.

[147]  MÖBIUS, A., FREISLEBEN, B., MERZ, P., and SCHREIBER, M. Combinatorial Optimization by Iterative Partial Transcription. *Physical Review E*, 59(4):4667–4674, 1999.

[148]  MOSCATO, P. On Evolution, Search, Optimization, Genetic Algorithms and Martial Arts: Towards Memetic Algorithms. Technical Report Caltech Concurrent Computation Program, Report. 826, California Institute of Technology, Pasadena, California, USA, 1989.

[149]  MOSCATO, P. Memetic Algorithms: A Short Introduction. In CORNE, D., DORIGO, M., and GLOVER, F., editors, *New Ideas in Optimization*, pages 219–234. McGraw-Hill, 1999.

[150]  MUKHERJEE, B. *Optical WDM Networks*. Optical Networks. Springer, 2006.

[151]  NAGATA, Y. New EAX Crossover for Large TSP Instances. In RUNARSSON, T. P., BEYER, H.-G., BURKE, E. K., GUERVÓS, J. J. M., WHITLEY, L. D., and YAO, X., editors, *Procedings of Parallel Problem Solving from Nature - PPSN IX, 9th International Conference*, volume 4193 of *Lecture Notes in Computer Science*, pages 372–381. Springer, September 2006.

[152] NAGATA, Y. and KOBAYASHI, S. Edge Assembly Crossover: A High-Power Genetic Algorithm for the Travelling Salesman Problem. In BÄCK, T., editor, *ICGA*, pages 450–457. Morgan Kaufmann, 1997.

[153] NAGATSU, N., HAMAZUMI, Y., and SATO, K.-I. Number of Wavelengths Required for Constructing Large-Scale Optical Path Networks. *Electronics and Communications in Japan (Part I: Communications)*, 78(9):1–11, 1995.

[154] NEŠETŘIL, J., MILKOVÁ, E., and NEŠETŘILOVÁ, H. Otakar Borůvka on Minimum Spanning Tree Problem (translation of both 1926 papers, comments, history). *Discrete Mathematics*, 233 (1–3):3–36, 2001.

[155] ORAM, A., editor. *Peer-to-Peer: Harnessing the Power of Disruptive Technologies*. O'Reilly, February 2001.

[156] ORLOWSKI, S., PIÓRO, M., TOMASZEWSKI, A., and WESSÄLY, R. SNDlib 1.0–Survivable Network Design Library. In *Proceedings of the 3rd International Network Optimization Conference (INOC 2007), Spa, Belgium*, April 2007. http://sndlib.zib.de.

[157] PADBERG, M. W. and RINALDI, G. Optimization of a 532 City Symmetric Traveling Salesman Problem by Branch and Cut. *Operations Research Letters*, 6:1–8, 1987.

[158] PALMER, C. C. and KERSHENBAUM, A. Representing trees in genetic algorithms. In *Proceedings of the First IEEE Conference on Evolutionary Computation*, volume 1, pages 379–384, 1994.

[159] PALMER, C. C. and KERSHENBAUM, A. Two Algorithms for Finding Optimal Communication Spanning Trees. Technical Report RC 19394, IBM T. J. Watson Research Center, Yorktown Heights, NY, USA, January 1994.

[160] PALMER, C. C. and KERSHENBAUM, A. An Approach to a Problem in Network Design Using Genetic Algorithms. *Networks*, 26:151–163, October 1995.

[161] PELEG, D. and RESHEF, E. Deterministic Polylog Approximation for Minimum Communication Spanning Trees (Extended Abstract). In LARSEN, K. G., SKYUM, S., and WINSKEL, G., editors,

*Automata, Languages and Programming: 25th International Colloquium, ICALP'98,* volume 1443 of *Lecture Notes in Computer Science,* pages 670–681. Springer, 1998.

[162] PELEG, D. and RESHEF, E. Deterministic Polylog Approximation for Minimum Communication Spanning Trees. Technical Report CS98-01, Weizmann Institute, Israel, London, UK, 1998.

[163] PRIM, R. C. Shortest Connection Networks and Some Generalizations. *Bell System Technical Journal,* 36:1389–1401, 1957.

[164] RADCLIFFE, N. J. Forma Analysis and Random Respectful Recombination. In BELEW, R. K. and BOOKER, L. B., editors, *ICGA,* pages 222–229. Morgan Kaufmann, 1991.

[165] RADCLIFFE, N. J. and SURRY, P. D. Fitness Variance of Formae and Performance Prediction. In WHITLEY, L. D. and VOSE, M. D., editors, *Proceedings of the Third Workshop on Foundations of Genetic Algorithms,* pages 51–72, San Francisco, 1994. Morgan Kaufmann.

[166] RAMASWAMI, R. and SIVARAJAN, K. N. Design of Logical Topologies for Wavelength-Routed Optical Networks. *IEEE Journal on Selected Areas in Communications,* 14(5):840–851, June 1996.

[167] RECHENBERG, I. *Evolutionsstrategie: Optimierung technischer Systeme nach Prinzipien der biologischen Evolution.* Frommann-Holzboog, Stuttgart, 1973.

[168] REINELT, G.    TSPLIB – A Traveling Salesman Problem Library.    *ORSA Journal on Computing,* 3(4):376–384, 1991. See also http://www.iwr.uni-heidelberg.de/groups/comopt/software/TSPLIB95/.

[169] REINELT, G.    Traveling Salesman Problem library. http://www.iwr.uni-heidelberg.de/groups/comopt/software/TSPLIB95/, May 2007.

[170] RESHEF, E. Approximating Minimum Communication Cost Spanning Trees and Related Problems. Master's thesis, Department of Computer Science and Applied Mathematics, The Weizmann Institute of Science, Rehovot, Israel, April 1999.

[171] ROTHLAUF, F. *Representations for Genetic and Evolutionary Algorithms*. Springer Verlag, second edition, January 2006. First edition printed in 2002.

[172] ROTHLAUF, F. and HEINZL, A. Developing Efficient Metaheuristics for Communication Network Problems by using Problem-specific Knowledge. Technical Report 9/2004, University of Mannheim, Mannheim, Germany, 2004.

[173] ROTHLAUF, F., GOLDBERG, and HEINZL, A. Network Random Keys – A Tree Representation Scheme for Genetic and Evolutionary Algorithms. *Evolutionary Computation*, 10(1):75–97, 2002.

[174] ROTHLAUF, F., GERSTACKER, J., and HEINZL, A. On the Optimal Communication Spanning Tree Problem. Working Papers in Information Systems 10/2003, University of Mannheim, Mannheim, Germany, May 2003.

[175] ROWSTRON, A. and DRUSCHEL, P. Pastry: Scalable, Decentralized Object Location, and Routing for Large-Scale Peer-to-Peer Systems. In GUERRAOUI, R., editor, *Middleware 2001, IFIP/ACM International Conference on Distributed Systems Platforms*, volume 2218, pages 329–350. Springer, September 2001.

[176] SCHRIJVER, A. On the History of Combinatorial Optimization (till 1960). In AARDAL, K., NEMHAUSER, G., and WEISMANTEL, R., editors, *Handbooks in Operations Research and Management Science, Volume 12: Discrete Optimization (Handbooks in Operations Research and Management Science)*, pages 1–68. Elsevier, Amsterdam, 2005.

[177] SCHWEFEL, H.-P. *Evolutionsstrategie und numerische Optimierung*. PhD thesis, Technische Universität Berlin, Berlin, Germany, 1975. German.

[178] SHARAFAT, A. R. and MA'ROUZI, O. R. The Most Congested Cutset: Deriving a Tight Lower Bound for the Chromatic Number in the RWA Problem. *IEEE Communications Letters*, 8(7):473–475, July 2004.

[179] SHARMA, P. Algorithms for the optimum communication spanning tree problem. *Annals of Operations Research*, 143(1), March 2006.

[180] SINCLAIR, M. C. Minimum cost routing and wavelength allocation using a genetic-algorithm/heuristic hybrid approach. In *Proc. 6th IEE Conf. Telecommunications*, March 1998.

[181] SKORIN-KAPOV, N. Routing and Wavelength Assignment in Optical Networks using Bin Packing Based Algorithms. *European Journal of Operational Research*, 177(2):1167–1179, 2007.

[182] SOAK, S.-M. A New Evolutionary Approach for the Optimal Communication Spanning Tree Problem. *IEICE Transactions on Fundamentals of Electronics, Communications and Computer Sciences*, E89–A(10):2882–2893, October 2006.

[183] SOAK, S.-M., CORNE, D. W., and AHN, B.-H. A New Evolutionary Algorithm for Spanning-Tree Based Communication Network Design. *IEICE Transactions on Communications*, E88-B(10):4090–4093, October 2005.

[184] SOAK, S.-M., CORNE, D. W., and AHN, B.-H. The Edge-Window-Decoder Representation for Tree-Based Problems. *IEEE Transaction on Evolutionary Computation*, 10(2):124–144, April 2006.

[185] SPROULL, R. F. Refinements to Nearest-Neighbor Searching in $k$-Dimensional Trees. *Algorithmica*, 6(4):579–589, 1991.

[186] STEELE, J. M. Complete Convergence of Short Paths and Karp's Algorithm for the TSP. *Mathematics of Operations Research*, 6 (3):374–378, August 1981.

[187] STEIN, D. *Scheduling Dial-a-ride Transportation Systems: An Asymptotic Approach.* PhD thesis, Harvard University, Cambridge, U.S.A., 1977.

[188] STOER, M. *Design of Survivable Networks*, volume 1531 of *Lecture Notes in Mathematics*. Springer Berlin / Heidelberg, 1992.

[189] STOICA, I., MORRIS, R., KARGER, D. R., KAASHOEK, M. F., and BALAKRISHNAN, H. Chord: A Scalable Peer-To-Peer Lookup Service for Internet Applications. In *SIGCOMM '01: Proceedings of the 2001 conference on Applications, technologies, architectures, and protocols for computer communications*, pages 149–160, New York, NY, USA, August 2001. ACM Press.

304    BIBLIOGRAPHY

[190]  SVIREZHEV, Y. M. and PASSEKOV, V. P. Fundamentals of Mathematical Evolutionary Genetics. *Mathematics and Its Applications (Soviet Series)*, 22, 1989.

[191]  TAN, L. G. and SINCLAIR, M. C. Wavelength assignment between the central nodes of the COST 239 European optical network. In *11th UK Performance Engineering Workshop*, pages 235–247, 1995.

[192]  TANENBAUM, A. S. and VAN STEEN, M. *Distributed Systems: Principles and Paradigms*. Prentice Hall, 2nd edition, October 2006.

[193]  TANG, M. and YAO, X. A Memetic Algorithm for VLSI Floorplanning. *IEEE Transactions On Systems, Man, And Cybernetics—Part B: Cybernetics*, 37(1):62–69, February 2007.

[194]  THAIN, D., TANNENBAUM, T., and LIVNY, M. Distributed Computing in Practice: The Condor Experience. *Concurrency - Practice and Experience*, 17(2-4):323–356, 2005.

[195]  VALENZUELA, C. L. and JONES, A. J. Estimating the Held-Karp lower bound for the geometric TSP. *European Journal of Operational Research*, 102(1):157–175, October 1997.

[196]  VARELA, G. N. and SINCLAIR, M. C. Ant Colony Optimisation for Virtual-Wavelength-Path Routing and Wavelength Allocation. In *Proceedings of the Congress on Evolutionary Computation*, pages 1809–1816, 1999.

[197]  VOIGT, B. F. *Der Handlungsreisende - wie er sein soll und was er zu thun hat, um Aufträge zu erhalten und eines glücklichen Erfolgs in seinen Geschäften gewiß zu sein - von einem alten Commis-Voyageur.* Schramm, Kiel, Germany, 1832/1981. Reprint, in German.

[198]  VOLGENANT, T. and JONKER, R. A branch and bound algorithm for the symmetric traveling salesman problem based on the 1-tree relaxation. *European Journal of Operational Research*, 9(1):83–89, January 1982.

[199]  WALSHAW, C. A Multilevel Approach to the Travelling Salesman Problem. *Operations Research*, 50(5):862–877, 2002.

[200] WALSHAW, C. Multilevel Refinement for Combinatorial Optimisation Problems. *Annals of Operations Research*, 131:325–372, 2004.

[201] WANG, Y., CHENG, T. H., and LIM, M. H. A Tabu search algorithm for static routing and wavelength assignment problem. *IEEE Communications Letters*, 9(9):841–843, September 2005.

[202] WARSHALL, S. A Theorem on Boolean Matrices. *Journal of the ACM*, 9(1), January 1962.

[203] WAUTERS, N. and DEMEESTER, P. Design of the Optical Path Layer in Multiwavelength Cross-Connected Networks. *IEEE Journal on Selected Areas in Communications*, 14(5):881–892, June 1996.

[204] WOLTMAN, G. GIMPS – The Great Internet Mersenne Prime Search. http://www.mersenne.org, September 2006.

[205] WU, B. Y. and CHAO, K.-M. A note on optimal communication spanning trees, April 2004.

[206] XU, S., LI, L., and WANG, S. Dynamic routing and assignment of wavelength algorithms in multifiber wavelength division multiplexing networks. *IEEE Journal on Selected Areas in Communications*, 18(10):2130–2137, 2000.

[207] YANG, B. and GARCIA-MOLINA, H. Designing a Super-Peer Network. In *Proceedings of the 19th International Conference on Data Engineering (ICDE)*, March 2003.

[208] YAO, A. C.-C. On Constructing Minimum Spanning Trees in $k$-Dimensional Spaces and Related Problems. *SIAM Journal on Computing*, 11(4):721–736, 1982.

[209] YOON, W. J., KIM, D. H., CHUNG, M. Y., LEE, T.-J., and CHOO, H. Routing with Maximum EDPs and Wavelength Assignment with Path Conflict Graphs. In GAVRILOVA, M. L., GERVASI, O., KUMAR, V., TAN, C. J. K., TANIAR, D., LAGANÀ, A., MUN, Y., and CHOO, H., editors, *ICCSA (2)*, volume 3981 of *Lecture Notes in Computer Science*, pages 856–865. Springer, 2006.